ROUTLEDGE LIBRARY EDITIONS:
THE LABOUR MOVEMENT

Volume 40

THE INTERNATIONAL LABOUR ORGANISATION

THE INTERNATIONAL LABOUR ORGANISATION
The First Decade

ALBERT THOMAS

Routledge
Taylor & Francis Group
LONDON AND NEW YORK

First published in 1931 by George Allen & Unwin Ltd

This edition first published in 2019
by Routledge
4 Park Square, Milton Park, Abingdon, Oxon OX14 4RN
605 Third Avenue, New York, NY 10017

Routledge is an imprint of the Taylor & Francis Group, an informa business

British Library Cataloguing in Publication Data
A catalogue record for this book is available from the British Library

ISBN: 978-1-138-32435-0 (Set)
ISBN: 978-0-429-43443-3 (Set) (ebk)
ISBN: 978-1-138-32901-0 (Volume 40) (hbk)
ISBN: 978-0-429-44834-8 (Volume 40) (ebk)

Publisher's Note
The publisher has gone to great lengths to ensure the quality of this reprint but points out that some imperfections in the original copies may be apparent.

Disclaimer
The publisher has made every effort to trace copyright holders and would welcome correspondence from those they have been unable to trace.

THE INTERNATIONAL LABOUR ORGANISATION

THE FIRST DECADE

Preface by
ALBERT THOMAS

Published for the
INTERNATIONAL LABOUR OFFICE (LEAGUE OF NATIONS) BY
GEORGE ALLEN & UNWIN LTD
40 MUSEUM STREET, LONDON, W.C.1
Distributed in the U.S.A. by the
WORLD PEACE FOUNDATION
40 MOUNT VERNON STREET, BOSTON, MASS.

FIRST PUBLISHED IN 1931

PRINTED IN GREAT BRITAIN BY
UNWIN BROTHERS LTD., WOKING

PREFACE

THIS book is the work of certain officials of the International Labour Office who prefer to remain anonymous. It is something more than a sincere effort to describe, impersonally and simply but in as telling a form as possible, the work of this institution; it is a confession of faith.

It may be asked what justification exists for the publication of these 400 pages. Much has already been written on the first ten years of activity of the International Labour Organisation: articles, pamphlets, even books, published both in Great Britain and the United States, some of them of considerable value. The Office itself published an official album containing shrewd and impartial comments on the work of the past ten years by the Officers of the Governing Body. It may be asked then what is the need for this new study. First of all, it seemed useful to complete the record of the first ten years of international co-operation. Our colleagues of the Secretariat of the League of Nations have published a comprehensive volume giving a valuable survey of their work which covers every international sphere save one—that of labour. The public, or at least that section of it which wishes to help us and which is sometimes apt to complain of insufficient information, is entitled to expect this gap to be filled, remembering that the Treaties of Peace postulated that there could be no lasting peace without social justice.

And there is another reason. Surely among all the voices raised in praise, or it may be criticism, of our work, it is but right that a voice from within the Office should also be heard. It is this voice which finds expression here—a discreet, perhaps somewhat colourless voice, the voice of officials. Yet even if its tone is uniform and intentionally subdued it is vibrant with memories, with hopes, with emotion. We can say with joy and pride that in these ten years the conviction and enthusiasm of the staff of the International Labour Office have never failed or weakened.

In order to make this a convenient handbook, the authors have, of course, been obliged to give a full and systematic description of all the activities of the Organisation, enumerate all the problems, follow the standardised and obvious plan of discussing successively the origins and principles of the institution, its work, the results obtained and its position in the general movement for justice and peace. It is true also that they have had to abstain more than others from offering ingenious but sometimes dangerous suggestions or from passing too daring judgments. Nevertheless, even in this well-trodden field they have brought out new points which would seem to be of great value. And they have done more, as no one can appreciate better than the Director who has been dealing with the subject in his reports every year since 1921: they have produced a living and interesting study.

Their first great merit is that they have brought out the immense difficulties of our task, difficulties which are perhaps still growing or at least changing their angle. The members of the Commission on International Labour Legislation (in 1919) certainly imagined that it would be comparatively easy to obtain the ratifications which States were asked to give to International Labour Conventions, and that the development of international labour legislation would proceed almost automatically along the lines laid down in Part XIII. Some members even went so far as to suggest the institution of an international assembly with full legislative powers for all countries; others proposed that the Conventions should automatically come into force and be binding on all so long as no States made any reservations. The wording of Part XIII, careful as it has been to respect national sovereign rights, clearly reflects this early confidence. Not many months had elapsed, however, before the first difficulties arose. I well remember my feelings at the end of the First Session of the Governing Body in Paris in January 1920, when, having scarcely entered on my duties as Director, I was informed by Mr. Rufenacht, Swiss Government Delegate, of the difficulties which his Government had found in the Eight-Hour Convention adopted practically unanimously at Washington a few weeks before, but destined to cause us so much trouble in future years. Thus began our stiff task which was to encounter so many other complications and obstacles later: administrative delays, national prejudices, constitutional contradictions, legal objections, economic apprehensions, press of Parliamentary work, Government negotiations, opposition manœuvres, indifference or hostility in public opinion, mutual misunderstandings and suspicions, and so on. Not only for the Eight-Hour Convention but for every Convention without exception ratification has become in the fullest sense of the term an affair of State. Yet there are already thirty Conventions and fifty-five members of the Organisation. As long as this Organisation lives and is governed by its present constitution, there will be an annual debate on the results obtained and on the value of the total figure for ratifications. In the album for the tenth anniversary, Mr. Arthur Fontaine, Chairman of our Governing Body, showed by skilful mathematical reasoning the true significance of this figure. The present writers have reproduced this proof (p. 279) and have shown what unremitting effort, what insistence, what politic indiscretions are reflected in the total of 415 ratifications by January 1931. They have made a perfectly fair comparison with the results obtained by the League of Nations. They even point out, not without a touch of humour, that the United States of America have for several years past possessed a kind of international labour conference for harmonising the social legislation of the federated States, which are without a doubt more closely united than the States Members of the International Labour Organisation; yet all things considered, their progress towards standard legislation has been much less rapid than our own. The argument (p. 282) is worth reading; it is quite a novel idea.

New also, as far as we know, is the lucid proof of the usefulness, the direct value of International Labour Conventions. Much has been heard of the worthlessness of their texts. If critics were to be believed, the Conference generally adopts merely minimum Conventions, more or less consolidating the national legislation of the majority of countries and stabilising, one might say, the reforms already carried through, but involving no fresh progress. Consequently, these critics maintain, the ratifications which are obtained with so much difficulty are nothing more than a hollow farce. In reply to this criticism the "effective results" of each Convention are analysed in turn. The classification of the Conventions into groups according to whether they have been widely, less widely or sparsely ratified, and have involved considerable, little or no legislative progress, may appear rather artificial. But the detailed analysis which has been outlined (pages 288 *et seqq.*) is instructive, showing as it does that these Conventions have, in the words of the Treaty, conferred lasting benefits on numbers of workers; it will also be a welcome reassurance to those who, like ourselves, are firmly convinced of the effectiveness of the international methods of procedure established in 1919.

We are also heartily grateful to those writers who planned and composed the whole of the second and largest part of the volume, entitled "The Work." A study of these pages will give a faithful impression of the International Labour Organisation, the Office and the Conference "at work" in every branch of social life and in every field with which they are competent to deal. Our constant and I think legitimate reply to those who complain of the small number of ratifications registered has been that ratification is often merely the final seal placed on our work, that it is in some sense the ultimate goal of every effort at reform, but that it is the movement itself which is of primary and essential, if not exclusive, importance. In the anniversary album Mr. Olivetti, Employers' Vice-chairman of the Governing Body, brings out clearly in an important passage the fact that the results of our activities do not lie merely in the resolutions of the Conference, and that the Office has found its most fruitful function in promoting and stimulating social progress in every country. Year by year, in the second part of the report of the Director to the Conference, we ourselves have sought to show how in every sphere—hours of work, wages, hygiene, safety, employment and unemployment, etc.—whether for all workers or for some large occupational group, the work of the Office was supported and developed by the demands of the workers, by currents of public opinion and by scientific research, and how in return our actions, our decisions, our methods helped to guide, define and clarify these movements and efforts, so that they could only reach their fullest possible utility when co-ordinated round our own work. So far, however, no general picture had been drawn of this process. Now it has been done, and in masterly fashion. These keenly suggestive pages reveal all the actions and reactions which go to form the network of social progress: the indirect influence of the Conventions, which, even if not ratified, serve as standards for national legislation (in particular, the enormous influence of the much-maligned Eight-Hour Convention which, although only sparsely ratified, has been almost universally accepted as the code for hours of work) and the real but rarely recognised effectiveness of the important Recommendations, such as that on inspection, which is now the recognised standard for the young inspection services in countries which were revived or unified by the War or which are only now launching out upon industrial life, or the Recommendation on workers' spare time, which may already be said to have become the charter of the new humanism at which the world of labour aims. They also show the organising power of the social insurance Conventions, which are at the origin of the new international groups of insurance funds and provide a clearly defined framework for their activities (it is even said that these Conventions have indirectly led to organised resistance on the part of doctors). They bring out, too, the value of our scientific studies, of the *Encyclopædia of Industrial Hygiene*, of the *Safety Survey*, of our studies on finding employment, on social insurance and public works, which have led to the imitation of the most successful schemes in other countries and thus sometimes proved as useful for the defence of human life as the Conventions themselves, even when ratified. These pages tell of the fruitful meetings in our commissions of experts and men of science separated by the War or by circumstances; the revival of great scientific movements which have been more or less paralysed; the resurrection of ideas or aspirations which were being allowed to languish or were stifled. Through all the tangle of legal procedure, through all the confusion of committees, commissions and conferences, beneath the apparent emptiness of congress resolutions and the jumble of texts, we see with amazement the desired reforms being adopted in every part of the world—slowly, it may be, but surely, and sometimes even beyond our highest hopes. It is occasionally the habit of workers' meetings to cast doubts on the value of the International Labour Organisation; some, in moments of disillusion, have gone so far as to say that our international institutions are a sham. But that view cannot be accepted by anyone who reads these pages with an open mind. It must be frankly admitted that the movement for the protection of the workers would never have had the same vigour or the same success amidst all the political and economic difficulties of the post-War world had it not had at its centre the International Labour Organisation.

That is the impression which must be left by this objective

and quite impersonal description undertaken by our collaborators. They have studied only the past, the ten years since the Organisation began, but their unspoken thought for the future, which we share, is revealed on every page. Without such concern for the future there can be no good history. Is not history indeed the science of the future? An institution lives only in so far as it cares about its future.

No doubt our future is guaranteed by a number of considerations, but that will make it none the less difficult and arduous. The very intensity of our activity brings us face to face with new problems which are sometimes disconcerting just because of their novelty.

To what extent, for example, have the procedure and the mechanism created in 1919 proved in these ten years to be adapted to the conditions of our dawning international life? Have the permanent international bodies been endowed with adequate powers and competence? What place is there for the consultation of technical experts, the representation of interests, etc.? It is true that some attempts at reform have been made, but without much success. Valuable suggestions for amending the Standing Orders of the Conference or of the Governing Body have been rejected. The proposed amendment to Article 393 of the Treaty of Peace did not obtain the necessary number of ratifications to bring it into force. But sooner or later we must either agree to accept some new practices not specified in the Treaties, as may happen even with the best-regulated constitutions, or else have the courage to amend them.

The necessity for some such step becomes all the clearer when it is remembered that, as this volume shows, the reforms undertaken in the name of social justice will be more fully applied and more real year by year, so that they will involve more direct and more tangible consequences in national life and even in international relationships. The "Labour" Section of the Peace Treaties was based on two principles. In the first place it wished to abolish everywhere the "injustice, hardship and privation" which the workers had to suffer, and to guarantee "fair and humane conditions of labour" to all. As a general rule, and especially in the early years, the main object in view in drafting the International Labour Conventions was to achieve this end and apply the present ideals of social justice accepted in the Labour Charter. These Conventions were the direct outcome of the feelings of humanity and justice by which Governments were animated throughout that period. But Part XIII had a further object. The reforms adopted in the more advanced countries had to be protected against unfair competition by other countries which perhaps might not scruple to exploit their workers to the utmost for the sake of commercial advantage. This was the other aim of our work as defined in the texts voted. The post-War monetary, financial and economic crises which completely destroyed international equilibrium forced into the background the question of competition based on unequal conditions of labour. Now that many important Conventions on points of principle have been drafted for the compulsory and immediate protection, if need be in spite of economic conditions, of the weaker workers, of women and children; now that the most general rules for protection and safety have been laid down; now that a certain degree of international financial unity has again been reached and broken commercial relations re-established, we find that in several branches of industry, such as mines, glass works or textiles, the favourable or unfavourable effects of its labour conditions on a country's trade are becoming more apparent and more keenly felt. It is no longer merely a question of protecting the individual workers against too great hardships. There must also be a certain equality of burdens among the various national economic systems. Hence the demand for Conventions containing stricter and more precise regulations for a given industry than did the general Conventions. Hence also the idea of regional Conventions limited to a few States and the idea of new types of procedure, the institution of which must undoubtedly be considered by the Organisation even at the risk of certain dangers.

The same reasons lie at the root of the widespread but confused discussion which has been going on for years with regard to the interdependence of economic and social questions, the demarcation of the competence of the various organisations of the League of Nations, and the attention to be paid to economic conditions in the drafting of our Conventions. In one of the following chapters (Part II, Chapter VIII) the authors have traced objectively and without bias the successive phases of this controversy. This is not the place to consider the theoretical conclusions or to reopen the examination of the problem as a whole, but the discussions at our Conferences and at the recent meetings of the Unemployment Committee have shown with increasing clearness that the immediate future of our work and even the very future of our institution depend on the solution of this question and on the spirit which is to inspire national and international economic policy. One possible solution is that, having established a minimum of protection for humanity —what has been called "the sanitary cordon"—we may subordinate the ever-evolving conceptions of, and the ever-recurring aspirations after social justice to "economic necessity" and "economic laws," the "free play" of which must not be further disturbed. Or we may decide that, just because of these ideals of justice and because of the growing clearness of the voice of the human conscience, and sometimes even in the face of economic laws, which (to put it mildly) have perhaps not always the full force of natural laws, human intelligence must make every possible effort to organise the economic system and has in fact the power to do so. The social factor must take precedence over the economic factor; it must regulate and guide it in the highest cause of justice.

Doubtless many a long decade must still elapse, many a compromise, many a struggle and perhaps many a failure be faced and accepted before the economic system is finally regulated and organised for the common weal. The decade which is so well described in the following pages can at least claim to have defined all these problems in a practical form. The world in which we live and struggle is big with new ideas, still uncertain, indefinite, confused, but arising out of the great upheavals of the War and post-War periods and to some extent forced on the attention of every thinking man. Will our international institutions be able to clarify these ideas and translate them into facts? That is the question of the future. Whatever the answer may be, it is in the light of these ideas that they must seek their path and define their duties.

ALBERT THOMAS

January 1931

CONTENTS

PART I: STRUCTURE AND FUNCTIONS

PART II: THE WORK

PART III: RESULTS

PART IV: RELATIONS

PART I

STRUCTURE AND FUNCTIONS

On October 29th, 1919, the First Session of the International Labour Conference opened in Washington. In the same city a few weeks later the Governing Body met to take the necessary steps for organising the International Labour Office and appointed as its first Director Albert Thomas, former Minister of Armaments in France. Thus barely a year after the Armistice, five months after the signature of the Treaty of Versailles which contained its constitution, three months before that Treaty came into force and more than a year before the first meeting of the Assembly of the League of Nations, to which it was constitutionally attached, the International Labour Organisation came into active existence.

Nothing could show better than this simple comparison of dates the importance and the urgency which the international social problem had in the eyes of the post-War Governments. It is generally difficult for contemporaries to estimate the true importance of an event. Those who lived through the troubled months immediately following the War were impressed chiefly by the impassioned discussions at the preliminary Peace Conference and in the various countries on the vexatious questions of frontiers and reparations. The great eddies in which the world was still swirling after the storm of the War years had too strong a hold on the attention of the public to enable it to give due heed to the first tentative efforts at international organisation which were being made in the background. The apparently lukewarm interest shown in these attempts even by certain of the statesmen on whom their success depended and the seeming disproportion between the overwhelming problems of the hour and the proposed institutions whose possible stability could not be gauged by any past experience obscured the fact that the texts drafted in Paris would, after the painful task of winding up the past, prove the foundation on which, patiently and stone by stone, the new organisation of the world was to be built up.

It is true that the action taken by the statesmen was determined by the general longing for peace and the great dream of international reconciliation and social justice cherished by the peoples during the dark days of the War. But for this unanimous desire, deep-rooted in every country, there would have been at the Peace Conference no Commission for the League of Nations and no Commission on International Labour Legislation. But the masses had difficulty in recognising the objects of their hope behind the often lifeless formulae of legal texts submitted to them. They were faced with machinery, with a starting point the great daring of which escaped them, because they compared it with the ideal of which they had dreamt and not with the past on which they were deliberately turning their backs.

Ten years have passed. The institution has lived. It has survived the early struggles, and although it has not done more than begin to carry out its programme it has at least shown enough of the possibilities of realisation to make clear the boldness of the solutions imagined in 1919. We are beginning to see that the historian who a century later may analyse the facts of this memorable year will lay by far the greatest stress on the creation of the international institutions. What he will find it necessary to explain will not be the timidity but the boldness of their constitutions, not the hesitations of certain States but the rapidity with which an organisation was set up which in many respects ran counter to the traditional conceptions of the law of nations. This daring and this urgency can be seen even more clearly in Part XIII than in Part I of the Treaty. The constitution laid down by Part XIII establishes an entirely new type of international organisation on account of the representation of interests in the composition of the Conference and the Governing Body, the system of individual voting by delegates, the two-thirds majority in place of the rule of unanimity for the adoption of Conventions and Recommendations, the obligations which this adoption involves for the States Members and finally the measures taken for supervising the application of Conventions. The position which its constitution occupies in the Peace Treaties and the autonomy which the Organisation enjoys within the League of Nations are proof of the special importance with which its founders wished to endow it. Finally, the date of October 1919 fixed in the Treaty for the opening of the first International Labour

Conference, the agenda laid down in an additional protocol and the decision of the Peace Conference to give the constitution of the new Organisation executive force without waiting for the signature of the Peace Treaty, reveal the urgent desire of Governments to give the workers a pledge of their good will and their sincerity.

CHAPTER I

ORIGINS AND PRINCIPLES

Paving the Way: The Current of Thought in the Nineteenth Century

The special treatment accorded to the social problem by the peace-makers of 1919 can be understood only in the light of the past. In the history of institutions thought has always preceded action. For a century, indeed, the movement of ideas had paved the way for the new organisation and had even before the War taken concrete form and provided lessons for the future.

Every work which has analysed the constitution of the International Labour Organisation has devoted a chapter to this movement. At the beginning there were a certain number of striking individuals, the precursors, who at the very dawn of labour legislation asked that the social problems raised by large-scale industry should be dealt with by international collaboration. In 1818, Robert Owen submitted to the Congress of the Holy Alliance at Aix-la-Chapelle two memoranda asking the powers to introduce in every country measures for protecting the workers against the ignorance and exploitation to which they were exposed and inviting them to appoint a labour commission. From 1838 to 1859, Daniel Legrand, a Mulhausen manufacturer, sent innumerable memoranda and petitions to Parliaments and Governments "with a view to the adoption," as one petition says, "of national laws and also international legislation for the protection of the working class against work excessive in amount and at too early an age, the primary and principal cause of its physical deterioration, its moral degradation and its deprivation of the blessings of family life."

Interesting as these declarations are in the history of ideas, their real value must not be over-estimated. They do honour to the foresight of their authors, but they had no direct influence on later developments. The idea of international collaboration for labour legislation could not become strong enough to lead to positive results until the movement for labour legislation itself had gained strength in each country and had proved victorious over the doctrine of economic liberalism which had previously opposed its progress.

This is what happened in the second half of the century. Under the influence of the growing social movement and the humanitarian ideas propagated by the revolution of 1848, the theory of *laisser-faire* lost some of its power. Legislation for the protection of the workers became more frequent, the demands for such legislation grew more urgent and the idea of international labour legislation received a fresh impulse. In France, Germany, Switzerland, in the universities as well as in Parliament, men of various shades of opinion expounded the idea that the progress already made in the social sphere could be consolidated and further progress made only by eliminating the disadvantages which such progress and the consequent rise in production costs could have for the industries of the more advanced countries in international competition.

First Practical Results: The Berlin and Berne Conferences

This current of ideas, which insisted chiefly on the economic justification for international labour legislation, was to reach its first very modest practical results at the end of the century. In 1889, the Swiss Government proposed for the first time to convene an international labour conference. The idea was taken up by the German Government, and a conference was held in Berlin in 1890, attended by representatives of fourteen countries. The results were limited and were not followed up. The conference merely adopted a certain number of resolutions on the limitation of the work of women and children, work in mines and the weekly rest.

This first experiment had at least one salutary effect. It brought to light the defects of the method and showed that no progress could be made without careful technical preparation and continuous and regular action.

The credit for drawing the correct conclusion from the experience of the Berlin Conference lies with a group of scholars and economists who in 1900 founded the International Association for the Legal Protection of the Workers in Paris. While official circles hesitated and failed to act, private initiative stepped in and undertook to convene international labour conferences, to prepare their agenda and by constant propaganda to have the texts adopted incorporated in national legislation. An international office was set up in Basle to centralise the research work and the collection of information. The Association had national sections through which it could get into touch with official circles. Support was asked from the various Governments. Finally, when the ground seemed to have been sufficiently prepared, the Swiss Government convened a conference at Berne in 1905, which was attended by experts and technicians from about twenty countries. Two sets of texts were adopted, one dealing with the use of white phosphorus in the match industry and the other with the night work of women. Next year a further conference was held in the same city, consisting this time of plenipotentiaries, which adopted the texts in question in the form of international conventions. Two successive conferences, the first technical and the second diplomatic—such was the method invented to get round the double difficulty arising from the fact that the experts were not empowered to sign conventions and the diplomats lacked the technical knowledge to draft them.

The encouraging results of this step decided the Association to prepare for a new conference of experts, which was held at Berne in 1913; texts were adopted on the limitation of hours of work for women and young persons and the prohibition of night work for children, but the outbreak of hostilities prevented the meeting of the diplomatic conference which was to have transformed these texts into conventions in the following year.

The Workers' Demands

Although the War interrupted the activities of the Association, in another way it won for international labour legislation new and indispensable support: that of the organised proletariat. Up to that time the masses of the workers had remained rather in the background. It is true that the progress of trade union action had always exerted an influence by drawing attention to the social problem. It is true also that certain of the workers' leaders had expressed their sympathy for the aims of the international movement for the legal protection of the workers. But the masses had appeared unwilling to commit themselves until they saw positive and effective results. The Berlin Conference and its pious resolutions had aroused their distrust rather than confidence. The work of the Berne Conference seemed to them doomed to be slow and uncertain so long as the initiative lay entirely with a private association which could count only on the personal authority of its members and its propaganda to obtain the support of Governments and the application of the

Conventions. They considered that this new international legislation dealing with the questions they had most at heart should not be made for them but with their collaboration and thus savour less of philanthropy. In place of the somewhat narrow idea of legal protection, they would have preferred that of a code of workers' rights, which they hoped to win from Governments as a recognition of their just due and not as a favour obtained by the generous and altruistic intervention of a group of intellectuals. They hoped also that the application of international legislation would not be left to the good will and good faith of States but would be guaranteed by a system of supervision and sanctions.

Before the War, however, the workers' organisations had hardly attempted to define their attitude to these problems. The courageous but modest efforts of the International Association had brought to light the obstacles in the way of any attempt at infringing the sovereign rights of States. Efforts had been made, as in 1905 for example, to arrive at an agreement to set up an international supervisory commission for the application of the conventions ratified, but this proposal was rejected, even though the commission was only to be of an advisory nature, and all that could be done was to adopt a resolution on the subject. The War, by the change it wrought in men's minds and the tremendous increase in the power of the trade unions which followed, brought within the workers' grasp possibilities which a few years earlier had seemed unattainable. The appeal which was made by Governments in every country to the working class not only developed in it a consciousness of its solidarity, but also turned the attention of the whole nation to that class and to the necessity for raising it to a higher material and moral standard of life.

Thus, when the delegates of the workers of the allied countries, and later of the neutral countries, met at Leeds in 1916, at Stockholm in 1917 and at Berne in 1918, and demanded that the terms of peace should "safeguard the working class of all countries from the attacks of international capitalist competition and assure it a minimum guarantee of moral and material order as regards labour legislation, trade union rights, migration, social insurance, hours of work and industrial hygiene and safety," their demands met with the support of public opinion and a sympathetic hearing from Governments. The sufferings of the

War had developed in every stratum of society a feeling that peace must mean something more than a return to the conditions of 1914. A new order must be created which would guarantee the peace of the world and give to everyone the just reward of his labour.

The Labour Problem at the Peace Conference

This vague idealism, sustained by the promises of statesmen who were indeed not a little troubled by the agitation among the workers, ensured the triumph of these claims. The League of Nations, which was intended to safeguard the peace of the world, seemed the natural institution for achieving that social justice without which peace would be meaningless. But there could be no waiting for the ratification of the Peace Treaties or the beginning of the activities of the League of Nations before deciding what form the international organisation should take which was to deal with labour questions within the framework of the League. *Festina lente* might be a suitable motto in other fields, but the social problem required rapid and bold decisions. Any delay, any indecision might have destroyed the confidence of the working class and turned it against those who had encouraged it with promises. Moreover, the ground was less new than in other spheres. It had to a great extent been cleared by the Berne Labour Conferences, and their work, interrupted by the War, had merely to be taken up again in a manner which would meet the workers' wishes.

All these circumstances explain why the Peace Conference decided at its sitting of January 25th, 1919, to set up a Commission of fifteen members "to enquire into the conditions of employment from the international aspect and to consider the international means necessary to secure common action on matters affecting conditions of employment, and to recommend the form of a permanent agency to continue such enquiry and consideration in co-operation with and under the direction of the League of Nations." Thus the Conference, before it knew what form the League itself might take, began to study the creation of one of the institutions which was to be attached to it.

The Commission for International Labour Legislation began its work on February 1st. Its composition recalled its double origin: what may be called the "scientific" movement for the legal protection of the workers and the great urge towards social reform after the War. The Governments saw to it that the delegates on this Commission should include not only important figures like Messrs. Ernest Mahaim and Arthur Fontaine and Sir Malcolm Delevingne, the moving spirits of the Berne Conferences, but also men more intimately connected with labour and sometimes directly appointed by the workers: Samuel Gompers for the United States, E. Vandervelde for Belgium, G. N. Barnes for Great Britain, Léon Jouhaux for France and A. Cabrini for Italy.

The Commission worked for almost two months under the chairmanship of Samuel Gompers. Its task was no easy one. From the outset it accepted as a basis for its discussions a draft put forward by the British delegation after having been submitted to the workers' and employers' organisations in Great Britain for their examination. It was not long before very divergent views began to appear as to the nature of the institution which was to be set up. The question of the powers which should be granted to it was the subject of a long battle between the United States delegation and the other delegations and might indeed have endangered the whole work of the Commission but for the fact that all the members were conscious of the great disappointment which such a failure would cause to the world.

Finally, on April 11th, after thirty-five sittings, the Reporter, Mr. G. N. Barnes, was able to submit to the Peace Conference the first results of the work of the Commission—a Draft Convention creating a permanent organisation for the international regulation of labour questions. This Draft was immediately approved, subject to amendments in detail which might be thought necessary by the Drafting Committee in order to bring it into harmony with the Pact of the League of Nations. At the same time, measures were taken to constitute as soon as possible the Preparatory Committee for the First Session of the International Labour Conference, which was to be held at Washington in the following October, so that it could set to work without waiting either for the ratification or even for the signature of the Treaty of Peace. On April 28th the Peace Conference met again and adopted, with certain formal amendments, the second part of the Report of the Commission on International Labour Legislation, which took the form of a draft declaration to be inserted in the Peace Treaty. These two documents, the Convention and the declaration, have, under the title "Labour," become Sections

I and II of Part XIII of the Treaty of Versailles, and were later inserted in corresponding positions in the other Peace Treaties concluded in 1919 and 1920.

The forty Articles which compose Section I of Part XIII form the actual constitution of the International Labour Organisation, regulating its composition, its working and the obligations assumed by the States Members. But these provisions do not form the whole of Part XIII. The mere creation of a new institution would not have satisfied the workers. The authors of the Treaty realised that this institution must, so to speak, be given a soul, and to this end they placed the constitution in a setting of two solemn declarations reflecting the main currents of thought and general tendencies out of which the International Labour Organisation arose. The first is the Preamble, which defines, more or less in terms of ideals, the aims and guiding principles of the Organisation. The other is the final Article, which, starting out from the ideas contained in the Preamble, sets forth with a view to immediate action a certain number of principles, the progressive realisation of which seemed to the High Contracting Parties to be of special and urgent importance.

The Preamble: Aims of the Organisation

"Universal peace" and "social justice" constitute the double object which the authors of the Treaty had in view in setting up the International Labour Organisation. The Preamble opens: "Whereas the League of Nations has for its object the establishment of universal peace, and such a peace can be established only if it is based upon social justice. . . ." In so far as its ultimate aim is to contribute to the establishment of universal peace, the work of the Organisation is linked up with that of the League of Nations. For that reason the Treaty provided certain organic bonds between the two institutions, the chief of these being the compulsory membership of the International Labour Organisation for all States Members of the League of Nations and the inclusion of the budget of the Organisation in the general budget of the League.

But social justice is not merely a means of establishing universal peace; it is also an end in itself. As such its moral value is so high and its realisation so urgent that it seemed fitting to entrust the task to a special organisation whose structure and method of work would be peculiarly adapted to its object, and which, by its independent position among the other institutions of the League of Nations, would be able to work in complete liberty for the accomplishment of the task assigned to it. The High Contracting Parties, when summing up at the end of the Preamble the lofty motives which form the basis of Part XIII, abandoned the apparent subordination of social justice to the work of peace and placed on an equal footing "the sentiments of justice and humanity and the desire to secure the permanent peace of the world" which led them to agree to the succeeding Articles.

The affirmation of the ideal of social justice in the first paragraph of the Preamble is immediately followed by a recognition by the High Contracting Parties of the existing abuses and the urgent necessity for doing away with them: "And whereas conditions of labour exist involving such injustice, hardship and privation to great numbers of people as to produce unrest so great that the peace and harmony of the world are imperilled; and an improvement of those conditions is urgently required. . . ." This is the minor premise of the syllogism of which the major premise is the desire of the world for peace and social justice, while the conclusion will be the necessity for creating a permanent Labour Organisation. In recognising the existence of the evils of which the working class complains, the Powers took the first step towards relieving them and gave the sufferers hope for a brighter future. They went further; in order that there might be no misunderstanding and that the labour world should see in the programme of the new institution the points about which it was particularly anxious, the Preamble gave by way of example an enumeration of the improvements which it seemed particularly urgent to effect. These are: "The regulation of the hours of work, including the establishment of a maximum working day and week, the regulation of the labour supply, the prevention of unemployment, the provision of an adequate living wage, the protection of the worker against sickness, disease and injury arising out of his employment, the protection of children, young persons and women, provision for old age and injury, protection of the interests of workers when employed in countries other than their own, recognition of the principle of freedom of association, the organisation of vocational and technical education and other measures."

But it may be asked what necessity there was for an international organisation to improve these conditions. What necessity was there for the adoption of measures drafted in conferences that were world-wide in their scope and possibly involving binding reciprocal undertakings for the States which adhered to them? It is true that the universal nature of the evils which were being attacked is a sufficient justification for the universal action undertaken to suppress them; the natural feelings of justice and humanity, as well as the collective instinct for self-preservation, render universal mutual aid imperative in a matter affecting the happiness and sometimes even the existence of large groups of individuals. Side by side with these considerations, however, there is an economic argument mentioned in the third paragraph of the Preamble in the following terms: "Whereas also the failure of any nation to adopt humane conditions of labour is an obstacle in the way of other nations which desire to improve the conditions in their own countries. . . ."

How far is this economic objection really valid? To what extent is it true to say that a piece of social legislation is a burden on the country which adopts it and is liable to place the industry of that country in an unfavourable position on the world market as compared with the competing industries of foreign countries which have not adopted the same legislation? To take some of the examples quoted in the Preamble itself, can one say that countries which make efforts to regulate the labour supply, to introduce vocational and technical education or to protect the workers against sickness and injury arising out of their employment are *ipso facto* at a disadvantage in international competition? And even the reduction of hours of work, the improvement of wages, the protection of children or social insurance surely repay their immediate cost by advantages and incentives of which national industry finally reaps the benefit? Experience appears to show that the countries with the most advanced labour legislation are by no means the least successful in the competition for world markets. The whole question has often been discussed and doubtless will be discussed for long years to come, for social experiments are not carried out in a laboratory where factors of secondary importance can be eliminated, and consequently it is difficult to establish a definite connection of cause and effect in this subject, and the conclusions advanced on both sides are necessarily in the nature of conjectures.

Be that as it may, one fact remains, namely, that since the beginning of the modern industrial system, whenever a measure for the protection of the workers has been proposed or demanded—whether it was the prohibition of the employment of children under nine years of age in the early nineteenth century, or the limitation of the hours of work of all workers to eight in the day in the early twentieth century—the economic objection has in every case been raised. Whether well founded or not, the fear of foreign competition has alarmed industrialists and has paralysed or hindered social progress. It may be said that even if the conditions governing international competition are less incompatible than has often been thought with an improvement in working conditions in any one country, the fear inspired by such competition is clearly an obstacle to improvements of a social nature. Add to this the fact that the present pace of industrial development has, especially in periods of depression such as that through which every country is now passing, made this competition a veritable obsession, and it will readily be understood how necessary it is to find some means of calming these apprehensions which bar the way to all further progress and even endanger the reforms already achieved. The remedy which suggested itself to the authors of the Treaty as likely to lead to a reasonable and systematic improvement in working conditions, safeguarded from the risks of sudden panic in times of depression, is the one advocated since the days of Daniel Legrand and tried out before the War at the Berne Conferences, namely, to induce a parallel improvement in working conditions in every country and fix the minimum standard which every country would undertake to maintain. All that was required was to establish regulations for the application of the system and to improve its working and its efficiency. This was the purpose of the authors of the Treaty in drafting the constitution of the International Labour Organisation.

The Final Article: The General Principles

Although the Preamble set forth clearly the aims and the programme of action of the International Labour Organisation, the authors of Part XIII were clear from the outset that such a solemn proclamation was not in itself sufficient to dispel all distrust. The Preamble certainly contained a list of questions with which the Organisation was requested to deal urgently, but there was nothing to show to what point Governments were prepared to go in the way of reforms. To take one example only, the Preamble mentioned the regulation of hours of work and the fixing of maximum hours for the day and the week, but what was of importance to the workers was to know whether they were to obtain satisfaction in their demand for an eight-hour day. Now the state of mind in 1919 was such that a reply to these definite questions could not be put off. As Mr. Barnes forcibly stated before the Peace Conference, the worker of 1919 was living with the memory of his pre-War situation; he feared a return to former conditions and was determined not to accept it.

When the Commission on International Labour Legislation was set up by the Peace Conference, many people thought that its deliberations would result in a kind of international labour code the provisions of which, when inserted in the Peace Treaty, would immediately apply to all the Member States. The International Trade Union Conference, which met at Berne about the same time, drew up a programme of fifteen Articles summarising the demands of the workers. The political, and even more the legal, difficulties in such a step prevented its being taken, and it was left to the new Organisation to reach definite formal decisions on each point. But the Commission, while declining to draw up proposals which could be accepted in a definite form, unanimously recognised "that their work would not be complete if it were simply confined to setting up a permanent machinery for international labour legislation." "So impressed were they," as their report says, "with the urgent need for recognising explicitly certain fundamental principles as necessary to social progress, that they decided to submit a series of declarations for insertion in the Peace Treaty." The High Contracting Parties were not invited to give immediate effect to these declarations, but merely to subscribe to them in a general manner, leaving it to the International Labour Conference to examine them thoroughly and put them into the form of Recommendations or Draft Conventions. The mere fact, however, that the Commission decided to retain and submit to the Peace Conference only those declarations which were supported by at least two-thirds of the votes (in point of fact, many of them had obtained unanimity) gave these proposals considerable moral authority.

It is these declarations, which the Peace Conference decided to insert in the Treaty of Peace at the end of the actual constitution of the International Labour Organisation, which form Section II of Part XIII, under the title "General principles." With the

Preamble they certainly represent the most impressive provision of Part XIII. This Section, which forms a counterpart to the Preamble in which a number of urgent improvements in conditions of labour are enumerated, has with justice been called the International Labour Charter. It indicates in nine points the direction in which improvements must be sought. It reveals the desire of Governments to give the workers a pledge with regard to a certain number of definite reforms on which the workers' demands were most urgent: the right of association for all lawful purposes by the employed as well as by the employers; the right to a wage adequate to maintain a reasonable standard of life; an eight-hour day or a forty-eight-hour week; a weekly rest of at least twenty-four hours, which should include Sunday wherever practicable; the abolition of child labour; the principle that men and women should receive equal remuneration for work of equal value; equality of treatment for national and foreign workers; the organisation of a system of inspection to ensure the enforcement of legislation for the protection of the workers; and, dominating all the rest, the solemn affirmation, reflecting the whole idealist current of thought of the period, "that labour should not be regarded merely as a commodity or article of commerce."

In making these declarations the High Contracting Parties made two reservations: the one refers to the difficulty of immediately attaining "strict uniformity in conditions of labour" as a result of "differences of climate, habits and customs, of economic opportunity and industrial tradition." The other refers to the necessarily provisional and incomplete character of the programme set forth. The Commission on Labour Legislation had already pointed out in its report that it did not feel called upon "to draw up a charter containing all the reforms which may be hoped for in a more or less distant future"; it had confined itself to "principles the realisation of which may be contemplated in the near future." Similarly, Sir Robert Borden, in submitting to the Peace Conference the final text of Article 427, pointed out the impossibility of drafting immediately a code which could apply permanently over a long period and of foreseeing all the future developments of these principles and the ideals which might be aimed at later. It was this difficulty which led to the declaration in Article 427 that the principles and methods referred to above should not be considered as "either complete or final" and that when enumerating them the High Contracting Parties wished merely to emphasise "their special and urgent importance." Having made these reservations, the authors of the Treaty immediately proclaimed solemnly that, "if adopted by the industrial communities who are Members of the League, and safeguarded in practice by an adequate system of inspection, they will confer lasting benefits upon the wage-earners of the world."

Such declarations were calculated to reassure the world of labour. The new machinery would not be beating the air. A plan of work had been laid down, and the impulse and definite direction for that work had been given. The success of the Organisation would depend on its fidelity to this programme.

CHAPTER II

THE STATES MEMBERS

The Desire for Universality

"Universality" is a word which appears in the very first sentence of the Preamble to Part XIII: "Whereas the League of Nations has for its object the establishment of *universal* peace and such a peace can be established only if it is based upon social justice"; and the idea recurs later: "And whereas conditions of labour exist involving such injustice, hardship and privation to large numbers of people as to produce unrest so great that the peace and harmony *of the world* are imperilled"; and yet again: "Whereas also the failure of *any nation* to adopt humane conditions of labour is an obstacle in the way of other nations which desire to improve the conditions in their own countries." Thus, the universality at which the International Labour Organisation must logically aim is three times emphasised in the Preamble.

Universal the Organisation should be in the same way as the League of Nations as a whole, since the peace of the world may be endangered by the ferment of social agitation which can arise in any country where the working classes are subject to poverty and privation. Universal the Organisation must be also to an even greater extent than the political organisations of the League, since the maintenance of inhuman conditions in even a single country may, through international competition, arrest or compromise social progress in every other country.

In view of that fact it is not surprising that one of the chief preoccupations of the Organisation since the beginning has been to increase the number of its Members as much as possible.

Compulsory Participation of Members of the League of Nations

The close connection between the ultimate aims of the two institutions led to the inclusion in Article 387 of the Treaty of the provision that the original Members of the League of Nations should be the original Members of the International Labour Organisation, and that hereafter membership of the League of Nations should carry with it membership of the said Organisation. It seemed indeed impossible that any State adhering to the Covenant and accepting its programme should decline to accept Part XIII. Under Article 23 of the Covenant States undertook "to secure and maintain fair and humane conditions of labour for men, women and children . . . and for that purpose to establish and maintain the necessary international organisations." Part XIII merely gave this undertaking more definite form and contained the constitution of the proposed Organisation.

The compulsory participation of all Members of the League of Nations in the work of the International Labour Organisation was, however, contested in one case. In 1920 the State of Salvador maintained that while it had become a Member of the League of Nations by adhering to the Covenant, it had no obligations towards the International Labour Organisation because it had not signed any of the Treaties of Peace containing its constitution and had accepted only the Covenant, which, it asserted, did not explicitly mention the International Labour Organisation. Salvador therefore refused to share in the cost of this body. Its assertion, which raises a very important point of principle, was several times discussed by the Council and Assembly of the League of Nations in 1921 and 1922, and a financial arrangement was finally arrived at, Salvador undertaking to pay its arrears of contributions. At the same time, it maintained its argument and stated that it reserved the right which it had claimed, but in point of fact it has since sent delegates to two Sessions of the Conference.

New Members since 1919

The principle that membership of the League of Nations compulsorily involves membership of the International Labour Organisation may therefore be considered as firmly established and accepted at the present day. But while such a bond seems necessary and natural, it is not sufficient to give the International Labour Organisation that universality which its aims and functions imply. It would suffice only if the League of Nations itself were a world-wide institution. It will be remembered that when the International Labour Organisation was set up in 1919 the list of original Members of the League of Nations or of States which could become Members contained only 45 States, of which 32 had signed the Treaty of Versailles and 13 had been invited to accept the Covenant. There was no mention for example, of Germany, Austria, Hungary, Bulgaria, Turkey, the new Republics created by the Russian Revolution or Mexico. From the point of view of the League of Nations, these omissions might be justified by political considerations. It was clear that some of them, and particularly the omission of Germany, were in direct contradiction with the task imposed on the International Labour Organisation. Assuming that for reasons of economic competition the regulation of labour and the protection of the workers should progress along parallel lines in every country, how could one of the chief industrial Powers of the world possibly remain outside the movement? Moreover, how could the Organisation proceed without the very wide experience of social legislation which that Power possessed?

This question had already received serious attention from the members of the Commission on International Labour Legislation of the Peace Conference. The Italian Delegation had formally proposed the admission of all nations without exception to the new Organisation. Messrs. Vandervelde and Jouhaux had both stressed the necessity for making the new Organisation as universal as possible. The Commission was interpreting this general wish when in drafting one of its Resolutions it pointed out that "an international code of labour legislation which will be really effective cannot be secured without the co-operation of all industrial countries." Consequently, when the question was raised during the peace negotiations with Germany and Austria of the collaboration of these countries in the International Labour Organisation, the Supreme Council, after having consulted its Labour Commission, finally decided to place no obstacle in the way of the admission of these countries but to grant the Washington Conference the power to settle the question as it wished. The matter was placed as the first item on the agenda, and the Conference decided at its second sitting on October 30th, 1919, to admit Germany and Austria to the Organisation with the same rights and obligations as the other States.

It is worth stressing the fact that the first act of the International Labour Organisation represented an effort towards complete universality. It is worthy of note also that on the first occasion when the question of the boundaries of the International Labour Organisation and those of the League of Nations arose, the idea of identity was dropped and the special needs of the Organisation for as wide a field of action as possible were recognised by the authors of the Peace Treaty. It should also be observed that when the Supreme Council decided to permit the admission of Germany to the Labour Organisation before it was admitted to the League of Nations, Mr. Arthur Fontaine, who was then General Secretary of the Commission on International Labour Legislation, sent a letter to the Secretary-General of the Peace Conference asking whether this decision did not necessitate some change in the drafting of Article 387 of the Treaty; neither the Supreme Council nor the Drafting Committee felt the necessity for adopting such a suggestion.

At that time it could be taken as accepted that the connection established by Article 387 between membership of the League of Nations and membership of the International Labour Organisation did not make it impossible for the latter to recruit members outside the number of those which had adhered to the Covenant. In reply to a request from Finland for admission to the Labour Conference at Washington the Supreme Council decided once again to let the question be settled by the Conference itself. When Finland's request was examined by the competent committee of the Washington Conference, a proposal was made by four votes to one to admit that country on the same footing as Germany and Austria and to decide that in principle any State which applied for admission to the International Labour Organisation in accordance with the procedure laid down could be admitted.

The minority of the Committee, however, was strongly opposed to this view and set out in its report the legal arguments which seemed to preclude the admission to the International Labour Organisation of any State which did not belong to the League of Nations. This report pointed out that if the authors of Part XIII had considered such a possibility they would have indicated clearly by what authority and subject to what conditions a State could be admitted. The minority further believed that the organic connection between the two institutions was such that it prevented the adherence of a State to Part XIII unless it adhered at the same time to the Covenant of the League of Nations. They argued that the case of Germany and Austria should be considered as quite exceptional; the decision of the Supreme Council on that point should be viewed as a special agreement entered into between those two States and the Allied and Associated Powers for the purpose of and as a condition of their acceptance of the Peace Treaties. According to this view the decision of the Council could not be taken as an interpretation of Article 387, for as such it would have been null and void, since the power to interpret the Treaties was reserved to the Court of International Justice. In the absence of any formal provision in the Peace Treaties, the right to admit members could not be conferred on the International Labour Conference by a decision of the Supreme Council, and still less by a decision taken by the Conference itself.

In spite of its desire to extend the territorial competence of the Organisation, the Washington Conference did not dare to ignore these legal arguments, and "without passing on the question of principle" it contented itself with inviting the delegates of Finland to take part in the Conference on the same footing as other countries not belonging to the League of Nations. An identical decision was taken at Washington in the case of Luxemburg and again at Genoa with regard to Finland. The position of these two countries with reference to the International Labour Organisation was, however, automatically settled when the First Assembly of the League of Nations in December 1920 decided to admit them to the League. The same Assembly also admitted Albania, Bulgaria and Costa Rica, which, according to the basic principle of Article 387, at the same time became members of the International Labour Organisation. The applications of certain other States—Estonia, Latvia and Lithuania—were rejected for political reasons which do not concern us here; the important fact to be noted is that the Assembly, although it replied to these applications in the negative, at the same time recognised that the need of the International Labour Organisation for universality could not easily be reconciled with the considerations which might dictate the limits of the League of Nations. It was decided that if these States requested to be admitted to the International Labour Organisation their applications should be submitted to the Conference. There is no doubt that the Conference would have taken advantage of the right thus granted it if the Second Assembly had not admitted these States to the League before the next Conference met.

Hungary was admitted to the League of Nations in 1922, Ethiopia and the Irish Free State in 1923, and the Dominican

Republic in 1924, all these becoming States Members of the International Labour Organisation. Germany, which had been admitted as a member of the Organisation by the Washington Conference, became a member of the League in 1926, and as Austria had been in the same position since 1920, the boundaries of the International Labour Organisation were for a time the same as those of the League of Nations.

The Case of Brazil

The question of principle raised at Washington and left unsettled by the Conference at that date was bound to arise later. It almost did so in 1922, when it was thought that Mexico would apply for membership of the International Labour Organisation. There is no knowing what might have been the attitude of the Conference at that time when the Assembly had recently recognised its power to admit a number of States. As it happened, it was not called upon to take any decision, since the Government of Mexico did not carry out its original intention.

The problem came before the Assembly and the Conference in a new form in 1926. As a result of certain incidents which the reader will recall, Spain and Brazil declared their intention of withdrawing from the League of Nations, but stated at the same time that they wished to remain members of the International Labour Organisation. The question which thus arose was no longer whether the Conference had power to admit new members, but whether a State which withdrew from the League of Nations could continue to belong to the International Labour Organisation, or whether the boundaries of the two institutions must be considered identical notwithstanding the exception created at the beginning by the Supreme Council in favour of Germany and Austria. Spain returned to membership of the League of Nations before the expiry of the period of notice of two years prescribed in the Covenant, so that in the case of that country the question did not arise. But Brazil held to its decision and actually left the League in 1928, so that in 1929 the Assembly was forced to take a decision.

Once again legal scruples were set aside in favour of practical necessities and the obvious interests of the two institutions. When the Fourth Committee of the Assembly was about to discuss the budget of the Organisation, which allowed for income from the Brazilian contribution, the Secretary-General of the League of Nations read a statement in which he requested that if the Fourth Committee accepted that contribution it should be on the understanding "that its action in so doing in no way prejudiced any constitutional questions arising under the Treaty provisions which had established the Labour Organisation. Under the present circumstances the question of the precise legal situation with regard to the continuance of Brazil's membership of the Labour Organisation could be considered as being of so theoretical a character that there did not seem to be any need to endeavour to solve it."

In reply to the Secretary-General the Director of the International Labour Office agreed "that it would be incorrect to attribute any theoretical or absolute value to the incorporation of the Brazilian contribution in the budget of the Labour Organisation. The Secretary-General's reservation could not, however, constitute at some future date an argument against the legal consequences of the positive fact that this contribution had been paid. In any case it would not affect the rights of Brazil and the obligations that it had assumed in virtue of its participation in the International Labour Organisation." The Fourth Committee and the Assembly, when adopting the budget of the Organisation, confined themselves to taking note of these two declarations.

Constitutionally the question was thus left entirely open, and this is important from the point of view of law. But from the point of view of practical life the most important fact is that the need of the Organisation for universality has been recognised and met. In practice Brazil has remained a member of the Organisation, and it sent complete delegations, whose credentials were accepted by the Conference, to the three Sessions of the Labour Conference following its withdrawal from the League.

Present Extent of the Organisation

The International Labour Organisation at present consists of a total of fifty-five States which participate in its work. Through these States its competence extends to the territories which they administer as colonies, possessions, protectorates or mandated territories. By Article 421 the members engage to apply Conventions which they have ratified to their territories which are not fully self-governing, subject to the double reservation that the Convention need not be applied if inapplicable on account of local conditions and that modifications may be made if necessary to adapt the Convention to local conditions.

The Organisation has thus a very wide range of competence covering four-fifths of the population of the world. It extends to every continent, and it is particularly noteworthy that the Organisation numbers among its members more of the Pacific countries than any of the institutions or organisations specially set up in recent years for strengthening the bonds between these peoples and for studying their common interests.

Non-members: United States

Wide as is the geographical extent of the Organisation it has not yet reached the universality which it logically requires.

Three States mentioned in the appendix to the Covenant as original members of the League of Nations have never actually become members. Two of these are Hedjaz and Ecuador, which have never taken any decision either way with regard to ratification of the Treaty of Versailles. The third is the United States which, as the reader knows, formally declined to ratify.

There is no doubt that the absence of the United States is at present the most serious gap in the structure of the International Labour Organisation. As the most powerful industrial country in the world and one which is increasing its hold on the international market year by year, its absence constitutes a hindrance to the future progress of international labour legislation. It is true that for ten years the Organisation has been able to accomplish valuable work, even in the realm of international legislation, without the collaboration of the United States. In this it was aided by the peculiar economic circumstances of the post-War period. Now that the world is faced by an economic crisis of unprecedented extent which is intensifying the competition in the world's markets, there is a danger that the countries will be less ready to bind themselves by Conventions which do not apply to one of their most formidable competitors. On the other hand, the fact that the United States has become a large exporter of manufactured goods implies that the labour costs of American industry are brought into daily comparison and competition with those of other exporting countries. It has therefore become increasingly important from the American standpoint that their standards should not be endangered by lower standards elsewhere. The maintenance of the wage-levels which have given the American workman a high standard of living is now no longer dependent solely on domestic conditions in the United States, but is directly influenced by international conditions and considerations. It is therefore not surprising that the International Labour Office should frequently have dealt with the question and that the Office should have done all in its power to induce the United States to take part in its work. Fruitful relations have been established with official and private bodies, and these will be dealt with in another chapter of this work. In 1923 there was even some hope that a delegation of employers and workers might attend the Conference as observers. The idea was abandoned at the last moment and has not again been suggested, so that officially the situation is still the same as in 1920. Hopes of a change in the near future are entertained, but without much conviction. For the time being at any rate the attitude of the International Labour Organisation can only be one of expectation, which of course does not prevent it from seizing every opportunity of getting into touch with official or private circles.

Mexico

Close beside the United States, Mexico makes another blank on the map of the Organisation—a blank which it is difficult to understand in view of the fact that the trend of social development of this country for several years has been exactly parallel with that followed in Geneva. It is not surprising that from time to time attempts have been made on both sides to arrive at an understanding. As early as 1922 negotiations were entered into with the Government of President Obregon, and the Director in his report to the Conference felt justified in announcing that Mexico would shortly apply for admission to the Organisation. Internal troubles in Mexico prevented the Government from carrying out its intention at that time, but in 1924 negotiations were again opened with the new President, General Calles, who met Mr. Albert Thomas in Paris during his visit to Europe. Their interview revealed the lively interest which the President took in the development of international labour legislation and at the same time the difficulties which prevented his country from entering the Organisation. The normal way of entrance is through the League of Nations, but Mexico had not forgotten its lively resentment of the attitude of certain Powers in 1919, when its name was omitted from the list of States invited to accede to the Covenant. Moreover in 1924 its diplomatic situation was still such as to give grounds for the belief that a request for admission might not be accepted without discussion. In view of this fact, the Mexican Government preferred to take no definite step as regards membership of the League. While it was prepared to give a cordial reply to any invitation coming from Geneva it decided not to make an application until it was certain of receiving a unanimous welcome.

Mention has already been made of the legal objections to entrance into the International Labour Organisation prior to admission to the League of Nations. Just when President Calles was endeavouring to make his position clear, Mr. Oudegeest placed the question before the Governing Body and requested it, in the name of the Workers' Group, to invite Mexico to apply for admission to the Organisation. The Workers' Group obviously wished to give Mexico a guarantee in advance that its application would be accepted, but the Governing Body, while sympathetic to the proposal, could not forget the discussion at Washington with regard to Finland's application and did not consider that it was advisable under the circumstances to lay the matter before the Permanent Court of International Justice.

Since then there has been no official change in the position of Mexico. The country is still outside the Organisation but ready to join it as soon as circumstances permit. In the meantime, it has on several occasions shown its willingness to collaborate in scientific and technical work, and in 1930 it sent an official observer to the Conference who spoke during the discussion on the Director's Report.

Turkey

In the case of Turkey, just as with Mexico, purely political reasons are responsible for its absence. Immediately after the signing of the Treaty of Lausanne it was hoped that this estrangement would soon come to an end. So far, however, Turkey has not applied for admission to the League of Nations and consequently remains outside the International Labour Organisation. This abstention has not, however, precluded a sincere desire for collaboration, as is clearly shown by the fact that official observers have attended recent Sessions of the Conference.

Egypt This country also has shown a desire to collaborate. As far back as 1924 the Prime Minister expressed the hope that the task in which the Egyptian Government was busily engaged might be extended and consolidated by the participation of Egypt in the work of the international institutions for maintaining the peace of the world. Since then the Organisation has been in frequent touch with official and private circles, and the only apparent obstacle to the full participation of this country in the work of the Organisation and of the League of Nations as a whole would seem to be the delay in settling the constitutional problems at present under negotiation between Great Britain and the Egyptian Government.

The U.S.S.R. The position with regard to the U.S.S.R. is unfortunately quite a different one. In the last three countries mentioned above, a desire for active participation exists but has so far been prevented from coming to fruition by external circumstances. The Union of Socialist Soviet Republics, on the other hand, has never ceased to express, in terms which have varied only in their degree of forcefulness, its hostility towards the International Labour Organisation—an attitude to which the Organisation could not be indifferent. At the same time, the great economic changes brought about in Russia by the Bolshevist Revolution and the uncertainty existing abroad with regard to the social consequences of the new regime, made it incumbent upon the Organisation to study these conditions impartially and collect first-hand information. As early as the Second Session of the Governing Body, in January 1920, Mr. Sokal, Polish Government delegate, drew attention to the Russian problem. The Governing Body decided to send a mission to study these conditions, but after lengthy negotiations the Soviet Government refused its consent and it has not since then changed its attitude.

As a result of the Genoa and the Hague Conferences in 1922, certain relationships were established with Russian representatives or administrations. Gradually an exchange of publications was instituted, and about 1928 it was thought that a further step might be taken and scientific co-operation organised for the study of certain questions, particularly that of wages, between the Office's research services and those of the People's Commissariat for Labour. It was hoped that the Soviet Government, which had recently taken part in the International Economic Conference of 1927 and in the sessions of the Preparatory Commission for Disarmament, would gradually change its attitude towards the International Labour Organisation, but in the last months of the year these hopes were dashed to the ground. The scientific co-operation which had been begun was abruptly brought to an end. The Executive of the Red Trade Union International, at its meeting in Moscow in December 1929, reaffirmed its resolution to combat the "reformist agencies of world imperialism," among which it quoted the International Labour Office, and about the same time the Commissariat for Labour published an article stating that all attempts at collaboration with the International Labour Office must be stopped once for all. The leaders of the U.S.S.R. have rejected any form of collaboration, even in the scientific sphere, between Soviet institutions and international institutions because, according to the article referred to above, such collaboration involves divorcing science from politics and separating the study of facts from analysis in the light of Marxist doctrines, which is considered as being the only true science.

This return of Moscow to its original uncompromising antagonism to the Office is no doubt connected with the general evolution of the policy of the Soviet Government. A few faint attempts at establishing relationships were made when the New Economic Policy was introduced, but the Communist reaction of recent years has forced the leaders in Moscow to return to their fighting policy. This fact suggests that there may be further changes in the future. In the meantime, however, the gap continues to exist and its seriousness cannot be overlooked.

This survey of the important States which have not adhered to the International Labour Organisation shows that, with the exception of two (which are, however, the two most powerful), a desire for collaboration exists and a mere change in circumstances would be enough to make them Members.

Certain Anomalies

This survey would not be complete if it failed to mention Afghanistan in Asia and certain small States and territories in Europe which are still outside the Organisation.[1] In the

[1] To this list should be added Iceland, since the Danish Act of November 30th, 1918, giving it almost complete independence, appears to have withdrawn it from the jurisdiction of the International Labour Organisation.

case of Afghanistan there is no reason to expect any early application for membership, but its absence cannot be said to be of great importance for the progress of international labour legislation. The position of the tiny European States of San Marino, Monaco, Liechtenstein and Andorra is more abnormal. The Assembly of the League of Nations considered the question in 1921 but found it difficult, in view of their small size, to admit them as ordinary Members. So far no decision has been arrived at, and we thus find adjoining advanced industrial countries small districts to which international labour legislation does not apply. In the case of the territories administered by the League of Nations—the Saar and Danzig—the situation constitutes a still more flagrant paradox. In consequence of provisions the results of which were certainly not foreseen by their authors, these territories, which are densely populated, highly developed economically and advanced in social matters, are unable to participate in the work of the Organisation. The fact that the position of the Saar is merely transitory makes this anomaly less serious. Moreover, since 1925 the Commission for the government of that territory has, as a result of a resolution adopted by the International Labour Conference, endeavoured to some extent to meet the situation. It has set up a Joint Chamber of Labour to which the resolutions adopted by the Conference are regularly submitted with a view to considering the possibility of applying them in the territory.

The Free City of Danzig has also felt the need for participating in the work of the Organisation. In 1930 it applied for membership, but doubts were raised as to whether the request was in order in view of the rather peculiar legal position of the City, which is more or less under the double protectorate of the League of Nations and Poland, the latter being responsible for its foreign affairs. In view of this rather complicated situation the opinion of the Court of International Justice was asked, and the reply was in the negative. In this case, therefore, some other method of collaboration, distinct from ordinary membership, will have to be found if the City of Danzig is going to collaborate in the work of the Organisation and if the International Labour Conventions are to be regularly applied in its territory.

These exceptions and anomalies, paradoxical as they may be, do not prevent the International Labour Organisation from becoming a universal body. They are merely temporary difficulties which will be solved by the exercise of good-will. The important fact to note, and one which is a happy augury for the future, is that during the first ten years of its existence the cohesion of the Organisation has never been imperilled, and that if it does not yet cover as large a part of the globe as could be wished, the reason can be found in many cases in legal or political difficulties which have formed an obstacle to the wishes of those concerned and the aspirations of the Organisation itself for complete universality.

CHAPTER III

STRUCTURE OF THE ORGANISATION

Permanence

As was pointed out some time ago by Mr. Elihu Root, the famous American lawyer, speaking of international peace, abstract good-will is not enough: there must be some organisation for carrying it into effect. In 1919 the desire for social justice existed with every Government. There is no saying what might have happened to this desire in the midst of the various crises which followed if no institution had been set up to put it into practice. The great waves of public enthusiasm recur but rarely, and the origin of many a social or political crisis can be traced to failure to carry out promises given in a moment of enthusiasm or emotion. The authors of Part XIII therefore set up an institution which would fulfil the pledge given to the workers in 1919. Before describing how this institution fulfilled its task, it will be well to analyse its structure and elements, for the results obtained by such an organisation often depend on the quality of its constitution. The structure of the International Labour Organisation has triumphantly stood the test of ten years.

The first characteristic of the new institution is its permanence. The first Article of Part XIII states: "A *permanent* organisation is hereby established for the promotion of the objects set forth in the Preamble." In putting the fact of its permanence in the foreground the authors of the Treaties wished to bring out at once the difference between this Organisation and the pre-War experiments. The Berne Conferences had only established temporary contact between the Governments which took part. Once the Conference had dissolved there was no official body to follow out the decisions taken or prepare for the next meeting. Everything depended on the initiative and tenacity of the International Association for the Labour Legislation. Before each Conference could be convened there were interminable discussions between Government departments, and these discussions continued to work in another form after the Conference had concluded its work.

These difficulties have now been removed. A permanent organisation has been set up, consisting, as is stated in Article 388, of (1) a General Conference of representatives of the Members, and (2) an International Labour Office controlled by a Governing Body.

Regularity of Sessions and Effective Participation of States

The Conference shares in the permanent character of the institution as a whole. It has nothing except the name in common with the Berne Conferences, which were held at no fixed interval and were not continuous. Article 389 states that "the meetings of the General Conference shall be held from time to time as occasion may require and at least once in every year." These meetings, and consequently also the progress of the work, are thus not dependent on political contingencies or on the temporary good-will or ill-will of a State.

During the first years of the Organisation it was sometimes thought that the authors of the Peace Treaty had perhaps gone too far in their endeavour to assure the continuity of the work. It was suggested that the range of activity of the Conference was not wide enough to justify annual sessions, and that too frequent meetings might prove a strain on the good-will of Governments, particularly in distant countries which had to send delegations to Geneva at great expense.

Experience has shown that these apprehensions were unfounded. Not only have the annual Sessions been fully occupied, but they have even proved insufficient to deal with all the questions demanding attention. Twice during the first ten years the Conference has had to hold two Sessions in one year. In October 1930, when the Governing Body had to select a question to complete the agenda for the Sixteenth Session, it had before it a list of fifty subjects previously suggested by the Conference, by members of the Governing Body, by Governments or by industrial organisations. There is therefore no fear of the agenda of the Conference being exhausted at an early date. The new questions which are constantly being brought to light by the study of labour conditions and the new problems arising out of economic and social progress and out of the evolution of the problems already dealt with will easily keep it fully occupied.

Nor has there been any sign of waning interest on the part

of States up to the present time. The contrary is indeed the case. Forty States were represented at the Washington Conference in 1919; at the last Session held in Geneva in 1930 there were 51. This is the record figure to date. Moreover, since the origin of the Organisation the number of States taking part in the Conference has never fallen below 39, except at the Maritime Sessions, which are of interest only to a limited number of countries.

It is reassuring to find that the interest in the work of the Organisation, far from declining, has increased steadily during recent years: 39 delegations in 1926, 43 in 1927, 46 in 1928 and 50 in 1929. The 51 States represented at the 1930 Session included 26 European States and 25 non-European, of which 15 were States of Latin America, 5 from Asia, 1 from Africa and 4 from the British Dominions. One of these Dominions, New Zealand, was taking part in a Session of the Conference for the first time, thus testifying to the growing prestige of the Organisation throughout the world and to the fact that it is in the long run impossible for a country, even when situated in the Antipodes, to hold aloof from the work of the Conference.

Of the 55 States Members of the Organisation only 4 were absent in 1930—Argentina, Norway, Salvador and Ethiopia. In the case of the first two, absence cannot be attributed to habitual indifference, but merely to certain misunderstandings or incidents, such as are inevitable within any large family, whether it be composed of States or of individuals.

There have been strange vicissitudes in the relations between Argentina and the International Labour Organisation. At Washington in 1919 and at Genoa in 1920 that country sent complete delegations, whose active participation was frequently commented upon. A seat was granted it on the Governing Body, and everything seemed to point to fruitful collaboration. At the end of 1920, during the first Assembly of the League of Nations, the Argentine delegation received instructions from President Irigoyen to withdraw as a protest against the rejection of one of its proposals, but for a time it was thought that this would not affect the normal relations of the country with the Organisation. The Argentine Government delegate continued to attend the meetings of the Governing Body until July 1921 and, although he has not appeared since that date, he has never officially resigned his position. For two years there was no

Argentine delegation at the Conference, but in 1923 a second change took place. When Mr. de Alvear was elected in place of Mr. Irigoyen as President of the Argentine Republic relationships were immediately re-established. Argentina still remained absent from the Assembly of the League, but sent delegations to every Session of the Conference from 1923 to 1928. In 1928 a special tribute was paid to the country by the election of Mr. Saavedra Lamas as President of the Eleventh Session. In the same year, however, Mr. Irigoyen again became President of the Republic and his election led to a fresh breach between that country and the Organisation. It is hoped that recent events may close that breach. It is at all events noteworthy that the Argentine Government delegate resumed his place at the October Session of the Governing Body, which was held immediately after the disturbances in Argentina.

Norway has been absent from the last two Sessions of the Conference, but it is not expected that this situation will continue. The reason is again one of internal politics. The Government was unable to send a delegation because the Storting refused the necessary credits for 1929–30. There is no reason to suppose that this will occur again, and in the meantime the Government showed its desire to collaborate by sending observers to the two Sessions of the Conference to which the decision of the Storting prevented it from sending official delegations. The Association of Norwegian Shipowners also sent an observer to the Thirteenth Session, who let slip no opportunity of explaining how the Storting's decision could jeopardise the international and maritime interests of Norway within the International Labour Organisation.

The importance of the temporary absence of any one country from the International Labour Conference should not be exaggerated. What would be serious for the Organisation would be indifference or waning interest reflected in general absenteeism. The Conference cannot hope to be immune from passing incidents, but such incidents settle themselves in time when they run counter to some recognised need. That the International Labour Organisation meets such a need is amply shown by the fact that 51 States out of 55 took part in the last annual Ses ion of the Conference, while official observers were sent by 2 non-Member States: Turkey and Mexico. Very few private associations can show such a high rate of attendance. When such extensive participation is assured it may be said that the States which remain absent are thereby wronging themselves more than the Organisation, since they voluntarily renounce the influence which they might exert on international life.

The Representation of Occupational Interests

A further characteristic of the International Labour Conference, in addition to its permanence and the obligation to hold regular Sessions, is its peculiar composition and more particularly the presence of representatives of the occupational interests of employers and workers in addition to Government representatives. In this it differs not only from pre-War conferences, but also from other international institutions set up in virtue of the Peace Treaties.

To find an explanation of this innovation one must study the circumstances of the year 1919. The authors of Part XIII wished to give the workers a pledge of their sincerity. Now, an organisation in which only Governments were represented would not have sufficed to inspire confidence. Notwithstanding the programme laid down in the Preamble, notwithstanding the general principles set forth in Article 427, it was to be feared that when the great wave of post-war idealism had passed and the Governments were once more at grips with their everyday difficulties, the longing for social justice might disappear into the background and an International Labour Conference at which only the voice of Governments was heard might fall asleep. If the Organisation was to be kept alive its assemblies had to be democratic and represent the parties concerned, thus enabling them to influence Governments or remind them of the lofty aims which they had undertaken to pursue. Moreover, such a system of representation was one of the most urgent demands of the labour movement. As early as September 1914 the American Federation of Labour had expressed the hope that the representatives of the organised workers of every nation would meet before the general Peace Conference so as to make known their proposals for the establishment of a lasting peace. This resolution proved the starting-point for a number of conferences of workers, both during and after the War, at which the workers' general claims were formulated. The last of these conferences, held at Berne in February 1919, formally demanded that an International Labour Office should be set up in the form of a real inter-occupational and international labour parliament, with direct representation of the workers' trade union organisations of every country.

Two rival systems of representation claimed the attention of the Commission on International Labour Legislation of the Peace Conference. Certain members, obsessed by the principle of equality, wished each State to be represented at the Conference by one Government delegate, one employers' delegate and one workers' delegate. Others considered that the Government should have the preponderance and that its delegates should carry as much weight as the employers' and workers' delegates together. This second solution was finally adopted and is prescribed in Article 389, which states that the Conference "shall be composed of 4 Representatives of each of the Members, of whom 2 shall be Government delegates and the 2 others shall be delegates representing respectively the employers and the workpeople of each of the Members." In order to ensure that the employers' and workers' delegates should not be appointed arbitrarily, but should actually be the authorised representatives of these industrial groups, Article 389 further provides that "the Members undertake to nominate non-Government delegates and advisers chosen in agreement with the industrial organisations, if such organisations exist, which are most representative of employers or workpeople, as the case may be, in their respective countries."

Article 390 adds that "every delegate shall be entitled to vote individually on all matters which are taken into consideration by the Conference."

As a consequence of these provisions, the aspect of the International Labour Conference is entirely different from that of any other official international assembly. Although the seats at the Conference are arranged by countries, so that the employers' and workers' delegates of any country sit side by side with their Government delegates, the voting is not by countries. The employers' representative and the workers' representative have complete freedom to vote in opposition to their Government representatives, and their votes are generally determined by the occupational interests of the category which they represent.

The Group System

The arrangement described above has led to the constitution of groups. Even at the Washington Conference the solidarity of their occupational interests led the employers' delegates and the workers' delegates to hold separate meetings for discussing the questions on the agenda from the point of view of their respective interests and endeavouring if possible to arrive at an agreement among themselves which would enable them to influence more effectively the result of the voting. The Government delegates followed this example, so that to-day the "group," although not provided for in Part XIII, has become part of the normal mechanism of the Conference. It is sanctioned by the Standing Orders, which give the groups important prerogatives in the constitution of the committees of the Conference, thus accentuating the resemblance which is sometimes found between the Conference and a Parliament. Instead of an assemblage of national representatives such as is found in most international assemblies, we have under the group system an assemblage of Government representatives, employers' representatives and workers' representatives, corresponding in some sort to parties in the parliamentary sense of the term. It is for this reason that a delegate of the employers or of the workers often seems to be not so much the spokesman of the workers or employers of his own country, as the representative of the workers or employers as a whole.

The group system has not always escaped criticism. At the 1928 Session Mgr. Nolens, Netherlands Government delegate, attacked what he called group discipline. He showed that the result of the voting on a Convention might be distorted if for reasons of discipline the minority in a group agreed to vote with the majority, or if the whole group decided to abstain because no agreement could be arrived at. The fear has also been expressed that the secret meetings and the slogans of groups tend to accentuate mutual distrust and suggest that the important thing for each group is to maintain its unity in attack or defence rather than seek reasonable and acceptable terms of peace. It has further been argued that the autonomy granted to the groups, especially for the appointment of members of committees, gives the majority in these groups the power to exclude the representatives of certain minority views from the work of the committees.

It must, however, be observed that these criticisms have never led to a suggestion that the groups should be abolished. It is not their existence but their policy which is attacked. The groups sprang up at Washington so spontaneously, so irresistibly and as such an obvious result of the representation of occupational interests at the Conference, that there could be no question of abolishing them. Even if they were deleted from the Standing Orders of the Conference, they would continue to exist unofficially, and the alleged dangers would merely be aggravated. The way to overcome these dangers is not to attack the groups but to seek a remedy for the unfortunate consequences of some of their practices. In 1928 Mgr. Nolens expressed the hope that the workers' and employers' groups "would consult together instead of taking up hard-and-fast attitudes in advance." Until such time as "the joint meetings of the employers' and workers' groups" to which Mgr. Nolens looked forward take place, the Conference has taken steps to protect the minority of the group against the power of the majority to exclude it from committee work. It has authorised any delegate, even when not appointed by his group, to take part in the work of a committee without the right to vote.

The Question of Incomplete Delegations

The composition of the delegations to the Conference, as defined in Article 389, has in practice raised two rather important problems: that of incomplete delegations and that of selecting the "most representative" industrial organisations.

The first point arose at the Washington Conference, and has constantly forced itself on the attention of the Organisation ever since. The authors of the Peace Treaty, when they decided that there should be one employers' and one workers' delegate in addition to two Government delegates, assuredly intended that the participation of those directly concerned in the work of the Conference should be one of the essential characteristics of the Organisation. If the workers had had any suspicion in 1919 that this provision would remain a dead letter, they would certainly never have placed confidence in the new institution. They would rather have turned their backs on it, and sought other means of obtaining satisfaction for their demands. It will, therefore, readily be understood that a strong feeling arose at Washington when it was found that sixteen States out of forty had sent incomplete delegations. There was, naturally, a protest by the workers' delegates, who considered that the position of the workers in the Conference was damaged by the absence of incomplete delegations. The Standing Orders Committee of the

Conference, which dealt with the protest, expressed the opinion that Article 389 required Governments to appoint four delegates, and that, strictly speaking, they were not entitled to send Government delegates only, "if," as Article 389 says, "workers' and employers' organisations exist in their respective countries."

This finding of the Committee illustrates the difficulty which the Conference must encounter in satisfying itself that the obligations of Article 389 have been respected. Incomplete delegations tend, beyond all doubt, to change the aspect of the Conference and to disturb the balance at which the Treaties aimed. But if countries in which employers' or workers' organisations are still in an embryonic state appointed delegates of little or no qualification to represent the employers and workers, this balance would be purely artificial, and the satisfaction given to the workers would be illusory, for these delegates might in fact be merely disguised Government delegates. On the other hand, if States which found difficulty in appointing workers' and employers' delegates simply abstained from taking part in the work of the Conference, the interests of the Organisation would suffer as the result of a rigid enforcement of its own rules.

For this reason the Conference, while maintaining the rules in theory, has in practice had to exercise tolerance. It has had to recognise that it possessed no legal or other means of compelling States to appoint non-Government delegates, and it has hesitated to suggest such means. It has, in fact, decided merely to exert a moral pressure by inviting those Members who have not sent complete delegations to state their reasons to the International Labour Office when communicating the credentials of the delegates, and leaving it to the Credentials Committee of the Conference to ask for supplementary information from the delegates of the States in question.

This procedure, which was first adopted by the Washington Conference, has been in regular use since 1923. It has had the threefold advantage of constantly reminding the States concerned of their obligations under Article 389, of dissipating many understandings by enabling States to explain their genuine difficulties, and sometimes of bringing to light a means of overcoming these difficulties. It is doubtless due as much to the successful application of this method as to the progress of industrial organisation throughout the world that the number of complete delegations at the Conference has risen in recent years. In 1919, only 24 out of a total of 40 delegations were complete; after falling to 20 out of 39 in 1922, the number rose to 29 out of 46 in 1925, and to 35 out of 51 at the 1930 Session. The number of States sending complete delegations to the Conference has thus increased more rapidly since 1922 than the total number of States represented; and this should help to reassure those who feared at the beginning that a disproportion between the number of Government delegates and that of non-Government delegates might distort the machinery and vitiate the general spirit of the International Labour Conference.

The Most Representative Industrial Organisations

The question of selecting the most representative industrial organisations has troubled the Conference at every Session even more than the problem of incomplete delegations.

According to Article 389, paragraph 3, of the Treaty, "The Members undertake to nominate non-Government delegates and advisers chosen in agreement with the industrial organisations, if such organisations exist, which are most representative of employers or workpeople, as the case may be, in their respective countries." The same Article gives the Conference the right to see whether States have faithfully observed this provision. Paragraph 7 states that: "The credentials of delegates and their advisers shall be subject to scrutiny by the Conference, which may, by two-thirds of the votes cast by the delegates present, refuse to admit any delegate or adviser whom it deems not to have been nominated in accordance with this Article." If the Conference refuses to admit a non-Government delegate, the position is the same as if that delegate has not been appointed by the State in question, and the other non-Government delegate is not entitled to vote.

So much for the regulation, in virtue of which the validity of credentials has many a time been disputed. It was even found necessary in 1921 to ask for an interpretation from the Permanent Court of International Justice. The point at issue was whether paragraph 3 of Article 389 meant that the employers' or workers' delegate ought to be appointed by the Government in agreement with the only organisation which could be considered as the most representative of the employers or workpeople of the country, or whether the plural employed in the text for the word "organisations" meant that in countries where there were several industrial organisations the Government was at liberty to appoint the employers' or workers' delegate in agreement with a group of organisations, none of which might be the most representative in itself, but which as a whole were the most representative of the employers or workpeople of the country.

In the case under discussion the Government of the Netherlands had appointed as workers' delegate Mr. Serrarens, Secretary of the Federation of Catholic Trade Unions, in agreement with four out of the five most important workers' organisations in the Netherlands. These four organisations had together 280,000 members. The fifth organisation, the Federation of Independent Trade Unions, which had 218,000 members, and was therefore the most important single organisation of the five, claimed that the workers' delegate should be chosen in agreement with it alone, and protested against a nomination which it deemed contrary to the terms of Article 389. The Conference, after the question had been considered by its Credentials Committee, accepted the credentials of the Dutch delegate. At the same time it thought the question of interpretation involved so important that it asked the Governing Body to obtain the opinion of the Court upon the point. This opinion was given on July 31st, 1922, and supported the view of the Netherlands Government. The Court held that the object of each Government must certainly be to obtain agreement between all the most representative organisations of employers or of workers. If that could not be done, it was the duty of the Government to do its best to obtain such an agreement as seemed most calculated in the circumstances to ensure the adequate representation of the employers or workers of the country, subject always to the right of the Conference to decide whether the result was in conformity with Article 389.

In succeeding years this opinion served to guide Governments in making the appointments under Article 389, and the Conference in examining credentials. But in spite of that, the credentials of several non-Government delegates or advisers have been objected to at each Session. The recurrent discussion on the credentials of the Italian workers' delegate is a familiar feature of the Conference. The workers' group, believing that freedom of association does not exist in Italy and that consequently there can be no organisation which really represents the working classes, has regularly—although unsuccessfully—protested at every Session against accepting the credentials of this delegate. The political interest of this discussion is apt to overshadow the innumerable and important questions of law and fact, often of a very delicate nature, which have to be dealt with each year by the Credentials Committee. The task of determining which are the most representative organisations, even in the wide sense accepted by the Permanent Court of International Justice, involves many difficulties. Is a Government which considers that the workers' organisations in its country are not sufficiently developed to be really representative entitled, as the Japanese Government used to do, to consult the workers directly? What should it do when the country has no organisation of workers only, but merely mixed organisations? Or supposing that there exists side by side with the central organisation a special industrial organisation not affiliated to the central body and having a larger membership? Or supposing a special organisation appears to be more representative of the particular class of workers or employers affected by the business of any given Session? Or supposing that there is no central organisation, but instead a number of trade unions of varying shades of opinion, with no regular relationships between each other? Such examples might be multiplied. These are sufficient, however, to show the complexity of the questions which may be raised by objections to credentials. The Conference has never yet refused to accept credentials. It has sometimes concluded that the conditions of Article 389 had not been complied with, but it was always of the opinion that the Government in question had acted with sufficient good faith for its choice to be accepted, and it confined itself to making recommendations as to the procedure to be followed in future in order to avoid fresh disputes. Thus the Credentials Committee has gradually developed an unwritten law which enables it to settle more surely than in the early days the difficult problems submitted to it, and which also guides Governments in appointing their workers' and employers' delegates.

The Composition of the Governing Body

The composition of the Governing Body presents a certain analogy to that of the Conference. Governments, employers and workers are represented on it, in the same proportions as at the Conference but in smaller numbers—12 Government representatives, 6 employers' representatives and 6 workers' representatives.

No serious difficulties have occurred in connection with the representation of industrial groups on the Governing Body, because the system is one of indirect representation, and the question of the most representative organisations does not arise. The employers' and workers' representatives on the Governing Body are elected by the employers' and workers' representatives respectively at the Conference. They are appointed by name, so that they act on the Governing Body not so much as spokesmen of the employers and workers in their own countries, but as delegates of the whole group of employers or workers represented at the Conference.

The appointment of the Government members has proved a more delicate matter. Article 393 provides that: "Of the twelve persons representing the Governments, eight shall be nominated by the Members which are of the chief industrial importance and four shall be nominated by the Members selected for the purpose by the Government delegates to the Conference, excluding the delegates of the eight Members mentioned above."

This provision calls for two remarks. In the first place, in contrast to the representation of employers and workers, the representation of Governments has remained on a purely national basis; it is the States, and not the Government delegates at the Conference, which appoint the persons to represent them on the Governing Body. Further, as in the Council of the League of Nations, an exception is made to the principle of equality of States. The authors of the Treaty of Peace believed that the Governing Body could not be really representative unless the twelve Government members included representatives of the eight countries of chief industrial importance. It is true that the Treaty does not mention which countries these shall be; it merely provides that any disputes on the subject shall be settled by the Council of the League. As might be expected, such disputes have arisen.

The Eight States of Chief Industrial Importance

The Washington Conference, when called upon to constitute the first Governing Body, met with great difficulties. Following a preliminary selection made by its organising committee on the basis of four objective criteria, it drew up a list of the eight chief industrial countries, comprising Belgium, France, Germany, Great Britain, Italy, Japan, Switzerland and the United States. Denmark was to take the place of the United States until that country ratified the Peace Treaty.

Numerous protests were made against this list, but most of them were subsequently withdrawn. India, however, brought its claim before the Council of the League, which, after due consideration, recognised the justice of the demand, and granted India a seat in place of Switzerland. The enquiry made by the Council of the League at that time showed that, in the absence of the United States, the eighth permanent seat should be given to Canada. Thus, at the present day, the eight Powers recognised as being the most important from the industrial point of view are Belgium, Canada, France, Germany, Great Britain, India, Italy and Japan. This list has not varied or been contested since it was finally established.

The Demands of Non-European Countries

The discussions to which the composition of the Governing Body gave rise at Washington brought to light a wider and more serious problem than the mere allocation of the eight permanent seats. Considerable discontent was shown by the non-European delegations over the small number of seats reserved for their countries. As the Governments, workers and employers voted separately, in conformity with the provisions of the Treaty, it was found that the Governing Body as a whole included 20 European members out of 24—a regrettable fact in view of the need for universality in the Organisation. The non-European delegates did not conceal their feeling that it was difficult for them to place their confidence in a body so composed, and the Conference, at the last sitting of the Washington Session, adopted by 44 votes to 39 a resolution expressing its disapproval of the composition of the Governing Body.

As the members of the Governing Body hold office for three years, the next election was due to take place at the 1922 Session. In 1921 the Conference took the first step towards avoiding a recurrence of the incidents which had happened at Washington. It found on examination that it was impossible to give complete satisfaction to European and non-European countries without changing the constitution of the Governing Body. This question was therefore placed on the agenda of the 1922 Session, and it was then decided that the number of members of the Governing Body should be increased from 24 to 32, of whom 16 would be Government representatives (8 being appointed by the Powers of chief industrial importance), 8 employers' representatives, and 8 workers' representatives. Six Government representatives out of the 16, 2 employers' representatives and 2 workers' representatives were to belong to non-European States.

The Amendment to Article 393

This reform could be carried out only by amending Article 393. According to Article 422 of the Treaty, however, any amendment to Part XIII adopted by a two-thirds majority in the Conference must, before coming into force, be ratified by the States whose representatives constitute the Council of the League, and by three-quarters of the Members. Neither of these conditions has so far been fulfilled as regards the amendment to Article 393 adopted by the Conference in 1922. Forty of the necessary forty-two ratifications have so far been obtained, but the ratification of certain States represented on the Council of the League is still required. At one time the number of these States had been reduced to two, but it is now four, in consequence of changes in the composition of the Council. The States in question are Italy, Venezuela, Peru and Guatemala. It is strange that three of these four States belong to the non-European countries for whose benefit the amendment was adopted. On the other hand, that is a reason for hoping that ratification will come in due course. In the meantime the re-elections of the Governing Body in 1922, 1925 and 1928 were carried out under the conditions laid down in the original Article 393. In order to avoid fresh protests from non-European countries, the groups at the Conference have at each election adopted certain recommendations laid down by the Conference in 1921. The Government group has arranged that one of the four non-permanent seats at its disposal should go to a non-European country. Thus, as three of the eight permanent seats are occupied by non-European Governments, the total number of Government seats held by non-European countries is four out of twelve. The employers' and workers' groups also have each granted at least one seat out of the six at their disposal to representatives of these countries.

The International Labour Office

The International Labour Office differs from the Conference and the Governing Body in that it is not of a representative nature. It is a purely administrative department. Its Director is appointed by the Governing Body and chooses his staff, within the limits of the resources granted to him, with a view to the greatest possible efficiency. It is true that the Director must select persons of different nationalities, so that the Office may glean information from all possible sources and assure the growth of that international spirit which is essential to its work; indeed, Article 395 imposes this obligation in so far as it is compatible with efficiency. Every official thus appointed is responsible in the exercise of his duties to the Director alone. In the fullest sense of the term he is an "international official," and when he accepts his appointment he pledges himself, according to the Staff Regulations, "to discharge his functions and to regulate his conduct with the interests of the League alone in view." The regulations add: "He may not seek or receive instructions from any Government or other authority external to the International Labour Office." In 1921 the Office staff consisted of 262 officials, belonging to 19 nations; to-day there are 399 officials, belonging to 35 nations. It will be seen that a real effort has been made to make the Office as international as possible.

Correspondents

In order to preserve the necessary contact with the administrative authorities and with the economic and social life of different countries, the Office has found it essential to set up a series of Correspondents' Offices, the constitution and work of which will be described in another part of this volume.

Committees

However great the authority and competence of the experts and specialists on the staff of the Office, they obviously cannot fall out of touch with scientific, economic or social life, or they will find themselves left in a backwater. A number of committees have therefore been set up to keep the officials informed of the views and desires of those concerned and to assist them in certain particularly difficult scientific work. These committees bring a healthy fresh breeze from without into the research work of the Office and enable it to have wider and more varied relations with the industrial world than it could have through the members of the Governing Body. There are now twenty-two committees, on the assistance of which the Office calls when necessity arises. Some are of a statutory nature, such as the Joint Maritime Commission, which has to be consulted on every maritime question submitted to the Conference. Others are permanent advisory bodies which can be consulted by the Office at will on any questions falling within their competence. Such are the Permanent Migration Committee, the Advisory Committees on Salaried Employees and Professional Workers and the Correspondence Committees on Industrial Hygiene and Accident Prevention. Still others are of a purely temporary nature and are set up merely to assist the Office in carrying out some given study or enquiry by collaborating with its services and supervising their work. The composition and size of these committees vary as much as their functions. Some of them consist of only three members representing the three groups on the Governing Body. More often experts are added, the number of whom varies according to the nature of the questions under discussion. These experts are selected on varying grounds; some are specialists chosen on account of their scientific ability; others are appointed as direct representatives of certain interests or because they are qualified to express the point of view of a special class of workers or branch of industry. There is no need to give here a complete survey of the committees, since their activities will be described in the chapters dealing with the work of the Organisation.

Relations with the League of Nations

No description of the International Labour Organisation would be complete which failed to give some indication of its relationships with the League of Nations. We have seen already the motives which led the authors of the Peace Treaties to give the Organisation a special place within the League of Nations. Probably the workers' confidence would have been shaken if the actions and decisions of the Organisation, taken with the support of their representatives, had to be submitted for approval to an Assembly consisting only of Government representatives. Moreover, the social problem in 1919 demanded urgent solutions, which could not wait until the League of Nations itself had been finally established.

At the same time the authors of the Treaty wished to link the two institutions together for the sake of organic unity and for the purpose of emphasising their common aims. The Treaty prescribes that the Office shall form part of the organisation of the League of Nations; that it shall be established at the seat of the League (Article 392); that the meetings of the Conference shall, as a general rule, be held at the seat of the League

(Article 391); that the Secretary-General shall pay the expenses of the Organisation to the Director (Article 399); that the Director shall be entitled to the assistance of the Secretary-General in any matter in which it can be given (Article 398); finally, that the Secretary-General shall register the ratification of Draft Conventions and the adoption of Recommendations voted by the Conference in the same way as he registers all other international Conventions. The situation has been well summed up in the statement that, in general, the Secretariat acts for the Office as Chancellery and Finance Ministry.

On the basis of the above provisions, which are sometimes a little vague, the two institutions have built up their system of everyday collaboration. This collaboration is founded in essence on a division of labour. There are numerous questions in the economic sphere, in the field of hygiene, in humanitarian and social matters, in connection with transit and communications, mandates, etc., which are of interest to both institutions, though from different points of view. In the course of time it was necessary gradually to draw the line of demarcation between the respective competences of the institutions. The Office has made it a rule to refer to the Secretariat all questions which do not fall within its field of activity. Specialists from the Office have been invited to submit reports on the social aspects of certain questions on the agenda of the Committees of the League of Nations. In many cases they have been asked to attend the meetings of these Committees. A representative of the Office attends as a member the meetings of the Mandates Commission and another the meetings of the Child Welfare Committee. The Office is constantly represented in an advisory capacity on the Committee on Intellectual Co-operation, on the Health Committee and, when the agenda affects the Office, on the Economic Committee. For certain questions which are of equal interest to the Office and to some other organisations of the League, mixed committees have been set up, half the members being appointed by each institution; examples are: the Mixed Commission on Economic Crises, the Joint Committee on Hygiene and Health Insurance and the Mixed Committee on Inland Navigation. When the World Economic Conference was convened in Geneva in 1927 the Office was asked to help in preparing for the meeting by drafting a number of reports.

The most delicate point in the relations between the International Labour Organisation and the League of Nations would appear to be the financial link. The Organisation, jealous of its independence, must obviously be in a position to settle its own programme of work. Article 399 fully respects this principle when it says that the expenses of the Organisation "shall be paid" to the Director by the Secretary-General. The Secretary-General, however, cannot pay these expenses without asking the Assembly for the necessary votes and submitting to it the budget of the Organisation as prepared by the Governing Body after careful examination by its Finance Committee. Thus, it is the Assembly which finally passes the budget of the Organisation. Normally, the power of adopting a budget implies a scrutiny of the votes demanded and the power to discuss them, reduce them or even refuse them. If, however, such a power were used too freely in the present case it would infringe the autonomy of the Organisation. There is, therefore, a possibility of conflict between the prerogatives of the Assembly, which is the supreme financial authority, and those of the Organisation, which is an independent institution.

In practice, no such conflict has arisen. A *modus vivendi* has been arrived at, according to which the Assembly accepts in practice the supervision of the budget by the Governing Body. When changes or reductions have been asked for, they have never affected the international work of the Organisation as laid down by resolutions of the Conference or decisions of the Governing Body. At times, it is true, some slight inclination for stricter supervision has been shown by the Fourth Committee of the Assembly. On each occasion the difficulty has been met by arrangements designed to safeguard the prerogatives of both institutions. So long as the danger of a conflict of competence does not become more acute (and there has been no fresh sign of such a conflict during the last two years), it seems probable that both parties will prefer not to seek any formal or rigid solution for a problem which essentially calls for tact and discretion.

CHAPTER IV

FUNCTIONS AND METHODS

THE functions of the International Labour Organisation can be summed up in two words: legislation and information. The chief means proposed by the authors of Part XIII for carrying out the programme laid down in the Preamble was the drafting and application in every country of a system of international labour legislation. The special function assigned to the International Labour Office was to collect and distribute information concerning working conditions throughout the world.

I. INTERNATIONAL LABOUR LEGISLATION

The Provisions of the Treaty

When we speak of international labour legislation we are using an expression which is useful but which requires explanation. The International Labour Conference can give its decisions the form of Draft Conventions or of Recommendations. In the first case its decisions can be formally ratified, and this implies that the States which ratify have accepted certain commitments; in the second case there is no ratification and States are merely asked to carry out the Recommendations. In neither case have the decisions of the Conference a really legislative character. They do not become binding on the States Members by the mere fact of their adoption by the Conference. It may be recalled that when the Peace Treaty was being drafted the suggestion was made that the Conference should be given more extensive powers. The French and Italian delegations in particular supported the workers' demands that the International Labour Conference should be a legislative assembly in the full sense of the term, adopting laws which would be obligatory upon all the States Members of the Organisation. The British proposal, which was taken as a basis for discussion, did not go so far, but proposed that each Member should undertake to communicate within one year of the close of the Conference its formal ratification of the Conventions adopted, unless its legislative authorities were definitely opposed to such a course.

The Treaty did not even go so far as the British proposal. It did not make the decisions of the Conference in any way compulsory, nor did it force any State to ratify them. Nevertheless, the special provisions concerning the drafting and application of these decisions constitute an important step forward as compared with the rules applying to the former diplomatic conferences or to other international assemblies.

In the first place, the idea of unanimity which appeared to be a natural corollary of the sovereign rights of States has been definitely set aside. The agenda of the Conference is drawn up by the Governing Body after it has considered proposals put forward by Governments or by important industrial organisations. If any State Member wishes to object to one or more questions being retained on the agenda it is entitled to do so, but its opposition does not necessarily invalidate the item or items concerned, for the Conference can decide by a two-thirds majority to keep the question or questions on the agenda. Similarly, when the final vote is being taken on Draft Conventions or Recommendations proposed to the Conference, a hostile vote by one State cannot force a negative decision, because in this case also the two-thirds majority has been substituted for the rule of unanimity.

The full force of these provisions will be seen when they are taken in conjunction with those governing the composition of the Conference and the voting of delegates. It must be remembered, for instance, that half the Conference normally consists of employers' and workers' delegates voting individually, so that it is possible, if not probable, that in an extreme case a Draft Convention or Recommendation might be adopted even when the majority of the Government delegates voted against it.

The legal effects of the decisions of the Conference are the same whether a Government votes for or against these decisions. Although States are not compelled to apply the provisions thus adopted, they are at the same time not permitted to ignore them entirely. In the old diplomatic conferences, Governments were only morally bound through their plenipotentiaries. They were not even obliged to submit to their Parliaments Bills for authorising the ratification of Conventions signed by their representatives. Under Part XIII of the Treaty, the situation is changed.

No matter how its delegates vote at the Conference, a Government is bound to submit the Draft Conventions and Recommendations to the competent authorities—in the majority of cases, Parliament—for approval, so that they may be transformed into laws or that other measures may be taken. Governments are allowed one year, or in exceptional circumstances eighteen months, within which to fulfil this obligation. Thus, in the extreme case mentioned above, if a Draft Convention were adopted by the Conference in spite of the fact that the majority of Government delegates voted against it, the Government of every State Member of the Organisation, irrespective of its vote, would be bound to submit the Draft Convention to its Parliament within the prescribed time, and so give public opinion an opportunity of making itself heard. This obligation, moreover, binds not only the States represented at the Conference or those which took part in drafting the Convention, but all the States Members, even if they did not send a delegation.

If the competent national authority decides not to take action on a Recommendation or to accept a Draft Convention, the State has no further obligation. If the national authority does approve, the next step differs according to whether the decision concerned is a Recommendation or a Draft Convention. In the case of a Recommendation the State Member informs the Secretary-General of the League of Nations of the measures which have been taken, and its liabilities are thereby fulfilled. In the case of a Draft Convention, on the other hand, the State notifies the Secretary-General of its formal ratification and takes the necessary action to put the provisions of the Convention into effect.

As soon as a Convention is ratified it ceases to be a mere proposal and becomes a piece of international labour legislation. But legislation entails the supervision of its enforcement. Even at the Berne Conference in 1905, when the first two international labour Conventions were adopted, this fact was recognised; but it was found impossible at that time to agree to the institution of an international supervisory commission, even although its functions were to be purely consultative.

The authors of the Peace Treaty took up a much bolder attitude. Under Article 408 each of the Members agrees to make an annual report to the International Labour Office on the measures which it has taken to give effect to the provisions of Conventions to which it is a party. These reports have to be made in such form and contain such particulars as the Governing Body may request. The Director submits a summary of the reports to the next meeting of the Conference.

Thus a system has been set up for providing information and enabling supervision to be carried out. The Conference, and consequently also public opinion, can satisfy itself whether the States which have ratified a Convention actually apply it and in what manner they do so. In addition, there is a complete system of procedure for complaints, enquiries and sanctions, which occupies no fewer than ten Articles of Part XIII. There is no need to enter into details here, since the system has not had to be applied during these ten years.[1] Suffice it to say that the system is clearly inspired by a desire to delay the application of sanctions as long as possible, so as to allow the State implicated to justify itself at every stage of the procedure or to fulfil its obligations under the Convention. The sanctions provided, moreover, are of a purely economic nature, and the power of imposing them rests with the Permanent Court of International Justice.

The industrial associations of workers and employers share in supervising the application of the Conventions, as in their drafting. If any such organisation considers that a State has not taken sufficient steps to ensure the application of a Convention to which it is a party, it is entitled to make representations to the International Labour Office. The Governing Body may communicate these representations to the Government in question and invite it to give an explanation. If no reply is obtained from the Government within a reasonable period of time or if the reply does not satisfy the Governing Body, the latter

[1] It is true that in 1924 the Japanese Seamen's Union, considering that the method in which the Japanese Government was applying the Convention concerning facilities for finding employment for seamen did not correspond to the conditions laid down in that Convention, made formal representations to the Office under Article 409. Their complaint was submitted to the Governing Body, which examined it at its Twenty-fourth Session, in October 1924. According to the terms of Article 409 the Governing Body had to decide whether this representation should be communicated to the Japanese Government with a request that the Government should make such statement on the subject as it thought fit. That would have been the first stage in the procedure for enquiry laid down in the Treaty. The explanations supplied at that meeting by the representative of the Japanese Government led the Governing Body to decide that in the case under consideration the obligations entailed by the Convention had been fulfilled by the Japanese Government and that consequently there was no necessity to institute the proceedings provided for in Article 409.

has the right to publish the complaint received and the reply of the Government, if any. As a result, all the States Members would be given the opportunity, if they thought fit, to make a formal complaint, and so to open the procedure for enquiry and sanctions.

The Work of the Conference

Such in brief are the provisions of the Treaty regulating the legislative action of the Organisation. A considerable amount of work has already been accomplished in virtue of these provisions. From 1919 to 1930 the Conference has adopted thirty Conventions and thirty-nine Recommendations. The rhythm of this progress has not been the same at every stage. Three separate periods can be distinguished.

At the beginning, when the Organisation was confronted with the programme outlined in the Peace Treaty and was still under the direct influence of the aspirations from which it had taken its birth, it had a tendency, if one may use the phrase, to "bite off more than it could chew." The Peace Treaty itself had drawn up the agenda of the First Session, and that agenda included all the chief elements of a labour code: hours of work, the employment of women and children during the night and on unhealthy work, the minimum age for the admission of children to employment, the employment of women before and after childbirth and questions concerning the prevention of unemployment and means of dealing with its consequences. These problems were studied at Washington from the point of view of industry only. The Second and Third Sessions of the Conference were to consider successively the application of the principles adopted at Washington to maritime and agricultural work. The Third Session even added certain new questions, including the application of the weekly rest in industrial undertakings.

During its first three Sessions the Conference adopted sixteen Conventions and eighteen Recommendations, or more than half the number adopted up to the present. Experience showed that such a pace could not easily be reconciled with the slowness of parliamentary procedure in the different countries. It was thus found necessary to moderate the creative activity of the Conference, so that ratifications should not linger too far behind the drafting of Conventions. At one time a reduction in the number of Sessions was contemplated, and it was even suggested that the Conference should be convened only once in every two years; but this would have necessitated an amendment of Article 389, paragraph 1, of the Treaty, and would have met with active opposition from the workers; the idea was therefore dropped. As an alternative, the Governing Body endeavoured in 1922 and the ensuing years to keep the agenda of the Conference within narrow limits, so as to allow Parliaments time to give effect to the decisions so far adopted. At each of the Sessions held from 1922 to 1924, only a single Recommendation was adopted. In 1925 the output again became more intensive; in that year the Conference adopted four Draft Conventions and four Recommendations, dealing mainly with questions relating to workmen's compensation for accidents and occupational diseases. Generally speaking, the tendency since 1925 has been to proceed more slowly than during the first three years and to restrict the output of the Conference to one or two Draft Conventions, accompanied by two or three Recommendations.

The Discussion Procedure

This decline in the rate of progress is not merely the result of a deliberate limitation of the agenda; it is also a necessary consequence of a more thorough procedure for discussion which was adopted in 1924. During the respite of 1922 and 1923, the Conference was able to give some attention to its methods. It found, in the light of experience, that in many cases provisions of minor importance contained in Conventions could prevent their ratification. A number of suggestions were made for getting over this difficulty. In 1922 the Conference considered the institution of a procedure for amending Conventions when it was found that their ratification by certain States was conditional on such amendment. In view of the serious constitutional difficulties involved, the proposed procedure was not adopted. The Conference preferred another system, which was tested in 1924. This was known as "the second-reading procedure" and consisted in submitting Draft Conventions to two successive Sessions of the Conference. The vote given at the first Session was regarded as being merely provisional, and intended to give the delegates and Governments time to consider at their leisure the provisions of the Draft Convention. Each Government was entitled to submit amendments before the final vote, which would be taken at the Conference in the following year.

This procedure, which was applied for the first time in 1925, did not prove as advantageous as had been hoped. It certainly helped to slacken the speed at which the Conference worked, by spreading the discussion of each question over a period of two years. But, in practice, it had certain serious drawbacks. While it had been hoped that the interval of a year would enable the holders of opposing theories to arrive at an agreement, and produce a formula which would make ratification possible for a greater number of States, events showed that the exact opposite was the case. The intervening period was, in fact, used by all parties as an opportunity to defend and justify their attitude at the Conference in the eyes of public opinion. When delegates met a year later, they were more closely tied than before to the views which they had supported. These views were sometimes embodied in proposed amendments to the texts adopted at the first reading. Instead of suggesting amendments on points of detail, as had been the original intention of the authors of the system, they proposed to alter the Drafts adopted at the preceding Session in some of their essential points. The Conference consequently found it necessary in 1925 to go back on the step taken in 1924 and to discuss afresh the problems which it had considered in the previous year.

As a result, the "second-reading procedure" was abandoned; it was replaced in 1926 by a new system known as "the double-discussion procedure." The idea of spreading the consideration of a question over two years was retained; but under the new system each of these stages was of a distinct character. The first stage consisted of a general discussion which more or less cleared the ground; at the close, the Conference would decide by a two-thirds majority whether the question should be placed on the agenda of the following Session, and if so on what points decisions should be taken by the Conference. The second discussion would take place at the next Session, and it would only be then that the text of a Convention or Recommendation might be adopted. In short, at the first Session the Conference would discuss a problem on a general basis, and at the second it would discuss the draft of a Convention on the subject.

This double-discussion procedure, first tried in 1927 and 1928, has since been maintained with certain minor changes. It is still too early to say to what extent it has helped ratification; but in any case it has not met with the same objections as the second-reading procedure. It does not leave a formal draft lying open to prolonged criticism for a year. By keeping the first discussion entirely general, it prevents the adoption in advance of stubborn and uncompromising attitudes which would preclude any agreement and probably render the second discussion fruitless.

Preparatory Study

While the Conference was thus trying to improve its methods of discussion, the Office was asked to develop the preparatory study of the subjects discussed. According to Article 396 of the Treaty, the Office has to study all questions which are to be submitted to the Conference for decision and also to prepare the agenda for its Sessions.

The Office at first followed the method adopted by the Organising Committee of the Washington Conference. It sent to Governments a questionnaire dealing with the points which seemed suitable for treatment in the proposed Convention or Recommendation; it then prepared a report analysing the replies received from the Governments and embodying a proposed Convention or Recommendation based on these replies, the report being designed to provide the Conference with a basis for discussion. These reports have come to be generally known as the "Blue Reports" on account of the colour of the cover.

By 1921, however, the Office began to feel that it was necessary to go further and to give the Conference not only "Blue Reports" on the main items on the agenda, but also a technical report summarising for the information of the delegates the existing law and practice on the questions to be considered. These reports, which have now been recognised in the Standing Orders of the Conference, especially since the double-discussion procedure was adopted, are known as "Grey Reports."

By present practice, therefore, the preparatory work done by the Office falls into the following stages: On each question figuring on the agenda of the Conference for a first discussion, the Office prepares a study intended to inform delegates of the legislative or other measures already adopted for dealing with the problem in different countries, the possibility of an international agreement on the question, and the various points which might be covered by such an agreement. On the basis of this report, a first, general discussion is held by the Conference. This discussion enables the Office to draft a formal questionnaire, which is sent to all Governments. Finally, in the light of the replies received from the Governments, the Office prepares a report which, a year later, forms the basis for the second discussion by the Conference.

It may be added that the Governing Body never places a question on the agenda of the Conference until it has received from the Office a preliminary report on the general position of the problem, a fact which in itself demonstrates the constant effort of the Office to make its work more mature and more thorough.

The Principle of Continuity

Behind the successive improvements in the methods of work of the Conference lies the firm desire of the Governing Body to ensure continuity from one Session to another.

It might have been possible for the Governing Body to limit the agenda of the Conference each year to some special question, and thus indirectly to encourage the States to send representatives who were particularly qualified to deal with that particular question. If, for example, the conditions of work of transport workers, miners, painters, glassworkers, bakers, or salaried employees were to be considered, the Government delegates in each case might have been experts particularly conversant with the special industry concerned, while the employers' and workers' delegates might have been chosen in agreement with the most representative organisations and from the industrial circles most directly interested in that industry. At a first glance, this method would seem to have considerable technical advantages. But it would mean that the delegations would change from Session to Session, and the continuity and permanence of the Conference—which are insisted upon by the Treaties—would have been more apparent than real. This would have been particularly serious in the early days, since it would have prevented the Organisation from acquiring that tradition which is indispensable for really effective work, and also from correcting year by year the defects revealed by experience.

The Governing Body chose the opposite method. In 1920, when it had to draw up the agenda of the Third Session and to carry out the desire of the Washington Conference by including questions relating to agricultural labour, it stressed the fact that the Session was intended to be of a general character. In order to dissuade Governments from sending merely experts in agricultural questions or representatives of agriculture, as they would doubtless have done for an exclusively agricultural conference, the Governing Body placed on the agenda of the Session two questions quite unconnected with agricultural work: the weekly rest in industrial undertakings and the use of white lead in painting. Later, as a result of the Second Session of the Conference, it added two maritime questions: the minimum age for the admission of young persons to employment as trimmers or stokers, and the compulsory medical examination of children and young persons employed at sea.

This variety in the agenda enabled the Director to point out in a letter to Governments that the Third Conference would not be a special Conference dealing with one restricted field, but that it would have to deal with agricultural questions, maritime questions, industrial hygiene, and general questions such as the weekly rest. He therefore recommended to them, in pursuance of a Resolution adopted by the Governing Body on March 25th, 1920, that they should consult the central organisations of employers and workers rather than special industrial organisations when appointing the non-Government delegates. He explained that if there were too many expert delegates, the Conference would be in danger of losing sight of the general principles on which international labour legislation was based, and the decisions taken might not be in complete conformity with the spirit and aims of the International Labour Organisation. He also pointed out to the Governments how desirable it was to send the same Government delegates to each Session of the Conference, so as to ensure the utmost continuity in its composition. Whenever possible, the Government delegates should be those who had participated in the work of the Washington or Genoa Conferences. Finally, he reminded Governments that according to the Peace Treaties every delegate was entitled to be accompanied by two technical advisers for each item on the agenda, and that it was thus possible to reconcile the claims of specialised knowledge with the need for homogeneity in the Conference.

Although these hints given to Governments by the Office in 1920 and 1921 were no more than suggestions, dictated by a desire for the successful progress of the Organisation, they were generally followed; and they have proved so valuable for the efficacy, unity and continuity of the Conference and of its work, that there is no thought of abandoning them. Thus, there are very few delegates at any Session of the Conference who have not had experience of several previous Sessions.

An Exception: Maritime Sessions

From the outset there has been one exception to the principle of continuity, namely, that of the Maritime Sessions. This exception can be explained on historical grounds. As was rightly pointed out by Mr. Arthur Fontaine when opening the last Maritime Session, in October 1929, maritime transport would seem to be the most international of all industries and the one most subject to the laws of international competition. It follows that seamen have special need of the protection of international labour legislation, if their conditions of work are to be safeguarded and improved. This was realised in Paris when Part XIII was being drafted. At that time certain associations of seamen proposed that a special organisation should be set up for the introduction of international legislation on maritime labour. Aversion to a useless multiplication of international institutions led to the rejection of this proposal. At the same time, the Commission on International Labour Legislation recommended that the special problems of the minimum guarantees to be granted to seamen should be dealt with at special Sessions of the Conference devoted exclusively to this purpose. In accordance with this resolution, the Governing Body decided immediately after the Washington Conference that the work of the Second Session of the Conference should be restricted to questions bearing on the conditions of work of seamen. The tradition of Maritime Sessions was thus set up, and two other Sessions of this kind have been held since that date, the one in 1926 and the other in 1929.

But while the Governing Body took account of the special needs of shipowners and seamen, it did not forget the importance of ensuring continuity in the work of the Conference. In 1920 it set up a permanent Commission—the Joint Maritime Commission—consisting of a number of members of the Governing Body and of representatives of shipowners and seamen elected by the employers' and workers' delegates to the Maritime Sessions of the Conference. This Commission, which has since been enlarged, is in principle merely an advisory body; but the Conference itself has decided that no question touching maritime work should be placed on the agenda without being previously submitted to the Commission. Hence, in the interval between the Maritime Sessions (which are of necessity irregular) a special body exists to ensure continuity in dealing with maritime questions. This body also serves to link up the special interests represented at Maritime Sessions with the general interests represented on the Governing Body, for in addition to representatives of the shipowners and seamen, it includes a member of the employers' group and a member of the workers' group on the Governing Body, and the chairman of its meetings is the President of the Governing Body; moreover, its resolutions are invariably submitted to the Governing Body for ultimate decision.

Experience alone can show whether the system thus improvised for dealing with the special interests of the mercantile marine and the peculiarly technical questions raised by the regulation of working conditions for seamen is the best possible. It must, however, be admitted immediately that the composition of the Maritime Conferences has in practice raised difficulties, and has even led to rather serious disputes, with prejudicial effects in some cases on the work of the Conference.

The first such problem concerned the attitude of non-maritime countries. According to the constitution of the Organisation, such countries had to be convened to the Conference, seeing that the General Conference of the Members is the only body which has the power to adopt Draft Conventions and Recommendations. Certain States, such as Switzerland, abstained on principle from sending representatives to the maritime Sessions, but others, such as Czechoslovakia, sent delegates who obviously could have no claim to be specially representative of maritime interests. Again, certain countries which were maritime, but whose mercantile marine was in a very elementary stage of development, were tempted to send the same delegates to Maritime Sessions as to ordinary Sessions. Those most directly interested had thus grounds for complaining that the maritime character of these special Sessions was impaired by the presence of too high a proportion of delegates having no special competence to deal with the questions under discussion. For the purpose of overcoming this difficulty, the shipowners' representatives have insisted in recent years that ordinary and Maritime Sessions of the Conference should not be held consecutively, as in 1926, but at different periods of the year, so as to prevent certain States, anxious to economise, from appointing the same delegates for the special Session as for the ordinary Session.

The most serious constitutional difficulty met with in connection with Maritime Sessions has been that of the method to be adopted by Governments in appointing non-Government delegates in countries where there are strong organisations of shipowners and seamen. Should the Government, as in the case of any other Session, consult the central organisations of employers and workers when appointing delegates, and merely draw attention to the special maritime character of the proposed Conference, or should it, on the other hand, apply directly to the organisations of shipowners and seamen, and agree with them on the delegates to be appointed? The majority of the Governing Body has always upheld the first of these solutions. As early as 1920, the Governing Body pointed out in a resolution, adopted with a view to the Maritime Session to be held in Genoa, what seemed to it to be the only possible interpretation of Article 389. But the shipowners' organisations and several organisations of seamen were not satisfied, and declared that such a solution was incompatible with the promise made at Paris in 1919 to devote special Sessions to the Conference to the study of maritime labour questions. In their opinion, only the organisations specially representing the maritime transport industry were competent to advise Governments as to the choice of their representatives.

This difference of opinion led to a rather serious crisis during the Thirteenth Session of the Conference, in October 1929. The British Shipping Federation, upholding the protest of two associations of seamen against the composition of the British workers' delegation, refused to appoint an employers' representative. The absence of the representative of the most powerful mercantile marine in the world was a very serious blow to the representative character of the Conference and to the authority of its decisions, more especially as it deprived the workers' delegate of that country of his right to vote. The employers' group at the Conference pointed out the gravity of this situation and suggested that, in order to avoid a recurrence of such difficulties, it should be formally decided that the non-Government delegates and technical advisers for Maritime Conferences should in future be nominated "in agreement with the organisations, if such organisations exist, which are most representative of shipowners and seamen respectively." In other words, the employers' group asked the Conference to repudiate the view hitherto held by the Governing Body. This resolution was rejected by sixty-four votes to twenty-four, whereupon the employers' group decided to abstain from taking further part in the work of the Session. Although after considerable negotiation the employers' delegates returned to the Conference a few days later, the seriousness of these incidents from the standpoint of the Organisation could not be overlooked. The Conference accordingly adopted a resolution recalling the difficulties met with at Maritime Sessions and instructing the Governing Body to take all possible steps to avoid a recurrence of these difficulties.

An Experiment: The Preparatory Technical Conference

When, in 1930, the Governing Body came to examine these problems, it had just witnessed an experiment in another sphere which seemed to offer a possible solution for the maritime difficulty. We refer to the Preparatory Technical Conference on conditions of work in coal mines, which may perhaps prove to have been a landmark in the constitutional progress of the Organisation.

In September 1929, it will be remembered, the Assembly of the League of Nations invited the International Labour Organisation to try to find an international solution of the problem of working conditions in coal mines. The Governing Body, in view of the urgency and the special nature of the problem, decided to convene a Preparatory Technical Conference in January 1930, to clear the ground and ascertain on what points an immediate international solution was possible. This Conference, which was of a purely advisory character, was to consist of one Government representative, one representative of the mineowners, and one representative of the workers in mines for each of the nine principal coal-producing countries in Europe, these being the only countries for which the immediate adoption of regulations could be considered practicable. The Governing Body was also to be represented by a delegate from each of the groups.

There is a considerable divergence of views as to the success of this Conference. It must be admitted that, in so far as the Conference was originally intended to be a means of hastening the solution of an urgent problem by saving the general Conference the delays of the double-discussion procedure, it was not a success; for the Fourteenth Session was unable to come to an agreement and finally adjourned the question of hours of work in coal mines to its next Session. But this partial failure must not be allowed to obscure the importance of the innovation.

It was thought that procedure by way of a similar Preparatory Technical Conference might help to solve the maritime difficulties which arose at the Thirteenth Session. Since this procedure is not provided for in the Treaties, the Organisation would not be bound, as it is in connection with special Maritime Sessions, by the statutory provisions governing the composition of the Conference. The Governing Body could quite easily restrict the invitations to countries directly interested in maritime questions, and particularly to those with a mercantile marine of a certain minimum tonnage. The Governments taking part could appoint their non-Government delegates in agreement with the organisations of shipowners and seamen, and thus give satisfaction to the urgent claims of these organisations. The study of the special questions raised by the regulation of the working conditions of seamen would thus be entrusted to a Conference whose composition, from the technical point of view, would no longer be open to the objections frequently raised by the shipowners. At the same time there would be no infringement of the provisions of Part XIII, since the Conference in question would be purely advisory and the final deliberation would be left to the General Conference of the States Members. Finally, the representation of general as well as special interests would be assured, as it had been at the Coal Conference, by the presence of a delegation from the Governing Body at the sittings of the Preparatory Maritime Conference.

After much discussion, the Governing Body accepted the Director's proposals, and decided to call a first Preparatory Technical Conference on maritime questions for October 1931; this Conference will continue the work left unfinished by the Thirteenth Session and try to arrive at a conclusion. This is unquestionably an experiment. The results will show whether it should be repeated and become an established method of procedure. If it succeeds, those concerned may even come to the view that there is no need to maintain the tradition of special Maritime Sessions; they may decide to submit the conclusions of the Preparatory Conference to an ordinary Session of the General Conference, and thus finally put an end to the difficulties raised by these special Sessions.

Whether this attempt succeeds or not, the problem which it is sought to solve will have to be dealt with by the Organisation in the next few years. Far from disappearing, it is more likely to increase in importance. Maritime questions are not the only ones which have a highly technical character and must be studied by Conferences with special qualifications. In the early years, the Conference dealt with very general and purely universal problems; but since then there has been a tendency to submit to it questions affecting special industries, or special groups of countries, which cannot well be dealt with by the ordinary methods of discussion at the Conference. For example, the question of work in coal mines and that of the regulation of forced labour have been discussed, and for these the Organisation had to find some means of ensuring the closest collaboration of the coal-producing countries and the colonial countries respectively, in the drafting of decisions. At some future date the Conference will doubtless be called on to consider the questions of work in the textile industries or in glass works, and possibly certain problems of Asiatic conditions, with regard to which the workers of Asia are urgently requesting the Organisation to take action. Whether the method of the Preparatory Technical Conference or some other method be finally accepted as the most effective, the Organisation will certainly have to find a means of reconciling the general and universal character of the Conference—an indispensable condition for the continuity of its work and a symbol of the oneness of the labour problem throughout the world—with the technical study which is essential in connection with special problems which may be submitted to it.

On the whole, then, the forms of procedure adopted by the International Labour Organisation in carrying on its legislative work are still in an evolutionary stage. To regard this as a sign of uneasiness or instability would be a mistake. It indicates, on the contrary, that a living organism cannot be tied to hard-and-fast rules, but must constantly adapt itself to the diversity of situations and circumstances. Throughout the experiments and tentative efforts described above, two very clear tendencies can be distinguished: the one is to safeguard the general authority, the homogeneity, and the continuity of the work of the Conference in accordance with the letter and the spirit of Part XIII; the other is to guarantee, by the most appropriate procedure, the fullest possible technical and specialised study of the problems under consideration.

Application of Conventions: Examination of Reports under Article 408

Closely linked up with the problem of the preparation of the decisions of the Conference is the problem of their application. The Organisation has never dissociated these two questions. In point of fact, it is precisely for the purpose of making its decisions suitable for general and effective application that the Organisation has on several occasions revised its methods of study and discussion. Every year the debate on the Director's Report at the Conference has given delegates an opportunity for collective self-criticism in this respect. When it is found that there have been difficulties in the progress of ratification or in the application of Conventions ratified, it is natural to ask whether these difficulties are not due to faults in the drafting of the Conventions. At the same time, the Conference has been led to take a growing interest in the fate of the Conventions and Recommendations adopted at previous Sessions, and particularly in the effective application of Conventions which have been ratified.

It was mentioned above that every State Member is obliged, under Article 408, to submit to the International Labour Office an annual report on the measures taken to apply any Convention to which it has adhered. These reports are drafted in a form indicated by the Governing Body, and must contain such information as it may request. A summary of them is submitted by the Director to the ensuing Session of the Conference.

At first, perhaps, the Conference did not give due attention to these documents, because it was interested chiefly in the progress of ratification. Perhaps also it was asking too much of the Conference, in a Session lasting three or four weeks, to undertake, as an addition to its special agenda, the detailed and careful scrutiny of these technical reports, the number of which was rapidly increasing. Be that as it may, at the Eighth Session (in 1926) the Conference took steps to deal with this situation. It recommended that in future each Session of the Conference should appoint a special Committee to examine the reports presented under Article 408; it also invited the Governing Body to consider the possibility of appointing a Committee of Experts to carry out a preliminary study of the reports. This procedure was put into practice in the following year, and has been maintained ever since. It will be seen that there are two successive phases: first, an examination of the reports by a committee of experts of a purely advisory character, which submits its observations to the Governing Body; in the next place, an examination by a special Committee of the Conference, which has before it the summary of the reports of the Governments prepared by the Office as well as the report of the Committee of Experts. The observations of this special Committee are submitted to the general Conference.

At the outset, this new procedure created some difficulties. The authority of the report of the Committee of Experts was called in question on the ground that Part XIII made no provision for such mechanism, and it was contended that the Committee of the Conference should not be allowed to take into consideration the conclusions of the Committee of Experts. On similar grounds, it was held that the Committee of the Conference should not be permitted to request delegates present at the Session to provide supplementary explanations with regard to reports sent in by their Governments.

For the first two years after the adoption of the new procedure, the attention of the Committee of the Conference was largely taken up with the discussion of such general and constitutional questions; but these difficulties settled themselves as soon as the advantages of the new system became clear. The Conference realised that the task of supervising the application of Conventions was complex and delicate, but that to neglect it would compromise the future of the Organisation. Moreover, the task demanded, as Mgr. Nolens pointed out, frankness, impartiality and a certain amount of independence and courage. The Governments themselves recognised that there was nothing to be gained by concealing the real situation with regard to the application of Conventions and giving free course to rumours about the alleged indifference of States to the Conventions they had ratified. Indeed, even from the first year of the new procedure, it was noted that the representatives of those Governments which had had the strongest doubts about the system were the first to come forward spontaneously and give the Conference the explanations which had been requested.

Since that time the careful study of the reports under Article 408 has become an integral part of the business of the Conference. Already the work of the Committee of Experts, backed up by the Governing Body and the Conference, has produced considerable results. Governments have sent in their annual reports more regularly; the forms sent to Governments for these reports have been improved and supplemented so as to elicit fuller or more explicit replies; differences in the interpretation of a clause by different Governments have been brought to light; the reports have shown in what directions the application of a Convention by certain Governments was insufficient. In all these ways the system has helped to enlighten all the Governments concerned as to the extent to which Conventions are applied by the other countries which have ratified them, and, as the conclusions have generally been more favourable than was expected, they have strengthened the mutual confidence between Governments. As a consequence it has been possible in some cases to arrive at a more uniform or more complete observance of Conventions without any necessity for having recourse to the procedure of enquiry and sanctions for which provision is made in Article 409 and the following Articles of the Treaty. Finally, this system has thrown light on the real difficulties which are involved in the application of the Conventions, and which are sometimes due to points of drafting.

At present the general tendency is not by any means to suggest that the new procedure is unwarranted or to restrict it to narrow constitutional limits, but rather to extend it, if possible, and make it more effective. In this connection two recent decisions are worthy of attention. The first directs the attention of the Committee of Experts to the importance of studying closely not only the degree of conformity between national legislation and the provisions of a Convention, but also the actual application of that national legislation. The other invites Governments to supply information as to the difficulties met with in ratifying certain Conventions. It is true that this latter resolution goes beyond the mere examination of the application of Conventions, since, according to Article 405, a Government has no further obligations if a Convention is rejected by its competent authorities; but it is also apparent that the information so requested would in itself be of great value for the future development of international labour legislation.

Procedure for the Revision of Conventions

A further problem with which the Organisation has had to deal in recent years is that of the revision of Conventions. This problem is not mentioned in the Treaty, but it was bound to arise sooner or later. In a few decades international labour legislation might be nothing more than a group of formulae divorced from reality, if its provisions could not be adapted, after their original adoption, to the circumstances, needs and ideas of succeeding years. During the first ten years the field to be covered was so vast that the Conference was constantly called upon to face new problems, and there was no urgent need for revising the work already accomplished with a view to bringing it up to date or extending it. Moreover, the question of revision was first raised in circumstances of such a kind that any later suggestion of revision was bound to inspire considerable apprehension in many quarters.

It was in 1921, when the world economic crisis had led to a noticeable reaction in several countries against the humanitarian and social movements from which the International Labour Organisation had taken birth, that the British Government asked that the Washington Convention on hours of work should be reconsidered with a view to greater elasticity on several points. The Governing Body definitely rejected this proposal, being of opinion that the Convention had not been in existence sufficiently long for it to be amended. Nevertheless, the request of the British Government disturbed the workers to such an extent that revision came to be regarded as synonymous with reaction against the reforms already adopted, particularly as, on every subsequent occasion when the idea of revision was mooted in the Governing Body or in the Conference, it was always in connection with the Hours Convention, which the workers regarded as the keystone of the new international labour legislation.

That in itself explains the prudence—if not the actual repugnance—with which many members of the Governing Body and delegates to the Conference have always approached the question of revision. But the problem could not be put off indefinitely. All the Conventions adopted by the Conference, beginning with those of its First Session, contain a formal Article inviting the Governing Body to submit to the Conference at least once every ten years a report on the application of each Convention, and to decide whether the question of its revision or amendment should be placed on the agenda of the Conference. Since five of the Draft Conventions adopted at Washington came into force in June and July 1921, the question of their possible revision would have to be placed on the agenda of the 1931 Conference at the latest.

The procedure for revision and the legal effects of revision raise a host of very complex and delicate problems, and it was obviously expedient that these should be settled in advance. After long discussions, reflecting the mixed feelings with which the delegates regarded the very notion of revision, the Governing Body and the Conference succeeded in settling these questions in 1929, and in April of the following year the Governing Body began its examination of reports prepared by the Office on the application of eight Conventions which would have been in force for ten years by 1931. The Governing Body had before it a number of formal proposals for revision made by various Governments; one of these, submitted by the Swedish Government, was for the revision of the Washington Hours Convention. As regards seven of the Conventions under consideration, including the Hours Convention, the Governing Body decided that no revision was necessary, and that the reports prepared by the Office on the application of the Conventions should merely be communicated to the Conference. In the case of the eighth Convention, that on the night work of women, the Governing Body agreed to consider certain proposals for revision, and instructed the International Labour Office, in accordance with the revision procedure recently adopted, to obtain the opinion of Governments on the proposals in question. Finally, in the light of the replies received from Governments, the Governing Body decided, at its Session in January 1931, to place the question of the revision of this Convention on the agenda of the 1931 Conference.

This year, then, the Conference will have its first experience of the operation of the revision procedure which it has instituted. The results will doubtless determine to a great extent the attitude of delegates to future proposals for revision. It should be emphasised that, if the Governing Body decides to submit the question of the revision of a Convention to the Conference, it does not necessarily follow that the Convention as a whole is thrown open to discussion. The Governing Body can suggest total revision, but it can also, in accordance with the regulations drawn up in 1929, which reflect the apprehensions already referred to, decide that only a partial revision is required. In that case the Governing Body must state definitely which provisions it is proposed to revise, and the discussion in the Conference is restricted to these Articles of the Convention.

Summing up

This section does not exhaust or even enumerate all the vital and absorbing problems involved in the mechanism of international labour legislation. To be complete, it would have to deal with the growing importance of committee work as a preliminary to legislation; it would have to describe the different conceptions which have been expressed, and have sometimes clashed, in the Conference with regard to the general form of Conventions and the amount of elasticity they should possess; it would have to show how Recommendations, originally intended as an expedient for adapting the provisions of Part XIII to the peculiar situation of certain federal States—and particularly to the Constitution of the United States, where the Federal Government has not the general power to legislate on labour matters or to ratify Conventions on them—have developed a position of their own; how, side by side with the Conventions, they supplement the minimum general standards laid down by the Conventions, pointing out the lines on which they might be applied, or suggesting solutions which the Conference can commend to the States Members but cannot ask them to accept as mutual commitments. Reference might also have been made to the advantage so far taken of the provision of Article 405, paragraph 3, by which the Conference may permit exceptions or transitional measures in countries "in which climatic conditions, the imperfect development of industrial organisation, or other special circumstances make the industrial conditions substantially different." Unfortunately, space precludes the discussion of these points of detail.

Enough has been said, however, to show how the International Labour Organisation has in these ten years created, improved and tested a series of rules and systems of procedure, not based on any general theoretical programme but improvised thoughtfully to meet the day-to-day demands of life and action, and to comply with the requirements alike of facts and of ideals.

This policy of prudent opportunism, if one may so describe it, has not been unfruitful. In a recent report, the committee set up by the League of Nations to study the question of the ratification and signature of Conventions concluded under the auspices of the League, included among its suggestions for expediting ratification a recommendation that there should be a more thorough preparation; and it quoted the example of the International Labour Conference, even reproducing in full the rules of the double-discussion procedure which has been described above. The same report proposes the insertion in future Draft Conventions of a formal clause, couched in the spirit of Article 405, paragraph 5, of the Treaty, whereby the signatory States would undertake within a specified period to bring the Draft Convention before the competent authorities for ratification or to inform the Secretary-General of other action taken with regard to the Convention.

This suggestion, that other international organisations might with advantage adopt some of the rules governing the activity of the International Labour Organisation, is the highest compliment that could be paid to that Organisation.

II. International Information

A Clearing House of Information

When the International Association for Labour Legislation set up the first International Labour Office at Basle in 1901, it did so in the belief that this office, in addition to acting as a permanent secretariat and preparing the ground for its conferences, could do valuable work for the furtherance of social progress by collecting and publishing information on labour legislation. There can be no question that the services rendered in this direction before the War had some influence on the drafting of Article 396 of the Treaty, which defines the functions of the International Labour Office. This Article states that: "The functions of the International Labour Office shall include the collection and distribution of information on all subjects relating to the international adjustment of conditions of industrial life and labour, and particularly the examination of subjects which it is proposed to bring before the Conference with a view to the conclusion of international conventions and the conduct of such special investigations as may be ordered by the Conference." The Office was also instructed "to edit and publish in French and English and in such other languages as the Governing Body may think desirable, a periodical paper dealing with problems of industry and employment of international interest."

The Collection of Information

The Office has consistently proceeded with its research work and its collection of information along three lines.

The first concerns the work of the Conference. Here the task of the Office is governed by the agenda for each Session and runs parallel with the work of international labour legislation carried out by the Organisation as a whole. The Office, following the instructions and rules of the Governing Body and the Conference, prepares "questionnaires," "grey" and "blue" reports and any other documents which may be required of it.

The second line of action relates to current international events. The Office follows the development of social ideas and movements in all countries; it endeavours to deduce general trends; it notes those events which appear to be of real international interest—in certain selected cases, it studies the chief of them more intensively.

Thirdly, the Office is a centre of scientific investigation. On instructions from the Conference or the Governing Body, it carries out enquiries or special studies in specified fields which may be wide or restricted. Sometimes it has to collect information on a given question, to be placed at the disposal of the enquirer. As an example, mention may be made of industrial hygiene, the results of enquiry into which constitute a veritable encyclopædia. In other cases, the Office may be called upon to study a problem in the light of all the information available, analysing the different factors and perhaps foreshadowing possible international solutions. As an example of this kind of investigation may be cited the Enquiry into Production, undertaken by the Office during the first post-War economic crisis.

Obviously, there is a close connection between the study of current events and the scientific research work of the Office, for it is only by noting the events and tendencies of the day that the Office can respond to demands for special studies. For instance, the unemployment problem has for several years past been the subject of a permanent study, and it is this that has made it possible for the Office, during a period of intense depression such as now prevails, to place at the disposal of the Governing Body or of Governments, without the slightest delay, a wealth of authentic and valuable information on the subject, compiled on an international basis.

A chapter might be devoted to showing how the sources of supply of the Office have been developed since the day when the original little groups of officials set to work in Seamore Place, London—an international institution unknown to the world but anxious to prove its value—or to describing how its methods of investigation have been improved and how, after experimenting (with varying success) by means of questionnaire, external collaboration, committees of experts, the study of documents, and first-hand enquiries, the Office has succeeded in combining these different methods, concentrating on the one most suitable for any given enquiry. These methods will not be discussed at length here, as they will be seen in action in the second part of this work. It will suffice for the moment to quote two sets of figures which demonstrate the development of the Office's supply of information. The Library, which in 1923 received 10,228 works, received 34,484 in 1929. The number of newspapers and periodicals received in 1929 was 3,800, as against 1,570 in 1924.

The Distribution of Information

The collection of information necessarily implies its distribution, for which the Office depends chiefly on two channels: direct replies to requests for information, and publication, the latter being the chief method.

The number of requests for information to which the Office replied (not counting those with which its National Correspondents could deal without referring to Geneva) was over 1,000 in 1928 and again in 1929, as compared with 920 in 1927 and 800 in 1926. Many of these requests necessitated extensive research or the collection of a mass of information; for example, a request of the Greek Government for information concerning the cost and source of social charges; an enquiry of the Ford Company, in London, concerning real wages in certain towns; a demand of the Polish Government for data concerning the wages of workers in mines and other industries; of the Japanese Government concerning the training of workers in France and in the U.S.S.R.; of the Italian Ministry of Corporations concerning economic councils in different countries; of the Spanish Employers' Association concerning accident insurance legislation and institutions; of the Belgian Wood and Building Federation and the Rumanian Union of Employers concerning holidays with pay in different industries; of the German Ministry of

Labour concerning systems of work by shifts in the glass industry; of the Scientific Department of the People's Commissariat for Labour of the U.S.S.R. concerning the legislation on and institutions for invalidity, old age and survivors' insurance; of the French Ministry of the Mercantile Marine concerning international maritime legislation, etc. The variety of the subjects mentioned shows the wide area over which the International Labour Office, as an intelligence department, can influence the progress of social legislation and the workers' conditions of life.

Publications

The publications of the Office are intended to serve a similar purpose. The Treaty of Peace definitely instructed the Office to publish a periodical paper dealing with problems of industry and employment of international interest. In practice, not one periodical but a whole series of publications have been found necessary. It has also been necessary to adapt the programme of publications to the varying needs of the times. For instance, the *Monthly Record of Migration*, which was at one time in great demand, was later incorporated in a publication of a general nature. Other periodicals, such as the *Industrial Safety Survey*, which were originally parts of general periodicals, have been separated from them and adapted to the requirements of the specialist rather than those of the general reader.

But, in spite of changes in detail, it is noteworthy that the broad lines of the Office's programme of publications have not changed since it was first launched.

Directly bearing on the work of the Conference are the *Documents of the International Labour Conference*, which include the questionnaires, the "grey" and "blue" reports, the Annual Report of the Director, the verbatim report of the proceedings, the minutes of committees and so on. Allied to this group is the *Official Bulletin*, which appears at irregular intervals and contains official documents relating to the work of the Organisation.

Next, the Office publishes two general periodicals, *Industrial and Labour Information*, which appears weekly, and the *International Labour Review*, appearing monthly. The first covers systematically, under a series of standard headings, the whole field of activity of the Office. The latter contains more exhaustive studies prepared by the Office or by outside contributors on trends and facts observed in different countries; it also contains current statistics, compiled by the Office on such matters as the cost of living, wages, unemployment and migration. Two annual publications of a purely documentary character are published, designed to provide the reader with the necessary textual basis for any international study of labour law. These are the *Legislative Series*, each yearly volume of which contains the texts or translations of the principal labour laws and regulations promulgated in many countries during the year; and the *International Survey of Legal Decisions on Labour Law*, which analyses the chief legal decisions on labour law in five selected countries: England, France, Germany, Italy and the United States.

In the same group of publications may be included certain special periodicals: The *Bibliography of Industrial Hygiene*, the *Industrial Safety Survey*, the *Bibliography of the International Labour Organisation*; formerly also the *Monthly Record of Migration*, and in future, perhaps, a *Native Labour Review*. These cannot be embodied in the general periodicals either for technical reasons or because of the peculiar nature of the subjects with which they deal.

Finally, the considered results of the day-to-day research work of the Office are published in the seventeen series of its *Studies and Reports*. One or two exceptionally voluminous reports not falling inside the main framework have appeared outside this series as "Special Studies"; among them are the report of the *Enquiry into Production*, the *Encyclopædia of Industrial Hygiene*, and the *International Labour Directory*.

These three main groups of publications—official, periodicals and studies—may be considered as so many different headings in the periodical which the Office was instructed by the authors of the Peace Treaty to publish. All overlapping between the groups is carefully avoided. The only other publications of the Office consist of a few pamphlets and a brief *Monthly Summary of the International Labour Organisation*, the primary purpose of which is popular intelligence.

These publications do not appear merely in French and in English. Most of them, including almost all the Conference documents, are published in German, and many appear in Spanish. A selection from the articles in *Industrial and Labour Information* and the *Review* is made by the National Correspondents of the Office in Rome, Berlin, Madrid and Tokyo and published in Monthly Reviews in the languages of their respective countries.

The number of the publications of the Office has sometimes been criticised, and it has been described as "a mill for grinding out publications which no one wished to read." By way of reply to this criticism attention may be called to the volume of business done in the sale of these publications. The receipts have risen more or less steadily from 99,000 Swiss francs in 1923 to over 250,000 Swiss francs in 1929, while the sums voted for printing have remained practically constant. But the sales returns must not be taken as anything like a complete index to the utility of the Office publications or the extent to which they are actually utilised. The Office has never aspired to produce a "best seller." What it desires, and what it must desire, is to place at the disposal of all those who are interested in or working for the improvement of conditions of labour the necessary impartial and exact information which they may require for their studies or their activities. Such a purpose is not compatible with sensational sales returns.

It would seem to be generally recognised to-day that during the past ten years the Office has achieved to a large extent the aim set before it. As one of many testimonies given to the work of the Office, an extract may be quoted from a study on the International Labour Organisation published in 1928 by an employers' organisation in the United States, the National Industrial Conference Board, whose general attitude is by no means sympathetic towards the aims of the Organisation. This study recognised that the Office has become "an agency for the centralisation of information concerning all phases of the labour problem. Prior to its organisation there was no medium through which interested persons and organisations could keep in close touch with the development of labour legislation and the changes in the broader fields of employment relationships. The special investigations of the Office have assembled information which would not be otherwise available. . . . As a fact-finding and research agency the International Labour Office has functioned as satisfactorily as the breadth of its field of investigation in comparison with its resources permits."

CHAPTER V

THE COMPETENCE OF THE ORGANISATION

The Terms of the Peace Treaty

One may search in vain through the whole of Part XIII for an exact definition of the competence of the International Labour Organisation. The first Article, already quoted, states merely that "a permanent organisation is hereby established for the promotion of the objects set forth in the Preamble." Turning to the Preamble we find that the aims of the Organisation are set forth in extremely general terms: "social justice," "improvement of conditions of labour which involve injustice, hardship and privation to large numbers of people," "the adoption of humane conditions of labour." When the document does become more definite and leave general expressions for an enumeration of the improvements which are urgently required, it begins with the words "for example" and ends with "and other measures," thus precluding any restrictive interpretation. Consequently, when the Preamble speaks of "the regulation of hours of work," "the establishment of a maximum working day and week," "the regulation of the labour supply," "the prevention of unemployment," "the provision of an adequate living wage," "the protection of the worker against sickness, disease and injury arising out of his employment," "the protection of children, young persons and women," "provision for old age and injury," "protection of the interests of workers when employed in countries other than their own," "recognition of the principle of freedom of association," and "the organisation of vocational and technical education," it cannot be maintained that these are the only measures which the Organisation may adopt in order to establish the humane conditions of labour at which it aims. The sole purpose of the authors of the Peace Treaties in drawing up this list was to give the Organisation some lines of action and an initial impetus by drawing its attention to certain reforms which seemed particularly urgent.

The final Article of Part XIII, which repeats more definitely, in the form of nine general principles, some of the points already mentioned in the Preamble, is equally non-restrictive in character, for it expressly states that the High Contracting Parties do not claim "that these methods and principles are either complete or final."

It must not be imagined that this absence of a clear definition of the field of activity of the Organisation is due to an omission. Definition always implies to some extent limitation. The authors of the Peace Treaties wished to avoid any formula which, being inspired by the circumstances of the moment, might impede the future progress of the Organisation by preventing it from taking such action as later circumstances might require. They pointed out the ultimate and ideal aims which it must seek to realise; they pointed out certain immediate means which appeared to them appropriate in the existing circumstances for the realisation of these aims; but they carefully emphasised the fact that they did not consider these to be the only possible means, and that later developments might call for the adoption of measures which they could not foresee.

Social justice is thus looked upon as a movement, and not something static. It was for the very reason that its realisation requires a continuous effort, not limited in time, that a *permanent* organisation was set up to achieve it; it is precisely because this effort has to be constantly adapted to new circumstances arising out of the economic and social development of the world that the Organisation was given so wide a competence. The only word which can sum up this competence and mark both its extent and its limits is "Labour," which is the title given to Part XIII of the Treaty of Versailles.

Competence Called in Question

Although this idea of the extensive competence of the Organisation would now seem to be generally accepted, it has not invariably been so. At times efforts have been made to prevent the International Labour Organisation from dealing with certain classes of workers on the ground that they were not expressly mentioned in the Treaty. Sometimes it has been denied the right to protect persons not bound by a contract of service to an employer, a prohibition which would have prevented it from dealing with unemployment. Proposals have been made to withdraw certain problems from its sphere of activity by labelling them "national questions" or "domestic affairs." The validity of its decisions has been called in question because, in order to protect certain classes of workers, it incidentally regulated the work of the employer himself or touched on problems of production.

Whenever the contention of incompetency has been advanced at the International Labour Conference, it has been rejected by a large majority. In three cases the authors of the objections would not accept defeat, but requested that, in accordance with Article 423 of the Treaty, the provisions of Part XIII should be submitted to the Permanent Court of International Justice for an opinion.

The Opinion of the Court

In 1922 the French Government, in view of decisions taken by the 1921 Conference on agricultural questions, requested the Council of the League of Nations to ask the Permanent Court whether the competence of the Organisation covered the conditions of work of persons employed in agriculture. A few months later it further asked whether the consideration of proposals for organising and developing the means of agricultural production fell within the Organisation's competence.

In 1926 the employers' members of the Governing Body, objecting to a provision which the Conference had inserted the previous year in the Draft Convention for the prohibition of night work in bakeries, requested the Governing Body to obtain an advisory opinion from the Permanent Court as to the competence of the Organisation to regulate the personal work of employers.

The Court gave its opinion on the first two questions on August 12th, 1922, and on the third on July 23rd, 1926. In each case it fully confirmed the views upheld by the Organisation, as represented by the Conference, the Governing Body and the Director of the Office.

In reply to the first question it stated that the competence of the International Labour Organisation did extend to the international regulation of the conditions of work of persons employed in agriculture. In reply to the second question it noted the declaration made by the Director of the Office, in which he formally disclaimed any competence in questions of production, but at the same time it added that "the Organisation cannot be excluded from dealing with the matters specifically committed to it by the Treaty on the ground that these may involve in some aspects a consideration of the means or methods of production or of the effects which the proposed measures would have upon production." The third question was also answered in the affirmative, the Court confirming the competence of the Organisation "to draw up and to propose labour legislation which, in order to protect certain classes of workers, also regulates incidentally the same work when performed by the employer himself." These were the exact terms of the question submitted to it by the employers.

The Theory of "Extended Competence"

This is not the place in which to discuss the legal arguments invoked in each case against the extended competence of the Organisation, nor the way in which the Court refuted them one by one when explaining the reasons for its opinion. Indeed, these arguments have only a technical and one might say passing interest. The important fact from the point of view of the history of the Organisation is that the tendency lying behind these appeals was kept in check. The year 1921, when the competence of the Organisation was first called in question, marked the beginning of the great post-War economic depression, and a period of depression always entails the spread of reaction against social progress. The attempts to limit the competence of the Organisation in 1921 were not unconnected with the resistance which began to be shown in many circles and many countries at that time to the humanitarian views which had dictated the terms of Part XIII. Since it was impossible to make a direct attack on the existence of the Organisation without provoking serious discontent among the workers, efforts were directed towards excluding from its competence certain classes of workers whose inadequate trade union organisation made their claims the least insistent. This was the tendency, directly opposed to the spirit of 1919, to which the Court replied by interpreting the provisions of the constitution, thereby making it plain for the first time that the permanent mechanism set up after the War did not allow States to escape easily from their commitments. The Court rejected the theory of restrictive interpretation. On the contrary, a study of the Treaty led it to the conclusion that the aims entrusted to the International Labour Organisation were stated in such general terms that "language could hardly be more comprehensive."

The same conclusion was repeated and further developed in

the third advisory opinion, given by the Court in 1926. It noted once again that the competence of the Organisation was extremely wide, and that the documents on which it is based should be interpreted in their widest sense. But the Court added on this occasion certain general considerations tending to prove that this extended competence of the Organisation not only derives from a literal interpretation of the documents, but is also in complete harmony with its mission and with the nature of the powers granted to it. It pointed out that if the Organisation really possessed international legislative powers—that is, if it could take decisions which were binding on States—then a restrictive interpretation of its competence could be justified with a view to preventing it from infringing the sovereign rights of States. But, as has already been seen, this conception, although suggested at Paris in 1919, was not accepted, and the International Labour Conference has only the power to make proposals. The Draft Conventions and Recommendations which it adopts by a two-thirds majority do not automatically become binding on States. Governments have merely to submit them within a certain period to the competent authorities, who are free to reject or approve them; and if they are rejected the State Member is released from all further obligations. In view of this, it is difficult to understand how the sovereignty of States can be endangered by the actions of the Organisation. That sovereignty is protected by sufficient guarantees for the extended competence of the Organisation to be accepted without fear.

When the Permanent Court gave this opinion, it not only reiterated the wide interpretation it had already given to the text of Part XIII, but it also dissipated any apprehensions which this interpretation might have aroused and thus helped to prevent further disputes.

The results of the several appeals to the Permanent Court for its opinion on the scope of the competence of the Organisation must therefore be regarded as reassuring from the point of view of the future of the Organisation. Nothing would have been more dangerous than to allow the opinion to take root that the Organisation was an intrusive institution, wishing to meddle in every field, to exceed the competence granted it, and to menace the rights of States at every point. As it is, the Organisation, reinforced by the consistent decisions of the Permanent Court, has been able to develop its international action without again encountering the objection of incompetency which for a moment had threatened to paralyse its work. It would be too much to assume that its competence will never again be called in question; but, if fresh doubts should ever arise on the point, the principles by which they must be settled are at least known.

Nothing would be gained by trying to describe the precise scope of the competence of the Organisation in this part of this volume. The extent and diversity of its activities will be realised on perusal of the following part. But even a description of the past and present activities of the Organisation cannot convey an exact and complete idea of its competence, because that competence cannot be exhausted by any enumeration. The evolution of social conditions alone can show, as time goes on, with what problems the Organisation must grapple if it is to accomplish to the full the lofty aims of social justice and humanity assigned to it by the Treaty of Peace.

PART II

THE WORK

THE whole work of the International Labour Office has been, and always must be, based on enquiry and study. Even if the Office were only a centre for the collection and distribution of information—one of the two functions assigned to it by the Peace Treaty—study would still be required, for the Office has never considered that it was being completely true to its functions if it confined itself to broadcasting its information in the rough and often incoherent state in which it is received. The first essential is a systematic arrangement of information, such that international comparisons can be deduced therefrom, provided, indeed, that such information lends itself at all to an international survey.

The second purpose of the enquiry work initiated is even more important, because it is the basis of the action taken by the Organisation. The system of international labour legislation which is gradually being constructed by the Organisation cannot be built up in the void, but must live in a world of events and be based on the principles of a judicious opportunism. An international labour Convention is of importance for the Organisation only in so far as it has a chance of being ratified by as many States as possible. It can stand such a chance only if national legislation and custom in a certain number of countries are reasonably close (either above or below) to the standard laid down in the Draft Convention. The sole means of discovering whether this is so is the study of national law and practice. The Governing Body does not place a question on the agenda of the Conference until it is in possession of a preliminary study on it from the Office. A more detailed study is presented before such question is discussed by the Conference. Any examination of the constantly widening activity of the Organisation which tended to separate its enquiry work from its policy in adopting decisions for the international adjustment of labour conditions would give a false idea of the nature of the Organisation. The range of this activity is immense; each year the Organisation reaps its harvest from certain fields, selected in the light of a preliminary survey and clearing of the ground by the Office and the Governing Body.

All the questions which have been made the subject of study—themselves the result of selection among a multitude of items—are not equally ripe for action. In some cases the final stage of a Convention or Recommendation can be attained; in others preliminary enquiry, or sometimes discussion in the Conference, has sufficed to show that a problem is not yet ready for international solution. Nevertheless, that enquiry has at least served to illuminate the state of the problem, and is sometimes a part contribution towards such international solution.

To attempt to give any idea of the whole field of enquiry and of action of the International Labour Office during its first ten years of existence means reviewing in one comprehensive glance those parts of this field which have been surveyed, which have been cleared, which have been sown, and which have been reaped, not to mention those which have still to be explored.

All progress for the legal protection of workers in the international sphere must be preceded by a comparative study of the law and practice in different countries. Therein lies the fundamental importance of the Office's *Studies and Reports*; these deal with various factors in the life of all classes of workers, and already constitute in themselves a substantial library.

National practice is based on law, and on the same principle this series of original studies is based on the annual publication of the Office known as the *Legislative Series*. This work, which is a continuation and an enlargement of the *Bulletin of the International Labour Office* (until 1919 the official organ of the International Association for Labour Legislation), is an annual publication reproducing in three languages—English, French, and German—the texts of the principal legislation for the protection of workers enacted in every country in the course of the preceding year. It provides the best possible indication of the growth of social legislation year by year. The advance of this legislation, however irregular and unsteady it may be, leads to the encouraging conviction that social progress is slowly but surely being consolidated, in spite of all the vicissitudes of national life and international policy. In fact, side by side with public law and private law, a third system has now appeared, deriving from the other two: labour law.

CHAPTER I

CONDITIONS OF WORK

I. Hours of Work

The Eight-Hour Day

The eight-hour day was the principal demand of the workers' organisations long before the War. During the War a whole series of attempts was made in more than one country to improve the working conditions of all wage earners; means were sought for reconciling better output with better working conditions, and certain experiments seemed to show that this could be done by adopting the eight-hour day and combining it with a scientific organisation of the work. Finally, the misery, horror and barbarity of the War itself evoked a general desire to build up a nobler, more understanding and more sensitive humanity; but a life worth the living was impossible so long as the whole day was taken up by toil in factories, in offices or in the fields, leaving the worker no time for reading, reflection or education.

The minds of men were therefore prepared to give a favourable welcome to the old demands of the workers when they were brought forward at the end of the War by the international trade union organisations, not entirely in their old form but incorporated as part of a complete plan for the international organisation of labour conditions. The eight-hour day appeared as the first article in a general programme the realisation of which was to be entrusted to an international and permanent labour organisation. Reference was made to it in the Preamble to Part XIII of the Treaty of Peace, and Article 427, which is more explicit, states that one of the first objects of the new Organisation must be "the adoption of an eight-hour day or a forty-eight-hour week as the standard to be aimed at where it has not already been attained."

The text did not specify any categories of workers either by reference to the industries in which they were employed or to their occupations. There could be no denial that the item embraced the whole body of labour. When the International Labour Conference held its first Session at Washington in 1919, the first item on its agenda was "the adoption of the principle of the eight-hour day and the forty-eight-hour week," without further qualification.

From the outset, however, the Conference met with a difficulty which appeared insurmountable, namely that of defining in one and the same Convention the various adaptations of the eight-hour-day system which would be compatible with occupations so widely different as industrial work, work on board ship, agricultural work and office work, to mention only the main branches. Moreover, certain minds had already perhaps more or less consciously grasped the idea which was to be publicly put forward two years later, that the International Labour Organisation was not competent to regulate the conditions of work of all categories of workers, but only of industrial workers. Be that as it may, two decisions were taken: firstly to restrict the task of the 1919 Conference to the drafting of a Convention on the eight-hour day in industrial undertakings, including mines and railways, and secondly to convene a special Session of the Conference to study the regulation of hours of work in maritime occupations. Such a Conference was, indeed, explicitly provided for in the text of the Washington Convention. The question of extending the principle of the eight-hour day to other categories of workers was reserved for the future.

The "Washington" Convention

The Convention adopted by the Washington Conference thus referred only to workers in industrial undertakings, including mines and railways. It limited the hours of work to eight in the day and forty-eight in the week in industrial undertakings in general and to 56 hours in the case of work which must, by its nature, be continuous. It admitted the possibility of a Saturday half-holiday. The methods of applying these principles were to be decided in consultation with the representative organisations of employers and workers, or even by agreement between these organisations. Special systems were permitted for countries of the Far East. Overtime was allowed, when agreed to by the organisations concerned, as a temporary measure, but the wages paid for such overtime had to be one and one quarter times the normal rates.

There is no necessity for tracing here the whole history of

the Washington Convention since that date. It will suffice to mention certain essential facts which are of particular importance for the life of the Organisation and the Office.

In 1919 the Convention was adopted almost enthusiastically by the very great majority of the delegates of the different States present at Washington. Indeed, the principle on which it was based—the eight-hour day and the forty-eight-hour week—was already applied in many national systems of legislation. The States which have since that date introduced the eight-hour day have endeavoured to conform with the provisions of the Convention, and those which altered their system of hours have all tried to keep these alterations within the limits of the framework laid down by the Convention. Although the International Labour Office has at present no power of interpreting the text of a Convention, the Director has on several occasions given an unofficial opinion, when consulted, as to the meaning of one or other Article, so that States should not run the risk of unintentionally breaking through these provisions. The desire to know what commitments the Convention implied has also led the representatives of the important industrial Powers of Europe to hold two meetings, the one in Berne and the other in London, to arrive at an agreement as to the exact meaning and scope of certain clauses. In these cases also the International Labour Office was consulted.

During these ten years the Office has had to reply to innumerable requests for information as to the hours of work in various industries and in different countries, and this is surely the best possible proof of the general interest in the question. It has published many brochures and articles analysing the tenor of the Convention, reckoning the progress made and showing the state of ratification each year, while at the same time noting the effects of the shortened working day on industry, on the economic system as a whole, and on the well-being of the worker. Practically every Session of the Governing Body and every Session of the Conference have dealt with the same questions. The ratification of the Washington Convention may be said to have become one of the vital problems of the Organisation, just as before the War it was the essential article in the workers' programme.

This situation is due to the fact that the enthusiasm which led to the adoption of the eight-hour-day principle in 1919 has, in the case of many Governments, given place to a state of mind full of apprehensions and reservations when it came to consecrating the principle by law. States did not wish to bind themselves irrevocably for the future unless their economic competitors did the same. This is the reason for conditional ratifications, which are not uncommon in the case of the Diplomatic Conventions of the League of Nations but are quite exceptional in the history of the Labour Organisation. France and Italy, for example, have ratified subject to the condition that they will not put the Convention into force until it is ratified by certain other States, in the former case by Great Britain and Germany and in the latter by these States plus France and Switzerland. Similarly, purely conditional ratifications have been registered by Austria, Latvia and Spain. The only States which have ratified the Convention unconditionally are Belgium, Bulgaria, Chili, Czechoslovakia, Greece, India, Luxemburg, Portugal and Rumania, a total of nine States, of which only two are numbered among the eight States Members of chief industrial importance which are permanently represented on the Governing Body. Recently, however, Germany has stated its intention of ratifying the Convention as soon as the Bill for the Protection of Labour has been adopted, and the Italian Government has introduced a Bill which will enable it to renounce the conditions to which the application of the Convention was subject. In April 1930 the Labour Government in Great Britain introduced a Bill which is in agreement with the Convention.

There is therefore no need to despair of the final complete success of this Convention, which has for ten years absorbed so much of the activity of the Office and the Organisation. On three occasions the Governing Body has rejected proposals for revision: in 1921; in 1929, even though the proposal was made by one of the greatest industrial Powers, Great Britain; finally in 1930—a still more important occasion, because in this case it was a question of the ten-yearly examination to which every Convention must be subjected, and there was a formal proposal for revision submitted by the Swedish Government.

With regard, then, to the Washington Convention and the international regulation of hours of work in industrial undertakings, progress is being made. The Office has accomplished its task of inspiring legislation, and has even successfully passed the test of revision after the first ten years. There seems no doubt that this success and the recently expressed intentions of

Germany and Great Britain will now hasten the progress of ratification. The task of the Organisation and the Office will be merely that of following up and facilitating the application of the Convention.

Hours of Work in Maritime Occupations and Agriculture

The regulation of hours of work in industrial undertakings was urgent on account both of the number of workers to be protected and of the importance of these undertakings in economic and social life at the present day. At the same time it may perhaps be admitted that it was the easiest step to take on the hours question. There is a certain uniformity and comparability between every type of industrial work, and it is perhaps in such work that the two conceptions of presence at the work place and effective work (the latter being so strongly insisted upon by the employers) most nearly coincide. Moreover, it was in respect of industrial undertakings that the old and powerful industrial organisations were best able to take or support any action.

But while industrial workers are an important factor in the labour world, they do not comprise the whole of labour. A mere glance at the latest Statistical Year Book of the League of Nations will show that industrial workers, including those in mines and quarries, constitute about 22 per cent. of the working population of the globe; workers in agriculture, fisheries and forests constitute about 60 per cent., and professional workers and employees in commerce, banks, ports, domestic service, etc., about 18 per cent. It was therefore natural that the Organisation, when it had dealt with the regulation of hours of work in industrial undertakings in 1919, should not consider this effort to be by any means complete. It will be remembered that the Washington Convention itself made provision for a special Session of the Conference to be convened to study the regulation of hours of work in maritime occupations. This Session was held at Genoa in 1920, but succeeded in adopting only two Recommendations on limitation of hours, for the fishing industry and for inland navigation. The question was not brought up again until 1929 at the Thirteenth Session of the Conference, held in Geneva, which was also devoted entirely to maritime work. The difficult conditions under which the Office then pursued its stubborn search for a solution will be recorded later. On the basis of a report by the Office, the Conference adopted a questionnaire requesting the Governments to express their opinion on the limitation of hours of maritime work on the principle of the eight-hour day and the forty-eight-hour week. Replies have been received from the Governments during 1930, and when they have been examined by a technical Conference a Session of the full Conference in 1932 will decide whether a Draft Convention should be drawn up, and, if so, in what terms.

In the case of agricultural work, matters are not so far advanced. As early as 1921 the Office considered that the question should be brought before the Conference, but at that time the competence of the Organisation to cover every branch of labour had not been generally admitted. The French Government in particular declined to recognise its competence to deal with agricultural work, and the question was therefore removed from the agenda of the Session. Since then it has been left untouched. The competence of the Organisation to deal with agricultural questions can no longer be contested, since the Permanent Court gave its opinion in 1923. The neglect of the question is due to other reasons. One is, possibly, that the regulation of agricultural work presents difficulties which, if not insurmountable, are at least very special, the chief one obviously being the inequality in the amount of work to be done at different seasons. Another is, possibly, the fact of the agricultural depression at present raging throughout the world, which has (surely unjustly) forced the question into the background. Finally, there is no doubt that the strength and unity of the associations of agricultural workers, which are smaller than those of industrial workers, are not sufficiently developed to enable them to assert their claims and take action. In any case the question remains entirely one for the future.

The Hours of Work of Employees in Commerce and Offices

In the case of this category of workers, the regulation of hours of work has reached the stage of an international Convention after less than four years' work. It was in September 1926 that the question was first raised by the International Association for Social Progress, which, at its first meeting held in Montreux, requested the International Labour Organisation to place on the agenda of the Conference at the earliest possible date certain questions concerning the conditions of work of employees, and particularly that of hours of work. The Association, backed up by various national and international organisations of salaried employees, further requested the Office to prepare a study on the present state of the regulations for the closing of commercial establishments. In 1928 the Office issued a study, restricted to European States, which showed that the majority of these States had already adopted shop-closing regulations.

These preliminaries brought to light one fundamental question, namely that of the angle from which the problem of hours of work in commerce and offices should be studied if it were to be considered at all. The issue was whether the regulations should deal with the hours of work of "all salaried employees" or with the hours during which shops should be open. The advocates of the second method desired to abolish the excessively long hours of work of the staff of small establishments, particularly shops. That mode of settling the question would lead to a restriction in the hours of work not only of the employee but also of the small shopkeeper. The decision of the Permanent Court with regard to the Draft Convention on Night Work in Bakeries showed that such a proposal was not outside the competence of the Organisation. To lead shopkeepers to a mutual compact which they were unable to conclude on their own initiative really meant contributing to their own obvious interest and well-being.

But when the question was raised in the Governing Body in 1928 with a view to its being placed on the agenda of the Conference, the decision taken was that the hours of work of salaried employees should be regulated first. The argument which carried the day was that such regulation would have the advantage of protecting more numerous bodies of workers than regulation on the closing of shops, quite apart from the fact that indirectly it would probably lead to shorter hours for shops. The question was therefore placed on the agenda of the Twelfth Session of the Conference (May–June 1929) in this form. After a preliminary discussion, the Conference adopted a questionnaire to be sent to Governments, and in June 1930 the Fourteenth Session adopted a Draft Convention limiting the hours of work in commerce and offices to eight in the day and forty-eight in the week.

The Convention, however, does not apply to "salaried employees" as a body. The Conference declined to attempt a definition of a term which is so vague and which has such varied meanings in different languages and countries. It merely specified the groups of establishments to which the Convention should apply. The Convention permits the hours of work to be increased to ten in the day to meet the special requirements of commercial establishments. The hours of work so regulated are defined as being the time during which the employee is at the disposal of the employer. Exemption from the scope of the Convention is possible in the case of establishments in which only members of the employer's family are employed, or in the case of offices in which the staff is engaged in connection with the administration of public authority. The employer is entitled to make up each year thirty of the hours lost by a collective stoppage of work. Hours of work may be extended by permanent exception in the case of shops or other establishments when the nature of the work, the size of the population, or the number of persons employed makes the forty-eight-hour system inapplicable. These exceptions must, however, be authorised by regulations issued by public authority after consultation with the organisations of employers and workers concerned, due account being taken of collective agreements, where they have been concluded by these organisations. Finally, hours of overtime permitted by way of a temporary exception must be paid for at one and a quarter times the normal rates.

Three important categories of establishments are not covered by the Convention: hotels, restaurants and similar establishments; theatres and other places of public amusement; establishments for the treatment or the cure of the sick, infirm, destitute or mentally unfit. Three recommendations were adopted requesting the States Members to carry out special enquiries into the conditions of work existing in these three types of establishments, and to communicate the results to the International Labour Office within a period of four years, so as to enable it to prepare a special report providing the Governing Body with the necessary information for deciding whether the question of the hours of work of the persons employed in these establishments should be placed on the agenda of an early Session of the Conference.

This question, then, is more than half settled. There is already a Draft Convention covering the majority of the workers known as salaried employees. The others have grounds for hoping that in a few years this protective legislation will extend to them if such an extension proves possible. The immediate task of the Office is to do all in its power to obtain ratification of the Draft Convention adopted, and to prepare studies with regard to those persons not covered by it.

The Hours of Work of Miners

Among industrial occupations there is one which has always been subject to special legislation because it is particularly strenuous, injurious to health and perilous: that of underground workers. Most national legislations and collective agreements prescribe shorter hours of work for miners than for other industrial workers. It is true that miners fall within the scope of the Washington Convention, but coal miners, arguing from precedent and the reasons lying behind the precedent, which they maintain still hold good, have, ever since the Washington Convention was adopted, demanded that a more liberal system should be applied to them.

The question was first laid before the Organisation in 1925, when the coal industry in European countries was faced with economic difficulties, the consequences of which threatened to be extremely serious for miners and for mining companies. The Committee of the International Federation of Miners, at its meeting in Brussels on April 28th, adopted and transmitted to the International Labour Office a resolution pointing out that the differences between the conditions of work in the chief coal-producing countries intensified competition. The remedy which it advocated was international uniformity in the conditions of work of miners, with a view to which it requested the Office to collect and distribute comparable data on the conditions of work in coal mines in the different producing countries, and especially on the questions of hours of work, holidays with pay and wages.

The Governing Body instructed the Office to carry out this enquiry. Two years later, at the beginning of 1928, the Office published a volume on hours of work and wages in European coal mines in 1925; in 1929 a second volume gave similar data for 1927. With regard to hours of work, the Office enquiry showed that in spite of their apparent uniformity there were important differences from one country to another, due chiefly to the variety in the methods of calculating the duration of the shift. This showed that the Miners' Federation was right in stressing the differences in hours of work.

In the meantime, the coal crisis was becoming more severe

and its international character more marked. More and more international solutions of an economic or social nature were being advocated to deal with it.

In 1928, two important workers' organisations, the International Federation of Miners already referred to and the International Congress of Christian Miners' Trade Unions, requested the League of Nations and the International Labour Organisation to take urgent measures to arrive at a practical solution. The Council of the League instructed its Economic Committee to study the coal problem as a whole and requested the Office to continue its examination of the social aspects.

At its Tenth Session in September 1929, the Assembly of the League of Nations, after hearing a report by Mr. Graham, President of the British Board of Trade, on the subject of the international crisis in the coal industry and the necessity for finding remedies of an international character for this crisis, adopted a resolution proposed by the British and French delegations, inviting the Governing Body of the International Labour Office to consider "the advisability of convening at an early date a Preparatory Technical Conference consisting of representatives of the Governments, employers and workers of the principal coal-producing countries of Europe, in order to advise it as to what questions relating to conditions of employment in coal mines might best be included in the agenda of the International Labour Conference of 1930 with a view to arriving at practical international agreement." The Council of the League endorsed the resolution of the Assembly, which was then transmitted to the Governing Body of the International Labour Office, which decided to convene for January 6th, 1930, the Preparatory Technical Conference suggested by the Assembly of the League. The Governments invited to take part were those of the following countries: Austria, Belgium, Czechoslovakia, France, Germany, Great Britain, the Netherlands, Poland and Spain.

The Preparatory Technical Conference, thus composed, and including three representatives of each of the nine countries mentioned above (one for the Government, one for mine-owners and one for workers), was held in Geneva from January 6th to 18th, 1930. It had to consider questions concerning hours of work, wages and other conditions of employment in coal mines, and its main purpose was to suggest to the Governing Body which of these questions it considered could most usefully be placed on the agenda of the next Session of the International Labour Conference with a view to arriving at an international agreement. The only question which it recommended for this purpose was that of hours of work. Taking as the basis for discussion the preliminary text of a Draft Convention on hours of work in coal mines prepared by the Office, the Conference then gave quite definite, if not complete, suggestions as to the form which such a Draft Convention might take.

On February 5th, 1930, the Governing Body decided to place on the agenda of the next Session of the Conference (June 1930) the question of hours of work in coal mines. That Conference, realising the urgency of the problem and observing that the work of the Preparatory Technical Conference had thrown light on many points on which international regulation was possible, decided to treat the question as if it were already the second discussion. The Draft Convention prepared by the competent committee and approved by the preliminary vote of the Conference applied only to hard-coal mines; it fixed the time to be spent in the mine at 7 hours 45 minutes per day without any possibility of overtime for economic reasons and with provision for a possible further reduction in hours of work within a period of three years from the date on which the Convention came into force. The Convention was to come into force when ratified by the following countries: Belgium, Czechoslovakia, France, Germany, Great Britain, the Netherlands and Poland. The question of hours of work in the lignite industry was referred to the 1931 Conference. When the final vote was taken there were 70 for and 40 against the Draft Convention, which thus did not obtain the necessary two-thirds majority as the result of the abstention of certain States, including Germany, this abstention arising out of the rejection of an amendment permitting a certain amount of overtime for economic reasons. The Conference immediately decided, however, to place the question on the agenda of the Conference for the 1931 Session.

Such is the present position of the question of hours of work for the International Labour Organisation. The question was solved ten years ago for industrial workers, subject to ratifications, which are a matter for the sovereign rights of States; it was solved in 1930 for the majority of salaried employees; it is on the way to solution for seamen and miners; it has not yet been dealt with either in studies or, *a fortiori*, by the Conference in the case of agricultural workers, with regard to whom it is entirely a question for the future.

II. The Weekly Rest and Holidays with Pay

Those who instituted the eight-hour day did so not merely in order to prevent the worker from being overworked and his health thereby endangered; they had another and perhaps higher aim, namely, to give him sufficient leisure for physical recreation and for mental culture; in short, for life as a human being. This is the double aim of two measures for the protection of the worker which also deal with hours of work: the weekly rest and the institution of annual holidays with pay.

The Weekly Rest

One of the general principles laid down in Article 427 of the Treaty of Peace for guiding the policy of the League of Nations is "the adoption of a weekly rest of at least twenty-four hours, which should include Sunday wherever practicable." At the very first Session of the Conference at Washington in 1919 the question of the weekly rest was raised; the principle was then considered as the logical complement of the regulation of weekly hours, and the Washington Convention implicitly accepts the principle, since Article 2 fixes the daily hours of work at eight and the weekly hours at forty-eight, thus showing that the work is intended to be distributed over six days, leaving the seventh for rest. Similarly, Article 4, which lays down a special system for establishments in which work is continuous, adds that "such regulation of the hours of work shall in no case affect any rest days which may be secured by the national law to the workers in such processes in compensation for the weekly rest day."

In many countries, moreover, large bodies of workers in industry and commerce already enjoyed a weekly rest guaranteed by legislation, collective agreement or custom. Public opinion supported this and was in favour of its extension, sometimes for religious rather than for social reasons, in which case the weekly rest was intended to coincide with Sunday.

In 1921 the question was placed on the agenda of the Third Session of the Conference, and a solution was found for workers in industry and transport, while a Recommendation dealt with the application of the weekly rest to commercial establishments.

The protection of industrial workers once again preceded that which must sooner or later be applied to all workers, no doubt for the same reasons as operated in the case of the eight-hour day. The Weekly Rest Convention provides that in all industrial and transport undertakings a minimum rest period of twenty-four consecutive hours must be granted during each working period of seven days; this rest should as far as possible be enjoyed at the same time by the whole staff of the undertaking and it must coincide whenever practicable with the weekly rest day consecrated by tradition or custom in the country or district in which the undertaking is situated. The same principles are laid down in the Recommendation referring to commercial establishments. This Convention has so far been ratified by seventeen States: Belgium, Bulgaria, Chile, Czechoslovakia, Estonia, Finland, France, Greece, India, Italy, Latvia, Luxemburg, Poland, Rumania, Spain, Sweden and Yugoslavia. The Recommendation concerning commercial establishments has been a source of inspiration to a certain number of national systems of legislation. In many cases, indeed, the weekly rest is granted not only to commercial employees but also to agricultural workers, domestic servants and fishermen. Along these lines the International Labour Organisation will one day have to follow, for the question has advanced rapidly since 1921 for these groups of workers.

Annual Holidays with Pay

Here the first step in international regulation has still to be taken, though the problem has been under discussion for some considerable time. At the First Session of the Conference in 1919 the Swedish Government Delegate expressed the hope that it would be placed on the agenda of a very early Session, and the matter has been brought before the Governing Body by Government and Workers' Delegates on several occasions since then. In February 1930 the Governing Body had to consider it as a possible item of Conference agenda, but it failed to secure a place for the 1931 Session. It seems probable, however, that it must do so soon.

It is not a question of instituting a new practice. The custom of the annual paid holiday is already widespread, either in national legislation which is already in force or in proposed legislation. Provision is also made for annual holidays with pay in a number of collective agreements. The value of an international Convention on the subject would be that it would extend and consolidate the practice. This was never more clearly shown than at the Preparatory Technical Conference on Conditions of Work in Coal Mines in January 1930; during the discussion on hours of work the Polish Government Delegate pointed out that the question of hours could not be separated from that of holidays, and that if a really equitable system of hours of work was to be established in every coal-producing country, then the same rule for annual holidays with pay for miners would have to apply in each case, or else provision would have to be made for overtime in compensation for the holidays in those countries where they are granted. The Preparatory Conference did not completely accept the reasoning of the Polish Government, opining that the two questions were not so closely and necessarily bound up with each other as was maintained. At the same time it pointed out to the Governing Body that the question of annual holidays with pay for miners was one which urgently required to be regulated internationally. At its Fourteenth Session, in June 1930, again at the suggestion of the Polish Government, the Conference adopted a resolution in favour of annual holidays with pay for all wage-earners. There may be room for doubt as to the closeness of the logical connection between the international regulation of hours of work and that of holidays with pay, but it is certain that the former could not but gain from the institution of the latter.

This question, then, is still under discussion and in course of being studied. The Office has already undertaken a considerable amount of work. In 1925 it published a comparative study of national systems of legislation which granted holidays with pay to the workers; in 1928 it examined the principles on which holidays were guaranteed to certain groups of workers in numerous European States by collective agreement; in 1930 it described the regulations in force for miners; very shortly it will publish a complete comparative analysis of the system applied to salaried employees, who are granted holidays with pay of shorter or longer duration in every country. Thus the material for building up an international Convention has already been got together. When the work will be put on the stocks depends on the future decisions of the Governing Body.

III. Night Work

The number of hours during which he works is the most vital question for the well-being of the worker. But the period covered by these hours is also an important factor, for work during the night, at least in the temperate zone, is more prejudicial to the health of the worker and to his family life than work during the day. The Treaty of Peace made it incumbent on the International Labour Organisation to suppress night work wherever possible, and in all other cases to regulate it, prohibit it for the weaker workers, that is for women and children, and ensure that other workers employed during the night were not so employed without interruption.

The Employment of Women and Children at Night

As early as 1906 a diplomatic Convention was concluded at Berne prohibiting the employment of women in industry during the night. In this Convention, however, industrial establishments employing less than ten persons or employing only members of one family were excluded from the field of application. A number of persons of experience objected with regard to the first of these exclusions that it was precisely in these small establishments employing less than ten persons that the conditions of work during the night were most harmful

At its 1919 Session the Conference adopted a Draft Convention prohibiting the employment of women in industry during the night and applying to all industrial undertakings except those employing only members of one family. The term "night" in the text of the Convention means a period of at least eleven consecutive hours, which must include the period between 10 p.m. and 5 a.m. Exemptions are granted in cases of *force majeure*, interruptions which it is impossible to foresee and which are not of a recurring character, work with materials subject to rapid deterioration when such work is necessary to preserve them from certain loss. In seasonal industries the duration of the "night" may be reduced to ten hours for sixty days in the year. In countries in which the climate makes work particularly strenuous during the day the "night" period may be shortened, provided that a compensatory rest is granted to the worker during the day. Special conditions were laid down for the application of the Convention to India and Siam.

In 1921 the Session of the Conference which dealt chiefly

with agricultural work adopted a Recommendation on the employment of women in agriculture during the night. This is much less strict, not only because it is a Recommendation, but also because of its terms. Agricultural work depends mainly on climatic and atmospheric conditions and that in certain climates work in the fields is impossible in the heat of the day; it therefore merely recommends that the States Members should take measures to regulate the employment of women during the night in agricultural undertakings so as to ensure a rest of at least nine hours, which should, wherever possible, be consecutive.

This Recommendation has no history, but the Convention has. It is true that it has been ratified by nineteen States, but at the same time objections have been raised. Some of these have come from various women's organisations which are hostile to any special protection for women workers. They consider that this Convention and any other dealing solely with the employment of women may, or even does, close certain occupations to women. These objections will be dealt with later in the discussion on the desirability of and the warrant for international regulations concerning the employment of women. Other objections have been brought forward recently in connection with the question of revision, which has to be considered for each Convention after it has been in existence for ten years. The British Government Delegate on the Governing Body pointed out that the Convention as drafted in 1919 prevented women from occupying certain posts in industry which were perfectly suited to them, for example, in small provincial electric power stations employing a small staff. The Swedish Government Delegate objected to the definition of "night" as including the period between 10 p.m. and 5 a.m., because this inclusion is contrary to the geographical situation and the customs of Sweden. The Governing Body therefore decided to submit the question of revision to Governments. This is the only one of the Conventions voted in 1919 on which such a decision has been taken. But there must be no misapprehension: those who took the decision by no means wish to overthrow a Convention for the protection of women; on the contrary they wish to make it more effective in the future.

Here, again, it will be noted that only industrial undertakings are covered by this Convention.

Another Convention prohibiting night work in industrial undertakings was adopted at Washington in 1919 for the benefit of children and young persons under eighteen years of age. In the case of this Convention there has been no criticism and no proposal for revision, and it has been ratified by twenty-one States. Its provisions are similar to those of the Convention concerning women, the only special feature being that in certain continuous process industries the minimum age for the employment of children during the night is sixteen years.

Night Work in Bakeries

There is one industry in which night work is not due to continuous work, but has become the rule through long custom: this is the baking industry. For a long time certain sections of public opinion protested vehemently against this custom, which is not based on any inevitable necessity, but merely on the selfish desire of the consumer to have fresh bread in the morning, and which is at the same time very prejudicial to the health of the baker and to his enjoyment of family life. During the past forty years night work in bakeries was prohibited in a certain number of countries, and the War may be said to have accelerated the movement, because the necessity for economising wheat and flour led to prohibiting the sale of new bread, which is more easily consumed. When peace came, many of the measures taken in this direction were repealed by law with little or no protest from public opinion.

It seemed an opportune moment for agreeing to an international Convention prohibiting night work in bakeries. At the Third Session of the International Labour Conference in 1921, eight Government delegates and four workers' delegates submitted a resolution to this effect, which was adopted by the Conference. The Governing Body placed the question on the agenda of the Sixth Session of the Conference in 1924, and at the Seventh Session in 1925, after a second discussion, a Draft Convention was adopted prohibiting any person engaged in the manufacture of bread in bakeries from working during the night, that is to say, for a period of at least seven consecutive hours, which must include the hours between 11 p.m. and 5 a.m. This latter period could be altered to between 10 p.m. and 4 a.m. when the climate or the season of the year made such a change desirable.

Up to the present the Convention has been ratified only by Bulgaria, Cuba, Estonia, Finland and Luxemburg. The competent authorities have recommended ratification in Colombia, Czechoslovakia, France, Germany, Greece, Latvia, the Netherlands, Poland and Uruguay.

It has already been pointed out that this Convention raised a point of law which had to be settled by the Permanent Court of International Justice. The Convention prohibited night work for all persons engaged in the manufacture of bread, thus including the employer. The employers' organisations protested and asked the Court whether the International Labour Organisation was competent to draft and propose regulations concerning the personal work of the employer. The Court replied that the Organisation was competent to draw up and to propose legislation which, in order to protect certain classes of workers, also regulated incidentally the same work when performed by the employer himself. That is a decision which, in its import and possible extensions, goes far beyond the case of bakers, important as that case may be.

IV. Industrial Hygiene

The Preamble to Part XIII of the Treaty mentions among the essential tasks of the International Labour Organisation the protection of workers against general and occupational diseases and industrial accidents. This is an immense field, which is constantly growing and changing with the development of working conditions and production methods. A danger which formerly menaced the workers' health may be abolished by a change in technique, while some other danger may arise. Moreover, all these dangers are not equally urgent or equally easy to remove; in such a vast field progress must be made by gradual stages.

The Organisation attacked this difficult and complicated task without losing time. At its first Session in Washington, the Conference discussed an industrial hygiene topic. The Office has from the beginning had an Industrial Hygiene Service. This has been small, and even to-day numbers only six officials, of whom three are doctors. The principal task of this Service has been to establish contact with associations and persons engaged in the work of industrial medicine in every country and ensure the necessary collaboration. The months immediately following the institution of the Service were almost entirely devoted to rebuilding and extending this international scientific collaboration which had been largely destroyed by the War, and for which the experts in some of the former belligerent countries were not always particularly enthusiastic, or which they preferred to delay for a certain period. The matter was urgent, because the Conference had decided at its Washington Session to place certain questions of industrial hygiene on the agenda of the Third Session in 1921. Thanks to the assistance of experts in countries which had been neutral during the War, and to the relations which the Office's technical adviser had established with the majority of specialists, either through the International Commission for the Study of Occupational Diseases set up at Milan in 1906, or through the technical committees of the International Association for Labour Legislation, a first consultation of specialists was held in Geneva a few days before the Third Session opened.

This was in embryo the Advisory Committee on Industrial Hygiene which the Conference of 1919 had wished to establish. The Committee itself was created soon afterwards. Its members are consulted by correspondence, but every year a certain number of them are convened to discuss certain questions of industrial hygiene on which they are particularly competent, selected by the Governing Body at the suggestion of the Office.

The work thus initiated has been continued without interruption. This work has comprised the discussion of special and general questions at the Conference, studies by the Advisory Committee, and publications by the Office.

Questions dealt with by the Conference

In 1919 the Conference adopted a Recommendation requesting the Governments of the States Members to ratify as soon as possible the diplomatic Convention drawn up at Berne in 1906 prohibiting the use of white phosphorus in match factories. The Organisation thus decided to take over a Convention prepared by its predecessors, without waiting for technical studies on which to base fresh decisions. Since 1919 the Berne Convention has been ratified by fifteen States, and there is no doubt that the Washington Recommendation has been an important factor in this success.

Another 1919 Recommendation referred to the prohibition of the employment of women and children in any industry dealing with lead oxide, which is a source of lead poisoning. The same Session of the Conference also placed on the agenda of its Third Session, to be held in 1921, the prohibition of the use of white lead in painting, and the disinfection of wool infected with anthrax spores.

The white lead question was regulated by a Draft Convention in 1921. According to this Convention, every member of the Organisation undertakes to prohibit the use of white lead, lead sulphate, or any products containing these pigments, in interior painting work in buildings, with the exception of railway stations and industrial undertakings in which the use of these substances is declared to be necessary by the competent authorities after consulting the organisations of employers and workers. These provisions were not to apply to artistic painting or fine lining. It was further forbidden to employ young persons under eighteen years of age or women on industrial painting work involving the use of these substances. Finally, in the case of work for which the use of these substances was permitted, the States Members which ratify the Convention undertake to regulate their use in accordance with a certain number of principles laid down in the Convention.

So far the White Lead Convention has been ratified by nineteen States; some of the most important industrial powers are on the point of ratifying, and their example will certainly encourage others; and in any case will involve the complete application of the Convention by many States whose ratification is at present conditional. Few Conventions, with the exception of the Eight-Hour Day Convention, have given rise to such high feeling and such high words. The Convention has met with numerous adversaries who would have preferred a series of regulations and preventive measures rather than complete prohibition. In point of fact, however, it would seem that the preventive measures adopted in certain systems of national legislation have not been successful, and that the method of prohibition laid down in the Convention will have to be adopted. Since the Convention has begun to take effect the classic examples of large-scale lead poisoning have gradually disappeared. There are, however, still many cases on a small scale which are due to the use of lead. This is the explanation of the Office studies on lead poisoning in the two industries which seem to be most seriously affected: the manufacture of enamels and metal enamelling and the manufacture of accumulators.

Anthrax infection coming from wool infected with anthrax

spores is a danger not only to wool-workers, and particularly those employed on wool pulling, but also to workers on hides and skins, and even, although less severely, to those manipulating bones, horns, hoofs, and animal hair. When the International Labour Conference dealt with the question in 1921, it endeavoured to consider it as a whole. It came to the conclusion that sufficient data were not available for a Convention or even a Recommendation. A temporary Committee was set up to examine the whole question of occupational anthrax. This Committee met in London in 1922, and drafted a series of recommendations adopted by the Conference in 1923. On this basis the International Labour Office, in collaboration with the Health Committee of the League of Nations, set up a Mixed Committee for studying the best means of disinfecting hides and skins. So far laboratory research has given encouraging results, but it does not yet seem possible to apply these results in industrial practice. In the meantime the Office submitted to its Industrial Hygiene Committee in 1930 draft regulations for the protection of workers engaged in the transport or manipulation of hides and skins; the Committee has discussed the matter, and the draft will shortly be submitted to the Governing Body which, if it approves, will publish it. Similar regulations will then be drawn up for the transport and manipulation of bones, horns, hoofs and animal hair. Since it does not seem possible at the moment to abolish the source of the danger, the Organisation is thus concentrating on preventing the spread of infection.

The Governing Body placed on the agenda of the Seventh Session of the Conference in 1925 the question of workmen's compensation for accidents. In certain countries, particularly Great Britain, a single phrase, "workmen's compensation," covers compensation for industrial accidents and for occupational diseases, which are assimilated to accidents. For this reason the Governing Body decided to place both questions on the agenda, probably with a view to two separate Conventions. Moreover, public opinion demanded legislation on both points, and the Convention on compensation for industrial diseases was adopted without difficulty. Under this Convention the States which ratify undertake "to provide that compensation shall be payable to workmen incapacitated by occupational diseases or, in case of death from such disease, to their dependants, in accordance with the general principles of the national legislation relating to compensation for industrial accidents." This Convention has now been ratified by nineteen countries.

The most important feature of the Convention is the definition of "occupational diseases." The Committee of the Conference which had to prepare the Draft Convention spent much time on endeavouring to find a definition, but without success. It finally decided, as did the Conference, and as many States had previously done in their national legislation, to enumerate in a schedule those diseases for which compensation should be granted as occupational diseases. This list contains three items, namely, two diseases—lead poisoning and mercury poisoning, and an infection—anthrax infection. It has been suggested that this is a very narrow field. The objection is justified, but at the same time these three items cover on an average between 80 and 86 per cent. of the cases of diseases recognised as being of occupational origin. Moreover, the Convention provides that the list can be revised and extended by the Conference at a future Session. The Industrial Hygiene Committee of the Office has already twice examined the list, in 1926 and 1928, with a view to its extension.

Special Studies

In the sphere of industrial hygiene more than in any other the work of the Organisation is based on a science which has only recently started. The Office Service, with the support of the specialists on the Committee, has therefore had to do all in its power to encourage the progress of this science by choosing the most urgent questions for discussion—the most widespread and most harmful diseases, the use of the most dangerous substances and the hygiene of certain particularly sensitive organs of the human body. These studies have occupied the attention of the Office since 1925, the last year in which an industrial hygiene question was dealt with by the Conference.

The diseases studied have been silicosis and cancer. The former of these is a dangerous disease of the respiratory organs caused by silicious dust. The workers' organisations submitted the question to the Office at an early date. A questionnaire was sent to specialists in 1924, and in 1929 the Office's technical adviser secured the placing of this question on the agenda of the Fourth International Congress on Occupational Diseases at Lyons. Partly under the impulse of these events a number of studies are being undertaken in Belgium, France, Germany and Italy. At the suggestion and with the financial assistance of the South African Bureau of Mines, which is particularly interested in the question because of the ravages of silicosis in that country, a meeting of experts was convened for Johannesburg in August 1930 to study it thoroughly.

This Conference, composed mainly of experts, adopted a series of resolutions which the Office has sent to the Governments concerned. Further, in accordance with the wishes of the Conference, the Office will undertake research with a view to reaching agreement on a uniform terminology and a uniform radiographic technique for discovering silicosis; ensure the co-ordination of the scientific studies undertaken by various institutions, and collect additional information as regards the incidence and development of the disease and the investigation of rehabilitation schemes. At the request of the British Government delegate on the Governing Body, the Office will collect information and inform the States concerned as to the measures taken in different countries for the classification of silicosis as an occupational disease and the use of apparatus for absorbing dust, which is one of the principal factors in the spread of the disease.

In the case of cancer, the Office is naturally concerned mainly with occupational cancer, and particularly cancer of the skin. Enquiries carried out by the Health Committee of the League showed the seriousness of this occupational cancer, and a Mixed Sub-committee, consisting of members of the Health Committee and the Committee on Industrial Hygiene of the Office, instructed the Office to carry out an enquiry. This has already progressed sufficiently to show the danger of cancer involved in the use of certain industrial substances, more particularly the by-products of tar. The information collected and arranged by the Office will be published shortly along with that collected by the Health Committee of the League with regard to cancer among the Schneeberg workers.

Other Office studies into the effects of certain substances employed in industry on the health of the workers cannot be recorded here in detail. It must suffice to mention some of the more characteristic ones: that on the employment of lead tetraethyl in motor spirit; on the employment of alcohol ether in the artificial silk industry; on the use of radio-active substances in watch-making; on the effects of benzene in many chemical industries, and on the dangers to the eye of the "sunlights" used in cinema studios.

The eye is one of the particularly delicate organs of the body which the Office has studied. In 1923 it published a work entitled *The Protection of Eye-sight in Industry*, dealing with the influence of bad conditions of natural and artificial lighting on the eye. In 1930 a study was published on colour-vision tests as applied to railwaymen and seamen.

Another subject which has been studied is muscular fatigue. In collaboration with the associations dealing with industrial fatigue in France, Germany and Great Britain, the Office has attempted to cast light on the highly controversial question of the limitation of weights which have to be lifted, carried, pushed or dragged. The first results seemed to be based on theoretical rather than practical considerations, whereas the purpose of the study was a practical one. The Office set up a Sub-Committee of its Industrial Hygiene Committee to study fatigue and asked it when making its report to consider the question from the point of view of repeated effort, and not of a single exceptional effort, because the worker is not concerned with athletics or sport, but with the repeated lifting, carrying, or dragging of heavy objects. The study is still being carried out, and in 1929 the International Labour Conference dealt with the problem, but adjourned its examination until the studies had produced practical conclusions. It may be hoped that this will be the case at an early date, because although the use of cranes and hoisting apparatus is spreading and making the problem much less acute in the case of transport workers and dockers, it is nevertheless true that the problem still exists for workers in the foodstuffs industry, agriculture and even a large number of factories.

Under modern working conditions, muscular fatigue is not the only fatigue to which the worker is exposed; there is also nervous fatigue, which, in this age of rationalisation and mechanisation, may result from the speed, intensity or even the monotony of the movements required of a manual worker. The problem is dealt with later in connection with the more general problem of the relation between the health and output of the worker and a system of rationalisation, whether good or bad.

General Studies The questions raised by the International Labour Organisation and the studies undertaken, however numerous, do not exhaust the field of industrial hygiene and industrial medicine. As long as the International Labour Office exists it will have problems of this kind to solve. There are an immense number of such problems not yet dealt with, and fresh ones are constantly being raised by technical advances. There are also some questions touching the whole field of industrial hygiene and medicine.

One of those problems requires consideration apart from any international Conventions which may be adopted or any specific measures which may be taken for the protection of the workers' health: it is the organisation in every country of a medical inspection service capable of supervising the application of Conventions and the execution of such measures. In 1919 the Conference adopted a Recommendation asking Governments to create a special service for protecting the health of the workers which would supplement the work of factory inspection. In this connection the Office prepared a report for the Fourth Session of the Conference in 1922, which had to study the question of factory inspection. A Recommendation was adopted on the latter point, but the question of the medical inspection of labour was adjourned. It was taken up again later when, in 1926, at a meeting held in Düsseldorf, the Committee on Industrial Hygiene considered reports on the position in various countries given by officials in charge of the Medical Labour Inspection Services; these reports were subsequently published by the Office. Systems of medical inspection will sooner or later have to be generally adopted and organised, but an adequate staff must be found with the necessary competence and experience to take charge of them. Therein lies the value of the international exchanges of doctors instituted by the Health Section of the League of Nations; on two occasions, in 1925 and 1929, the Industrial Hygiene Service of the International Labour Office was invited to organise these exchanges, and on these occasions the subject studied was medical institutions dealing with labour.

This would seem to be the beginning of a comprehensive effort towards training the staff of these institutions, which will one day have to supervise and organise the complete protection of the health of the workers. This protection presupposes not only certain special health regulations for each industry, but also agreement as to more general rules applying to all undertakings, all occupations and all workers. The Office has attempted to draft such general rules under the title of "A Standard Code of Industrial Hygiene." These are not regulations which may one day be embodied in an international Convention, but a collection of general but quite definite precepts which may be taken as guiding principles for the legislation of those countries where no such regulations at present exist. In May 1930 the Committee on Industrial Hygiene established the basis of these regulations, and it has requested the Industrial Hygiene Service of the Office to draft them, with the assistance of a special committee of four experts. They will be published and sent to Governments, probably in the course of 1931.

It has already been pointed out that the programme of industrial hygiene of the Organisation could be extended to an infinite degree. The essential point is to regulate as soon as possible the most urgent and easiest questions. There is no doubt that the support of the experts of the Committee on Industrial Hygiene is extremely useful for pointing out these questions, but the Committee since its first meeting has expressed the hope that the Office would undertake certain studies which have not yet been attempted. These desires will help to guide the Office in its future work. In 1921 the Committee adopted resolutions with regard to health conditions and occupational diseases among transport and railway workers and on the pathological effects of carbon monoxide; in 1926 resolutions on the protection of women workers before and after childbirth and on the institution of a periodical medical examination in certain unhealthy establishments; in 1928 on the extension of the schedule of occupational diseases given in the Convention of 1925.

The Encyclopædia of Industrial Hygiene

This brief review of the work of the Office with regard to industrial hygiene shows that that work is encyclopædic in its nature. It can be carried out only through permanent contact with the experts on the Industrial Hygiene Committee and with other international institutions working in the cause of health, such as the Health Committee of the League of Nations, the International Committee on Industrial Medicine, the Hygiene Service of the League of Red Cross Societies, the Union of National Associations of Medical

Inspectors of Labour and many others. The task will be a long one and progress slow and gradual. The Office therefore decided that, in order to bring home to itself and to experts, and still more to employers and workers, the immensity and urgency of the task, it was desirable to examine the position by collecting a compendium of a popular and analytical nature, with no claim to original scientific value, of all the important data on the dangers which threaten the health of the workers in different industries. This led to the publication of *Occupation and Health*, which is an encyclopædia of hygiene, pathology and social welfare. This publication carries out a Resolution adopted by the Conference at its 1919 Session, requesting the Hygiene Service to draw up an international list of unhealthy industries. There are in fact very few industries which are unhealthy in themselves. There are, however, numerous industries, if not all, in which under certain conditions, dealing with certain products, working up certain materials or living in certain premises heated, lighted or ventilated in a certain way, the worker finds himself exposed to avoidable dangers to his health. The encyclopædia describes these conditions and these dangers, as well as the methods adopted or suggested for eliminating them. In preparing it the Office has had the assistance of ninety-five collaborators belonging to fifteen different countries. The work is now almost complete; it comprises 400 articles (about 2,500 pages) published in parts, which will be collected to form two volumes. The first volume has appeared; a number of parts of the second volume have also been published, and the whole work will be completed in 1931.

V. The Prevention of Industrial Accidents

When the International Labour Organisation was set up the question of accident prevention was in the grip of one of the most revolutionary changes which have overtaken it since it first arose in the industrial world. The doctrines on the subject which had been accepted in Europe for more than half a century and which were based on the principle of the protection of the worker by the public authorities were being attacked by a new doctrine born in the United States and known as "Safety First," according to which the worker himself is the essential factor in his own protection against industrial accidents. No account of the work of the Organisation in this sphere would be complete if it did not take account of and examine this fact.

European and American Doctrines

In Europe the principle that workers should be protected against accidents was recognised and applied long before the idea of compulsory accident insurance was accepted. The protection then given consisted solely in a number of regulations which the public authorities compelled employers to observe. At that time the majority of industrial accidents were attributed to the development of machinery, and it was therefore natural that the public authorities should intervene and supervise the degree of "safety" of the machines, so that suitable protective devices could be made compulsory where required. Thus, the methods of accident prevention which were generally in force were of an administrative and technical character. It would be unjust to condemn them as ineffective, since in Germany, for instance, in spite of the enormous development of machinery during the last forty years, the proportion of industrial accidents due to machines has remained the same: 25 per cent. of the total number of industrial accidents for which compensation was paid. This proportion in itself shows that the spread of machinery cannot be held responsible for all industrial accidents.

The American doctrine of "Safety First" came into being in the early twentieth century. For a long time the doctrine of social protection according to which the worker is entitled to compensation for an industrial accident was not applied in United States legislation. Now numerous States in that huge federation have made the employer legally responsible for the payment of compensation. The employer thereupon insured himself, and the possibility of having to pay large sums drew the attention of insurance companies and employers to the problem. In this way the systematic struggle against industrial accidents began. The double principle was soon established that an industrial accident is as costly for the worker, who loses the whole or part of his capacity for employment, as for the employer and the insurance companies which have to pay compensation, and that, in the second place, at least three-quarters of industrial accidents are not due to any fault or lack of protection in the machine which the worker has to manage, but to the faulty manner in which he carries out his task. This led to the suggestion that those who restricted the work of accident prevention to technical regulations were on the wrong track, and that what was necessary was to inspire in the worker and in the employer the will to avoid accidents, while at the same time giving them by appropriate training the means of carrying out their resolve: Safety First.

The Organisation did not feel called upon to choose between these two theories, each of which contains part of the truth and each of which has given valuable results in practice. It thought it more reasonable and more useful to accept both, since they are not irreconcilable.

The Function of the Organisation

The ideal course of accident prevention might be briefly outlined in the following manner. An industry arises which uses a certain appliance, and the manufacturers believe that its use is perfectly safe. When it is used accidents occur. Public opinion and the authorities are stirred to action, and it is decided to make notification compulsory for all such machines in use. Statistics show the number of machines and the number of accidents to which they give rise during a given period. The Government inspectors make a report on the apparent causes of the accidents, and the employers who use them, the manufacturers who construct them and scientific institutes carry out studies with a view to making them harmless. If a protective device is found necessary its use is made compulsory by order of the authorities, and the Government officials ensure the application of this rule. If, on the other hand, the enquiry shows that it is not the appliance which is at fault, but the manner in which the workers use it, then it is a question for propaganda and instruction, both of which should be applied to all those concerned in production: employers, managers and workers.

Where is there an opportunity for effective action by the International Labour Organisation in this scheme? In the first place it can study national methods of technique, propaganda and instruction, recommending those which seem best. It can take all the necessary steps to facilitate an exchange of information between States, between occupational groups, between technical experts. Finally and above all it can help in the general movement for international agreement by which Governments can be led to encourage the work of accident prevention within their countries.

The Work of the Conference

Three Sessions of the Conference have devoted part of their attention to accident prevention: the Fifth in 1923, the Eleventh in 1928 and the Twelfth in 1929. In addition to seven different resolutions on the subject, these conferences adopted two Draft Conventions and five Recommendations. The Draft Conventions deal with the protection against accidents of workers employed in loading or unloading ships and the marking of the weight on heavy packages transported by vessels (1929).

The five Recommendations deal with the general principles for the organisation of a system of inspection to secure the enforcement of the laws and regulations for the protection of the workers (1923); the prevention of industrial accidents in general; the responsibility for safety devices of those who sell or buy power-driven machinery; reciprocity as regards the protection against accidents of workers employed in loading or unloading ships; the consultation of workers' and employers' organisations in the drawing up of regulations dealing with the safety of these workers.

There is no necessity to analyse all these texts here. Attention may be directed to the first Draft Convention and the first two Recommendations mentioned because their texts show particularly clearly the services which the Organisation can render with regard to accident prevention and the methods which it can employ to this end.

Factory Inspection

It is obvious that a factory inspection service is useful not only for the prevention of accidents, but also for various other purposes connected with the legal protection of the workers, but up to the present the Office's studies and enquiries have considered chiefly, indeed almost exclusively, the services rendered by factory inspectors in the prevention of accidents. The conditions of engagement of factory inspection staff and the organisation of such staff depend chiefly on accident prevention requirements, and an inspection service which can adequately carry out prevention work will be able to do all the other work required of it. The Recommendation of 1923 urging States Members to take all possible steps to organise a factory inspection service deals chiefly with the need for accident prevention, while the important Recommendation of 1929 on accident prevention stresses the importance of factory inspection.

The Recommendation of 1929

This Recommendation, which might almost, without exaggeration, be called the gospel of the Organisation on accident prevention, shows that the Conference fully realised the great value of private initiative, that is of the Safety First movement. The Recommendation invites States Members to encourage this movement by all means in their power and to undertake all possible research work concerning industrial accidents, their causes and the accompanying circumstances. It also draws attention to the importance of accident statistics, which cannot provide complete and comparable data unless governed by legal provisions. It further advocates certain propaganda measures and instruction methods for giving the workers the will and the power to avoid accidents by frank collaboration with their employer in the cause of industrial safety. The Recommendation does not conceal the fact that these spontaneous forces, if granted full play, will be more effective than any compulsory measures, however carefully they may be planned. It even appeals to insurance institutions and companies for their co-operation in the work of accident prevention and particularly for support of the Safety First movement, urging them to "take into account in assessing the premium for an undertaking the measures taken therein for the protection of the workers."

At the same time the Recommendation states that "any effective system of accident prevention should rest on the basis of statutory requirements ensuring an adequate standard of safety." Public authorities should prescribe and supervise the equipment of the undertaking from the point of view of safety, the training of the workers in safety methods and the periodical examination of the premises to ensure that they are constructed in a manner compatible with safety. Officials of the inspection service should be empowered to give orders in particular cases to the employer as to the steps to be taken by him to fulfil his obligations, subject to a right of appeal to higher administrative authorities. The Recommendation thus entrusts these officials with an onerous and delicate task and one which implies co-operation by the workers, because the Recommendation provides for the appointment of workers not only to the safety committees, but also "to positions in the official inspection service."

Convention for the Protection of Dockers

The Draft Convention adopted in 1929 for the protection of workers employed in loading and unloading ships is extremely technical and will not be analysed in detail here. One of its special provisions should, however, be noted, because it is the first of the type which has been adopted by the Organisation and may form a precedent for the future. The text of this Draft Convention insists on the necessity for adequate supervision of the application of these provisions in countries which have ratified. Fear was expressed that many States will find it difficult to draft national regulations which can be applied in their ports and which are in complete conformity with the provisions of the Convention, the technical requirements of which are somewhat complicated and difficult. For this reason the Conference, in a special Resolution, requested the Governing Body to set up a technical committee to prepare, on the basis of the Draft Convention, standard regulations for the protection of dock workers which might guide the States Members in drafting their national regulations and would ensure their being in harmony with the principles of the Convention which they had ratified.

The Office's Studies

Accident prevention, like industrial hygiene, must be based on a scientific study of facts. In this case such study is particularly complex because it comprises the technology of engineering, chemistry, statistics, physiology and even psychology. This means that the Office's Safety Service, which is quite small, would be quite unable to advance this science and must therefore seek rather to stimulate and co-ordinate its progress and make known the results.

The Safety Service was instituted in 1921 and spent its first years in preparing items on the agenda of the 1923 and 1925 Sessions of the Conference which directly concerned it.

The 1925 Session had to deal with conditions of work in mechanical and automatic glass-works, questions on which the Conference took no decision. The field was, however, mapped out and explored. In 1925 the Governing Body gave the Safety Service the assistance of a committee of experts, which was originally a sub-committee of the Correspondence Committee on Industrial Hygiene but has since 1930 been independent. This Committee originally met every two years, but it now meets annually, dealing on each occasion with certain questions placed on its agenda by the Governing Body. On each of these questions it appoints a Reporter who prepares a draft plan of study, which, after being discussed by the Committee, is amended by the author and the Office and published by the latter. In this way the Office has published studies on the prevention of accidents in the use of chains, hydro-extractors and presses; a fourth study is at present being made on the use of acetylene.

The scientific work of the Office itself has consisted chiefly in preparing for the Sessions of the Conference mentioned above, and collecting and distributing information of interest on various aspects of accident prevention. Since 1925 the Safety Service has had its bi-monthly review, the *Industrial Safety Survey*, which publishes original articles on special questions, reports on the work of some fifty industrial safety associations, institutions and museums, information concerning safety legislation, etc., and a certain number of official reports. The Office has also published a preliminary study on the methods of compiling accident statistics, but this study is far from exhausting the subject, which is one of the most difficult and most complex in the whole field of statistics. Yet, until exactly comparable numerical data are available showing the frequency and gravity of industrial accidents, their causes and the preceding and accompanying factors, there can be no certainty as to the countries and the industries in which accident prevention is most efficiently organised, what examples should be followed and what should be avoided. This must be one of the future tasks of the Organisation. There are, however, others. On the basis of the general Recommendation on accident prevention adopted in 1929, it would appear to be in the interests of the Organisation to continue along the road on which it set out in the same year when adopting two special Conventions for the protection of dock workers and for marking the weight on heavy packages—a difficult road, but one offering vast possibilities. The desire for accident prevention must be general and must animate all systems of legislation, all employers and all employees. But at the same time the methods of applying it to different forms of work must necessarily vary. The types of employment which require to be most urgently dealt with either by the Office or by the Conference itself would seem to be work in mines, the production and use of acetylene, the fitting up and working of high tension electrical installations, railway coupling and the work of professional motor drivers. These are mere indications of some of the questions suggested in various quarters, on which indeed international action has already been taken. In 1930, for example, the Office convened the first meeting, to be followed by a second in 1931, of a Committee of Experts for examining the possibility of introducing automatic coupling on European railways. In continuing this work this Committee will take into consideration the observations made by the International Union of Railways.

The field of accident prevention is immense, for there is always the possibility that continued technical development may at any time bring to light fresh problems, the solution of which will be more urgent that any of those mentioned. The important thing for the Office is to have at its disposal information which is constantly kept up to date and to keep in close touch with all the experts and scientists dealing with accident prevention, and with the organisations of employers and workers directly concerned.

VI. Employment of Women and Children

The Preamble to Part XIII states that the International Labour Organisation must deal with the "protection of children, young persons and women."

Precedents

The authors of Part XIII cannot be said to have introduced anything new in this field. Many States inaugurated their national systems of labour legislation by Acts on the employment of women and children, while international labour legislation when it first began to take shape, before the Organisation came into being, directed its initial efforts towards protecting women and children. Large-scale industry started in Great Britain, and it was in this country that the cruel conditions which it involved for women and children were first brought to light. The British Act of January 6th, 1844—in the middle of the nineteenth century, a period at which the full liberty of the individual to dispose of his services was still accepted as an inviolable dogma—prohibited the employment of women in industry during the night. During the second half of the nineteenth century Prussia, France,

Switzerland, Austria, Russia, Sweden, Norway, the Netherlands and Belgium followed the example of Great Britain. With regard to children, as early as 1802 the British Parliament, at the instigation of Sir Robert Peel, passed an Act abolishing night work for them, and in 1819 a further Act made the provisions still stricter. Legislation for the protection of children continued to progress in many countries up to the end of the nineteenth century. In 1905 the first of the two diplomatic Conferences at Berne, which attempted to formulate international labour legislation, adopted a Convention prohibiting night work for women, while in 1913 the second adopted a Draft Convention prohibiting the employment of young persons in industry during the night. For a long time also the protection of women before and after childbirth had been urgently demanded.

Thus, when the International Labour Organisation came into being, the way had to some extent already been cleared and had merely to be followed. Up to the present that is practically all that the Organisation has done, but the time will soon come when it must prepare to strike out in new directions.

Employment of Women

At its First Session in Washington the Conference had on its agenda, together with the basic question of hours of work, certain questions particularly affecting women workers: the employment of women in industry during the night, the employment of women before and after childbirth and the employment of women in so-called unhealthy industries.

We have seen that in 1919 a Convention was adopted prohibiting night work of women in industry. As has already been stated, the Governing Body of the Office recently discussed the revision of this Convention with the intention not of decreasing the protection at present granted to women workers, but of enabling fresh ratifications to be added to the nineteen which have already been registered. It should be noted that of these nineteen ratifications, thirteen are by European States, while in five other European States the competent authorities have recommended ratification. It may therefore be said that the Convention has already been accepted by all the States of Europe, which is certainly by far the most important continent from the point of view of the employment of women in factories.

The Washington Conference also adopted a Draft Convention on the employment of women before and after childbirth, the provisions of which apply, without distinction of age or nationality, to all women, married or not, employed in any industrial or commercial undertaking, with the exception of those employing only members of one family. A period of six weeks' rest is granted before childbirth and a compulsory rest of six weeks afterwards. It is further provided that the woman worker shall be paid benefits "sufficient" for the full and healthy maintenance of herself and her child, provided either out of public funds or by means of a system of insurance. It will be noted that the Convention carefully avoids making the employer responsible, lest the possibility of having to pay these benefits might prevent him from employing women, particularly married women. Moreover, it is made illegal to dismiss a woman worker who is absent under these conditions, and adequate time is allowed her for nursing her child.

At the Third Session of the Conference in 1921 a Recommendation was adopted inviting States Members to guarantee similar protection to women wage-earners in agriculture. These provisions lead towards the goal which must be aimed at, directly or indirectly, by any special Convention dealing with the employment of women, namely, the preservation of the maternal function.

This Convention has so far been ratified by eleven States only. Several reasons have been suggested for this lukewarm enthusiasm for a Convention which is so much in harmony with long-advocated humanitarian principles. They are said to lie in the text of certain clauses: the extension of protection to unmarried women, the proposal to institute an insurance system, which might be difficult if sufficient benefits are to be granted to the mother and child, and possibly also the six-week period, which some persons consider to be too long. In any case, the Governing Body, on examination, decided that revision was not necessary. This decision is approved by those who prefer Conventions setting a high standard of protection, even when they are not ratified, to Conventions which obtain numerous ratifications but set a lower standard.

In 1919 the Conference adopted a Recommendation inviting the States Members to prohibit the employment of women in a certain number of industries known as unhealthy; these comprise the reduction of zinc or lead ores and the manufacture of lead alloys, which involve a risk of lead poisoning.

Such has been the work of the International Labour Organisation up to the present for the special protection of women workers. Particular attention has also been given to women in the course of some of its general activities. Obviously all decisions of the Conference connected with hours of work, unemployment, social insurance, industrial hygiene, accident prevention and the conditions of work of salaried employees are protective measures which cover working women as well as men. In certain of these measures the Conference has had to make special provision for women.

In 1926, for example, at the Eighth Session, when a Draft Convention was adopted concerning the inspection of emigrants on board ship, the Conference supplemented the Convention by a Recommendation requesting that special measures should be taken for safeguarding women and girls who were migrating. Similarly, at the Eleventh Session in 1928, when dealing with the very complex question of the living wage, the Conference adopted a Draft Convention on minimum-wage-fixing machinery in those industries which were inadequately organised, and particularly in home-working trades, and in this connection it did not forget that women constitute the bulk of the persons employed in the latter group. Hence a Recommendation was adopted pointing out to States Members the necessity of devoting special attention to trades or parts of trades in which women are ordinarily employed. Measures were suggested for associating women in the operation of the wage-fixing machinery, and the principle of equal remuneration for work of equal value, irrespective of sex, which was already laid down in the Peace Treaty, was recalled and its application recommended to Governments when fixing minimum rates of wages.

The work of the Organisation for the special protection of women has been approved by the majority of women's organisations, and particularly by all the organisations of women workers, which contain the persons directly interested in this work. Certain women's organisations have protested against the Office's activities on the ground that they obviously accentuated the relatively unfavourable situation of women workers as compared with men and even closed certain industries to them. This question will be discussed later in dealing with the relations of the Office with outside institutions and associations. It will suffice to repeat here what was said above, that all special protection for women workers must, if it is to be true to its end, be based on the necessity for avoiding the serious consequences, often extending to future generations, of the physiological injuries which certain types of unhealthy or trying conditions of work may cause to women, or, in short, for protecting the maternal function. Any protective measure which aimed solely at restricting the scope of employment for women without being inspired by the above considerations would constitute an infringement of the principle of the equality of the sexes referred to several times in Part XIII of the Treaty of Peace.

This definite and limited task does not exhaust international effort on behalf of women workers. At its Twelfth Session in 1929 the Conference adopted a resolution to the effect that an international agreement should be arrived at for prohibiting the employment of women in underground work in those few countries where it is still permitted. The Office is at present studying the legislative position on this question in different countries. This study was begun in connection with the enquiry into conditions of work in coal mines instituted in 1925 and extended in 1930 on the occasion of the Preparatory Technical Conference.

The Office has recently also undertaken an enquiry into conditions of work in the chief textile industries. It is a well-known fact that the majority of the workers in these industries are women; practically everywhere they constitute two-thirds of the total, and in Italy as much as 77 per cent. The method chosen by the Office, with the approval of a special committee appointed by the Governing Body, provides that all the information collected should make a distinction between data referring to men, to women, and to children, so that ample material will be provided for consideration and perhaps for international decisions with regard to conditions of work for women. No doubt the study of the maximum weight of loads, to which the Office has for several years been giving attention, will also lead to particular conclusions concerning the female organism. There is probably not one of the Office's studies which has not to give special consideration to the employment of women, with a view to improving their conditions, not to restricting their chances of employment. A general comparative study is at present being made of the regulation of women's work in various countries, which will also doubtless provide material for reflection and action.

The Employment of Children

The International Labour Conference first dealt with the employment of children at its First Session in Washington. Article 427 of the Treaty of Peace mentioned among the urgent tasks of the International Labour Organisation "the abolition of child labour and the imposition of such limitations on the labour of young persons as shall permit the continuation of their education and assure their proper physical development."

A Convention adopted at Washington fixed the minimum age for the employment of children in industry at fourteen years. This Convention had been ratified by eighteen States on January 1st, 1931. In 1920 another Draft Convention fixed the same age for the admission of children to maritime work, and a third fixed the age for admission to work in the stokeholds of ships at sixteen years. These Conventions have obtained twenty-two and twenty-one ratifications respectively—figures which are relatively much higher than the eighteen ratifications mentioned in connection with the first Convention if account is taken of the number of maritime States among the Members of the Organisation. In 1923 a fourth Draft Convention fixed the age for the admission of children to agricultural work at fourteen years; this Convention however differed from the first in that it made provision for a number of exceptions and special arrangements, which can be explained by the special characteristics of agricultural work, and in particular its seasonal nature. This Convention has so far been ratified by twelve States.

It is perhaps doubtful whether the success of the first three of these Conventions is a matter for unqualified satisfaction. It may merely indicate that the Conventions did not aim high enough, and that their ratification involved practically no change in national custom even where that custom was quite unsatisfactory. It may indeed be asked whether the limit of fourteen years of age meets the demands of modern social life. Has a child completed its physical development at the age of fourteen? Has it acquired all the knowledge and all the education which will enable it to live a complete human life in this modern world?

This is the first question raised by the 1919 Convention, and the Office is preparing to reply to it by carrying out two studies; the first will deal with the present state of national legislation on the minimum age for the admission of children to industry, and the second will discuss the possibilities of complying with a resolution adopted by the Fourteenth Session of the Conference in 1930, which requested the Governing Body to consider means of giving future workers in their youth the necessary education so as to make accessible to them later the whole field of science, letters and art and equip them for a "really human life."

This raises a second question. The reason for not admitting a child too early to remunerative employment is that its physical development is not yet complete; moreover, the period of childhood ought to be the period of school attendance if the future worker is to have every opportunity of developing his adult personality to the full. Now if compulsory school attendance does not last until the moment when the child is admitted to employment there is an interval during which children, unable to be either at school or in the workshop, are left to their own devices, without supervision or education or earnings, and exposed to the "dangers of the street." The International Labour Office has recognised the importance of this question by beginning an enquiry into the period of compulsory school attendance in different countries; it will receive the assistance of the International Bureau of Education, which has its headquarters in Geneva. The results of this study will show whether the Organisation, in order to ensure the success of its decisions on the minimum age for admission to employment, should not endeavour to have the school age in every country raised to a point which will harmonise with these decisions.

The Conventions already adopted on the minimum age for the admission of children to employment cover a very large range of occupations. Those which still remain outside the scope of international regulation are some in which children are employed with special frequency, namely, shop and office work and in general all non-industrial urban occupations, including hotels, restaurants, cafés, theatres, cinemas and other places of entertainment. Many of these occupations—some have to be carried on partly at least in the street—can be clearly harmful both to the health and morals of children. The Governing Body was therefore justified in placing on the agenda of the Fifteenth Session of the Conference, to be held in 1931, the question of the minimum age for the admission of children to this wide group of occupations.

Thus during its first ten years of existence the Organisation has maintained to the impetus given in 1919 by the Peace Treaty and by the First Session of the Conference, and has concentrated its efforts on behalf of children to regulating the age for their admission to different types of employment. Age, however, is not the only factor to be considered. Even if the upward limit of compulsory school attendance were raised to sixteen years—which is far from being the case—the adolescent worker ought not be left to himself after leaving school, for at that age he is still a minor, legally, physically and intellectually, and requires protection in many directions. He must be protected, for example, against fatigue, which is particularly dangerous between fourteen and eighteen years, when the physical organism is still growing, and against industrial accidents, which the young worker is less able to avoid than the adult. Special regulations on hours of work (and not only on the number of hours but also on their distribution) ought to be considered for young workers, as well as special measures for decreasing the risk of industrial accidents. It would also seem desirable to prohibit or regulate their employment in occupations recognised as dangerous or unhealthy or immoral and to organise their work in such a way that they can continue their intellectual education and become capable of enjoying human life to the full. This task, like the task of protecting women workers, has a single aim, namely, that the employment of women or young persons should not under any circumstances endanger either before birth or during the period of growth the well-being of the future man.

CHAPTER II

SOCIAL INSURANCE

PUBLIC opinion—even pre-War public opinion—and the Treaty of Peace have dictated all the enquiries and activities of the first decade of the International Labour Organisation described above. With regard to social insurance its work is original.

Social Insurance and the Wage-Earner

The wage-earner has to distribute his small and precarious wages over an existence whose hazards are unknown. He lives under the constant threat of risks which, if they materialise, will stop his work and deprive him of his wages, the only source of income for himself and his family: industrial accidents, general or occupational diseases, invalidity, old age, early death, or unemployment. To remedy this insecurity, these risks must be covered. This cannot be done by the worker himself. All he can do is to accumulate savings, which are of little value until after a long and uninterrupted period of employment and remuneration, whereas danger threatens him every day of his life. Social relief is also of little value, because it takes effect only after the event. Social insurance alone can cover the wage-earner against all the risks which threaten his working and living conditions, and guarantee him a certain amount of economic security.

It is in the general interests of society to abolish the insecurity of the wage-earner. Since it is impossible for him to make provision, and since the absence of such provision may have evil consequences for society as a whole, it becomes the duty of society to make provision for all its members. Insurance must be made compulsory by law and the individual must be forced to insure. The principle of compulsory insurance is gradually replacing that of optional insurance and its social function is being extended.

Originally the function of insurance consisted merely in compensating the worker for the materialisation of certain risks by granting large or small benefits to those who had suffered. The second stage was to make good the injury rather than to pay compensation, but even that stage has now been passed.

The third stage which has been reached is that insurance takes part in preventive work so as to avoid the risk wherever possible and maintain working capacity. It endeavours to deal with the malady at its roots and not merely with its consequences.

The principle that every wage-earner should be protected by insurance is gaining ground not only in European countries but also in a great number of oversea countries. Every economic system, even that of the United States, is gradually adopting insurance for meeting the insecurity in the position of the wage-earner. In less than fifty years social insurance has conquered Europe and is well on the way to conquering the world.

This chapter will outline the position in 1919 and the early work of the International Labour Organisation, and will then proceed to discuss the way in which the insurance problem has in general been dealt with and advanced by the Organisation in the course of its first ten years' activities, finally giving an indication of the position in 1930, which has partly been the result of those activities.

I. The International Labour Organisation and the Problem of Social Insurance (1919–1921)

The Position in 1919

The first large-scale application of social insurance was the work of Bismarck in Germany. Within a period of seven years, from 1883 to 1889, he gave that country sickness insurance, accident insurance, invalidity insurance and old-age pensions. Other countries followed this example with hesitation and to a limited extent. Austria instituted sickness insurance in 1888, followed later by Hungary and in the beginning of the twentieth century by Luxemburg, Norway, Serbia, Great Britain, Rumania and Russia. In the case of old-age and invalidity insurance the German example found no imitator for a quarter of a century; a few years before the War France passed an Act on pensions for workers and peasants; a similar Act was adopted in the Netherlands, and general insurance was established in Sweden. Although the principle of the recognition of an industrial accident as an occupational risk and the right to compensation even where the employer was not proved to be at fault, was admitted before the War in the legislation of practically every industrial State, its application had not then given rise to compulsory accident insurance except in Central and Northern Europe. When the War interfered with the movement its extent and organisation were far from reflecting the conception of social insurance as a single social institution for covering the wage-earner against all occupational and social risks.

The Peace Treaty

The state at which national legislation had arrived when it was brought to a standstill by the War did not suggest that public or official opinion had any organic conception of social insurance as a corollary to the industrial system. The same is true of Part XIII of the Peace Treaty. The Preamble certainly states that the International Labour Organisation is set up to improve the position of the wage-earner, and in particular to protect him "against sickness, disease and injury arising out of his employment," and later, by means of "provision for old age and injury." This enumeration, like all the others in the Preamble, is intended merely as a suggestion and an example; it is neither complete nor co-ordinated. It mentions certain risks and the necessity for covering them, but it merely places the risks and the covering methods side by side without uniting them into a single or even a uniform system for ensuring the physical and economic protection of the wage-earners against every risk to which they are exposed by their working and living conditions.

The First Post-War Years

In spite of the great economic depression which followed the War, beginning with under-production and proceeding to under-consumption and involving monetary inflation and the collapse of several currencies, the progress of legislation on social insurance was resumed with fresh force immediately after peace had been concluded. The countries of Central Europe extended the principle of compulsory sickness insurance to all wage-earners; the Dutch Act on old-age and survivors' insurance was applied, and the compulsory principle was adopted in Italy and Spain, and subsequently also in Belgium, Denmark and Czechoslovakia. But although social insurance remained unaffected in countries where there had been no monetary crisis, and although certain particularly strong branches of insurance in other countries were able to stand the strain of inflation which revealed the defects in certain old institutions, the conditions were not favourable for concerted and systematic international action, and indeed such a possibility was not mentioned in the Peace Treaty.

It was thus quite natural for the International Labour Organisation during its early years to approach the problem of social insurance with prudence and to restrict itself to certain aspects.

At Washington in 1919, as has been mentioned, the Draft Convention on the employment of women in industry and commerce before and after childbirth referred to the part which might be played by insurance: during the period of authorised or compulsory absence the benefit to be paid to the mother was to be obtained either out of the public funds or by an insurance system. Thus, the cash benefits to women during childbirth under a sickness insurance or maternity insurance scheme were confirmed by international decision. The same suggestions were repeated in the 1921 Recommendation on the employment of women in agriculture before and after childbirth.

At Washington also the Conference adopted a Draft Convention and a Recommendation on the subject of unemployment among workers in industry and commerce, which will be referred to later and which mentioned among other things the establishment of a system of unemployment insurance. At Genoa in 1920 it adopted a Draft Convention on the unemployment benefit to be granted to seamen in case of loss or foundering of the ship, and a Recommendation suggesting the extension to seamen of the measures laid down in the 1919 Unemployment Convention.

At Geneva in 1921, in a Draft Convention on workmen's compensation in agriculture, the Conference demanded the extension to agricultural wage-earners of the legislation on workmen's compensation, and in a Recommendation it invited the States Members to extend to these workers the benefit of the legislation on insurance against sickness, invalidity, old age and other similar social risks in industry and commerce. In this case no formal decision was taken, nor was a minimum standard of protection for the worker established, but the principle was at least laid down that agricultural wage-earners should be covered by social insurance in the same way as all other groups.

In the meantime the general economic system, although shaken (and for a long time), was settling down, and the monetary crisis was being overcome. Out of the discussions on the subject of insurance at the 1919, 1920 and 1921 Sessions a doctrine was gradually taking form. The hour seemed to have come for dealing with the problem as a whole and drawing up a programme of international legislation on social insurance.

II. International Regulations on Social Insurance

A Programme of Study and Action

In 1924 the Governing Body requested the Office to submit to the Seventh Session of the Conference in 1925 a report on the general problems of social insurance, with a view to obtaining definite information as to the direction in which the Organisation should work and the order in which different insurance questions should be treated at later Sessions. The Office, after consulting a certain number of members of its Correspondence Committee on Social Insurance, prepared a report of this nature, which was examined and discussed by the Conference. The order in which the different questions should be placed on its agenda and the lines of a programme for studies and publications were thereupon fixed by the Conference.

Further the Conference in a Resolution defined the place of social insurance in the economic and social structure of the world: "A system of labour regulation, if true to the principle of social justice, must secure the effective protection of the workers against risks endangering their livelihood or that of their families. . . . This protection can best be obtained by means of the establishment of a system of social insurance granting clearly defined rights to the beneficiaries." This profession of faith was to be immediately translated into practical action and into a programme for the future work of the Organisation. The Conference invited the Governing Body to place on the agenda of early Sessions the question of sickness insurance and invalidity, old-age and survivors' insurance, while the questions of workmen's compensation for accidents and compensation for occupational diseases were already on the agenda of the 1925 Session.

At this Session the Office submitted, in addition to its report on the general problems of insurance, a comparative analysis of the national systems of legislation on workmen's compensation for accidents, occupational diseases, sickness insurance and unemployment insurance. The Conference requested the Office to continue the collection and distribution of such information for every branch of social insurance and to extend its studies to the results obtained by the application of such legislation in different countries and different branches of industry. A programme of action and study was thus laid down for the Organisation.

Workmen's Compensation for Accidents

The same important Session of 1925 saw the adoption by the Conference of two Draft Conventions and three Recommendations concerning compensation for industrial accidents.

The first Draft Convention is of fundamental importance. It provides that the basic principle of occupational risk set forth in legislation on workmen's compensation and accident insurance should cover all workers, employees and apprentices employed by any enterprise, undertaking or establishment, whether public or private, irrespective of its nature, its size or the degree of risk involved. The only persons who may be excluded are out-workers, the members of the employer's family working with him, and persons whose employment is of a casual nature. The compensation due in the case of a fatal accident or one involving permanent incapacity must be given in the form of periodical payments; in exceptional cases it may be paid in whole or in part in the form of a lump sum if the competent authorities are satisfied that such sum will be properly utilised. The compensation due for incapacity must be paid not later than as from the fifth day after the accident; the benefits should include cash compensation and such medical, surgical and pharmaceutical aid as is recognised to be necessary in consequence of the accident, as well as the supply and normal renewal of the requisite artificial limbs and surgical appliances.

For the purpose of guaranteeing the payment of these benefits, the Conference was not completely satisfied with the old system of ranking claims as privileged in insolvency, but at the same time it could not say that a compulsory system of insurance was the only sure guarantee. It therefore left it to national legislations to decide the method of guaranteeing payments most suitable to special national conditions.

These regulations do not apply to agriculture. The 1921 Convention previously mentioned provides, however, that wage-earners in agriculture shall be covered by any general legislation on workmen's compensation. Thus, in States which have ratified the 1921 and 1925 Conventions landworkers enjoy the benefit of the compensation provided for industrial workers.

Neither of these Conventions contains provisions regarding the amount of benefit. It was so difficult to reach agreement on this point that the Conference decided merely to give certain indications and not to lay down imperative rules. It therefore adopted a Recommendation dealing with the minimum scale of compensation: in the case of total incapacity it should be equal to two-thirds of annual earnings for permanent, and to two-thirds of the weekly or daily wage for temporary, incapacity; in the case of partial incapacity, to that fraction of the compensation due for total incapacity which corresponds to the degree of loss of earning capacity. The Recommendation also contains certain suggestions as to compensation in a lump sum, the supplement to be granted to injured persons who require the constant help of another person, and the question of dependants: husband or wife, children under eighteen years of age, and in certain cases ascendants, grandchildren, brothers and sisters.

Another Recommendation of the 1925 Conference deals with jurisdiction in disputes on workmen's compensation; these should be submitted to special tribunals or arbitration boards which should include, with or without the addition of regular judges, an equal number of employers' and workers' representatives appointed to act as adjudicators.

The second Draft Convention adopted in 1925, which is followed by a Recommendation for its application, binds every State Member which ratifies the Convention to grant to the nationals of any other Member which shall have ratified, who suffer personal injury due to industrial accidents happening in its territory, the same terms in respect of workmen's compensation as it grants to its own nationals, without any condition as to residence.

At present the Convention on workmen's compensation has been ratified by eleven States, and the Convention on equality of treatment for foreigners by twenty-seven.

Sickness Insurance

The question of sickness insurance was placed on the agenda of the Conference for its Tenth Session in 1927. The Office collected complete information on national systems of legislation for compulsory or optional insurance. The discussion led to the adoption of two parallel Draft Conventions on sickness insurance, one for workers in industry and commerce and the other for those in agriculture. These Conventions bind the States which ratify to institute compulsory sickness insurance for wage-earners and guarantee the latter sickness benefit for the first twenty-six weeks of incapacity, as well as medical and pharmaceutical aid from the beginning of their illness until at least the expiry of the period laid down for the payment of benefit. It is left to national legislation to determine the amount of the cash benefit; it may also authorise or prescribe the granting of medical aid to members of the insured person's family. Sickness insurance is to be administered by self-governing institutions under the supervision of the competent public authority. The insured persons and their employers should share in providing the financial resources of the sickness insurance system.

These are the minimum conditions laid down by the two Conventions for every sickness insurance system. In addition, in order to enable States to benefit by the experience already gained, a long Recommendation lays down the general principles which have been found in practice most efficacious for the reasonable and equitable application of sickness insurance. This Recommendation is in some sort a statement of the policy of the Organisation on sickness insurance, containing, as it does, instructions and suggestions for determining the amount of the benefit according to the wages of the sufferer and his family responsibilities, the improvement of benefits in kind, the organisation of the medical service, the co-operation of insurance institutions in the prevention of sickness, and the desirability of making the organisation of insurance more effective by concentrating action on a territorial basis. Even the most advanced systems of sickness insurance can profit substantially by studying the principles of this Recommendation, which deals with the three functions of a complete modern system of sickness insurance: compensation, cure and prevention.

It has already been remarked that of these three functions the last is the most recent and may become the most important, as was shown by the discussion of the committee of experts in 1926. The preventive rôle of sickness insurance and its share in combating social diseases have been studied jointly by the International Labour Organisation and the Health Organisation of the League of Nations. The aim of these studies is to draw up, if possible, a general plan for co-ordinating all the preventive work of health services and social insurance institutions. Important enquiries have already been completed and many preliminary decisions taken, which, if confirmed by the enquiries at present being carried out, will help to extend and render more effective the work of protecting the health of the workers.

So far eight States have ratified the Sickness Insurance Convention for workers in industry and commerce and four the Convention for agricultural workers.

Invalidity, Old-Age and Survivors' Insurance

There is so far no international system of invalidity, old-age and survivors' insurance, but the principle has already been accepted by the Organisation on several occasions. The Preamble to Part XIII of the Treaty expressly mentions "provision for old age and injury"; the Seventh Session of the Conference in 1925 adopted a Resolution inviting the Governing Body to place the question on the agenda of an early Session; the invitation was repeated at the Tenth Session in 1927 with the further resolution that the Conference, either previously or at the same time, should be called upon to consider the question of the maintenance of pension rights for workers moving from one country to another.

It has merely been the fear of overburdening the agenda of the Sessions and the desire to give the Office time for thorough technical preparation (which is being carried out and is proving particularly difficult) that have up to the present led the Governing Body to postpone its decision; this will, however, doubtless be taken in the near future. As it is, the principle which has been accepted and set forth has already proved an inspiration for action, as will be seen later.

The regulation of social insurance in the international sphere is still incomplete. Based on those principles in national systems which have best stood the test of time, it is a synthesis of all the characteristic trends of the insurance movement. It stimulates States to fresh progress and prevents any tendency to slip back. It is the point round which the national movements are coordinating their progress slowly or occasionally with rapidity, as is proved by the history of the last few years.

III. The Present Position of Social Insurance

Development from 1920 to 1930

In 1920 the number of systems of social insurance covering all physical risks was extremely small. Only two important industrial countries, Germany and Great Britain, had protected the wage-earners of all occupations against sickness, invalidity and old age. Elsewhere social insurance, if it existed, covered only one risk or one section of the wage-earners. That was the position in Europe; outside Europe there was nothing.

Between 1920 and 1930 the extension of social insurance over the European continent has been uninterrupted, overcoming all opposition and all doubts. The following list, although incomplete, is impressive: in Austria, old-age pensions (1927) and the extension of compulsory sickness and accident insurance to agricultural workers (1928); in Belgium, old-age and survivors' pensions (1920); in Bulgaria, compulsory insurance against sickness, invalidity, old age and accidents (1924); in Czechoslovakia, general application of compulsory sickness insurance and institution of invalidity, old-age and survivors' insurance (1926); reform of pensions insurance for salaried employees (1929); in France, compulsory sickness, invalidity, old-age and survivors' insurance for wage-earners in all occupations (1930); in Great Britain, compulsory pensions and survivors' insurance (1925 and 1928); in Hungary, old-age, invalidity and survivors' insurance for wage-earners in industry and commerce (1929); in Italy, insurance against invalidity and old age (1923), against tuberculosis (1928) and institution of a sickness insurance fund for commercial employees as the first step towards corporative sickness insurance (1929); in the Netherlands, compulsory sickness insurance for wage-earners in all occupations (1930); in Poland compulsory sickness insurance in a uniform scheme for the whole country (1920); extension of accident insurance (1924) and institution of pensions insurance for salaried employees throughout the whole country (1928).

The following examples refer to reforms which have been decided upon but have not come into force, or Bills which are under discussion at the time of writing: in Australia, a Bill for compulsory insurance against sickness, invalidity and old age; in Austria, an Act passed but not yet in force concerning invalidity and survivors' insurance for workers in all occupations; in Belgium, Bills for compulsory sickness and invalidity insurance; in Denmark, a Bill for general insurance against sickness, invalidity and old age; in Poland, a Bill for the general organisation of social insurance, and for invalidity, old-age and survivors' insurance for workers; in Rumania, a Bill for the reform and unification of sickness and accident insurance; in South Africa, a Bill for compulsory insurance against sickness, invalidity and old age; in Switzerland, a Federal Act, not yet in force, concerning general compulsory insurance against old age and for survivors.

This partial list suffices to show that the universal application of social insurance is no longer merely an item in a programme; it is an accomplished fact. The position of social insurance in the economic and social organisation of communities is steadily growing in importance, as can be seen by the increased budgetary provisions, the extension of its functions, the growing number of beneficiaries and the more active intervention of the insurance institutions over longer periods. Sufficient proof can be found in the progress made since 1913 by the German insurance system, which is the largest and most highly developed of its kind. From that date to 1929 its income has been more than trebled, rising from 1,370 to 4,700 million marks in the sickness, accident, invalidity, old-age and survivors' branches (including salaried employees' insurance), and to as much as 5,500 millions if unemployment insurance is included. This sum represents 15 per cent. of the wages of the insured persons, 11 per cent. of the total wages paid, and 8 per cent. of the national income. These funds have to provide subsistence for a multitude of unemployed and supply four million pensions (two million old-age and invalidity pensions, over a million widows' and orphans' pensions, and almost a million accident pensions). The sickness branch has to provide medical aid and maintenance to an average of 825,000 sufferers, not counting the members of the families of insured persons who claim medical attention.

The movement is everywhere the same, even if not so strongly marked. There is no doubt that the application of the insurance principle is more or less rapid and thorough according to the needs and capacities of each national economic system and the accepted principles of political and social organisation. But in spite of all differences, the movement is extremely homogeneous in every nation. In the main there are the same trends, which seem to be inspired largely by the results of the international discussions described above. A few of these trends in the different branches of insurance may be mentioned here.

Trends of the Movement

The general acceptance of the principle of occupational risks and its application to the wage-earners of every occupation required by the two Conventions of 1921 and 1925 are now accomplished facts, not only in the States which have ratified these Conventions, but also in a great number of others which have conformed to them or are bringing their legislation into harmony.

The same is true of the rules laid down in the 1925 Convention for estimating benefit: payment in the form of pensions of the compensation due in case of death or permanent incapacity; medical, surgical and pharmaceutical aid and the supply of artificial limbs. Similarly the principles contained in the Recommendation of 1925 concerning the fixing of the compensation in proportion to the wages of the victim, the extension of the circle of his dependants in case of death, and occupational rehabilitation have been largely applied in practice.

On another very important point, equality of treatment for foreign workers, which was dealt with in the second Convention adopted in 1925, great progress has been made. Twenty-seven States have ratified the Convention—a record figure.

The most important rule in the two Conventions of 1927 on sickness insurance is that which applies the benefit of such insurance to all persons engaged in any occupation in virtue of a contract of service. This rule has been included in the most important Bills introduced or Acts passed in recent years: the French Social Insurance Act, the Netherlands Insurance Act, the Belgian Sickness and Invalidity Insurance Bills, and the Italian plan for corporative sickness insurance.

The same is true of the extension of sickness insurance to members of the insured person's family. As a result the latter really become insured persons receiving medical and pharmaceutical aid.

The same holds good for the predominance of curative and preventive work over the work of compensation, which is set forth or suggested in the Conventions and the Recommendation of 1927, and in particular for the suggestion that insurance institutions should co-operate in the work of preventing social diseases and furthering the health of the people.

In the case of invalidity, old-age and survivors' insurance, national legislation is ahead of international regulations, which are still in course of being studied. Insurance legislation for invalidity, old age or survivors is already applied in a number of countries. In this case the aims have not been suggested by the International Labour Organisation, but the latter may obtain suggestions from the national legislations. The chief tendencies seem to be in favour of a reduction of the waiting period, a lowering of the retiring age and the substitution of pensions for lump sums for survivors.

The Task of the Future

The International Labour Organisation has had its share in the remarkable development of social insurance during the last ten years. Despite their recent origin, the guiding principles of its Conventions and Recommendations have penetrated into national legislations, helping to improve them or sometimes to create them. Quite apart from the definite commitments of the States which have ratified, the Conventions adopted by the Conference, by the mere fact of their being adopted and being international, prove a common desire for social insurance which stimulates progress.

This does not mean that the Organisation will have fulfilled its obligations when all the fundamental Draft Conventions on the subject of insurance have been adopted. If that were the case its task might be complete in a few years. But that is far from being so.

Social insurance has still a number of entirely honest adversaries. Their hostility is due to two reasons: they cannot see exactly the extent of the benefit which society can obtain from social insurance, and at the same time they believe that they have a very clear idea of what social insurance costs society. To draw up an exact balance-sheet of insurance would be a great undertaking worthy of States devoted to the cause of social progress and worthy of the International Labour Organisation. At present, however, everything, or practically everything, still remains to be done in estimating either the credit or the debit of insurance. It is true that there is hardly any country which could dispense with the need for examining regularly the social changes brought about by insurance, and particularly those which can be shown by statistics: the number of insured persons and beneficiaries, the income and expenditure of insurance institutions, etc. But it is difficult at present to obtain precise data on the quality of the results of social insurance as shown by a better distribution of the product of labour in point of time, by an improvement in the health of the workers, by the greater regularity of employment and higher output secured by curative and preventive action. All these benefits are proclaimed with faith and even with certitude, but at the moment there is no scientific proof.

Some day, no doubt, the International Labour Organisation, with the support of Governments, will have to undertake this task. It has not so far been asked to discover the value of social insurance to those who practise it, but it has been asked what it costs. Three years ago the British Government delegate on the Governing Body requested the latter to invite the Office to undertake a study of "social charges" as they exist at present in the chief industrial States. Does the term "social charges" mean all the burdens assumed by a community for covering the risks of those who depend on the product of their labour for a livelihood? This definition is doubtless correct, representing as it does the cost of social insurance and of social relief, or at least of such forms of social relief as are sometimes still employed to cover the risks which are now more generally dealt with by insurance: industrial accidents; general and occupational diseases, maternity, invalidity, old age, death and unemployment. Even this simple definition gives rise to one preliminary difficulty: is it possible by means of statistics to prepare a double table of the above social charges in a comparable form for all the chief industrial countries?

Moreover, the request of the British Government, which was accepted by the Governing Body, has a twofold purpose: on the one hand to estimate the social charges weighing on production and on economic life, on the other to measure the standard of social protection granted by each State to its insured workers and to those who are covered by social relief. This involves a second difficulty as great as that of determining the exact meaning of "social charges," namely, that of defining the criteria to be adopted in making these calculations.

In spite of these difficulties, the Office has set to work on this task. With the help of a Committee set up by the Governing Body, it prepared a plan of enquiry covering Czechoslovakia, Germany, Great Britain and Poland. After strenuous efforts a report was submitted to the Committee last October. It must be admitted that the first results obtained are not in proportion to the effort required, but the Committee examined them with interest and advantage. It proposed to the Governing Body that the Office should be invited to publish a year-book or at least periodical tables of the social charges in industrial States.

The Office will do so if requested by the Governing Body, but it does not wish the world to find in one of its studies arguments against the principles maintained by the Organisation or a supposed proof that the cost of insurance is too heavy for the economic system or that the more highly developed a State is the greater its burden of debt must be. In such a study the counterpart referred to above would be lacking; even supposing that the cost were correctly calculated, there would be nothing to show the advantage gained from insurance. The International Labour Office is convinced that the advantages are great. For that reason it is proud to be closely associated in the work of the Organisation for the furtherance of social insurance—a work which it considers particularly original and valuable and which it will continue to uphold with enthusiasm.

CHAPTER III

LABOUR STATISTICS AND WAGES

The Necessity for Wages Statistics

Among the causes of "unrest" resulting from a state of "hardship and privation" referred to in the Preamble to Part XIII of the Treaty of Peace as deserving the attention of the International Labour Organisation, there figures the question of wages. It is true that Part XIII does little more than mention among the most urgent tasks an effort to enforce the principle of equal remuneration for work of equal value. It is also true, however, that the question of wages is, along with those of hours of work and placing in employment, one of the most important for the workers. The International Labour Organisation included it in its programme during the very first years of its existence.

From the first also it has met with a difficulty which has not yet been entirely overcome. With regard to wages, as to every other question, the Organisation is aiming at an international solution both when collecting its information and when preparing decisions. The basic information must therefore be comparative, and the ultimate decisions must be universally applicable. It is therefore necessary in the first place to collect comparable data.

The basis for such data are the figures for wages, which are expressed in national currency. National currencies differ in value, and even when converted to a standard value, say the gold standard, the figures represent different purchasing power and different standards of living according to the different prices of the commodities required for existence. Accurate and solidly constructed methods of comparison are therefore necessary. Nothing, or practically nothing, had been done in this direction before the Organisation came into being.

From the outset the Organisation was faced by the problem of international labour statistics, and the same problem was raised not only in connection with wages but inevitably in connection with every other enquiry (as has already been noted, for instance, in reference to accident prevention).

I. The Organisation and International Labour Statistics

The study of labour statistics brought the Office face to face with the essential need for a continuous effort in the collection and distribution of comparable international data. During the early years the collection and publication of a large number of figures were less necessary than the study and criticism of existing national methods of statistics, with a view to their improvement and possible assimilation.

First Steps

In 1920, when the Statistical Section of the Office was set up, the output of labour statistics was far from satisfactory. The War had disorganised many administrative bodies and had forced them to cut down a certain number of their publications; at the same time new States had arisen for which a system of statistics had to be created. During the last ten years some of the national statistical services have been reorganised and others instituted, so that to-day working conditions are reflected in national statistics as they have never been before. The International Labour Organisation can claim a share in this very satisfactory result.

At first the Office merely collected and published data from the chief branches of labour statistics: cost of living, prices and unemployment—data which were already published periodically by the majority of the more important countries. At that date wages statistics, which are the most important for the Organisation, were so rare and so incomplete that they could not be regularly published.

The Office was already getting into touch with national statistical services so as to be kept informed of their work and their methods. The violent price fluctuations in certain countries in Central Europe and their effects on the standard of living and social conditions of the workers were attracting great attention. The Office published a study covering three of the States which were suffering most severely: Austria, Germany and Poland. This study analysed wages movements, cost of living and employment figures. The comparison of wages and social conditions in general with those of the pre-War period was also a principal object of attention. The Office published a series of studies on wages movements in different countries from 1914 to 1921, 1914 to 1922, and 1914 to 1925, endeavouring in each case to show the variation in "real wages," that is, in the purchasing power and standard of living of the workers. No comparison between various countries was attempted, for it was impossible.

More and more, however, it came to be realised that this comparison was desirable, especially as the economic situation in the majority of countries became more settled and the condition of the workers was fixed at a level which was sometimes above that of 1913, sometimes the same, and sometimes perhaps lower. From the very beginning of its studies on comparative wages the Office had to point out the differences in the methods of collecting statistics in various countries which prevented any useful comparison being made. Labour statistics often come from an indirect source: the data are not collected for the immediate purpose of such labour statistics but are the result or, one might say, the by-product of special systems of regulation or the special work of certain administrative bodies. If details of the same category come from different sources in different countries it is clear that they cannot be compared, because they do not refer to identical things. It was pointed out above, for example, that an exact, complete and comparable enumeration of industrial accidents would be of great service for the prevention of such accidents, but it is extremely difficult to compare enumerations when some are partial, while others claim to be complete; when some include among the victims of accidents persons who are incapacitated for one day only, others those who are incapacitated for at least five days, and yet others only those who are victims of a serious or fatal accident. In the same way unemployment statistics are of great general interest, particularly at the moment, but these statistics are sometimes based on the number of insured persons in receipt of benefit, at other times on the number receiving relief, and in other cases on the number of persons registered with the employment exchanges or on the figures provided by trade unions and referring to their members only. Moreover, even when the statistics come from a direct source, that is, when the figures have been collected for the purpose of these statistics and for no other, as is the case with wages, there is little uniformity in the methods of collection and compilation. In one case wages are given by industries, in another by occupations; in one case we have an average total, in another separate figures according to age and sex, in one case "rates of wages," in a second "earnings," in a third "minimum wages," in another "actual wages." Between such varying figures there can be no comparability.

But those who apply to the Office as an international centre for information on social questions demand comparable data. If the Office was to live up to its reputation and fulfil its duty as defined in the Treaty of Peace, it had to make a strenuous effort to achieve the fullest possible uniformity in the methods of compiling statistics in different countries.

The International Conferences of Labour Statisticians

The Office has undertaken that task with the help of the Conferences of Labour Statisticians held in October 1923, April 1925 and October 1926. These Conferences were attended by the official representatives of the labour statistics departments of the chief States. Their decisions in no way committed their Governments, nor was it the intention to prepare a code of strict and complete rules for the classification and compilation of statistical data. It was merely a question of pointing out the general line to be followed in certain special branches of statistics and the direction in which improvements should be sought.

At the first Conference thirty-three countries were represented, and the agenda dealt with the classification of industries and occupations, statistics of wages and hours of work, and statistics of industrial accidents. The agenda of the second Conference comprised, in addition to a second discussion on the classification of industries and occupations, the question of cost-of-living statistics, and statistics of employment and unemployment; the agenda of the third Conference dealt with family budgets and statistics of collective agreements, strikes and lock-outs.

On each of these subjects the Office made a preparatory technical study dealing with the aims of the statistics under discussion and the best methods of collecting and arranging the data, with illustrations taken from the practice of the countries where such statistics are used. After thorough discussion, resolutions were adopted on each point indicating, in the spirit defined above, the methods of improving and unifying the different systems. The replies which the Office has received from Government offices since that date have revealed several improvements; the progress towards uniformity and comparability is slow, but it is certainly being maintained.

These three Conferences covered almost the whole field of statistics, in so far as it concerns conditions of labour. There are, however, other subjects not falling within the scope of the International Labour Organisation alone, yet directly interesting it; for example, statistics of migration, of housing and of social insurance. A further difficulty arises here in that these statistics are often collected, compiled and published by administrative departments or organisations which have no connection with labour questions, so that it is rather difficult to have the problem examined by a Conference of Labour Statisticians. They have not, however, been neglected by the Office.

At its Third Session in 1921 the Conference adopted a Recommendation on migration statistics, and since that date the Office has studied the question and has introduced considerable progress merely by the help of the Governments which reply to its questionnaires. Studies have been published on migration movements from 1920 to 1923, from 1920 to 1924, and from 1925 to 1927. The Office's Migration Service, with the financial support of an American organisation, the National Bureau of Economic Research, has published the first general study of migration movements during the nineteenth century. The Office is also responsible for the statistical tables on migration published annually in the *Statistical Yearbook* of the League of Nations. In the near future a Conference of Migration Statisticians is to be convened and the Office has prepared a report on the methods of compiling such statistics.

Housing statistics are of interest to the Organisation in that they provide an indication of the conditions of life of the workers. In 1928 the Office published a study on these statistics, and a Conference of Housing Statisticians will meet at an early date.

Morbidity statistics are of interest to the Organisation because they indicate the standard of health of the workers and the degree of unhealthiness of various industries and occupations. Much has still to be done to achieve uniformity in the compilation of these statistics, not only as between countries but even between industries and occupations within one country. The Office has recently published a study on this subject and a conference of specialists may one day be convened if the Governing Body so decides.

Such is the work so far accomplished in the sphere of labour statistics, but there is much still to be done. On practically every point all that has been achieved is agreement on certain guiding principles. In some cases only part of the problem has been touched upon: for instance, in the case of accidents, only those occurring in industry have been studied, whereas the problems are quite different when it comes to enumerating the accidents occurring in transport services, mines and the mercantile marine, especially with regard to the calculation of the risks. In 1929 the Office published two studies on accident statistics in mines and railways; a third is being prepared with regard to maritime work. In 1931 the Advisory Committee on Accident Prevention will study the methods of compiling accident statistics.

There is thus a great deal still to be done, and this is particularly true of the main section of labour statistics: wages statistics.

II. Wages Statistics

This is a branch to which the Office has devoted much attention and which has at present shown the most tangible results.

Comparability of Wages Statistics

It was in respect of labour statistics that comparability was most necessary and most difficult to achieve. It was necessary not only on behalf of Governments but also on behalf of organisations of employers and workers; for the Office is more and more being overwhelmed by requests for information on this subject from all quarters. The First Conference of Labour Statisticians considered the possibility of improving national statistics so as to make them more easily comparable, but it did not study the necessary measures for establishing these comparisons on a solid basis. Such a study was impossible at the time in view of monetary fluctuations and the rapid changes in wages which resulted. In 1924, as currencies became stabilised, the Office began exhaustive research into the level of gold wages and real wages in a certain number of occupations in the capitals of the chief industrial countries. This was a continuation of a study begun by the British Ministry of Labour in 1923 for comparing wages in a dozen capital cities. The British Government asked the Office to continue the work, which was at the same time extended. The Office chose a list of nineteen occupations in the building, engineering, furniture manufacture and printing trades, for which rates of wages could be obtained for adult males; it published periodically the wages paid for a forty-eight-hour week in these occupations in twenty-two important cities.

This in itself was a great innovation at that time. Its most interesting feature, however, was the system of comparison adopted. The most simple method of comparing the wages paid in different countries with different currencies is to reduce them to one common currency, but the faults of this method have long been realised. The British Ministry of Labour had substituted for this a method consisting in estimating and comparing wages from the point of view of their purchasing power in foodstuffs, the standard of measurement being the standard of consumption revealed by enquiries into the family budget in Great Britain. The Office, continuing to apply the same method, could not of course use the same basis, which was by no means international. After examining the family budgets of foodstuffs in different countries it fixed six different budgets or "baskets of provisions" as standards. The prices of the goods included in these six baskets for each of the cities covered by the enquiry are collected and the purchasing power of wages in each city is calculated in relation to these baskets. The next step is to calculate the "international" purchasing power of wages in each city by taking an average of the purchasing powers for the six different baskets. These purchasing powers were expressed in index numbers on the basis of British purchasing power.

The method chosen by the Office aroused considerable interest, although with certain reservations. The Office itself was the first to admit the limitations and defects of the system. The Second Conference of Labour Statisticians examined it, approved it and suggested some further improvements, and the same was done at the Seventeenth Session of the International Institute of Statistics. The Office continued its discussions and negotiations with Government statistical services for improving and extending its permanent enquiry. In 1928 it received valuable assistance from the Social Science Research Council of the United States, which, with the Office, invited experts from the United States, Canada, Great Britain, France and Germany to attend a Conference in Geneva in January 1929 to examine the possibility of obtaining still more satisfactory statistical comparisons. A second Conference was held in June 1930, with the addition of Italian experts. This collaboration proved of great value to the Office.

Important improvements have been introduced as a result of these discussions. The tables, which are now published quarterly, cover thirty instead of nineteen occupations in sixty cities belonging to twenty countries instead of in twenty cities as formerly. The list of commodities used for calculating purchasing power is not merely a basket of provisions; the number of commodities has been increased, and heating and lighting have been added. Clothing and housing have not yet been introduced, but it would seem that such a step may be possible in the near future.

Since these comparative statistics refer only to large towns it is obvious that they can take into consideration only the industries practised in every town: building, engineering, furniture, printing, to which have now been added transport, the trade in foodstuffs and municipal services. Very important industries, such as mining, textiles, the iron and shipbuilding trades, which are generally practised in special districts, are excluded. Yet these are perhaps the most relevant industries, because they represent the essential form of industrial concentration, because they all belong to the key industries in economic life, without which modern society could not exist, and because they employ millions of organised workers.

Special Enquiries

In connection with hours of work it was mentioned that the Organisation and the Office had been engaged from 1925 to 1930 in studying the conditions of work of underground workers in coal mines. The reports on the conditions of work of miners in 1925 and 1927 deal in detail and at length with the question of wages. The Committee on Mines set up by the Governing Body examined and approved the methods suggested by the Office Statistical Section. By these means it was possible to determine, for each of the countries covered by the enquiry (Belgium, Czechoslovakia, France, Germany, Great Britain, the Netherlands, Poland and the Saar), hourly wages, wages per shift and annual earnings. But the most important figures were those given at the conclusion of the study for each country, which gave the enquiry its real value and utility: the figures for real wages, that is, for purchasing power, which provide an indication of the social standards of miners, and the figures for wages per ton of saleable coal, which show the wages costs for the industry and their importance in the economic life of mining countries.

This was the first occasion on which an enquiry into wages had enabled these two figures to be determined with such accuracy. Herein lies its exceptional importance, and to a certain extent its value as a precedent and an innovation. The survey of the theory and methods given in the introduction to the report for 1925 was certainly something new, and many of the sections, in spite of the special characteristics of remuneration in mines, could be applied to any enquiry into wages. Such are, for example, the sections on the composition of the total wages bill, money wages, allowances in kind (accommodation and free or cheap coal), family allowances and employers' contributions for social insurance.

One point only was left in the shadow: the method of determining the miner's wages in different countries, which varies very considerably. The Governing Body, on the suggestion of the Preparatory Technical Conference on Mines, which met in January 1930, decided that the Office should submit a report on the law and practice on this question to the 1931 Conference.

These studies on wages in mines will no doubt be the first of a series. Even if they do not lead to the immediate adoption of international regulations on the subject dealt with, they will be of undoubted value in providing a measure of the standard of living, often very unequal, of workers in one and the same occupation in different countries, and in throwing light on a question which is often discussed without much real knowledge of the facts, namely, wages as a factor in the cost of production. We must not forget the fact, which is forcibly brought home in the Preamble to Part XIII, that certain States still seek to gain an advantage in the field of international economic competition by reducing the cost of production and, consequently, the selling price of their products at the expense of the workers' remuneration. Studies on wages carried out in the same way as that on miners' wages can, if used with prudence and with due regard to all the scientific reservations accompanying the tables, help to measure the extent of this "social dumping."

The Governing Body has already asked the Office to consider the possibility of a similar study into conditions of work in the two chief textile industries, wool and cotton. A committee has been appointed, a questionnaire prepared and the preliminary study begun. It will deal with all working conditions: hours of work, holidays, wages, the employment of women and children, unemployment and placing in employment, hygiene and safety. The chapter on wages will very probably be the most difficult to prepare, but there is no doubt that the Statistical Section of the Office, after its experience with coal mines, will be able to carry it out successfully.

Importance and Dangers of the Study of Wages

This statistical study of wages is of cardinal importance. The Preamble to Part XIII pointed out that there was still in the world too much hardship and injustice. In the case of workers the main factor in injustice is inequality of remuneration for the same work according to countries, districts, industries, sex or age. Hardship can mean only inadequate remuneration for the work performed, either in comparison with the minimum necessary for the worker to live and support his family or in comparison with the profits gained in industry, in which labour is one of the essential factors. In 1927, on the occasion of the World Economic Conference convened by the League of Nations, the Office published a preliminary and very instructive study on the standard of living of workers in a certain number of important industrial States. The variations in this standard in different areas are shown to be impressive. On the same occasion another study was published on labour costs as a factor in the cost of production in agriculture.

Since such studies lead to reflection and may generate action, they are either very valuable or very dangerous, according to whether they have been well or badly prepared. The Office feels that its studies have been well done, being based on a method which is carefully thought out, weighed and prudently applied; but it is also the first to state that in inaugurating a particularly difficult type of work it realises its imperfections. It was with a view to removing some of these imperfections that the Governing Body appointed a Committee on Cost-of-Living and Wages Statistics, which studies, with the Statistical Section, methods for improving the value and exactitude of these statistics which are already exact and valuable.

III. The Organisation and Wages

It has already been pointed out several times that the scientific research services of the International Labour Office cannot live in splendid isolation. The Office is failing in its duty if it undertakes a study which is not intended sooner or later to improve the situation of the workers. This truth applies to the studies on wages as well as to all others, for they must be directed towards the useful and the practical. The utility of the publication of international and comparative tables of wages has already been noted above.

In addition to these statistical publications there are systems and even principles of remuneration which, if thoroughly studied and made widely known, could be of service to the workers. There are even some which might be made the subject of Draft Conventions or Recommendations by the Conference. So far the Organisation has approached three of these subjects: minimum wages, family allowances and the so-called doctrine of high wages.

The Minimum Wage

It was in 1926 that the Governing Body first placed on the agenda of the Conference the question of wages, with a view to the adoption of international rules for the creation of minimum wage-fixing machinery. The Conference discussed the question in 1927 and adopted a Draft Convention in 1928.

Each State which ratifies undertakes to create or maintain machinery whereby minimum rates of wages can be fixed for workers employed in certain of the trades or parts of trades (and in particular in home-working trades) in which no arrangements exist for the effective regulation of wages by collective agreement or otherwise, and in which wages are exceptionally low. For the purpose of this Convention the term "trades" includes manufacture and commerce. The Governments are left free, subject to consultation with employers' and workers' organisations where such exist, to determine the trades to which this minimum wage-fixing machinery shall be applied. These organisations have also to be consulted as to the application of the methods adopted. Once minimum rates of wages have been fixed they are not subject to abatement by individual agreement or by collective agreement, except with the general or particular approval of the competent authority. This Convention refers in the first place only to countries which are less highly developed socially and where masses of workers in industry are not yet organised in trade unions which can discuss working conditions with the employers and prepare collective agreements. If only on this account it would be of value, because it provides the workers in such countries with a means of raising their very low standard of living. Its greatest service, however, is in its application to home workers, who are as a class very inadequately protected and the majority of whom are women. The Convention has been ratified by seven States.

Family Allowances

The fixing of wages is based on two principles, which sometimes clash. The first, which is laid down in Article 327 of the Treaty of Peace, is that of equal wages for equal work. The second, which is inscribed in the Preamble to Part XIII, which states that workers must receive adequate remuneration to enable them to live and support their families, might be formulated: " To each according to his needs."

The former of these principles is generally applied and can be found in the scales according to which identical wages are paid to all workers of the same category in any given undertaking or district, irrespective of their family responsibilities and conditions of life.

The second principle would guarantee a wage which varies according to the needs of each family, so as to ensure a suitable standard of living to all. It is derived from the doctrine of real wages, which guarantees to the worker the minimum required for subsistence. In practice it frequently happens that the minimum laid down in collective agreements corresponds to the needs of an average worker's family: the worker, his wife and an average number of children. It tends very soon to become inadequate if the family increases, and certainly becomes so for a large family.

The opposition between these two principles comes to a head when wage agreements have to be drawn up: the employer considers wages as the remuneration for work performed and as an element in his cost of production; family responsibilities are scarcely taken into account in collective agreements, and in an individual agreement, when there is a plentiful supply of labour, the employer naturally tends to choose the applicant who asks for the lowest wages, thus automatically sacrificing the worker who has a family.

It is for the purpose of meeting this difficulty that the idea of a system of family compensation or allowances, which had been applied before the War in certain public administrations in France, has been extended since 1920. It has been applied to a greater or less extent in France, Belgium, the Netherlands, and later in Germany, Czechoslovakia, Poland and Austria. It is applied less widely in Yugoslavia, Denmark, Norway, Sweden, Finland, Switzerland, Italy, Great Britain and Australia.

This brief enumeration will suffice to show that the idea is far from being generally accepted in every country, and it is perhaps too early to think of international regulations. The Office has at least studied the question for some time. In 1924 it published a preliminary international comparative study analysing the systems applied in the countries mentioned above. Since then it has steadily followed the developments of the system.

High Wages

For several years Europe has been interested in the doctrine known as that of high wages, applied by industrial employers in the United States. Certain people regard these high wages not merely as an improvement in the standard of living of all classes of workers, but as a source of salvation for the economic system and for production. They believe that to raise wages and thus improve the purchasing power and consuming power of the workers, who constitute the great majority of consumers, is to strengthen the power of the whole market in each country and, therefore, encourage production. Others, again, believe that high wages are the result and not the source of prosperity in production; the latter leads to the former and not vice versa. It is further argued that in a collectivity of more than 300 million people, such as Europe without Russia, it would be imprudent to try and raise the earnings of every individual to the same extent as in a highly industrial community, such as the United States, which has only 120 million inhabitants and where the extensive use of machinery enables high wages to be paid to the small number of workers required. They maintain that the same intense development of machinery in Europe would lead to high wages for a certain number of workers, but would mean unemployment for many others.

These are the two extreme views, between which the truth must be sought. The Office has undertaken an objective search for truth by analysing first of all the American conception of high wages to discover what it contains and what it does not contain: for example, insurance contributions. The Office has barely begun its studies on this difficult and important question, but a chance circumstance has enabled it to develop the study indirectly at the moment.

A year ago the Ford Company asked the Office to determine for it the wages which would have to be paid to an unskilled worker in seventeen specified towns in Europe to enable this worker to live at the same standard as an unskilled worker in Detroit in the United States earning seven dollars a day. Mr. Edward Filene placed a large sum at the disposal of the Office for the purpose of this enquiry, which is now being carried out. It is the first occasion on which an objective study has been undertaken with a view to determining exactly what standard of living high wages represent to the worker in the district of America in which they are paid, and in the second place the amount which would have to be paid in European countries which are, perhaps wrongly, considered as paying low wages, in order to give the worker a similar standard of living. Such a study brings the question of high wages into the sphere of practical politics. There is no doubt that a number of similar studies will one day throw complete light on the theory and philosophy of high wages.

CHAPTER IV

EMPLOYMENT

Vocational Training—Unemployment—Emigration

One of the most important and most natural preoccupations of the worker, apart from hours and wages, concerns his chances of getting work and of keeping it. The idea of insuring this chance, i.e. the idea of guaranteeing the future, admittedly only took hold of the worker after long reflection; he accepts it fully only when he reaches a certain degree of insight and organisation. This is not to be wondered at in the case of men and women whose remuneration for their labour provides merely the minimum required for their day-to-day life and who, having scarcely any means of saving, live for a present which is taken up by the daily work necessary to provide the daily bread. Thus, the worker's first thought is to find his job and to hold it. One of the most essential and difficult functions of the International Labour Organisation is to help him. In this direction the Organisation, even if sometimes hindered by national preoccupations which will be referred to later, has done great and useful service.

I. Vocational Training

The Programme of Work

It was in 1924 that the International Labour Office began to study vocational training in industry. It drew up a programme for comparative studies referring to the three branches of vocational training: vocational guidance, apprenticeship and technical education. In 1924 and 1925 it published in the *International Labour Review* a series of comparative studies on a more or less opportunist, if not actually haphazard, plan, depending on the amount of the information collected in one or other branch of the subject.

This was merely preparatory work, but it enabled the Director in his report to the Seventh Session of the Conference in 1925 to state with justice that the Office had realised the extent to which vocational training was occupying the attention of States Members of the International Labour Organisation. The idea, based on experience, that skilled labour is necessary for intensive and continuous production had dispelled the illusion which had at one time been cherished as a result of the development of machinery, that modern industry required only labourers whose work would be restricted to the performance of certain quite simple movements or manipulations which could be learned in a few hours.

Thus the great development of machinery and the spread of rationalisation did not do away with the need for vocational training; it perhaps even widened its scope, because it was found necessary to give apprentices not only craft manual skill and practical knowledge, but also the ability to understand the scientific principles on which modern technical processes are based. Such an understanding is all the more necessary because the mechanism of which the worker is a wheel is becoming more vast and more complex. Even the humblest woodman must not be allowed to lose sight of the wood on account of the number of trees. The question of technical education is complicated and enriched by the wider question of general training and culture.

In response to the Director's suggestion, the Conference in 1927 adopted a Resolution requesting the Office to undertake preliminary studies and the necessary enquiries to form the basis of a discussion on vocational guidance, apprenticeship and technical education at a future Session. This enquiry is at present being carried out.

Vocational Guidance

The enquiry began with the question of vocational guidance—an idea which has now found general acceptance. The dominant aspect of vocational guidance varies according to different tendencies and needs: those who are guiding the future worker sometimes base their action on medical opinion, sometimes on the opinion of the teacher and sometimes on the state of the national or regional labour market and its future requirements, as far as they can be foreseen. In any case the movement has now everywhere got past the stage of vague generalities, and methods are gradually being worked out. If in some cases they are still rather too systematic and mutually exclusive it may be hoped that a study such as is being prepared by the Office will be of value in rendering them more elastic and more harmonious. Here, as on other problems, there are good suggestions to be found in most national systems, which are still being tested rather than are actually in force. They can be judged only by results, and an international study will bring to light the best features of each system.

Apprenticeship

Apprenticeship, after being practically neglected during the early period of extreme mechanisation and rationalisation, is now again becoming a point of interest for Governments, employers and workers. The question has been dealt with in many clauses of collective agreements and many recent legislative measures. The Office has several times noted in its publications, and tries to encourage by all possible means, the spread of the double tendency at present guiding the modern reorganisation of apprenticeship: on the one hand the desire to guarantee to each industry and each occupation a labour supply trained to meet its special needs; on the other hand the desire to give adolescent workers on leaving school a general vocational training, the principles of which, if widely inculcated, would enable them if necessary to leave the industry which they originally entered and pass to another industry without feeling absolutely lost.

Technical Education

In every country the number of general or special vocational schools is increasing rapidly. In industry particularly they often coincide, at least in the case of the special schools, with institutions for apprenticeship. The Office's study will not be able to discuss technical education apart from such institutions; the Office feels justified in proceeding slowly and with caution precisely on account of this difficulty. A discussion in the agricultural field has preceded one in the industrial field; at the end of 1929 an important study was published on vocational training in agriculture which will be referred to later.

International Co-ordination of Principles

The Office is studying and making known all the experiments in vocational training now being made in all countries to suit their own needs, customs and financial position. There is, however, the further question of whether it would not be desirable, while respecting national customs and tendencies, to try to establish a sort of epitome of the essential principles which every national system of vocational training should accept and apply. At a period when labour is no longer exclusively national, when emigration is tending to make part of the labour supply international, such an undertaking would certainly be of value. Resolutions of international scope have already been adopted by international congresses of industrial associations, teachers, specialists and trade-union organisations. The International Labour Organisation will be ready and able to help when the texts of resolutions have to be implemented in actions.

Vocational and General Education

Emphasis is everywhere being laid on the desirability of co-ordinating programmes of vocational training with those of compulsory school education. The complexity of industrial life demands to-day that everyone who enters industry, no matter at what stage, should have attained a certain degree of general education. This truth can be found explicitly or implicitly in resolutions adopted by the International Trade Union Committee on questions of youth and education, by the Congress of the International Society for Commercial Instruction, by the Biennial Congress of the International Federation of Teachers and by the General Assembly of the Association for Social Progress. The Office took part in the last two of these meetings. Similarly, the International Labour Conference adopted at its Fourteenth Session in 1930 a Resolution requesting that fresh efforts should be made towards the universal ratification of the Conventions on the minimum age for the admission of children to employment, and that the Office should do all in its power to raise the compulsory school age in every country and give all children, adolescents and workers the foundations of a general education. This Resolution sums up the whole problem. The Governing Body in October 1930 invited the Office to begin a preliminary study on the general tendencies of the movement for workers' education in different countries.

II. Employment and Unemployment

The Study of Unemployment

During the last ten years unemployment has reached a degree of gravity hitherto unknown. The lack or imperfection of earlier statistics formerly concealed much of the evil; many suffered unknown, and practically no attempt was made to enumerate them. In 1919 the problem was already serious, and the Conference adopted a Draft Convention on the subject at its First Session in Washington. To-day most industrial countries are only too anxious to reduce, cure and prevent unemployment, but the first need is to understand it. Those States which first recognised the responsibility of society towards the unemployed and their right to receive insurance benefit, or at least relief, and first accepted the social duty of finding and applying all suitable means of prevention, were also the first to use statistics in order to throw light on this problem.

The first Article of the Convention on unemployment adopted by the Washington Conference deals with the international centralisation of unemployment statistics and of information on all measures taken to meet or prevent unemployment. For ten years the *International Labour Review* has regularly published the absolute numbers of unemployed and the percentages in certain occupations for every country which supplies the necessary information (and there are 23 which have ratified the Convention). These tables originally referred to 9 countries only, but in 1930 they covered 27 countries. It is true that these figures are not yet comparable from country to country. Practically all that is possible is to follow the curve of unemployment for each country separately, but that in itself is of value. The Office has made efforts to make the figures more comparable; it was pointed out above that the question was submitted to the Second Conference of Labour Statisticians in 1925, whose resolutions have had certain satisfactory effects; and it is hoped that further improvements will be made in due course.

In addition to demanding the compilation of statistics and their increased comparability the 1919 Convention also recommended an exchange of information as to measures taken and the results achieved by different States in combating unemployment. The Office has analysed and compared all the information supplied, whether by the 23 States which have ratified the Convention or by other States, and has published numerous studies on different aspects of unemployment. Every topic has been dealt with; it would be possible to compile an encyclopædia of unemployment from the Office publications on the lines of its *Encyclopædia of Industrial Hygiene*. Two editions have already been issued of the *Bibliography of Unemployment*, which has proved of great value for the study of this terrible phenomenon, and the report of 1929, which will be mentioned later, outlines its essential characteristics.

Unemployment Insurance

The number of unemployed in the world has probably never been less than ten million during the last ten years; in certain countries the proportion of unemployed has probably never fallen below a tenth of the number of workers. There are even cases in which this proportion has risen to a third when winter unemployment came to aggravate the effects of an economic crisis. The insurance of workers against unemployment is the most convenient method of dealing with it, although it is only a palliative and not a remedy. This practice was recommended to States by the International Labour Conference in 1919.

This Recommendation has been followed by appreciable improvements. In 1919 there were only 3,700,000 workers compulsorily insured against unemployment, and that in one country only—Great Britain; a compulsory insurance Act had just been adopted in Italy, and in certain countries the Governments gave subsidies to unemployment funds set up by the workers themselves. To-day more than forty-four million workers are covered by compulsory unemployment insurance systems in ten countries: Austria, Bulgaria, Germany, Great Britain, the Irish Free State, Italy, Poland, Queensland, Switzerland (seven Cantons) and the U.S.S.R.; almost three million workers are covered by optional insurance systems in eight countries: Belgium, Czechoslovakia, Denmark, Finland, France, Norway, the Netherlands and Switzerland (remaining Cantons).

It may be asserted that the work of the Office is not unconnected with this result. The further question remains, whether the time has come to submit the question of unemployment insurance to the Conference with a view to the adoption of a Draft Convention. So far the Governing Body, which has several times considered the problem, has not accepted this view. The question is, however, one of those between which the Governing Body has to choose each year when preparing the agenda of the Conference.

Placing in Employment

Unemployment insurance provides for the maintenance of the unemployed, but it does not do away with unemployment, which is the essential problem from the economic and social standpoints. For this reason Article 2 of the Draft Convention of 1919 dealt with the organisation of employment exchanges. There is no longer any discussion as to the value and utility of the public employment services recommended in the Convention. All that is required is to improve their organisation so as to make their work more effective. Several studies of the Office have reported what has been done by certain countries in this direction: namely, the specialisation of exchanges by industries and occupations and the inter-local, inter-regional and international organisation of placing in employment.

This problem is not a purely national one, and it is tending to become more and more international. Accordingly, the 1919 Convention instructed the International Labour Office to co-ordinate, in agreement with the countries concerned, the operations of the various national systems of employment exchanges. Up to the present the efforts of the Office in this direction have unfortunately not met with great success. It must wait for or urge on the day when all national administrations will be fully convinced of the usefulness of international collaboration in the work of finding employment. There will then be some hope of assuring the stability of the international labour market.

The Real Causes of Unemployment

It is impossible to organise the work of placing in employment unless there is a demand for labour somewhere. As has been seen during the last ten years, it is possible to find little or no employment available anywhere. The general unemployment from which the world has too often suffered in recent times has deep-rooted economic causes which have to be dealt with.

At its Third Session in 1921 the International Labour Conference asked the Office to undertake an enquiry into the national and international aspects of the unemployment crisis of that period, requesting the assistance of the other competent bodies of the League of Nations in solving the economic and financial questions which might be brought to light during the enquiry. It recommended that a special International Conference be convened to examine remedies of an international nature. In accordance with this resolution the first World Economic Conference was held in Genoa in 1922, but it gave merely a formal satisfaction on the subject of unemployment, only adopting a recommendation which repeated the terms of the Convention of the 1919 Session of the International Labour Conference. In reality the importance of the Genoa Conference lay not in its work on unemployment but in its programme of monetary policy.

The Office meanwhile set about its enquiry, which it is continuing and which, indeed, may be assumed to be destined to last as long as any unemployment remains in the world. Quite a number of studies have been published on the results of this enquiry, and the Office has collaborated on the question with the Economic and Financial Organisation of the League of Nations.

The Mixed Commission on Economic Crises

In 1923 the Office and the Economic Organisation of the League set up a Mixed Commission on Economic Crises, the first task of which was to consider the indices of economic forecasting, frequently referred to as "economic barometers." In 1924 the Office presented a report on the subject to the Economic Committee of the League of Nations, and this led to a series of studies which are partly responsible for the progress made in research work by special institutes in various countries.

At the same time the Office began a general study of the unemployment crisis of 1920–1923, which showed that, in addition to several other causes, the monetary policy of certain States had been an important factor in the crisis. Several later studies confirmed these conclusions and showed that the application of the resolutions on currency adopted by the Economic Conference at Genoa could help to increase stability of employment for workers; one special study showed how the credit policy of the banking system controlled by the Federal Reserve Board in the United States was directed towards this end. In the light of the reports submitted by the Office the Mixed Commission recognised in 1929 that the cyclical fluctuations in economic activity which led to unemployment could to a great extent be restricted if account were taken in the distribution of credits of the various economic factors involved, and more particularly of the trends of the labour market and the movement of prices. Moreover, in order to ensure that monetary stability which is essential to any successful economic organisation and a condition for stability of employment, it recommended that all the national currencies should be stabilised on the basis of a gold standard and that collaboration should be instituted between the central banks of issue. These ideas have come to be accepted: the Bank of International Settlements is in one aspect an application of the latter recommendation, and in 1928 the Consultative Economic Committee of the League recommended to the Financial Committee the creation of a special committee to study the causes of fluctuations in the purchasing power of gold and their effects on economic life. This committee is now at work, and the Office is collaborating with it in studying the effects of these fluctuations on the economic position of the workers.

The Mixed Commission has also studied other international causes of unemployment: the undue development of certain industries set up for War purposes and maintained for reasons of economic nationalism after peace had been signed; the dislocation of international trade as a result of the exaggerations and instability of certain tariff policies and fiscal systems. In fact every ill to which the economic system of a country or of the world is heir may be a cause of national or international unemployment. This truth contains one of the strongest reasons, although by no means the only one, which compel the International Labour Organisation, set up to ensure social peace, to consider as well every one of the problems concerned with economic peace.

In compliance with a recommendation of the Conference in 1919 the Office has submitted to the Mixed Commission a plan for an international study of the policy of different States with regard to public works as a remedy for unemployment. The plan was approved and the results of the study have now been published.

Various Studies

The studies referred to above are far from having exhausted the activity of the Office in the sphere of unemployment. Unemployment as a social fact is as serious as it is complex: it may be accidental; it may also be periodical; and it has been seen that the cycles affecting economic prosperity have an influence on the extent of unemployment. In many occupations seasonal unemployment is common, and this phenomenon has also been studied by the Office.

At the request of the Conference the Office has also considered and is still considering the influence on unemployment of economic, technical or demographic factors, such as rationalisation and scientific management, the development of new industries at the expense of older ones and an increase in population. The enumeration of these studies is sufficient to show the variety of the aspects of the unemployment question and how this long and exhaustive enquiry, begun by the Office in 1921, may in the end prove the best means of diagnosing the disease and one day possibly finding the cure.

The Two Reports of 1929 and the Resolution of the Assembly in 1930

Among all the Office's studies, the two reports published in 1929 deserve special mention.

One was submitted to and examined by the Conference at its Twelfth Session, in accordance with a resolution of the Eleventh Session in 1928. This report deals with certain vital aspects of the present-day unemployment problem: its connection with monetary fluctuations, its special features in coal mines and the textile industries, of which the Organisation has made a special study, and its relationships with migration policy as at present in force.

It will be seen later that the Advisory Committee on Professional Workers was invited by the Governing Body in 1928 to place on its agenda the question of unemployment among professional workers. In 1929 the Office submitted a report on the subject, comprising a series of studies on unemployment among musicians, theatrical artists, journalists, teachers, engineers, architects, doctors, dentists, pharmacists and nurses. The Committee, with the approval of the Governing Body, has asked the Office to continue these studies and extend them to cover employment organisation and vocational guidance and selection. This is a vast field, as are all those which have to be studied by the Employment and Unemployment Service of the Office.

In 1930, a year which must have seen a larger army of unemployed than the world had ever known (possibly eighteen or twenty million), it was inevitable that the question of unemployment should be brought more urgently than ever to the notice of the International Labour Office. In fact, while one of the workers' representatives on the Governing Body drew attention to this terrible scourge in graphic and moving terms, the Assembly of the League of Nations in September, in accordance with the suggestions of its Second Commission, adopted a long resolution on the economic problems of the day, among which it mentioned unemployment as one of the most important, at the same time expressing the confident conviction that the International Labour Organisation was studying the question thoroughly in all its aspects. In October the Governing Body decided to enlarge its Unemployment Committee, authorise it to consult experts and entrust it with the study of the problem as a whole. The Committee met in January 1931 and made certain proposals for the further examination of various aspects of the problem.

The Work of the Organisation and its Effects

It may be asked what results have been obtained or can be expected from so many completed or pending studies. At the moment the results must of necessity be slight in view of the extent and importance of the problem to be solved. At the same time the International Labour Organisation can be said from the very first to have done all that it could in this field; in many cases it could do no more than throw light and stimulate action. Unemployment is to a great extent a national problem, and the causes of the unemployment in many countries must be sought in their national economic policy. It is none the less true that unemployment is partly the result of international difficulties which could be lessened or removed by a policy of international collaboration. But for the insistence of the Organisation in bringing up this question again and again in the name of the workers and demanding a solution for these international difficulties, it is very doubtful whether the leaders of national economic policy would have seen them or would want to see them. Yet these international difficulties certainly exist. There are, for example, commercial or financial difficulties which can be solved by boldly adopting a collective economic policy; the work of the Organisation in this direction will be referred to later. There are, on the other hand, the difficulties concerned with the harmonious distribution of labour by an international migration policy; the work of the Organisation in this direction is studied in the following section.

III. Migration of Workers

Nationalism and Migration

During the last ten years a large number of bilateral agreements on labour migration have been concluded. At the same time it cannot be denied that the most striking characteristic of this period has been a tendency to unilateral regulation in the matter of immigration and even of emigration.

The United States set the example in 1917 by prohibiting the immigration of "undesirables." In 1921 and 1924 much more restrictive measures were adopted under the Quota Acts, which affected all immigrants irrespectively. The British Dominions soon followed suit, and later certain States of Latin America.

This restrictive legislation is based on two principles: the power of absorption of foreign labour in each State, and its selection, either from the point of view of nationality or from the point of view of occupation. At the present time there is not a single immigration country which has not more or less protected its labour market by unilateral restrictive legislation. This is doubtless chiefly due to the economic difficulties of the moment, but post-War nationalism, which is so strong in many countries, also plays an important part; in many international discussions the representative of one or other immigration country has been known to say that immigration is a domestic question.

Now certain emigration countries are following the same movement. Here again it is claimed that emigration is a domestic question, and a vital one. When it involves the permanent settlement of the emigrant in the immigration country, and the loss of contact with his mother country, it is said to be undesirable; it is in the interests of the emigration country to permit only temporary emigration or emigration to colonies or protectorates of the mother country. Examples of this policy have recently been given by Italy and Spain; other countries in Southern Europe and also in Central and Eastern Europe have adopted stricter supervision over emigration, directing it only towards countries where conditions appear to be acceptable.

All these measures, whether their origin be political or economic and social (and the first is undoubtedly the most important at present), have an influence on the international labour market. It must also be said that they have often a favourable influence on the position of emigrants.

The International Regulation of Migration

That does not mean that these measures are sufficient or that they all have favourable results for the world as a whole. It does not even mean that there is no place for bilateral, multilateral or international agreements.

In 1926 the International Labour Office began to collect, analyse and publish systematically all texts regulating and controlling migration movements, both of emigrants and immigrants: national regulations, bilateral agreements, multilateral agreements and international conventions. This publication was completed in three years in three large volumes. An examination of these volumes will show that national regulations have proved no obstacle to bilateral agreements (on the contrary, they have sometimes given rise to them), nor to the first attempts at international regulation.

There can be no doubt as to the utility of this latter development. In a question so definitely international as that of labour migration, the non-existence of international regulations would appear to be a paradox. If, as seems most unlikely, this paradox should continue to exist, the International Labour Organisation would not be responsible. Since its earliest days it has devoted attention to the problem of regulating the migration of workers in its two main aspects: the international distribution of labour and the protection of migrants.

First Steps: the Committee of 1921

At its 1919 Session the Conference discussed the general question of migration in connection with unemployment and adopted a Recommendation suggesting that the recruiting of groups of workers in one country for employment in another should not be carried out except by agreement between the Governments of the countries concerned and after consultation with the organisations of employers and workers in the industries affected in the two countries. The Conference also requested the Governing Body to set up an international committee which, without infringing national sovereign rights, might find and propose suitable measures for regulating the migration of workers and protecting wage-earners residing in foreign countries; the number of representatives of European countries on this committee should not exceed half the total.

The committee was set up and met in August 1921, when it adopted numerous resolutions for submission to the Governing Body on the question of statistics, the international co-ordination of protective measures for migrants, the placing of migrants in employment, equality of treatment for national and foreign workers, State supervision over emigration agencies, the collective recruiting of workers for abroad, deductions from wages for the repayment of advances made to migrants, measures for dealing with the traffic in women and children, the inspection of emigrants before embarkation and on board, the health of emigrants, insurance, etc. This constitutes a wide and comprehensive programme which the Organisation is far from having completely carried out during its first decade of existence. What has been done is recounted below.

Migration Statistics

It was noted above that the migration statistics of the International Labour Office begun in pursuance of a Recommendation of the Conference in 1922 were far in advance of all previous statistics. Of the three general reports which have been published, the first, covering the period 1920–1923, referred to 60 States; the last, covering the years 1925–1927, deals with 95 countries. The volume on the history of migration already mentioned has been very favourably received. It is hoped that the next Conference of Emigration Statisticians will lead to fresh progress in the preparation of international information, which, thanks to the Office, has already made great strides.

Bilateral Agreements

The resolution of the Committee of 1921 concerning the collective recruiting of workers abroad was based on the Recommendation of 1919 and contained a certain number of guiding principles to be adopted by every State in which or for which the collective recruiting of emigrants was carried out: inspection and supervision of the operations by the competent authorities in both States; recruiting by offices or agents accredited by the said authorities; consultation of the organisations of employers and workers concerned; control of recruiting so as to prevent disturbing the labour market in either country; contracts signed in the country of emigration before departure and binding in the country of immigration; prohibition of recruiting of workers abroad to replace national workers on strike or locked out.

It must be clearly understood that this resolution was far from having the force of a Convention, since it was not subject to ratification and did not involve any legal obligation for the Governments of the States Members. It is none the less true that it has had a powerful effect on public opinion and an important and healthy influence on the bilateral agreements which have been concluded since 1921.

Even before the Washington Session of the Conference the French Government had instituted a policy of agreements with certain European countries for recruiting agricultural and industrial labour: on September 3rd, 1919, it concluded a preliminary agreement with Poland, quickly followed by others with Italy (September 30th, 1919) and Czechoslovakia (March 20th, 1920). The impulse thus given led to a multitude of other agreements which are still in force: France has signed agreements with Austria, Belgium, Czechoslovakia, Italy, Poland, Rumania and Yugoslavia; Austria with Czechoslovakia, Hungary and Poland; Belgium with Italy and Luxemburg; Germany with Czechoslovakia, Lithuania, Poland and Yugoslavia; Italy with Luxemburg and Yugoslavia.

Some of these agreements, in particular the ones to which France is a party, refer to temporary and permanent migration, whereas others deal only with seasonal migration among agricultural workers, as, for instance, the Austro-Czechoslovak agreement of June 24th, 1925, and the Germano-Polish agreement of November 24th, 1927. It may be noted that when bringing this latter agreement to the knowledge of the Labour Office the representative of the Polish Government pointed out that it was in conformity with the Recommendation of the Conference; the same remark was made by the two Governments concerned when the Franco-Polish agreement was communicated to the Office. All these agreements provide for a standard form of contract to be used in all cases of recruiting.

A certain number of bilateral agreements of the same type may be found outside Europe; for example, an agreement concerning immigration from Mozambique to the Union of South Africa and Southern Rhodesia and an agreement (pre-War) concerning the emigration of agricultural workers from Liberia to Fernando Po. In Asia, while there may be no formal agreements, there are at least customary rules, which are strictly observed; for example, in the case of the emigration of unskilled workers from India to Ceylon, the Straits Settlements or the Malay States, and of workers from the Dutch Indies to the two latter regions, to French Indo-China and to the French Establishments in Oceania. In America no bilateral agreements exist.

Certain attempts at bilateral agreements for regulating intercontinental migration have proved abortive: such was the fate of the Italo-Brazilian agreement of October 8th, 1921, and the agreement between Poland and the State of São Paulo of February 19th, 1927. It is much more difficult to conclude an inter-continental agreement, but there is no need to despair. In the British Empire an extensive plan of oversea settlement was inaugurated as a result of the Imperial Conference of 1921 and the Imperial Economic Conference of 1923, on the basis of bilateral agreements between Great Britain on the one hand and Australia, Canada, New Zealand, Southern Rhodesia and even certain private companies on the other.

It may therefore be said that the resolution of 1921 has been of partial and indirect service to a very extensive and still flourishing movement, which will have the effect of guaranteeing effective protection for migrants even before they leave their home country.

The Protection of Migrants during their Journey

The 1921 Committee also adopted a resolution on the inspection of emigrants before departure. It proposed among other things that agreements should be concluded between States as to the organisation of such inspection. At the present time the United States and Canada have already entered into agreements with numerous European States for a system of inspection by American or Canadian inspectors before the departure of the emigrants, thus to a great extent avoiding unfortunate rejections when the emigrants disembark. This example has been followed by Belgium, France and Germany.

At its Eighth Session in 1926 the Conference had on its agenda a question of a similar nature: that of conditions of transport of oversea emigrants. This question had not been dealt with by the 1921 Committee. A Draft Convention, accompanied by a Recommendation and a Resolution, was adopted. It provides that the inspection of emigrants on board ship should be carried out by a single inspector, so as to simplify the formalities, while a qualified woman will attend to unaccompanied women and children. It is also provided that each emigrant should have the services of an interpreter knowing his language.

This Convention has been ratified unconditionally by ten States and conditionally by two. On November 25th, 1925, the Spanish and Italian Governments concluded an agreement for co-operation in the protection and assistance of emigrants during the voyage. Later, on January 25th, 1929, an agreement was concluded between the Italian Government and those of Great Britain, Australia and India, in virtue of which these

Governments mutually recognise their respective regulations concerning emigrant vessels. This is a noteworthy achievement, because there was considerable difference of opinion during the discussions in 1926.

The International Labour Office has also collaborated with the League of Nations in studying measures for suppressing the traffic in women and children, and in connection with certain questions submitted to the Communications and Transit Organisation. In particular, in June 1929, it took part in a Conference which led to an international agreement concerning the issue of transit cards to emigrants leaving Europe for oversea countries. This agreement greatly simplifies their passage from Central, Eastern or Southern Europe to the ports of Western Europe.

The Protection of Migrants in the Country of Immigration

It was pointed out that when the Convention on Workmen's Compensation was adopted in 1925 the Conference also adopted a further Draft Convention concerning equality of treatment for foreign workers on this point, which has been ratified by the record number of twenty-seven States.

Moreover, numerous demands by workers' organisations and a Resolution of the Conference drew the attention of the Office to the desirability of guaranteeing to foreign workers who had paid contributions for invalidity, old-age and survivors' insurance in one country, which they had subsequently left, the maintenance of their right to a pension. The Office has begun to study this question.

The Rome and Havana Conferences

The work of the Organisation in connection with emigration and the protection of emigrants must not be underestimated. Yet, while the ground has been cleared, it cannot be said that the Organisation has touched rock-bottom. The Governing Body has hesitated to commit the Organisation too far in the problem of labour migration, because it realises the force of the political argument (which is theoretical rather than practical) that the problem is mainly a national and domestic one. Above all, it wished to be certain, before dealing with this question, that it would be followed by the majority of Governments, but up to the present it does not seem to be definitely convinced of this.

This hesitation, whether well founded or not, led certain

States a few years ago to take steps for international consultation on the migration question outside the International Labour Organisation and outside the League of Nations. At the suggestion of the Italian Government, a Conference of all Governments interested in migration problems was held at Rome in May 1924, and a second Conference took place at Havana in April 1928. The International Labour Office was invited to both Conferences, and took an active part at least in the material organisation and in the preparation of the minutes. Numerous resolutions were passed, but no Draft Convention was adopted. These two meetings served to strengthen the conviction that in migration problems, however much they may be considered to be domestic questions, there are international aspects which must be treated internationally, and that, if international Conventions are to be arrived at, the most direct and most convenient route is that which passes through Geneva.

This conclusion, although unexpressed, was quite obvious, and soon had consequences affecting the Organisation and the League of Nations.

The Migration Committee of the International Labour Office

In 1926 a World Migration Congress, held in London under the auspices of the International Federation of Trade Unions and the Labour and Socialist International, formally requested the Governing Body to adopt a more active policy with regard to the migration of workers.

Stimulated by these suggestions, and finding the atmosphere more favourable, the Governing Body in 1929 set up a Migration Committee composed of certain of its own members, with the assistance of five permanent experts from outside. The Office had submitted to the Twelfth Session of the Conference a report on certain international aspects of the unemployment problem already referred to in which a chapter was devoted to the possible assistance which might be obtained from an international organisation of workers' migration. The Governing Body placed a similar question on the agenda of the Committee for its first meeting in May 1930: that of the recruiting and placing in employment of foreign workers. A Recommendation on this question had been adopted at the Washington Session of the Conference; the question now was whether the time had come to take a fresh step, and possibly to prepare and adopt a Draft

Convention. The Committee has already had a first discussion, and Governments are being consulted; although the final aim may not be realised at once, it can at least be said that the period of doubts and hesitations has been left behind; the road may be long, but there is every reason to believe that it will not lead to a dead end.

The Diplomatic Conference on Equality of Treatment for Foreigners

In May 1928 the Economic Committee of the League of Nations prepared the draft of a Convention on equality of treatment for nationals and foreigners in every country. The Council of the League submitted the plan to a Diplomatic Conference, which held its first meeting in Paris in December 1929.

The questions of placing in employment and of the free introduction of labour were not dealt with in the Draft Convention either because they were considered (as some still hold) to affect national sovereignty or because (as may be concluded from the report of the Economic Committee) it was agreed that when these questions were treated internationally it should be done by the International Labour Organisation. The Draft Convention therefore referred only to migrants as individuals settled or living in a foreign country, and did not refer to their rights as workers. At the same time the Draft Convention contained by way of conclusion a sort of profession of faith in favour of the free exchange of labour as a counterpart, more apparent than real, to free trade in commodities. The Office was not consulted as to the desirability of including this formula; it accepts no responsibility for it, nor for the laborious discussions and somewhat uncertain results of the First Session of this Conference.

At its Second Session the Conference decided to suggest to the Council of the League that the opinion of the International Labour Office should be asked on two points: the consequences which the application of the proposed Convention would have for workers, and the principle of free access for immigrant workers to all countries. The latter is a very delicate point. Everyone must realise that free entrance for all foreign labour may meet with opposition, not only from Governments for political reasons, but also from workers' organisations for economic and social reasons, because it may lead to flooding of the labour market, and a fall in wages and in the standard of living of the workers in a highly developed country, while it may even prove a menace to trade union organisation.

Free entrance for foreign labour would be a less serious matter for the workers if equality of treatment with regard to hours of work, wages, insurance, trade-union organisation, etc., were solidly established as between national and foreign workers. In that case the former would not need to fear that the arrival of foreigners in large numbers threatened their existing rights.

In a world which is constantly growing smaller, and in which exchanges of all kinds—of workers, of commodities, of literature, of ideas—are becoming more general, the question of international migration has been little more than touched upon. It is a problem for the future even more than for the present. The International Labour Organisation has already done enough to show that it will be able to deal with the problem in all its aspects when asked to do so by the States Members.

CHAPTER V

SPECIAL CLASSES OF WORKERS

Seamen, Agricultural Workers, Professional Workers, Salaried Employees, Native and Colonial Labour

From its earliest days the International Labour Organisation has been familiar with the idea of "the unity of labour," and many speeches have been made on this subject at the Sessions of the Conference and the Governing Body. The International Labour Office, too, has always shown its attachment to this idea, which alone, in its opinion, would justify its competence to deal with all branches of labour. After all, from the standpoint of general working conditions there is no real difference between the factory worker, the land worker and those who, for a living, go down to the sea in ships. Conditions are fundamentally the same for the worker and the salaried employee, the manual worker and the professional worker. Nor do they really vary much for the white, yellow or black races. Thus as a rule the International Labour Conventions are universal in character.

There are, however, various methods of securing protection and equitable treatment for workers. The particular nature of the work performed by certain classes of workers necessitates the adoption of special regulations in addition to those of a general nature. From the outset therefore the Organisation has been obliged to consider the special measures of protection required by certain classes of workers, and here as elsewhere its activities (there could be no question of its competence) have developed; they have been extended to seamen, agricultural workers, native and colonial labour and, lastly, to professional workers and salaried employees.

I. Maritime Labour

The mercantile service is undoubtedly the most international of all trades: its work is transport from continent to continent, its sphere of activity the high seas, and it is therefore difficult without international agreement to protect the maritime industry of one country from the competition of others. Moreover, the necessary measures for the protection of its workers would prove an almost intolerable burden for the merchant fleet of any nation acting alone. Consequently, in maritime work even more than in work on land, international regulations are an indispensable preliminary to social progress.

In reality, international regulations are more easily conceivable in this branch of labour than elsewhere. The wandering life of a mariner changes but little with latitude, nationality and his port of registry. Throughout the world this occupation is the same, and from the Middle Ages it has always been regulated by a sort of international code, the custom of the seas, which applied to seamen of all nationalities employed side by side on the vessels of all countries. This code defined their obligations and rights; for, unlike their fellow-workmen on land, seamen have at all times been free agents. There seems no doubt, however, that the definite formation of the European States which coincided with the discovery of new lands from the sixteenth to the eighteenth century, resulted in breaking the unity of sea-law. On the basis of common principles taken from old customs and rights, national maritime codes were built up, which provided surer guarantees, especially as regards conditions of labour, for shipowners and seamen alike. These, in their turn, enabled the trade unions to make international comparisons and to demand the adaptation of the principles of labour legislation to sea-law.

There could, however, be no precise assimilation, for maritime labour is in a class by itself. This fact was so strongly recognised that, when the Peace Treaties were being prepared, the Commission on International Labour Legislation was asked by the seamen's associations to set up a special institution, side by side with the general Organisation, to deal with maritime questions. Happily, this proposal was rejected; but in the ideas prevailing at that time it is easy to trace the old conviction that maritime labour is a separate entity and that it is particularly suitable for international regulation.

The Organisation and Maritime Labour

The Second Session of the Conference, held in Genoa in 1920, was devoted to maritime questions. The Third Session, in Geneva, was required, among other tasks, to complete the discussion of a number of maritime problems begun in Genoa. Further Maritime Sessions were held in 1926 and 1929, while still another seamen's Conference will take place in 1932. So that almost a third of the Sessions of the Conference will have discussed maritime problems.

The frequency of these Sessions has ensured the efficacy as well as the continuity of the work undertaken on maritime matters. As far back as 1920 the Governing Body sanctioned the creation in the Office of a Maritime Section and, in order to assist the section, instituted the Joint Maritime Commission, a body which includes an equal number of shipowners' and seamen's representatives, who are elected by the employers' and workers' delegates to the Maritime Sessions of the Conference. In 1921 the Conference expressed the desire that no question concerning maritime labour should be put on its agenda without the previous approval of the Commission. The Governing Body, moreover, periodically consults the Commission on technical questions which seem to be of joint interest to shipowners and seamen.

The International Seamen's Code

One of the items on the agenda of the Genoa Conference was "the consideration of the possibility of drawing up an International Seamen's Code." As has already been said, the seamen's calling is everywhere the same and has been regulated since the Middle Ages by a sort of international maritime code based on the requirements and customs of the period. Here, then, were two excellent reasons for supposing that the matter could be dealt with nowadays without too much difficulty. Adopting this point of view the Conference proposed that a code should be drawn up in the form of "a collection of laws and regulations dealing with the condition and position of seamen as such, which it may be possible for the various maritime countries of the world to adopt as a common and uniform body of international seamen's law."

Now "a collection of laws and regulations" does not mean a single code which will regulate all branches of sea-law. For it is only by the adoption of a series of separate Conventions, each dealing with a specific aspect of maritime labour, that an international code can be ultimately evolved. The Genoa Conference itself decided to enumerate some of the questions which it considered essential and all-important. There was no question of scrapping national codes; the question was rather one of defining the general principles to be followed in the regulation of one or another branch of maritime work, and of getting national laws to conform to them. States which as yet had no national seamen's code but possessed a mercantile service were asked by the Conference to draw up a code embodying provisions based on principles to be laid down by the Conference in special agreements.

The main questions which the Conference recommended to the Governing Body for inclusion in the agenda of future Sessions were: seamen's articles of agreement, the accommodation for seamen aboard vessels, discipline, the settlement of disputes between individual seamen and their employers, and social insurance for seamen.

Seamen's Articles of Agreement

In 1925 the Governing Body put the question of the international codification of rules relating to seamen's articles of agreement on the agenda of the Ninth Session of the Conference. The preliminary discussion of the question by the Joint Maritime Commission revealed two conflicting views between which the Commission was unable to decide. The shipowners maintained that codification should be restricted to rules already accepted by the maritime States, whereas the majority of the seamen's representatives wished to base it on the more advanced systems of national legislation. The Office consulted the Governments. The majority of the replies favoured the second conception, and this led the Office to prepare three separate Conventions, the first dealing with seamen's articles of agreement as such, the second with the repatriation of seamen and the third with the maintenance of discipline on board ship.

A Convention was adopted on the first point. It deals with the nature, validity and various types of agreement, defines the compulsory clauses and proofs of engagement to be inserted therein and establishes the public character of the agreements and the conditions under which they expire or may be terminated. It thus standardises the essential principles of agreements on an international basis. And, though it cannot be hailed as a great social achievement in the majority of the maritime States, it is undoubtedly a most useful model for countries where legislation is less advanced or in the course of preparation.

The question of repatriation, which was well received in all quarters, led to a second Convention, which, besides guaranteeing that a seaman shall not be abandoned in a foreign port, lays down definite regulations as regards his repatriation. A seaman who is put ashore during the term of his engagement or on its expiration is entitled to be sent back without cost to himself to his own country, either to the port where he was engaged or to that at which the voyage commenced. Here again the Convention is an advance on backward national legislation. The Convention does not apply to masters and apprentices serving under special agreements or to seamen employed in the deep-sea fishing industry. States were recommended to extend the repatriation provisions to the first two groups by a Recommendation and to the third group by a Resolution.

Thus two of the main points were regulated by Conventions, the first of which has already been ratified by eleven States and the second by ten.

Things did not go so smoothly, however, as regards the disciplinary measures applicable in cases of breach of contract. Here also the Office had prepared a Convention including an article which, while being absolutely essential, was, however, bound to lead to much controversy. This article dealt with the offences of "desertion," "absence without leave" and "refusal to obey orders." The draft prepared by the Office did not mention imprisonment except where these offences were of such a nature as to endanger persons on board, the vessel or the cargo. Only in such cases was criminal liability to be incurred. No agreement could, however, be reached on this point, and the article was dropped by the competent committee without being replaced. The Conference thereupon rejected the Convention, feeling that it could not very well set up international regulations concerning discipline on board ship without settling the important question of disciplinary measures in case of desertion. It stated, however, that the question would be kept in view and instructed the International Labour Office to follow its evolution until it was considered opportune to bring it before the Conference afresh.

The General Protection of Seamen

Although unemployment, measures for placing workers in employment, the protection of young workers and inspection of labour conditions are general questions, they assume in the case of maritime labour such special forms that the Organisation has felt it necessary to deal with them separately for seamen.

Its action in connection with the finding of employment for

seamen has been based on the Convention adopted at the Genoa Conference in 1920, which stipulates that all such operations shall be performed not by private fee-charging agencies but by free public employment agencies managed jointly by the shipowners' and seamen's associations under the supervision of a central authority, or, in the absence of combined measures of this kind, by the State itself.

As to unemployment, the same Session of the Conference adopted a Convention which requires the shipowner to pay an unemployment indemnity equal to two months' wages to members of the crew of any ship which is lost or founders.

The Conference has voted three separate Conventions concerning the employment of young persons on board ship. The first, adopted at Genoa in 1920, prohibits the engagement of children under fourteen years on vessels other than those upon which only members of the same family are employed. The second, adopted at Geneva in 1921, stipulates that to be eligible for employment on vessels, subject to the same exception, persons under eighteen must produce a medical certificate which is renewable once a year; while the third, which was also adopted at the Third Session of the Conference, fixes at eighteen years the minimum age for admission of young persons to employment as trimmers or stokers.

Of these five Conventions the first has obtained 17 ratifications; the second, 16; the third, 22; and the fourth and fifth, 23 each.

Furthermore, at its Ninth Session in 1926 the Conference voted a Recommendation on the general principles for the inspection of the conditions of work of seamen, which, after defining the aims in view, provides for the organisation of inspection and the publication of an annual report on the work of the inspection services, and makes proposals concerning the powers and duties of inspectors, the safeguards necessary to prevent abuses and the co-operation of shipowners and seamen with the inspection authorities.

Questions under Consideration

In 1929 the Thirteenth Session of the Conference embarked on the study of a number of new questions. Under the double-discussion procedure which has now been applied for a number of years that Session was merely called upon to establish the principles on which a questionnaire for despatch to the

Governments should be based and to decide as to the inclusion of the said questions in the agenda of the next Maritime Session, when they would be the subject of definite decisions. All the questions were retained by the Conference. They related to hours of work, the protection of seamen in case of sickness or accident, the promotion of seamen's welfare in ports and the professional capacity of ship's officers.

Hours of Work on board Ship

Here, as for industry, it was the question of hours of work which led to the keenest discussion. When Part XIII of the Peace Treaty urged the adoption of an eight-hour day no mention was made of its limitation to certain classes of work. Nor was any such stipulation made in 1919 when the Washington Conference was called upon to examine "the application of the eight-hour day or of the forty-eight-hour week." Though that Conference limited the Convention which it adopted to industry and the transport services, it also definitely affirmed the necessity and urgency of convening a special Conference to determine the conditions which might suitably be applied to transport by sea, and even stated in the Convention that these conditions should include the principle of the eight-hour day.

The question therefore came up for discussion at the first Maritime Session held in Genoa in 1920. That Session adopted two Recommendations which called on the States Members to do all in their power to regulate work in the fishing industry and in navigation in accordance with the principle of the eight-hour day. But although the proposed Convention concerning an eight-hour day in the merchant service received a large number of votes—48 to 24—the two-thirds majority required was not obtained and the Convention was not adopted.

After a setback of this kind the Organisation was bound to take the question up again. At the Maritime Session in 1926 the Conference itself demanded that it should soon be again placed on its agenda, with the result that the question was brought up before the Thirteenth Session in 1929 under the title of "Regulation of hours of work on board ship." A break was thus made with theoretical formulae, future progress being no longer prejudiced by the idea that the Conference was discussing "the conditions in which the Washington Convention might be applied to seamen." Moreover, the preparatory work of the Office had been very thorough, and an attempt had been made not only to establish the usual comparative analysis of legislation but also to discover a real working basis for a practical solution. Everything then seemed favourable. The discussion of the matter led, however, to heated debates and to a number of lively incidents. The final outcome of the first discussion was the adoption of "conclusions" in which the Conference declared that the possibility of regulating hours of work by a Draft Convention based on the principle of "an eight-hour day or a forty-eight-hour week" should be considered and that, prior to the next Maritime Session of the Conference, the International Labour Office should ascertain the views of the Governments on the following main points: scope of the Draft Convention as regards vessels, trades, persons employed on board and special climatic conditions; the methods to be adopted in port, on sailing days, on passage, on arrival days; the possibility of providing that overtime for certain classes of work necessary for safety should not be subject either to limitation or compensation and the definition of such work.

The foregoing details are more than enough to show once again the peculiar situation of maritime workers, while they also bring out the complexity of the whole question and the likelihood of considerable differences of opinion in the answers received from the Governments. In order to give the Governments adequate time for reflection and to enable the Office to study and bring to the notice of all concerned the different opinions expressed, it was decided that the second discussion of the question should take place only at a Session to be held in 1932, and that in 1931 the Office should convene a preparatory technical maritime conference similar to that called in January 1930 in connection with the study of conditions of work in the coalmining industry.

Here the matter stands at present. There seems no doubt that a basis for future agreement will ultimately be found.

Protection of Seamen against Sickness and Accidents

The 1929 Session of the Conference also held the first discussion of the question of "the protection of seamen in case of sickness (including the treatment of seamen injured on board ship), i.e. (*a*) the individual liability of the shipowner towards sick or injured seamen; (*b*) sickness insurance for seamen." This is the formal title which the Governing Body drew up for this item.

It was on this text that the Office had to work and base its comparative studies, and it was on the same text that it had to draw up its questionnaire for despatch to the Governments with a view to the ultimate preparation of one or more Conventions. The wording of the text seems to indicate that the Governing Body did not contemplate the same studies and conclusions for sickness and accident alike. In the case of sickness, it suggests the regulation of the shipowner's obligations towards sick seamen on board ship and the establishment of a system of sickness insurance, while for accidents the regulation of the shipowner's liabilities is also intended, but without any question of accident compensation or insurance. The Office could not do otherwise than fall in with these proposals. It prepared two reports on the basic principles of questionnaires intended to lead to two separate Conventions, one dealing with the shipowner's obligations towards sick or injured seamen, the other with seamen's sickness insurance. Its conclusions, which were adopted by the Conference, will come up for second discussion in 1932. A certain amount of progress is certain to be made, although less than might have been possible.

Seamen's Welfare in Ports

The Conference drew attention in 1920 and 1926 to the moral and social importance of measures which would secure comfortable and respectable conditions for seamen during their stay in ports, where, far from home and with small means at their disposal, they are deprived of domestic and family comforts.

After consulting the Joint Maritime Commission the Office drew up a list of points on which the Governments might be consulted. Its proposals were accepted by the Governing Body without much change. The field covered by the list prepared by the Office included the organisation of methods and institutions for the study of the living conditions of seamen when in port and the co-ordination of certain measures, such as the regulation of the sale of alcohol in or near dock areas and the supervision of the use and sale of narcotics; the prohibition of the employment in public houses of attendants of either sex under a certain age; official supervision of taverns and hotels; the lighting and fencing of dock areas; the supervision of boatmen plying between ships and the shore; the removal from dock areas of persons of no definite occupation; the organisation of special police forces for dock areas; improved co-operation between consuls and the local authorities; greater practical facilities for seamen to communicate with their Consul; measures to ensure improved protection for seamen, such as the prohibition of soliciting and enticing seamen in harbour areas, the admission without difficulty of seamen of all nationalities and religious beliefs to hospitals and dispensaries, free and accessible treatment for venereal and other diseases, the installation and development of hostels, recreation rooms, canteens, libraries, sports organisations and opportunities for excursions.

Here, at any rate, there is every reason to believe that the 1932 Conference will lead to highly satisfactory results.

Professional Capacity of Officers

The question of the professional capacity of mercantile marine officers was discussed and subsequently put on one side at the Ninth Session in 1926. But, following the collision which occurred in August of the same year between the French liner *Lotus* and the Turkish collier *Boz-Kourt*, the International Association of Mercantile Marine Officers asked the Office to take it up anew. On the unanimous proposal of the Joint Maritime Commission the Governing Body included in the agenda of the Thirteenth Session of the Conference in 1929 an item conceived in the following terms: "Establishment by each maritime country of a minimum requirement of professional capacity in the case of captains, navigating and engineer officers in charge of watches on board merchant ships."

The importance of this question is easily understood, for on its solution depends the safety of passengers and crews as well as the professional reputation of the officers of the mercantile service. The points on which the Conference decided to consult the Governments related to the classes of persons required to hold a competency certificate and the nature of the certificate, the possible exceptions to the rules, the general conditions attached to the grant of certificates, the penalties to be established for non-compliance with the regulations and the supervision of their application.

Work still to be Accomplished

The brief description given above of the maritime problems which have been settled or are at present under consideration is sufficient to show the extent of the work already completed by the Organisation in this sphere. But here again, and perhaps more than in any other field, the immensity of the problems still to be solved strikes the imagination.

In order to give an approximate idea of the tasks ahead it is enough to mention some of the questions which the various services of the Office are studying at the request of Governments or official organisations. These include conditions of labour in the fishing industry, the study of which was decided on by the 1926 Conference, and the special conditions of workers employed in fishing for sponges, pearls, coral and other marine products, decided on by the same Session of the Conference. Then there is the protection of seamen's health, demanded by the Thirteenth Session of the Conference in 1929, which is being studied with the help of the Permanent Committee on Seamen's Welfare and the collaboration of the Health Section of the League of Nations and the League of Red Cross Societies. Another problem is the safety of seamen, a matter closely bound up with the problem of the general safety of navigation, for the solution of which the Communications and Transit Organisation of the League of Nations provides valuable assistance. Then there is a request made by the Joint Maritime Commission concerning the regulation of the loading of vessels, while another important question is that of the overloading of ships and load-line regulations, which is being studied as the result of repeated requests received from the Seafarers' Joint Committee of Great Britain, the International Association of Mercantile Marine Officers and the Joint Maritime Commission. Enquiries are also being made into technical maritime education at the request of the Genoa Conference; conditions of labour of Asiatic seamen at the request of the Thirteenth Session of the Conference in 1929; the penal consequences of professional mistakes committed on the high seas and resulting in collisions, the penalties to be incurred and the competent courts—questions raised by the International Association of Mercantile Marine Officers after the *Lotus* incident.

It is noteworthy that in each case the study of these questions has been undertaken at the request of the Conference, the Joint Maritime Commission or other important organisations concerned. This would seem to imply that sooner or later they are likely to come up for discussion or international adjustment. In dealing with them now the Office is merely exercising foresight.

In addition to maritime navigation consideration must be given to inland navigation on rivers and canals. It will be recalled that one of the Recommendations adopted at the Genoa Conference concerned the limitation of hours of work in inland navigation. Unfortunately that Recommendation had little effect. Later, in 1929, the Conference requested the Governing Body to bring the question again before the Conference. In the meantime as a result of suggestions made by the International Committee on the Unification of River Law (a technical body of the Communications and Transit Organisation of the League of Nations) the Office undertook the study of working conditions in general on the great international rivers of Europe. A small joint committee has been appointed, consisting of three representatives of the Communications and Transit Organisation and three members of the Governing Body (one each from the Government, Employers' and Workers' Groups). The Governing Body, as a result of the conclusions of the Joint Committee, later decided to set up a Committee of Experts of nine members, including four members of the Governing Body (two employers' and two workers' delegates). At present, this Committee is conducting the necessary enquiries.

Finally, there is the question of "air navigation." The Thirteenth Session of the Conference requested the Governing Body to undertake preparatory work with a view to establishing international regulations concerning the safety, the work and the technical training of persons employed in air navigation. This work has been begun. The profusion and intricacy of the technical, economic and legal problems which arise must be obvious to all.

To sum up, it can truthfully be said that despite the great difficulties which so frequently arise in associating the Governments of the maritime Powers and the shipowners' and seamen's associations in a common endeavour, the work already accomplished by the Organisation is substantial and effective. While the whole immense field has not yet been entirely delved, it has been marked off, surveyed and to a large extent cleared.

II. Agricultural Workers

The Organisation and Agricultural Problems

The International Labour Organisation has from its earliest days included agricultural labour in its programme. Since its constitution the International Labour Office has had an Agricultural Service, and never has the existence of this Service been questioned by the Governing Body. Indeed, it has frequently happened, even quite recently, that members of that body have asked for the Service to be enlarged. The initial plan of work drafted by the Service was vast, and perhaps even rather ambitious, but there is every reason to expect that it will one day be finally consummated. This plan, drawn up in London in February 1920, includes *inter alia* the following questions: right of association and combination of agricultural workers; collective agreements; all branches of social insurance, including unemployment insurance; wages and hours of work; regulation of the work of women and children; housing; prevention of sickness; supervision of conditions of labour; general and technical education; co-operation; credit.

It has of course been necessary to concentrate on certain questions within the limited means at the disposal of the Office. But the above enumeration is given to show that from the outset the International Labour Office had no intention of dealing with agricultural labour as the Cinderella of the industries and that it is not to be laid at the door of the Office if such labour has not been put on an equal footing with industrial labour. The industrial Session of the Conference at Washington in 1919, followed by a Maritime Session at Genoa in 1920, was also succeeded by an Agricultural Session in Geneva in 1921, when three of the four items on the agenda concerned agricultural workers. Although dating back to 1921, the technical report published by the Office in connection with that Session may probably still be regarded as the most complete and most useful international handbook on conditions of work in agriculture. All the above-mentioned subjects are covered, though the facts are not complete on all points. The 1921 Conference adopted a number of Recommendations concerning the night work of women in agriculture, the night work of children and young persons in agriculture, the protection of women wage-earners in agriculture before and after childbirth, the prevention of unemployment in agriculture and the development of technical agricultural education. These Recommendations in the majority of cases embodied a request to the Governments to extend to agricultural workers the protective measures laid down in the Conventions adopted at Washington two years previously on behalf of industrial workers.

There were, however, two essential differences in the measures proposed. In the first place the Conference restricted its efforts on certain points in favour of agricultural workers to Recommendations. Secondly, in dealing with agricultural labour, the vital question of hours of work, which had been settled at Washington for industrial workers, was withdrawn from the Geneva agenda. It was clear from the very outset that the Conference would not deal with questions of agricultural labour so sweepingly as with questions of industrial or even maritime labour. It is not without interest to study the reasons.

Special Aspects of Agricultural Problems

The most striking and unfortunate feature of agricultural labour problems seems to be the entire absence, prior to 1920, of any systematic and continuous study of them comparable to that carried out during the previous half-century in connection with industrial problems. Spasmodic, partial and irregular efforts have, of course, been made from time to time to study the matter, but as these generally occurred in connection with a depression they were usually ill-prepared and ceased with the passing of the crisis. It frequently happened that an enquiry would be made in one country without the slightest reference to or consideration of identical research work carried out some years previously.

The chaotic and desultory nature of enquiries into conditions of labour in agriculture is still common to all countries, though since the War the attention of Governments and of the public everywhere has been strongly drawn to these questions. No doubt it is exceptional nowadays to find an agricultural enquiry that does not refer in some way to the hours of work and housing conditions of agricultural workers, and particularly to their wages, and certainly a number of exhaustive national enquiries have been conducted on these questions. But it is still difficult to obtain complete information for a given period for any one country, or data which will permit of international comparisons. From this standpoint alone the effort made by the International Labour Office to publish a comprehensive article or documentary information on agricultural questions once a month in the *International Labour Review* or in *Industrial and Labour Information* (since 1921, sixty such articles have appeared in the *Review*), has rendered a great service to the agricultural workers.

A second characteristic of agricultural labour was gradually realised by the Office and eventually by those with whom it came in contact. At the outset the Office, the organisations with which it was in touch and the Conference itself were dominated by the idea of obtaining whenever possible the same conditions for agricultural labour as those secured for industrial workers. Subsequent enquiry proved that agriculture could not be entirely assimilated to industry. There is of course a close connection, and the essential principles and fundamental problems are the same, but it is not at all so certain that the same solutions are always practicable. It became apparent that although agriculture as a whole is not affected by certain intricate problems which arise in industry, it is nevertheless faced with other difficulties which have been overcome in industry many years ago.

The Conference was to encounter these obstacles from the very outset. For instance, the 1921 Recommendation concerning the prevention of unemployment in agriculture mentions a number of measures which go beyond the scope suggested by its title: modernisation of technical methods, intensification of production and measures to encourage the development of agricultural workers' co-operative societies for the working and renting of land. In spite of its desire to obtain equal protection for agricultural and industrial workers, the Organisation had to recognise at the very outset that the measures to be adopted could not always be the same.

The fact became apparent that there would probably be more difficulty in arriving at such measures in the agricultural sphere; this constitutes the third point of difference between agriculture and industry. The question of hours of work had been withdrawn from the agenda of the 1921 Session without any promise of future action. The Convention adopted at that Session concerning the minimum age for admission of children to employment in agriculture was much less rigid than that approved two years previously concerning the minimum age for admission to industrial work. For instance, the employment of children under fourteen years was prohibited in agriculture only during hours fixed for school attendance and provided it did not prejudice their attendance at school. Furthermore, the annual period of school attendance was stated at eight months, while the periods and the hours of school attendance might be so arranged "as to permit the employment of children in light agricultural work and in particular on light work connected with the harvest."

It was clear that these differences were not entirely due to the unequal social standards prevailing almost everywhere for these two classes of workers, but rather to different economic conditions. The question of the limitation of hours of work is obviously much more difficult to solve in agriculture than in industry, while the large amount of family labour employed in agriculture undoubtedly complicates the solution of the child labour question. Indeed, the solution of these two problems seems to have been postponed—totally in the first case and partially in the second, in so far as the solution at present adopted is inadequate and provisional.

It must be recognized that economic difficulties of a quite special character were among the motives which actuated those opposed to the activity of the Organisation in the field of agricultural labour. These motives even led those persons to bring the question of the competence of the Office before the Permanent Court of International Justice. But the award given by the Court in 1922 upheld the arguments of the Office and definitely proved its entire competence to deal with agricultural questions.

Swayed by these and other considerations, the Organisation has since 1922 proceeded on the principle that, in dealing with agricultural questions, it would have to adapt its methods to the special requirements of the case and advance by stages, without however abandoning the programme established in 1920 or the liberal aspirations expressed in 1921.

A Period of Research

The first matter to be settled, and one on which the solution of all others seemed to depend, was the representation of agricultural interests in the Conference and other institutions set up by the Organisation. It was, however, impossible to proceed with this without first ascertaining how and to what extent agricultural employers and workers were organised. Since the very inception of the International Labour Organisation it has always been considered that the success of its efforts on behalf of any particular class of workers would depend on the extent to which that class was organised and capable of supporting its demands by influencing national and international public opinion.

The Agricultural Service of the Office took up the study of this question, and in 1928 published a report on the *Representation and Organisation of Agricultural Workers*, which contains, among other things, an accurate summary of recent opinions expressed with regard to the constitution and competence of the Organisation and the representation of agricultural interests. The report also summarises the official decisions taken in connection with agriculture in 1919 by the Commission on International Labour Legislation of the Peace Conference, and discusses the attitude of other official bodies on this same matter. Another part of the report deals with the definition of an agricultural worker from a legal, economic and social standpoint, and his relation to tenant farmers and small-holders, the whole being concluded by notes on agricultural trade unionism in each of the States Members.

At the same time a series of articles was published on the spare time of agricultural workers, agrarian reform in the various countries and its effects on the land workers, the housing of agricultural workers, the education of agricultural workers' children, hours of work, wages, unemployment and the placing in employment of agricultural workers, contracts of service and the question of agricultural accidents in the different States.

As is customary, the Service responsible for this work maintained close contact with other official bodies interested in agricultural questions. It was in agreement with the Scientific Management Institute, then recently established in Geneva with the help of the International Labour Office, that it began work on a series of studies dealing with scientific management in agriculture, a question which, it will be recalled, was foreshadowed in the 1921 Recommendation concerning unemployment in agriculture. It was also in agreement with the Economic Organisation of the League of Nations that it published, in connection with the World Economic Conference, a study on the relation of labour costs to total production costs in agriculture which covered eleven important agricultural countries: Australia, Canada, Denmark, France, Germany, Great Britain, Italy, the Netherlands, Sweden, Switzerland and the United States.

Acting in conjunction with the International Institute of Agriculture, which was founded in Rome in 1905, the International Labour Office set up the Mixed Advisory Agricultural Committee, a body which, comprising representatives of the Governing Body and the Permanent Committee of the Institute, meets as a rule once a year to advise on collaboration between these two institutions in enquiries into agricultural problems. The questions which are at present the subject of collaboration in study by the two institutions include contracts of service, hours of work, wages and statistics, and the rural exodus.

Recent Attempts at International Regulation

Five years after the finding of the Permanent Court the Conference was again called on to discuss agricultural questions. When, in 1927, it adopted a Draft Convention concerning sickness insurance for workers in industry, it adopted a similar measure for agricultural workers. Again, in 1929 it was expressly stated that the Recommendation voted at that Session concerning the prevention of industrial accidents was to cover agricultural workers. In acting thus the Conference was undoubtedly making a further attempt to put industrial and agricultural workers on an equal footing, and it is interesting to see whether this attempt succeeded or failed. The mere fact that the 1927 Conference adopted two separate Conventions on identically the same subject shows that it was leaving the way open for the States Members to ratify the Convention affecting industry before taking action on the agricultural Convention. This is exactly what has happened, and at the moment the first has received eight ratifications as against two by the second. As to the Recommendation on the prevention of industrial accidents, it is to be noted that the proposal was qualified by the words "taking into account the special conditions of agricultural workers."

The Sessions of 1927 and 1929 may therefore be said to have accomplished much more than that of 1921. While great practical progress towards assimilation was made, complete equality still remained unachieved.

The Work still to be Accomplished

A state of complete equality will be reached only when the degree of organisation of agricultural workers becomes comparable with that of industrial workers, and when the studies and enquiries at present being pursued by the Office and other international bodies have served to determine what questions and what particular aspects of the problems common to labour as a whole are of special interest to agricultural workers. These special problems and these special aspects exist, whether they be due to the unequal development of technical methods or organisation, or to some essential difference due to natural conditions, or simply to the methods traditionally employed in dealing with agriculture. There are radical and superficial differences between the two branches of labour, and both have their effects on conditions of work. If they are ignored, there is a great risk that adequate measures for protecting working conditions in agriculture will never be evolved. For these reasons the agricultural studies undertaken by the Office are bound to be beside the mark if, in addition to their main object, which is social, they neglect the technical and economic aspects of the problem.

It is impossible not to perceive the immense differences in the methods of financing of industrial, transport or shipping undertakings and of financing agricultural undertakings. In the first case huge amounts of private capital are concentrated in mobile form. In the second case the land is divided up among millions of small undertakings, with little capital and still less reserves, which, owing to the difficulty of finding private credit, must perforce seek public or State aid. This gives rise to the organisation of agricultural credit, which is a democratic institution, in the first place because it draws on public funds and brings no profit to the credit institution, but only to the agriculturists, and secondly because it is society as a whole which, by regulating the flow of capital towards the different branches, guides and directs agriculture as a whole.

It is also impossible not to perceive the great organic differences between the powerful associations in industry, transport or shipping—where everything is in the hands of a few highly concentrated and independent combines—and the agricultural associations, which, co-operative in spirit, are formed to promote the use of machinery in common and to encourage production and commercial concentration. The situation of the agricultural workers and the small farmers who work the bulk of the land cannot be grasped unless all these factors, which are of economic as well as of social importance, are fully recognised.

Again, the agricultural depression at present affecting the whole world is an international problem which requires an international solution, because its causes are the same everywhere and must be sought in industrial States just as much as in agricultural countries. In the latter, the main causes are overproduction and the low price of agricultural produce in comparison with the manufactured articles which agriculture requires, while in the industrial countries the reasons are to be sought for in the general incapacity to absorb the whole of the agricultural production even at the low prices prevailing. The result is keen competition between agricultural countries, which one and all are trying to lower their prices by cutting their costs, often to the detriment of wages. This, in any case, is how the situation is generally described.

Whether it is actually so or not can only be shown by an enquiry. The report prepared by the Office in 1927 on the relation of labour costs to the total cost of production in agriculture was the first attempt to elucidate this question, the study of which is still going on. The field to be covered by research work is large, and includes technical and economic conditions in agriculture, agrarian reform, agricultural credit, the rural exodus, co-operation, profits, wage rates, the exploiting of women and children, the standard of living of small farmers and the effect on the agricultural labour market of the introduction of machinery and rationalisation methods in agriculture. All these questions are of equal importance, and in studying them the International Labour Organisation is bringing the time nearer when protection for agricultural labour will be claimed and obtained with the same rapidity, continuity and success with which it was secured for industrial workers.

III. Professional Workers

Competence of the Organisation

At its Third Session in 1921 the Conference adopted a Resolution couched in the following terms:

> The Third International Labour Conference, viewing with sympathy the efforts at organisation which have been made for some time past by the intellectual workers[1] (inventors, technical

[1] The Office has now adopted the term "professional workers" in place of "intellectual workers."

employees in commerce and industry, jurists, men of science, journalists, writers, artists, professors, etc.);

Being of opinion that it is its duty to assist those who derive their means of existence from imaginative or intellectual work to obtain better conditions of life and thus to assure full development to intellectual work, thanks to which humanity progressively advances;

Invites the Governing Body of the International Labour Office to consider means of creating a Commission on Intellectual Work composed of representatives of the national organisations of intellectual workers.

More than six years were to pass before any real effect was given to this Resolution. It cannot, however, be said that its object was less worthy than others to which the Office was already devoting its attention, or that the competence of the Organisation to deal with the working conditions of professional workers was in any way contested. The "unity of labour," so often affirmed at the Conference, implied the right of the Conference to deal with all branches of labour, and this right has only once been questioned—in connection with agricultural labour. The reply of the Permanent Court upon that occasion may well be said to apply to all classes of workers.

The Organisation and its permanent Office, while desiring to study every question thoroughly, were not in a position in the early days to deal with them all at the same time. It was necessary to adopt some sort of regular order and choice, based largely on circumstances. In 1921 the time was not ripe for a study of the professional workers' conditions, as the "injustice" and "hardship" of their position, to quote the Preamble to Part XIII, were not so crying as they were to become some years later.

At that time, too, the professional workers' organisations were in their infancy. They were only beginning to realise and feel the effects of the great mistake they had made in allowing the breach "which broke the unity of labour," as Mr. Justin Godart so aptly put it, to widen between them and the manual workers. Many national organisations were in process of formation; different types of associations, federations and confederations were being formed, some purely occupational, others technical, some loosely formed or otherwise based on the requirements of their members. These bodies sometimes closely resembled the trade unions, sometimes were entirely different. But it was only in 1923 that an international body, the International Confederation of Professional Workers, was constituted, and a certain interval was still to elapse before any precise form was given to the demands which were being expressed, more energetically than lucidly, in a spirit of general discontent.

Early Efforts

Called on at that time to deal with a large number of difficult problems, the International Labour Office was obliged to postpone the study of the constitution of the Commission proposed in 1921. Meanwhile it did all in its power to help in an indirect manner. In 1922 the League of Nations set up a permanent body called the International Committee on Intellectual Co-operation. The purpose of the Committee was clearly shown by its constitution and by its membership, which comprised the leading personalities in the world of science, philosophy and the arts. It was required to promote intellectual progress by personal contact and the exchange of ideas, and by such methods to build up, side by side with the treasures of national civilisation and thought, a sort of universal commonwealth of intellect, inspired by the principles of peace on which the League of Nations is founded and based on the mutual understanding and exchange of ideas, theories and works of literature and art. The fact that the material and economic position of professional workers did not come within its competence was repeatedly stressed by members of the Committee. It is obvious, however, that professional work has a material basis, and that the scholar, artist, man of letters and all who adopt a liberal calling can as a rule continue their labours only if the work provides them with a living. It was therefore natural that the International Labour Office, unable at that time to do all that it had to and later did do for professional workers, should endeavour to collaborate with the new institution by offering to help it to study the material conditions of professional workers.

The Committee accepted this offer. It was arranged that the International Labour Office should be represented at the meetings of the Committee by a member of the Office staff—a rule which has been regularly observed ever since—and that the Office should at the request of the Committee supply reports on the conditions of life and work of certain classes of professional workers. Reports of this kind were submitted on technicians in industry and on musicians in 1923, and on engineers and chemists in 1924.

By that time, however, requests for information began to be received from the professional workers' organisations themselves. In 1925 the Association of Journalists Accredited to the League of Nations asked the Office to prepare a study on the conditions of work and life of journalists. The Office immediately set to work on this task, in which it was aided by the International Federation of Journalists which came into being about that time. The study appeared in 1928 and was very favourably received.

The Advisory Committee on Professional Workers

In 1927 the Governing Body, in compliance with the 1921 Resolution referred to at the beginning of this section, set up the Advisory Committee on Professional Workers. This Committee, in addition to three members of the Governing Body—one for each group—comprises two representatives of the International Committee on Intellectual Co-operation of the League of Nations (who with the three Governing Body members constitute the executive of the Committee), four representatives of the International Confederation of Professional Workers, one member appointed by the International Federation of Journalists and one by each of the national organisations of professional workers in Germany, Italy, India and Japan, and three representatives of the International Organisation of Industrial Employers.

At the time of writing the Committee has already held two sessions, in 1928 and 1929. At the suggestion of the Office it was called upon by the Governing Body to study five main questions. In connection with the first question—unemployment among professional workers—the Office prepared a highly informative report, to which reference has already been made. It will be remembered that the Committee proposed and the Governing Body agreed that this study should be extended to cover the questions of vocational selection and guidance and the placing of professional workers in employment.

With regard to the second question—inventions by salaried workers—a resolution adopted by the Committee will be examined by the Governing Body with a view to necessary action as soon as it has been studied by the Advisory Committee on Salaried Employees, to which reference will be made later.

The Committee has not yet been able to form a definite

and unanimous opinion on the third question, that of the "radius" clause or clauses concerning the subsequent employment of engineers and technical workers leaving the service of an undertaking.

On the fourth question, concerning the finding of employment for theatrical artists, the decisions of the Committee have led the Governing Body to instruct the Office that Governments which have ratified the Washington Unemployment Convention should be asked to make special reference in the reports submitted in accordance with Article 408 of the Peace Treaty to any measures which they may have adopted for the organisation of free public employment agencies for artists.

As a result of the study of the fifth question—the conscience clause concerning the termination of the employment of journalists in cases where the outlook of their paper is changed—the Committee and the Governing Body have decided that the enquiry work undertaken should be extended to cover all the essential clauses of the contracts of service, and a sub-committee has been appointed to carry out this work.

A number of other questions are also bound to be studied; for instance, the measures to be taken to alleviate the unemployment prevailing among musicians as a result of the spread of mechanical music, and performers' rights in connection with broadcasting and mechanical music.

The criticism has been made that the activities of the Advisory Committee on Professional Workers are multifarious and dispersed. But where the field is wide, prospecting must be done. As in the case of agricultural workers, it would seem advisable to study all the essential conditions in order to determine whether there are any suitable for international regulation. It is encouraging that enquiry should have shown that at least one of these questions—the finding of employment for theatrical artists—not only lends itself to international adjustment but actually comes within the scope of an International Convention adopted as far back as 1919. It is also a matter of satisfaction to note that, thanks to the Office, journalists are already formulating a number of principles suitable for embodiment in the standard journalists' contracts of all countries. A resolution of the Committee even goes so far as to indicate the possibility of determining general principles for inclusion in the collective agreements of all professional workers.

Thus a good beginning has been made. But there are still a number of points which the Office is bound to take into consideration. For instance, it is practically certain that in the future questions of special interest to professional workers will be included on the agenda of the Conference, although it is still uncertain what these questions may be. Again, there can be no doubt that professional workers' conditions can be studied as thoroughly as those of industrial workers, but, as in the case of agricultural workers, the want of internationally comparable statistics is a great obstacle. This matter has, however, now been taken up by the International Institute of Intellectual Co-operation of the League of Nations; the International Labour Office will do all in its power to help the Institute in this work.

IV. Salaried Employees

Employees and Labour Conventions

The International Labour Organisation has sometimes been accused even by the salaried employees themselves of not having devoted any attention to their position until towards the very end of its first ten years of work. This statement does not quite conform to the facts. It is true that the special conditions of work of salaried employees were for a number of years not subjected to any general examination. But many of the Conventions and Recommendations adopted by the Conference apply alike to salaried employees and manual workers. This is true of the Conventions and Recommendations concerning unemployment, emigration, maternity, spare time and social insurance. Moreover, in 1921 the Conference adopted a Recommendation concerning weekly rest in commercial establishments. But as regards hours of work the Washington Conference restricted the application of the Convention to industrial undertakings and transport, postponing until some later date the study of the limitation of hours of work in commerce. It was found at that time to be impossible to incorporate in a single Convention the provisions required for both industry and commerce.

The Montreux Programme

It was in these circumstances that in 1926, at Montreux, the salaried employees' associations drafted a common programme of questions of special interest to salaried employees, which appeared to deserve the early attention of the International

Labour Organisation. This programme, which was endorsed by the first meeting of the International Association for Social Progress, mentioned among other objects the regulation of the hours of work of salaried employees, the regulation of shop-closing hours, the period of notice, the regulation of clauses restricting liberty of employment (radius clauses) in collective agreements and the protection of salaried inventors. The last two questions have also been put forward by professional workers.

The Hours Convention

After establishing the Montreux Programme, the employees' organisations insisted that the question of hours of work should be taken up before all others. The Governing Body decided to give effect to this suggestion and placed the question on the agenda of the Conference, with the result that it came up for discussion at the Twelfth and Fourteenth Sessions held in 1929 and 1930. As already stated (page 111), the outcome was the adoption in 1930 of a Draft Convention and three Recommendations.

Other Studies

The Office has made a number of comparative studies apart from the Conference agenda, including the regulation of shop-closing, the radius clause, gratuities in the hotel industry, conditions of labour of bank clerks and the various methods of remunerating commercial travellers and agents.

V. Native and Colonial Labour

Native Labour and the Peace Treaty

Native labour must logically be included among the questions which the International Labour Organisation is called upon to study. The terms of the Preamble apply indiscriminately to all workers. They have, as was pointed out by the Permanent Court of International Justice, a comprehensive character. Article 421 stipulates that States which ratify an International Labour Convention must endeavour to apply its provisions to their colonies, protectorates and possessions which are not fully self-governing, except in cases where local conditions prohibit their application or necessitate modifications.

Article 22 of the Covenant of the League of Nations lays it

down as a principle that the well-being and development of peoples as yet unable to stand by themselves under the strenuous conditions of the modern world shall form a sacred trust of civilisation, which means that it is impossible for the International Labour Organisation not to take steps to remedy the evils which in the past have accompanied the exploitation of labour in regions inhabited by primitive peoples.

Early Collaboration with the League of Nations

The initial efforts of the Organisation to protect native and colonial labour were made in connection with Article 22 of the Covenant. In the course of its earlier Sessions the Conference adopted a number of Conventions and Recommendations which had more effect on the working conditions in the economically advanced states than on those in tropical countries. Although the action taken under Article 421 of Part XIII of the Treaty had at an early period satisfactory results in the West Indies, where Western methods of production are being applied on an ever wider scale, similar action in the more primitive parts of the tropical zone had met with but little success.

By this time, however, the League of Nations, basing its activities on Article 22, had organised a system of territorial mandates. When in 1920 the League Council set up a Permanent Mandates Commission it invited the International Labour Office to appoint an expert on labour questions. The Office has been represented at all the sittings of the Commission, and the best proof of the utility of this collaboration is the continuous manner in which the latter has studied questions of native labour.

The Office was also represented on the temporary Commission on Slavery, the appointment of which in 1924 resulted in the adoption of the Slavery Convention in 1926. In adopting this Convention the Assembly of the League of Nations called attention to the work undertaken by the Office in order to study the best means of preventing forced or compulsory labour from developing into conditions analogous to slavery. The enquiries of the Commission on Slavery had definitely shown that besides the political and social problems investigated by that body there were many kinds of forced labour, more or less resembling slavery, which it was better to leave to an organisation specially competent in labour matters.

Direct Action by the Organisation

In 1922 the Governing Body decided that the Office should collect and circulate information on native labour. This work, which was started at once, has since 1927 completely occupied the attention of a special section. In 1926 an Advisory Committee of Experts, chosen from among recognised authorities on modern native policy, was appointed. The Conference at its Eighth Session congratulated the Governing Body on the steps it had taken, and in 1927 a further Resolution was adopted calling the attention of the Office to forced labour and contract labour. Since then the Organisation and the Office have devoted their main attention to these forms of labour, although other problems connected with native labour have continued to be discussed with a view to future investigation.

Special Nature of Native Labour Questions

For various reasons the study of the working conditions of native peoples, like the study of agricultural workers' conditions, cannot be strictly confined to the regulation of labour as such. The actual conditions under which natives work do not depend entirely on such regulation, but are determined to some extent by a number of political, economic and social factors which cannot be ignored if the whole question is to be understood.

The labour problems which arise in connection with primitive communities are much more closely connected with general economic, sociological and administrative questions than is the case among highly civilised peoples. For example, it is almost impossible to separate the study of the working conditions of African workers employed in the mines of South Africa from study of tribal life, of health conditions, standards of living and habits of these workers, including in many cases those relating to marriage and family life. Even the legislative method adopted, which may appear to be purely a political matter, may have certain effects on the native labour system: legislation based on native custom may artificially cause to survive primitive forms of relations between employers and employed, while more advanced laws may bring the native, as yet unprepared for such changes, face to face with modern conceptions of the relationship between capital and labour from which he would be unable to profit.

Never at any time has the International Labour Office shown

any inclination to go beyond the competence with which it was invested by the Peace Treaty; moreover it has always considered that the scientific study of a question should be preceded by a clear definition of the field to be covered. But in this case, perhaps more than in any other, it has had to recognise that labour was indissolubly bound up with a number of other factors from which it could not be dissociated without distortion. It is certain that the first inhabitant of the native village to sign a contract for the hire of his services unconsciously changes the life of the whole community. For these reasons the study of conditions of labour in an advanced native community must take into consideration a whole series of economic, social and even political factors. In the study of this question foresight, prudence and adaptability are required more than elsewhere.

Forced Labour

As already stated, in 1926 the Assembly of the League of Nations in voting the Slavery Convention drew the attention of the Office to the importance it attached to the continuance by the Office of its studies on forced labour. In 1927 the International Labour Conference adopted a Resolution in which it associated the question of contract labour with that of forced labour and expressed the hope that it would soon be possible to put both questions on the agenda of a future Session. These measures were justified by a number of practical reasons. In many of the Mandated Territories the fact that the old traditions of slavery still survived made it extremely difficult to introduce a constructive native policy likely to promote the evolution of economic conditions among the primitive peoples along the right lines. Those who have had the power of compulsion are reluctant to change to methods of persuasion, while those who are accustomed to be driven have never acquired the will to work. Native labour has not given the best results that might have been expected under a modern economic system, nor has it benefited from modern ideas as it might have done, simply because of the existence and the recent memory of compulsory labour.

The question of forced labour was by no means a new subject of international discussion. The Mandatory Powers had already accepted the restriction of their rights to use it in the Mandated Territories. The Slavery Convention also embodied an article concerning its restriction. The question was therefore both urgent and possible of solution. A report prepared by the Office in 1927 placed the problem before the Native Labour Committee. A chapter of this report was devoted to the formulation of principles calculated to serve as a basis for international regulation. The discussion of these principles occupied the whole session of the Committee and was continued afterwards by correspondence. During the session the Committee adopted a resolution which urged that the question of forced labour should be put on the agenda of the Conference and requested the Governing Body to take the necessary steps for that purpose with the least possible delay.

In October 1927 the Governing Body placed the question on the agenda of the Twelfth Session (1929) for a first discussion. The report on the subject by the Office was accompanied by a draft questionnaire, which was examined and approved by the Native Labour Committee during its second sitting in 1928. In 1929 the Conference adopted the questionnaire and, by 101 votes to 15, decided to send the item of forced labour forward for second discussion at the Fourteenth Session (1930), with a view to the establishment of a Draft Convention and Recommendations. Prior to that Session the Committee on Native Labour held a third meeting to examine the texts which the Office had prepared on the basis of the Government replies to its questionnaire and which it proposed to submit to the Conference.

The Controversy on Forced Labour

Great stress has purposely been placed on the details of the procedure adopted for the study of the question of forced labour, because it is felt that therein lies the answer to certain objections raised in the heated controversy which arose after the 1929 Session of the Conference against the attitude taken by the Office. One of the arguments of those opposed to the regulation of the matter by the Organisation was that the Slavery Convention had already done all that was necessary. The answer to this would seem to be that it was the League Assembly itself which had adopted the Slavery Convention and referred the question of forced labour to the Organisation in one and the same resolution. It is true that Article 5 of the Slavery Convention lays down certain principles concerning forced labour, but these principles are less comprehensive than those which have already been accepted internationally for the Mandated Territories and less rigid than the national laws of most of the colonial

Governments, which prohibit the employment of forced labour by private concerns (the Convention authorises it during the transitional period). The Assembly, that is to say the community of Governments represented at Geneva in 1926, considered it advisable that the International Labour Conference should establish a code of regulations against forced labour; and the Conference at Geneva in 1929, at which 60 per cent. of those who voted represented Governments, agreed on that point with the Assembly of 1926.

Another argument was that the non-colonial Powers were going to dictate to the colonial Powers. The details of the procedure set forth above show that there was not the slightest risk of this. At each stage the colonial Powers, through their representatives and by the replies to the questionnaire, were able to exercise a preponderant influence on the decisions taken, while the experts comprising the Committee on Native Labour—which was consulted three times—all belonged to colonial States. Again, the Committee appointed at the Conference to discuss the forced labour question consisted mainly of delegates from countries directly interested in the question.

There was only one argument that seemed likely to meet with success, and even this could prevail only if the Conference failed to study the question with the requisite attention and objectivity. It was affirmed, not without reason, that what was required above all was a constructive policy, and that any limitation of the rights of the colonial Powers could only result in hindering the vital work of economic and social development. This was indeed a powerful argument. But neither the Organisation nor the Office had lost sight of the necessity for a constructive policy. Their attention had first been turned to forced labour because this system has been shown to be an obsolete, uneconomic and anti-social method of employing natives, which must be abolished before any economic and social system can be established on modern lines. Surely those who make a clean sweep of the slums in order to prepare the way for modern dwellings are carrying out a constructive policy.

The Draft Convention of 1930

After a lively debate the Draft Convention was adopted by the Conference in 1930 by 93 votes. There was no opposition, but a considerable number of delegates abstained from voting.

The Convention is very long, and only the first Article, which embodies its essential principle, need be quoted:

> Each member of the International Labour Organisation which ratifies this Convention undertakes to suppress the use of forced or compulsory labour in all its forms within the shortest possible period.
>
> With a view to this complete suppression, recourse to forced or compulsory labour may be had, during the transitional period, for public purposes only and as an exceptional measure, subject to the conditions and guarantees hereinafter provided.
>
> At the expiration of a period of five years after the coming into force of this Convention, and when the Governing Body of the International Labour Office prepares the report provided for in Article 31 below, the said Governing Body shall consider the possibility of the suppression of forced or compulsory labour in all its forms without a further transitional period and the desirability of placing this question on the Agenda of the Conference.

It is interesting to note that on the final vote being taken on the Convention, five (Great Britain, Italy, Japan, the Netherlands and Spain) of the eight colonial Powers belonging to the Organisation and represented at the Conference declared in favour of it and three (Belgium, France and Portugal) abstained—Portugal, it would seem, on a question of principle, Belgium and France because they could not see their way to agree to certain clauses of secondary importance, such as the obligation to limit to sixty days the period of forced labour authorised under the conditions laid down in Article 2, and the prohibition of the employment of military forces on public works.

Other Questions

The 1929 Conference had associated the two questions of forced labour and contract labour. The Governing Body had, however, been unable to go so far, and had put only the first question on the Conference agenda. But in 1928 the Committee on Native Labour approved, at its second sitting, a plan for the study of native contracts of service, as well as a number of principles concerning the recruiting and engagement of natives by contract. The contract of service is the means whereby primitive peoples are introduced to and initiated into the economic necessities of modern life. When it is drafted unfairly it may lead to forced labour in its worst form, but when well and wisely drawn up it can be used to develop the idea of free employment in the primitive mind. Moreover, the contract of service has a great influence on such essential questions as housing, wages, hours of work and technical education, all of which are associated with voluntary labour. For these reasons it is obvious that the International Labour Office, by carefully studying, as it is doing at present, the application of contracts of service in native territories, can contribute towards the solution of the vital problems which the colonial Powers are bound to encounter if they really desire to make the primitive races capable of playing an effective part in the economic organisation of the world.

CHAPTER VI

THE WORKERS' LIVING CONDITIONS

I. Utilisation of Spare Time

Results of Reduced Working Hours

The reduction of working hours is not intended merely to give the workers the time necessary for eating and sleeping purposes. It should also allow them to live as human beings, to rest their bodies and minds, to indulge in family and social life, and to penetrate into the field of art, letters and science.

However, when in post-War years shorter hours were obtained, at any rate in most of the great industrial countries, no guarantee was thereby given that the workers would be provided with the means of utilising the spare time secured for them. The worker who has nothing but his earnings with which to maintain himself and his family cannot possibly find sufficient spare cash to procure these means. It is the duty of the community to provide them for him, which does not mean that it should *impose* them on him.

In the eyes of the worker the fundamental characteristic of spare time is liberty. Leisure which is in any way restricted ceases to be leisure, as the very etymology of the word will show, and enforced recreation prevents relaxation. The worker, weary of the discipline inseparable from labour, must be given full liberty to pass from sports club to cinema, from garden to library, and this implies that such things are at his disposal. The complete use of liberty presupposes a choice, and this choice must be available. The main object of those who took up the question of the utilisation of workers' spare time was to increase the range of this choice.

Such opportunities were numerous even before the foundation of the International Labour Organisation. Special associations set up to make the workers' spare time both pleasant and fruitful, not to mention public authorities, had already done good work in Austria, Belgium, France, Germany, Great Britain and a number of other countries. But practically no general ideas had been formulated, nor had there even been an international exchange of ideas when, during the First Session of the Conference in Washington, while the Hours Convention was still under preparation, Mr. Barnes, the British Government Delegate, declared that the workers should be "entitled outside of working hours to time for recreation, for education, and for the discharge of social and family duties."

Similar sentiments were expressed by different groups at the Fourth Session of the Conference in 1922 during the debate on the ratification of the Washington Convention and on the means of consolidating the reforms on hours which had been introduced into most national legislations. Then in 1923 the Governing Body placed the utilisation of workers' spare time on the agenda of the Fifth Session of the Conference, which was due to meet in October of the same year, although as a matter of fact the actual discussion of this item took place at the Sixth Session in June 1924.

The 1924 Recommendation

The 1924 discussion led to a Recommendation intended to guide the efforts of Governments in the organisation of workers' spare time. After affirming in the Preamble to the Recommendation that "whereas during such spare-time workers have the opportunity of developing freely, according to their individual tastes, their physical, intellectual and moral powers, and such development is of great value from the point of view of the progress of civilisation," the Conference proceeded to lay down a number of principles. The text of the Recommendation indicated certain methods likely to secure for the workers the undiminished preservation and enjoyment of the hours of spare time obtained for them. It then dealt with the question of social hygiene, surveying the possibilities of promoting the well-directed utilisation of spare time by encouragement of individual hygiene and legislative or public action against the misuse of alcohol and against tuberculosis and other social scourges, and by the adoption of a systematic housing policy. It urged the States Members to encourage institutions for the utilisation of spare time, making the necessary distinction between those which aim at the improvement of the worker's domestic economy and family life, the development of his physical health and strength, and the extension of technical or general education.

It further emphasised the desire for liberty felt by the workers and the advisability of avoiding any encroachment on that liberty. In conclusion the Recommendation exhorted the States to co-ordinate and harmonise the activities of institutions providing means of recreation by promoting the formation of district or local committees composed of representatives of the public authorities, of employers' and workers' organisations, and of co-operative associations. Effective propaganda, it was stated, should be undertaken "for the purpose of educating public opinion in favour of the proper use of the spare time of the workers."

The statements made and the active steps taken by Governments since the 1924 Session do not justify any claim that the Recommendation suddenly launched everywhere to a new, active and co-ordinated policy, for the utilisation of workers' spare time. However, the Recommendation has been neither ignored nor neglected. A number of Governments have caused enquiries to be made into the facilities possessed by the working classes for the utilisation of their leisure time. Two of them, the Italian and Belgian Governments, after making suitable arrangements in the provinces, have taken steps to deal with the problem from a national standpoint. In Italy a Royal Decree of May 1st, 1925, set up the National Workers' Spare Time Institute, a corporate institution endowed with the necessary funds, which under State control co-ordinates the whole movement in Italy for the utilisation of workers' spare time. The Institute, which deals with all aspects of the question mentioned in the Recommendation, has undergone rapid development, and at the end of 1925 had a membership of close on 1,250,000 workers. In Belgium, where the Provincial Spare Time Committees had for several years given a good example of what can be accomplished by co-ordination, an Act was passed by the House of Representatives in September 1928, whereby there was set up a Council of National Education, which is required to bring to the notice of the Government all measures which it considers likely to promote public education and ensure the best utilisation of workers' spare time. The Council took up its duties at the beginning of 1930. Other measures worthy of note include the Czechoslovak Act concerning public libraries.

It is in this connection that information and studies published by the International Labour Office can render useful service by describing, analysing and criticising the steps taken and methods applied in the various countries so as to permit of a general interchange of experience. A considerable amount of information has already been given in the Office publications; the opinion of a number of physical culture experts was obtained only recently. Finally, in a Resolution adopted at its Fourteenth Session in 1930, the Conference requested the Governing Body "to investigate the means of making the whole field of science, letters and art fully accessible to the workers." This resolution was a direct consequence of the principles invoked in the passage of the 1924 Recommendation on workers' spare time, which stated that the workers should have opportunity of developing their physical, intellectual and moral powers and of living as men worthy of the name. In the light of these ideas the Office is preparing to undertake a study of what is perhaps somewhat improperly termed workers' education, the full realisation of which certain minds see in what they describe by the term: "a University of Labour."

The problem of the utilisation of workers' spare time, which implies the adaptation of traditions and practice to present industrial labour systems, cannot be solved in a day. We are merely on the threshold of its evolution and there can be no doubt that fully satisfactory results can be obtained only by long enquiry and experience. The International Labour Organisation declared its principles in 1924, and has since then endeavoured to continue its contribution to this human advance by supplying information based on experience.

II. Housing

The Recommendation of 1924 concerning the utilisation of workers' spare time very aptly pointed out that the best way to enable the workers to enjoy their leisure hours and secure "the harmonious development of the worker's family life" was "to place within their reach a proper home." It therefore urged that an increase should be made in the number of healthy dwellings at low rentals in garden cities or urban communities, under proper conditions of health and comfort.

The class of dwelling to which a wage-earner can aspire depends not only on the wage earned, but also on the price at which comfortable and healthy quarters are obtainable. Any action taken to lower this price, either by a policy of direct or indirect subsidies or by promoting building facilities, has therefore an immediate effect on the workers' standard of life. As a result of the difficulties encountered in the building trade after the War and during the inflation period the whole problem has become so acute in Europe that the authorities have had to intervene to a large extent, and a new field of activity has thus been opened up for social policy.

On several occasions the International Labour Conference has shown its interest in these questions. Even prior to the 1924 Session and the Recommendation concerning workers' spare time, the Conference emphasised in a Resolution adopted in 1922 the opportuneness "of pursuing the study undertaken on this subject, having recourse, if necessary, to the collaboration of qualified experts." In 1928 again, it requested the Governing Body "to undertake an investigation of the question of industrial housing and the general living-in conditions of the workers, with a view to placing it on the agenda of an early Session of the Conference."

As a result of the 1922 Resolution the Office published two important studies on *European Housing Problems since the War* and *The Housing Situation in the United States*. The 1928 Resolution led to the preparation of a new study, intended to supplement the previous work on European housing problems. This study, which is now finished, deals mainly with the part taken by the authorities in the construction of cheap dwellings, a question which nowadays has a most important effect on building policy in all European States.

In spite of the desire expressed by the Conference in 1922, however, the question has not yet got beyond the period of study.

III. Co-operation

Co-operation and the Workers

There is no ground for surprise in the fact that from its very inception, and by a unanimous vote of the Governing Body in March 1920, the International Labour Office was led to keep in touch with the co-operative movement, especially when it is remembered that that movement embraces a network of institutions which, on account of their multifarious duties, are indissolubly bound up with practically every branch of economic activity. Co-operation is a mass movement which, amid the changes affecting the economic structure of the world since 1914, has been constantly growing, until to-day it includes more than 370,000 organisations, with an aggregate membership of 75 millions. Furthermore, it is a doctrine which, though employing other means than those at the disposal of the Organisation, is animated, like the latter, with the desire for equity, order and the emancipation of the masses. In attempting to further the solution of its own proper task, the International Labour Office could not do otherwise than utilise the vast amount of practical experience acquired by the co-operative movement. Co-operative activity is, indeed, so multiform and has penetrated so deeply into the different fields of labour organisation, that practically every general labour problem affects it in some way or calls for a solution which the co-operative movement can provide.

Distribution of Information

The Office is therefore bound to keep the workers regularly informed about the international co-operative movement. Such information covers a vast field, including the nature and importance of the co-operative movement in the different countries; the varied forms and activities of co-operative organisations, adapted to the special needs of all classes of workers —wage-earners or independent, rural or urban, of all races, all creeds and all economic and historical groups; the multifarious demands satisfied by co-operation in connection with family and personal requirements, housing, raw materials and equipment, the working up of raw materials and their sale, various services (motive power, irrigation, accountancy, etc.), credit, insurance; problems arising within the co-operative movement itself in connection with the application of co-operative democratic principles in the organisations, the management of undertakings, the peculiar relationship between the societies and their employees; and, finally, the revelation of the common principles reflected in uniform legislation or the desire for it, and of the converging tendencies and demands which have given rise to or reinforced the moral ties and the organic and economic relations between the various classes of co-operative organisations. Such is, broadly speaking, the ground covered by the co-operative studies of the Office during the last ten years.

Information on the national co-operative organisations is kept up to date and is published in the International Co-operative Directory, of which seven successive editions have appeared. The first, published in 1921, covered 34 countries and 120 central co-operative organisations; the latest, 1930, edition covered 48 countries and 728 central organisations—figures which show both the progress of the movement and the increased information supplied by the Office. One of the proudest achievements of the International Labour Office is that it has undoubtedly become one of the main centres for the study of international co-operation. Its archives enable it to supply information which is demanded of it, or which its work requires. Co-operation has been referred to in the Enquiry into Production (to which further reference will be made), in the work of the Mixed Advisory Agricultural Committee, and in that of the World Economic Conference of 1927. Out of a long list of studies published by the International Labour Office on co-operation, reference will be made to those which illustrate the originality of this movement as much as its undoubted power.

Studies on Co-operation and Labour

Attention may in the first place be called to those studies which directly touch labour interests, and which are naturally the most numerous. The mere list of such studies is suggestive in its variety: labour conditions in distributive co-operative organisations, with special reference to bakery societies; workers' producing societies and the movement in favour of labour co-operative societies and co-operative contracts of employment; the development of co-operative banks, their efforts to encourage the establishment and grouping of public savings banks working in the interests of depositors, and the possible utilisation of their mutual relations for the transfer of emigrants' savings; representation of different classes of society in co-operative organisations of all kinds; aspects of the co-operative movement for organising domestic life in urban and rural districts, providing the workers with opportunities of relaxation, recreation and culture, safeguarding their health, and providing guarantees against risks to which they are exposed; adaptation of certain classes of rural organisations, especially societies of the Raiffeisen type, to the requirements of urban workers, so as to enable them to hold their own against the moneyed interests of the big towns or to organise the life of the community in urban extension settlements; utility, in constructive schemes for the protection of native populations, of co-operative societies, which, by maintaining and even utilising the more primitive institutions, attach and assimilate the work of such populations to modern economic methods.

Agricultural and Distributive Societies

The Mixed Advisory Agricultural Committee has always attached importance to the question of co-operation. As a contribution to the enquiry which it had been invited to carry out in conjunction with the International Institute of Agriculture, the Office in 1924 prepared a preliminary report in which it examined the extent to which agricultural co-operative marketing societies might enable agricultural producers to organise their own marketing methods, the extent to which consumers might organise themselves so as to supply their own needs in agricultural produce, and, finally, what methods of contact and what institutions might be used by producing and by distributive societies in common, so as to establish a permanent relationship between producer and consumer. The Office has further made a study of the part played by agricultural co-operation, and especially by agricultural marketing societies and certain auxiliary societies (co-operative seed-testing societies, co-operative breeding societies, control (milk-testing) societies, etc.), in the standardisation of products, which, however possible for the individual producer in the manufacturing industries, in agriculture requires centralised collection and effort. An additional general study has been one on the original part played by distributive and agricultural producing societies in rationalising distribution methods, as a result of the improvement in their own respective fields of activity in this direction and of the creation of direct relations with each other.

At the request of the Preparatory Committee of the World Economic Conference, and as documentary information for the Conference itself, the Office prepared a memorandum on the part played by co-operative organisations in the international trade in wheat, dairy produce and several other agricultural products.

A memorandum was also prepared for that Conference on a comparison between retail prices in private trading and those of distributive co-operative societies. This report analysed a series of enquiries carried out by distributive co-operative organisations and public authorities in a number of countries.

Representatives of agricultural co-operative societies and distributive societies have been inspired by a resolution of the World Economic Conference to convene a mixed conference which will study and take measures to promote their common interests. This body has asked the International Labour Office to show in what way the most characteristic co-operative principles have found legal expression in various national legislations; to compile, in collaboration with the International Institute of Agriculture and other organisations, the information necessary to establish, product by product, a list of the supply and marketing requirements already met or capable of being met by distributive and agricultural producing societies.

Other Forms of Co-operation

The distributive and agricultural producing societies were bound to attract the initial attention of the International Labour Office by reason of their membership, their advanced development and the place they already occupied in the production and distribution of products of high importance to agricultural and industrial workers, whether producers or consumers. The Office now proposes to extend its enquiries to other classes of societies, such as co-operative fisheries, co-operative craft societies and co-operative societies of local rural industries. These societies, like the agricultural societies themselves, include workers who, though legally independent, can improve their situation only by uniting their feeble economic forces. For them co-operation is often the main, and sometimes the only, form of organisation. These enquiries will round off the work of the Office on co-operation, and will also help it in other ways, by bringing it into direct contact with a number of small units of the agricultural, craft and home labour systems, which cannot be overlooked if a complete picture is to be obtained of social conditions.

CHAPTER VII

THE WORKERS' GENERAL RIGHTS

When the State finally decided to abandon the policy of *laisser-faire* which it had always maintained towards the relations between employers and workers, and to replace it by legal intervention, it was only natural that its initial efforts should be directed towards the removal, or at least the mitigation, of the more acute causes of friction. It therefore began by introducing legislation for the reduction of working hours and the prohibition of night work for women and children. At the same time steps had been taken to deal with the legal problems which nowadays are usually referred to as labour law, and which comprise (1) collective labour law, covering freedom of association, collective agreements and conciliation and arbitration in industrial disputes, and (2) individual labour law, including contracts of employment and labour jurisdiction. At the outset these questions were not very clearly defined, and in certain quarters their study and solution were not felt to be so urgent. Evolution was particularly slow, for instance, as regards the wage-earners' right to combine for the collective defence of their interests.

The International Labour Organisation has followed similar lines and has already adopted many Conventions for the improvement of labour conditions as such. On the other hand, with the exception of the Convention—entirely confined to matters of principle—concerning the rights of association of agricultural workers, it has not voted a single Convention on labour law. This is no matter for surprise, as such a Convention would raise legal points and problems the solution of which varies from country to country—such as is no longer the case in regard to problems of labour protection in the strict sense of the term. A common solution acceptable to all is difficult to find. Nevertheless such matters must not be ignored by the International Labour Organisation. Indeed, a considerable amount of attention has already been given to them in the studies published by the International Labour Office. In such fundamental and difficult matters careful analysis, impartial comparison and the investigation of common principles must necessarily precede any attempt to embark on a constructive policy.

I. The Workers' Right of Association

The International Labour Organisation and the Trade Union Problem

Several reasons may be advanced to show that the International Labour Organisation is to some extent bound by its constitution to deal with the question of industrial association.

Let us recall, first, its origin. Even before the conclusion of hostilities, organised labour had been working for the inclusion of labour clauses in the future Peace Treaty and the creation of an institution to supervise their enforcement. These ideas were partly realised in Part XIII of the Peace Treaty.

Secondly, consider its procedure. The industrial associations enjoy joint representation in the Conference and the Governing Body; they may, in virtue of Article 409, exercise the right of making representations to the International Labour Office.

Take, in the third place, its programme. The Preamble to Part XIII of the Peace Treaty expressly recognises the principle of freedom of association as one of the means of improving the conditions of the workers and establishing universal peace. Article 427 mentions "the right of association for all lawful purposes by the employed as well as by the employers" among the principles of special and urgent importance.

In the early days the workers did not demand that this privilege should be guaranteed by a Convention, obviously considering that its full and entire recognition was the very basis of their collaboration in the work of the International Labour Organisation. This belief subsequently turned out to be insufficiently founded. After a certain number of complaints concerning the restriction of their rights had reached the Office, it was found to be legally impossible to require States to apply a principle laid down in the Treaty but not yet embodied in a Convention signed and ratified by them. Hence the impossibility of setting in motion the procedures laid down in Article 409 and the succeeding Articles.

Study of the Problem

It was necessary in the first place, before considering a possible Convention, to conduct an enquiry into freedom of association in order to bring out the general principles on which a Draft Convention might ultimately be based. It was considered that such an enquiry would also enable the Office to satisfy demands for special investigations received from Hungary and Spain without departing from the international comparative methods required in the work of the Organisation. In October 1923 the Office was authorised by the Governing Body to open the necessary enquiry. Two preliminary studies respectively dealt with the legal and judicial status of industrial associations in the different States Members, and tabulated the expressed wishes of employers' and workers' organisations. On the basis of these preparatory reports the Governing Body decided that enquiry should be continued and extended to legislation and legal practice governing freedom of association. The enquiries undertaken, which covered both trade union law in the separate States and a comparative study of the various judicial systems, appeared in the form of five substantial volumes during 1927–1930.

An Experiment in International Adjustment

The question of international regulation was raised at the Sixth Session of the International Labour Conference in 1924. A Resolution was adopted requesting the Governing Body to consider the advisability of placing the question of freedom of association on the agenda of a future Session of the Conference with a view to finding means of ensuring full respect for this principle. In 1926 the Governing Body decided to put this question on the agenda of the Tenth Session (1927). In the grey report and draft questionnaire submitted to that Session, the International Labour Office, convinced that detailed rules could not for the time being be made the subject-matter of an international Convention, confined the questionnaire to two fundamental principles, mutually complementary and capable of being embodied in a Convention, namely, the principle of the right of association, and the principle of the right of combination. The questionnaire, which was widely modified as the result of its discussion in committee, was finally rejected by the Conference by 66 votes to 28.

This set-back could only be of a temporary character. One

of the virtues of the Organisation, as was pointed out by the Director in his closing speech to the Conference, is that once a question has come up for discussion it can never be totally abandoned. And indeed at the very next Session the Conference adopted a Resolution urging that the enquiry should be pursued with a view to the future regulation of the question of freedom of association. As already stated, the publication of the initial results of this enquiry was completed in 1930.

Possibility of Future Regulation

The events of 1927 and the studies of the International Labour Office perhaps foreshadow the form which the final solution is likely to take. Trade association, it must be remembered, does not call for detailed regulations, but for the right to exist and to act. Moreover, it would be vain to attempt to lay down rigid limitations for a movement which is always in a state of flux. In trade union matters, as in all matters connected with industrial autonomy, the method of regulation employed must differ from that commonly applied to other kinds of social activities. When it is a question of measures for the protection of labour, a domain in which Government action is traditionally accepted, the procedure consists in demanding positive guarantees from the Governments. In trade association matters what is required is rather a promise to abstain from action. In short, when trade associations demand the right to take combined action, what they want from the authorities is not a promise of intervention, but one of non-intervention.

A simple promise to respect the principles of freedom of association would, however, have but little effect if it were not supplemented by some system for the supervision of its observance. Any such promise made by a State is bound to be relative and liable to be limited for reasons of public safety, which it is the duty of Governments to maintain. Now, the idea of public safety, and with it the extent of the liberty which it is proposed to guarantee, varies from country to country, from one period to another, and even with a change of Government.

Perhaps the solution is to be found, at least in the early stages, in an agreement concluded by States in the form of a Convention by which Governments, after recognising the principle of the right of association, would undertake to provide the Organisation, in conjunction with and under the supervision of the associations concerned, with the necessary information regarding any modifications made in their trade union legislation, their methods of applying such legislation and changes in the trade union movement (creation or dissolution of trade unions, etc., by legislative, judicial or other action, etc.). Official information of this character, supplied periodically to the International Labour Office in virtue of a Convention conceived in very general terms, would enable the Organisation to intervene when necessary.

Some such idea does not appear entirely foreign to the present intentions of the Governing Body on this subject. When it considered in October 1930 a Resolution adopted at the Fourteenth Session of the Conference, which demanded that the question of freedom of association should be put on the agenda of a future Conference, the Governing Body adopted the following resolution on the proposal of the representative of the Argentine Government:

> Considering that freedom of association is the most important question in all social legislation, and as such should take the first place in international social legislation,
>
> That, furthermore, as was shown by the unsuccessful attempt of 1927, the complexity of the question and the various difficulties which it raises make it impossible, in present circumstances, to submit, with any chance of success, the problem of freedom of association in all its aspects to the International Labour Conference,
>
> That, on the other hand, it is possible to deal with its regulation by successive stages, as, for instance, the guarantee of the principle of freedom of association itself, the organisation and recognition of trade unions, etc.,
>
> The Governing Body decides to instruct the Office to study the question on the lines of paragraph 3 above, and to submit the results of such study to the Governing Body at its session in January 1931, in order that, after having laid down the form under which the question should be approached, the Governing Body might decide to place the question, in that form, on the agenda of an early Session of the International Labour Conference.

Continued Study of the Problem

This effort to deal with the question, if it ever materialises, will have to be based on information constantly kept up to date. The enquiry into freedom of association sanctioned by the Governing Body in 1923 is completed—temporarily. Its results have been published in five volumes, the first of which contains a comparative international study of the question; the second includes reports on Great Britain, Ireland, France, Belgium, Luxemburg, the Netherlands and Switzerland; the third reports on Germany, the former dual monarchy of Austria-Hungary, Austria, Hungary, the Czechoslovak Republic, Poland, the Baltic States, Denmark, Norway, Sweden and Finland; the fourth reports on Italy, Spain, Portugal, Greece, Yugoslavia, Bulgaria and Rumania; while the fifth comprises studies on the United States, Canada, Latin America, South Africa, Australia, New Zealand, India, China and Japan. In addition, a special study has been published on the trade union movement in Russia, whilst still another, which will shortly appear as an appendix to the fifth volume, will deal with the movement in Mexico. All these studies have been confined to the position of trade unionism from the standpoint of legislation. It will undoubtedly be necessary one day to study trade unionism as a social factor, to describe its evolution in connection with other social factors (especially those of an economic character), and to analyse its action by comparing the results achieved, not only country by country, but point by point. Such a comparison would enable the legislative authorities in each country, who are all faced with the same difficulties, to choose the methods which appear most likely to give satisfactory results in their own country. Trade unions would find therein the best justification for their past activities and a plan for future action. In every case the study of the workers' and employers' associations would proceed concurrently.

As regards the task of the future. No subject probably, in all the wide field which it covers is the International Labour Office so fully conscious of the singleness of aim and purpose which unites its programme and its plan of action.

II. Collective Agreements, Conciliation and Arbitration

Here it may be pointed out that the right of association is closely bound up with two questions from which it derives its whole importance, namely, the question of collective agreements, which the organised wage-earners conclude with the employers or their associations with a view to regulating conditions of labour, and that of conciliation and arbitration, the procedure used when all other methods fail to promote the conclusion of collective agreements and guarantee their enforcement.

Conciliation and Arbitration

National legislation has always begun by dealing with conciliation and arbitration; demands addressed to the Office suggested that it should do the same. This was natural, for it is more important to prevent industrial troubles whenever possible than to formulate internationally acceptable principles as to the form of collective agreements. Moreover, the disturbed social conditions immediately following the War were characterised by many industrial disputes, for which it was of importance to find peaceful solutions.

At its Sixth Session in 1924 the Conference adopted a Resolution requesting the International Labour Office to include in its programme the study of collective agreements and of the methods of conciliation and arbitration commonly employed in different countries for the settlement of disputes. The Governing Body sanctioned work which included the preparation of separate studies on conciliation and arbitration procedure in fifteen countries, a number of slighter studies for other countries and a general comparative study. This work is now well advanced, and it is hoped that 1931 will see its consummation. A second Resolution voted by the Conference in 1927 requested the Governing Body to consider the inclusion of the question of collective agreements in the agenda of a future Session of the Conference; this resolution gave an added importance to the study originally undertaken.

It is still somewhat difficult to decide as to the advisability of attempting any international regulation of conciliation and arbitration procedure. But certain points are already clear. In almost every country where industry has attained any real importance the State has set up organisations which are intended to lend their aid in preventing overt industrial disputes or in settling them in a peaceful manner. The nature of these institutions varies largely in the different countries and even at different times in countries which have a compulsory system, such as Australia and New Zealand. It would seem at present that in no country is the doctrine established beyond question. Thus, in Germany strong protests continue to be made, especially in employers' circles, against the proposal to make arbitration compulsory and awards binding in certain cases. In fact, the fundamental difficulty of the question, whether from a national or international standpoint, seems to lie in the doubt as to whether the State should adopt a policy of coercion in the adjustment of labour conditions. Obviously, the reply to this query may depend not only on the prevailing idea of the State's prerogatives, but also on the results of any attempts hitherto made to apply conciliation and arbitration procedure, on which point opinions often differ. Nor does the question of coercion always present itself as a simple issue. Take, for instance, the Anglo-Saxon countries; with the exception of Australia and New Zealand they are opposed in theory to any form of compulsory State intervention, yet they recognise a system of binding awards for industries covered by minimum wage legislation, as well as for some public utility industries and some public services. Similarly, in many countries, certain formalities connected with conciliation and arbitration procedure are obligatory, even if the awards are not binding. These formalities include the obligation to appear in court, to supply the requisite information and to produce the necessary documents.

Thus, despite great divergency, a number of common trends are to be observed, such as a desire to promote the peaceful adjustment of labour conditions by means of legal procedure and collective agreements, the tendency to make awards binding only in respect of disputes affecting the public utility services, and an effort to introduce general methods of establishing reasonable wages rates—the chief source of industrial disputes.

Collective Labour Agreements

The main object of conciliation and arbitration procedure is to facilitate the use of collective agreements for the adjustment of working conditions. As it was called on to deal with the former question, the International Labour Organisation could not well avoid the latter. Its interest in the matter was further stimulated by a number of other powerful motives connected with the very nature of the collective agreement.

The drafting and application of a collective labour agreement practically amount, for the two parties concerned, to transferring the adjustment of labour conditions from individuals to industrial associations. The contract of employment loses its private character and becomes a sort of public transaction between organised industrial groups. The greater the part played by these groups in the preparation of collective agreements, the more their importance in modern society increases, as they thereby engage in laying one of the foundations on which society is based. The collective agreement is one of the sources of power to both employers' and workers' associations. The collective labour agreement in the second place is an instrument which enables the wage-earner, formerly helpless as against his employer, to obtain, through his union, the satisfaction of his demands when labour conditions are being arranged. Finally, the scope of collective agreements has gradually extended from the mere adjustment of wages to the regulation of hours of work, holidays, conditions for the cancellation of contracts, industrial hygiene, accident prevention, and, virtually, to all important features in the relations between employer and employed. It stimulates the evolution of social legislation on the one hand and supplements it on the other.

So important a subject was bound to come within the purview of the International Labour Organisation. In 1926 the International Labour Office began to make a collection of texts of collective agreements; this collection, which is kept up to date, now includes 2,500 texts. It is a valuable asset in the study of the nature of collective agreements and working conditions. When in 1927 the Conference adopted its Resolution on conciliation and arbitration, it at the same time requested the Governing Body to consider the possibility of placing the question of the general principles of contracts of employment—individual and collective—on the agenda of an early Session of the Conference. The Office has undertaken a comparative study of this question, which, when it is finished, will show whether there are any points in this branch of labour law to which a common solution may be applied. At present all that can be said is that the importance of the collective agreement grows from day to day in the principal industrial countries and that the necessity for its regulation by law becomes more and more urgent. Definite regulations are especially desirable concerning the prevention of departures from the terms of the agreements, the right to conclude agreements, the obligation of the contracting parties to observe the state of industrial peace guaranteed by agreements and the allied question of civil liability. The object of the study undertaken by the Office is to determine whether these questions lend themselves to an international solution, acceptable to all countries.

That the collective agreement has already acquired a certain importance in international labour legislation is shown by the two following facts. According to the Washington Eight-Hour-Day Convention collective contracts are to be utilised to ensure the local application of the eight-hour day; similarly, a mutual agreement between two States may take the form of a collective agreement applicable in both countries. This system is exemplified in the collective agreements concluded on the basis of an agreement concerning Upper Silesia, signed by Germany and Poland on May 15th, 1922. Somewhat similar methods are likely to be adopted in the attempt recently begun to regulate on an international basis the conditions of labour in inland navigation.

III. Individual Labour Law

The International Labour Organisation was called on from the outset and by its very constitution to study the nature of industrial associations and of the institutions bound up with the existence of such associations, namely, collective labour law including conciliation and arbitration, collective agreements and the right of combination in trade associations. The Organisation had also to study the question of individual labour law, or that branch which considers the employer and the worker as individual persons. The administration of labour law and the individual contract of employment are the main elements of this branch, which is only loosely connected with the subjects mentioned above.

The Administration of Labour Law

The importance of the part played in society by the authorities competent to administer labour law has increased with the extension of the scope of labour legislation. In addition to interpreting social legislation and applying it to particular cases these authorities are continually developing such legislation by their awards and their interpretations of the legislators' intention. Information as to legal decisions is perhaps as important as a knowledge of the substance of the legislation itself, if a comprehensive idea is to be obtained of its application and tendencies. Since 1926 the International Labour Office has published, in conjunction with a group of eminent jurists, an annual survey of legal decisions on labour questions, containing a selection of such decisions worthy of note from an international standpoint given during the preceding year in France, Germany, Great Britain, Italy and the United States—countries whose legislative procedures exemplify the principal existing types of legal organisation. This publication will in time enable a general opinion to be formed on the growth of ideas inspiring social legislation in the great industrial countries, and also perhaps on the possibility of harmonising them.

Side by side with the practice of the ordinary courts there is a simplified procedure which is cheaper and more rapid. This system, which in pre-War days consisted in appointing referees from among the employers and workers, has since led in many countries to the establishment of permanent labour courts. The International Labour Office has always endeavoured to keep the public informed about this movement. It now seems that it might go further and undertake a comparative study of these labour courts. Such a study would be very useful; it would show that these young institutions entrusted with the administration of labour law possess those qualities which are essential for the best administration of justice—namely, economy, rapidity and a constitution representative of the parties at issue.

The Individual Contract of Employment

The institution of collective bargaining has resulted in transferring the regulation of labour conditions from the individual to the industrial association. The collective contract fixes finally the lines of the individual employment contract, transforming it into a sort of agreement about the application of principles from which the parties may not depart. Yet, in spite of the restriction of the individual's contractual rights resulting from the position conferred by collective labour law on the industrial association, and in spite of the legal protection afforded to the workers under general legislation, it is the individual employment contract which governs the worker's living conditions. Otherwise it would be difficult to understand the reasons underlying the repeated attempts made to exempt the contract of service from ordinary civil law and to bring it under special legislation based on the requirements of modern society. Throughout modern labour legislation may be felt this tendency to restrict the right of command acquired by the employer simultaneously with his right to dispose of his employee's services and the desire to abolish the employer's personal rights over those in his employment.

When the Conference resolved in 1927 to request the Governing Body to consider the possibility of placing the general principles of contracts of employment on the agenda of an early Session, it was attempting to contribute to a development of which much may be hoped. The author of the resolution drew attention to several matters which, in his opinion, could be regulated on an international basis. These included the form of the contract, the period of its validity, factory discipline, deductions from wages and their justification, probationary periods, holidays, dismissal and compensation for dismissal. All these things are, as a matter of fact, involved in the progress of the individual employment contract, the tendency being to ensure that labour shall no longer be regarded as a mere commodity but shall be protected by all the legal guarantees inherent in a contract based on the principle of equality as between man and man. As in the case of collective agreements, the Office is on the point of undertaking a first study of the question, and until that is done it is not possible to say with certainty how far problems arising out of the individual employment contract are suitable for international regulation. However, it may be noted that several of them, including the right to paid holidays and the right to withdraw from contracts, have narrowly missed being included in the agenda of the Conference, and will probably appear on that agenda before very long.

IV. Industrial Relations

The 1928 Resolution

In 1928 the Eleventh Session of the Conference adopted the following Resolution:

Whereas it is contended that the policy of active collaboration between employers and employed, such as exists in certain countries, has resulted both in an improvement in the level of real wages and working conditions, and also in greater and more economical production; and

Whereas the economies resulting from such collaboration can

also be made available for the benefit alike of the employers, the employed and the community as a whole;

Therefore be it resolved:

That this Conference requests the Governing Body to consider the advisability of instructing the International Labour Office to follow with due attention the progress of the spirit of collaboration between employers and employed and to report on the subject from time to time.

Progress of Industrial Relations

This Resolution reflected the tendencies shown in the world of industry for several years back. The experimental policy governing relations between employers and employed which was launched boldly and on a large scale in the United States, regardless of traditions and class opposition, attracted the attention of a large number of countries belonging to the International Labour Organisation. During 1926 and 1927, official and private missions were despatched to the United States from Germany, Australia, Great Britain and a number of other countries; from all quarters of the globe numbers of individual employers and even workers set out on their own accord to study the new system at close quarters. The International Labour Office sent its Deputy Director to the United States in 1926 for a similar purpose.

This wave of curiosity seems to have given birth to a general movement for the reform of the relations which existed in the old world between employers and employed. But it has to be admitted that, although the example of America certainly played its part in originating the movement, the European countries were irresistibly drawn into it by a number of factors of purely European origin. The chaotic state of trade and commerce after the War had engendered numerous quarrels between the two parties, both equally exasperated by the general conditions, by strikes and by disputes, and some remedy had to be found. Reforms introduced into management and the organisation of industry had provided the employers and their staff with fresh opportunities of renewing personal relationships, which had had such fruitful results that there arose a general desire to systematise such relations. Finally, the need for co-operation between capital and labour was accentuated above all by rationalisation, which had spread in all directions with rapidity and success; for it is obvious that unless the workers show an intelligent interest in this question the employers can do but little.

Hence the different efforts made throughout the world in the years 1927 and 1928, which, although varying in form, all had the same object in view. National conferences on industrial relations, convened in some cases by Governments and in others by employers' associations, were held in Australia, Finland, Great Britain, New Zealand, the Netherlands and Sweden, while in France, Germany and Italy investigations were set on foot by the industrial organisations already equipped for such work. From 1928 onward the national movements showed a tendency to amalgamate on an international basis, and in the same year the International Association for Industrial Relations was set up for the purpose of carrying out comparative studies.

The 1928 Resolution merely asked the International Labour Office to associate itself during the preliminary period of study and development with this policy of investigation, and to give it the benefit of its experience of comparative international research work.

Research Work by the Office

As a result of the 1928 Resolution the Governing Body adopted a plan of research work for the Office which is now well under way.

It was arranged that members of the Office staff should pay a series of visits to undertakings which had already organised their industrial relations, in order to obtain material for studies which were to be published in the *International Labour Review* before appearing in book-form. These studies cover the present-day organisation of industrial relations in business undertakings, the history of earlier collaboration between employers and trade unions, and the functions of works councils and other bodies set up to promote a spirit of co-operation between employers and employed. They also show the manner in which such collaboration contributes towards the management of business and furthers vocational training, apprenticeship, industrial hygiene, accident prevention, pensions and insurance schemes, profit-sharing and workers' participation in management, and the various workers' welfare schemes (spare time, housing, etc.).

Reports have already appeared concerning industrial relations in the French State mines of the Saar Basin; the London Traffic Combine, which controls the greater part of the London underground railway, tramway and motor-omnibus services; the Bata Shoe Factory in Czechoslovakia; the Siemens Electrical Works in Siemenstadt, near Berlin; the Lens Mining Syndicate in France. A number of other visits have been made, and studies will be published in the near future.

In addition, the Office is preparing a series of national reports dealing with industrial relations in France, Germany, Great Britain, Italy and the United States. Rich in subject-matter, these studies will discuss the general state of economy and production; the workers' and employers' industrial associations; the methods of co-operation employed in the preparation of collective agreements and the application of conciliation and arbitration procedure; works councils; the scope of profit-sharing and workers' participation in management; the collaboration between employers and employed in the management of insurance and pensions institutions; plans to improve undertakings; trade exhibitions; the various social services; co-operative societies; rationalisation; the organisation of vocational guidance and education; national and district economic councils and allied organisations.

It was thanks to the financial aid of an active and influential American body, the Industrial Relations Counselors, Inc., of New York, that the Organisation was able to embark on an undertaking of this kind, and it is hoped that the resources at the disposal of the Office will allow it to continue on the same lines.

So far only large firms have been studied. It is often affirmed in managerial circles that it is easier to apply a satisfactory industrial relations policy to large firms than to firms of average size. It would indeed be interesting if the Office could show by a few studies bearing on undertakings chosen from the latter class that such statements are altogether too sweeping.

The national reports now being prepared cover five large countries. There are, however, a number of other countries where national experiments must certainly be worthy of study.

Finally, the Office will in all probability undertake comparative international studies concerning certain aspects of international relations. Perhaps some day it may even be in a position to place before the Conference a Recommendation, if not a Convention, concerning the fundamental principles applicable to industry in all countries, or a declaration of principles which will lay down the essential rules to which, with suitable adaptations based on national or local customs, habits, tendencies and opinions, all systems of industrial relations must adhere if they are to survive and render service to the community.

V. Profit-Sharing and Workers' Participation in Management

It is generally admitted that social progress is largely governed by economic conditions. The most sweeping social conquests, however final they may appear, have no real stability so long as organised labour has no hold or control over manufacturing processes. This truth is at the bottom of the trade union claim for the workers' right to collaborate in the management of business.

Purely theoretical before the War, this claim became a reality after the conclusion of hostilities. As a result of the collapse of the former political and social framework the workers in Russia, in the Central European States and elsewhere suddenly found themselves called upon to take an active part in the reorganisation of national life. Hence the mushroom growth of a whole series of new institutions—works councils, industrial boards, economic councils, factory committees, systems of labour co-partnership and profit-sharing—some officially recognised, others recognised *de facto*, with different functions, but one and all animated by the general desire to allow workers to collaborate in industrial life.

The growth of works councils was especially rapid in Central Europe, especially in Germany, Austria and Czechoslovakia, and subsequently in Norway, Luxemburg and the Free City of Danzig. In Great Britain and in some of the Dominions, Trade Boards and Whitley Councils were set up; in the United States, factory committees. In France and elsewhere it was the idea of labour co-partnership which was applied.

In a series of studies published in the *International Labour Review* the Office has followed, year by year, the development of this powerful movement in the different countries. Moreover, the question of works councils was officially submitted to the International Labour Organisation at the Twenty-ninth Session of the Governing Body. On that occasion the German Government representative, seconded by the Government representative of Czechoslovakia, proposed that the matter should be put on the agenda of a Session of the International Labour Conference.

Even though the international application of this reform cannot be considered for the time being, it is certainly the duty of the Office to prepare for it by a thorough study of the whole matter. If, as certain writers appear to believe, some system of profit-sharing is destined to replace, wholly or partly, the present methods of remuneration, it is obvious that the question will become one of the predominant features of the Organisation's plan of studies.

CHAPTER VIII

THE INTERNATIONAL LABOUR ORGANISATION AND ECONOMIC PROBLEMS

I. The Economic Evolution of the World since the War

The Position in 1919

The economic and social position of the world at the end of the War may be summed up in two words: poverty and disorder. The characteristic features of that period were a shortage of practically all kinds of raw materials; a breakdown in the land, river and maritime transport systems; budgetary deficits and heavy commercial losses, especially in Europe; inflation and shortage of capital; scarcity of labour, and especially of skilled workers, accompanied by unemployment; physical, moral and intellectual stagnation among the working classes, and a fall in the output of the workers, and even of machinery, which had been overworked and seldom renewed during the War; a general slump affecting commerce, banking, and what is commonly known as "business."

Most of the States directly or indirectly affected by the aftermath of the War were thus faced with a difficult, many-sided problem. Their efforts have been, and still are, directed towards solving these questions, with the help of the international institutions centralised in Geneva.

Remedial Measures

The efforts made to meet and overcome the economic depression of the last ten years went through a number of different phases. Any hard-and-fast division of these phases into fixed periods must necessarily be purely arbitrary, as the events affecting the various branches of economy naturally had no uniformity. Extreme scarcity of some of the world's most vital requirements was sometimes accompanied by an abundance of others.

Nevertheless, the reconstruction work of 1919–1929 can be divided into two main periods.

From 1920 onwards, underproduction rapidly gave way to

overproduction and a slump in markets. This situation was further aggravated by an unprecedented financial crisis and culminated in acute unemployment. Thus it was that, up to the end of 1924, all national and international efforts were directed towards the mitigation and removal of these evils. From 1924 onwards, although the same evils still persisted and unemployment was on the up-grade, the world, which, besides being enfeebled, was also disorganised, was nevertheless able to set about reorganising its economic activities on new principles which it was hoped would prevent the return of a similar situation. During these two periods—one spent in overcoming the depression and the other in reconstruction and the organisation of preventive measures—the International Labour Organisation shared in the common effort. Nor could it do otherwise without failing to justify the trust placed in it by the Peace Treaty.

II. The Organisation and Economic Questions

Affinity of Economic and Social Questions

During the last ten years a contrast has frequently been drawn between the international organisations, creations of the human mind, which, with its passion for logic and analysis, sifts facts, classifies them in groups and sets up institutions to deal with each separate group, and the realities of a world where all facts intermingle and react on each other, often with very little respect for analysis and logic. It would indeed seem that the authors of the Peace Treaty and those called on to interpret it have striven to endow Geneva with two independent institutions of different character, the first to promote political and economic peace, the second—the International Labour Organisation—to bring about social peace.

It is clear that the League of Nations aims jointly at political peace and economic agreement, proving by its very existence and nature the oft-repeated assertion that the best method of creating an economic understanding is to co-ordinate it with a political *entente*, and vice-versa. The fact that the International Labour Organisation was purposely invested with complete autonomy does not in any way imply that it should refrain from dealing directly with most economic questions, as social peace is at one and the same time a condition and a result of economic peace.

No astonishment need therefore be felt that both the Employers' and Workers' Groups have repeatedly called the attention of the Conference to the necessity for the Organisation to keep in touch with international economic problems.

Theoretical Affinity

The Preamble to Part XIII of the Peace Treaty concludes with the words: "Whereas also the failure of any nation to adopt humane conditions of labour is an obstacle in the way of other nations which desire to improve the conditions in their own countries. . . ." Can this be read otherwise than as meaning that under present conditions of economic competition a State which declines to assume the social charges necessary to the prosperity of its workers—charges which are met by taxes and ultimately by an increase in working costs and consequently in market prices—has a distinct advantage in foreign markets over States which assume such charges and that it consequently practises, consciously or unconsciously, a most immoral form of dumping at the expense of the working classes?

Economic conditions are thus influenced to some extent by social conditions, and all attempts to standardise the latter as between nations help to equalise and stabilise the former. Social policy, when carried out on international lines, tends to set up a sort of code of economic morals.

Actual Affinity

At the same time it is only too obvious that the economic stability or instability of the world does also in fact influence the conditions of work and existence of the labouring classes. The standard of living of these classes has its effect on the economy of the country to which they belong, for when it is high the purchasing power of the largest section of the consumers is increased. It is also true that a satisfactory economic position makes it easier for a State to apply a humane and liberal social policy, which, although obviously entailing expenditure, certainly gives profitable though perhaps less obvious results. It is incontrovertible that a sound and stable economic situation guarantees employment for the worker and exorcises the spectre of unemployment. Nor can it be questioned that well-organised markets and methods of production enable the worker to be certain of finding well-paid work at home and abroad, just as carefully-planned workers' migration enables the producer to be sure of being able to obtain the requisite supplies of suitable labour. Even that modern economic phenomenon, rationalisation, has its social aspect, since, as will later be shown, it can accomplish nothing if an attempt is made to apply it against the will or without the help of labour.

III. The Period before the World Economic Conference

The Enquiry into Production

At the First Session of the Conference, held in Washington in 1919, an Italian member of the Workers' Group, Mr. Baldesi, proposed on behalf of that Group that, with a view to promoting a trade revival in Europe, the question of the international distribution of raw materials, then extremely scarce, should be added to the tasks allotted to the League of Nations. This motion was rejected by the very small majority of 43 votes to 40. Thus, at the very beginning, the International Labour Organisation showed that it took an interest in the more important economic problems and indicated the lines along which it might proceed.

In 1920, when the industrial crisis was at its height, the Governing Body, acting this time on a suggestion of the Employers' Group, decided to entrust the International Labour Office with the making of "an enquiry into industrial production throughout the world, considered in relation to conditions of work and cost of living." One of the main objects of the enquiry was to determine to what extent production had been affected by post-War conditions of labour, such as the eight-hour day, the partial abolition of payment-by-result systems, etc. But at the request of the Workers' Group it was decided that all factors likely in any way to affect production should be taken into account.

The enquiry was spread over four years, and the results filled five volumes published in eight parts, containing a detailed examination of the information provided by Governments on production in general and the workers' output; on the shortage of raw materials, plant, transport, capital, markets, currency and exchange, and other elements important to production; and on the evolution of conditions of labour, such as the demographic consequences of the War, difficulties connected with vocational training, the shortage of labour and changes in the workers' living conditions, food, housing, wages and standards of life. The last volume summarised and discussed the steps taken or advocated to deal with the various slumps in production and to improve and render more normal the conditions of labour and existence of the workers.

Space does not permit of a longer description of this monumental work. It need only be added that during the World Economic Conference, to which reference will be made later, many speakers mentioned the help they had obtained from it. The least that can be said is that this vast work of analysis and classification is a living proof of the intention of the International Labour Organisation to carry out a wholehearted study of all economic factors in so far as they affect conditions of labour or are themselves affected by the latter.

The Mixed Commission on Economic Crises

Reference must here be made to this Committee, the work of which was surveyed in connection with unemployment. It may be recalled that its main duties, which are based on the principles of the International Labour Organisation and the Economic Organisation of the League of Nations, are to study economic crises, to seek their causes and remedies and to submit the studies made to one or other of the above institutions respectively according as they are of an economic or social character.

Special Economic Conferences

The first steps taken by the League of Nations to promote concerted international action in economic matters consisted in a number of Conferences, each devoted to one of the aspects of the general problem, namely, the Brussels Financial Conference of 1920, the Conferences held in Barcelona in 1921 and Geneva in 1923 which dealt with communications and transit, and the Genoa Conference of 1923 which was restricted to the study of a renewal of relations with the Soviet Union, and in which the International Labour Organisation took an active part. The time had not yet come for the affinity of economic and social problems to be definitely recognised in all quarters, although a tendency in that direction had been evident since the Washington Conference.

Nevertheless, in 1920, at the First Session of the International Labour Conference held in Geneva, when the world was faced with that slump in markets which succeeded the production crisis, two workers' delegates, Mr. Jouhaux and Mr. Schürch, moved a Resolution in which, rightly stressing the connection between unemployment and economic problems in general, they requested the International Labour Office to undertake an international enquiry into unemployment and suggested the convocation of an international conference to study international remedies calculated to put an end to unemployment.

It will be remembered that the Office immediately initiated this enquiry and has continued it ever since. A conference to find remedial measures for unemployment could not be other than an economic conference.. This conference was to take place in 1927, but it should be remembered that certain members of the Labour Conference had called for it six years previously.

IV. The World Economic Conference, 1927

Participation of "Labour" in the Conference

It is of interest to note that it was a worker, Mr. Jouhaux, a member of the Governing Body of the International Labour Office, who in 1924, when member of the French Delegation to the Assembly of the League of Nations, first called the attention of the latter to the necessity of establishing "economic peace." When a year later another French delegate to the Assembly, Mr. Loucheur, persuaded the League to convene an International Economic Conference, he did no more than consolidate the work begun by Mr. Jouhaux.

The International Labour Organisation was well represented at this Conference. The Chairman of the Governing Body of the International Labour Office was specially invited by the Council of the League of Nations. One of the most important committees, the Commission on Industry, was presided over by another member of the Governing Body. In addition, nine other members of the Governing Body were present at the Conference, either as delegates appointed by their countries or as representatives of institutions such as the International Institute of Agriculture or the International Chamber of Commerce or as technical experts. Finally, eleven of the fifty delegations present included a workers' representative—a fact, be it said, which shows that not enough Governments had followed the suggestion made by the Preparatory Committee of the

Conference to the effect that all interests should be represented. Yet the fact remains that it was proved impossible to convene an economic conference of world-wide importance without calling on Labour.

The International Labour Office collaborated closely with the Secretariat of the League of Nations in the documentary preparation and the organisation of the Conference. It presented the Conference with a report on the standard of living of the workers in various countries, the Commission on Industry with a study on scientific management in Europe, and the Commission on Agriculture with studies concerning the relation of labour costs to the total cost of production in agriculture and the part played by co-operative organisations in international trade. Furthermore, although this question was not included in its agenda, the Conference gave a part of its time to two studies prepared by the Office, dealing respectively with the statistics and the regulation of international migration movements.

The Conclusion of the Conference

In its Final Report the Conference gave a complete picture of the burdens which were oppressing the economic life of the world in 1927 and which to a great extent are still oppressing it. In addition to the purely political and economic causes of unrest, the Report drew attention to a number of others which have a direct and important effect on the workers' lives: the influence of Eastern competition on the cotton industry of the Western Hemisphere, the depression in the coal industry, the reduced purchasing powers of industrial communities affected by unemployment, the want of proportion between wages in various trades in Europe and America, that of prices in the different branches of production, and that between wages and prices, which is a prime cause of industrial disputes.

It was, moreover, a matter of considerable satisfaction to Labour that the Conference affirmed the same interdependence of States in the economic field which the Preamble to Part XIII of the Peace Treaty had proclaimed in the social-economic field in 1919. It was also a matter of satisfaction for the workers to be assured that there could be no return to pre-War conditions and that a new economic order must be built up, even as the Charter of the Labour Organisation had demanded a new social order in 1919. Economic and social questions were now recognised as being indissoluble. And if, among the resolutions adopted by the Conference, the widest, the most definite and those which raised the greatest hopes for the near future (since shown in part to be vain) referred to commerce, those concerning agriculture drew attention to the achievements and the possible future development of the co-operative movement, a matter which, it will be recalled, has long been studied by the International Labour Office. These resolutions declared that agricultural workers must obtain the same working conditions and attain the same standard of living as industrial workers—exactly what the International Labour Organisation has been striving for since 1921. The Conference also extolled the merits of technical education in agriculture, a matter which had at that time been preoccupying the Office for over two years.

Further, the resolutions concerning industry laid great emphasis on two questions of direct interest to the International Labour Organisation, namely, rationalisation (the Office had submitted a report on scientific management in Europe) and international industrial agreements. The Office submitted to the Conference two memoranda on the latter question, or rather on the possibility of regulating industrial agreements—a matter of extreme importance for the consumers and workers—which had been prepared by two of its most distinguished outside collaborators. The resolutions adopted on these two matters did not forget the workers' interests. That which dealt with rationalisation urged the Governments "to give special attention to measures of a kind calculated to ensure to the individual the best, the healthiest and the most worthy employment, such as vocational selection, guidance and training, the due allotment of time between work and leisure, methods of remuneration giving the worker a fair share in the increase of output, and, generally, conditions of work and life favourable to the development and preservation of his personality." Is this not, indeed, a definition of the "humane conditions of labour" mentioned in Part XIII of the Peace Treaty? As regards industrial agreements, although the Conference did not go so far as to recommend that supervision which was so strongly advocated by the workers, it nevertheless considered that the League of Nations "should closely follow these forms of international industrial co-operation and their effects upon technical progress, the development of production, *conditions of labour*, etc." It will be realised on reading these excerpts that the activities of the International Labour Office and of the representatives of the Organisation who took part in the Conference in various capacities had a deep and favourable effect on the proceedings at that famous international meeting.

V. From 1927 to 1930

The Conference outlined the economic work which the League of Nations was called on to undertake and drew up its initial programme. Since then the work has progressed, and the programme now begins to become a reality, in spite of difficulties of all sorts which do not require discussion here. The International Labour Organisation has made a sustained effort to accomplish with the modest means at its disposal the various tasks indicated as coming within its competence.

The Consultative Economic Committee

The success of the World Economic Conference led the Council of the League of Nations to set up a Consultative Economic Committee, which meets once a year to study the measures taken during the previous year to give effect to the decisions of the Conference, and to call the Council's attention to those decisions which have to be dealt with or studied during the coming year. The International Labour Office co-operates with the Secretariat of the League of Nations in the preparation of documentary material for the meetings of the Committee. Moreover, the Committee includes a number of labour representatives, whose election to the Committee was proposed to the Council of the League by the Workers' Group of the Governing Body of the International Labour Office.

The Organisation and Economic Questions of the Day

Viewed from the standpoint of the League of Nations the question of industrial agreements has made very little progress since 1927. All that has been accomplished is the inauguration of a technical enquiry into their working. Although the International Labour Office is deeply interested in this study it is unable for the time being to take any definite action.

The International Labour Organisation has never lost sight of the necessity of following the rationalisation movement, which, emanating from the United States, continues to extend in

Europe to all branches of activity, including industry, agriculture, commerce, banking, and public administration. Healthy rationalisation measures, it must be repeated, can only be applied in these spheres with the collaboration of labour. For these reasons, when opportunity arose to set up in Geneva an information office—the present Scientific Management Institute—to study and promote the movement in Europe the International Labour Office played its part. It was within the grounds of the Office and under its protecting influence that the Institute first saw the light of day. Although the Institute is entirely independent, its Board includes several members of the Governing Body of the International Labour Office, while several officials of the latter organisation have been seconded to the Institute.

Close and fruitful collaboration unites the Institute to the International Labour Office: the former deals with the technical and economic aspects of rationalisation, the latter with the social side of the question. The Office is on the point of publishing an international study on rationalisation in relation to hours of work, output, working conditions, wages, industrial hygiene, fatigue, accident prevention, unemployment, etc. This study, which is of an objective character, will help to dispel a number of prejudices and draw the attention of "rationalisers" to the necessity of taking some account of the social aspect of the problem if they are desirous of ultimate success.

Three of the agricultural enquiries undertaken by the Office, dealing with the effects of agrarian reform on agricultural workers, the rural exodus, and the present agricultural crisis, touch on the economic structure of agriculture. The question whether the deep depression which has been affecting agriculture throughout the world for a number of years has influenced or is likely to influence the land worker's wages, standards of living and possibilities of employment, can have different answers, which depend on whether the question covers present or future conditions, European or oversea countries, or is confined to certain forms of agricultural undertakings, certain branches of agriculture, etc.

It would be superfluous to enumerate the reasons why the International Labour Organisation studies and must study the unemployment crisis, which at present affects the whole world, and which is also an economic phenomenon, because it is the cause (as well as the effect) of underconsumption. Reference has already been made to the measures adopted for the study and mitigation, if not the abolition, of the unemployment scourge.

The two elements of the present economic system which are most deeply affected by crisis conditions are the coal-mining industry and agriculture, and it is interesting to note that when dealing with the coal-mining question the Economic Committee of the League of Nations and the Assembly were obliged to refer what was perhaps the most important part of the whole question to the International Labour Organisation, whose recent action in the matter will be recalled.

As to the agricultural depression, the International Labour Office is taking an active part in the studies required before any definite remedy can be tried. The question of main importance for the Office is undoubtedly that of the effects of the depression on the working and living conditions of agricultural workers. There is also, of course, the question of the slump in the markets, which, as always, is the result of overproduction or of underconsumption, according to the angle from which it is viewed. How and to what extent this slump can be overcome or reduced by increasing the purchasing power of the consuming masses, i.e., the workers, are queries which once again bring the International Labour Office face to face with the problem of "high wages," a social-economic question as difficult to define as it is to solve, and one which will doubtless have a place among the great problems of the future.

PART III

RESULTS

As has already been shown, the chief object of the International Labour Organisation is to prepare and bring into force binding international agreements relating to conditions of labour. The whole work of the Organisation is directed towards such positive results, and the work already accomplished in many spheres has led to the adoption by the Conference of thirty Conventions and thirty-nine Recommendations.

We shall now endeavour to show the extent of the results which have been attained by means of these international agreements during the first decade of the Organisation's existence.

These results are of two kinds. On the one hand we have the formal results as represented by the ratification of Conventions; on the other, the positive results achieved by the development of the legal protection extended to workers in various countries as an outcome of the adoption of Conventions. The Recommendations have also borne fruit, and a third chapter has been devoted to a survey of their results.

CHAPTER I

RATIFICATION OF CONVENTIONS

THE first International Labour Conventions, adopted at Washington in 1919, obtained the practically unanimous vote of the Government, employers' and workers' delegates present.[1] It was therefore not unnatural to suppose that their ratification would not give rise to much opposition in the various States, but would be obtained everywhere in a relatively short time. But by October 1921—that is to say, about two years after their adoption—they had been ratified by a very small number of countries, the actual ratification figures being 4 for the Hours Convention, 7 for the Unemployment Convention, 2 for the Maternity Convention, 6 for the Convention concerning night work of women, 4 for the Minimum Age Convention, and 4 for the Convention concerning night work of children. Although these results are by no means negligible, it has to be admitted that they fell far short of general expectation.

There can be little doubt that there was too much indulgence in that facile optimism so common after the War, and that the economic depression caused many Governments to reflect before committing themselves. At the same time, it soon became clear that the absence of ratifications was due in part at least to the difficulties inherent in the new procedure set up by the Peace Treaty.

In order to form an unbiased opinion of the results obtained during the first ten years it is essential to understand the character of these difficulties and to ascertain to what extent and by what means they have been overcome.

[1] The figures recorded were as follows:

Convention fixing hours of work	83 votes to 2
Convention concerning unemployment	88 votes to 4
Maternity Convention	67 votes to 10
Convention concerning night work of women	94 votes to 1
Convention concerning minimum age of children	92 votes to 3
Convention concerning night work of children	93 votes to 0

I. Initial Difficulties

Difficulties of Procedure

A number of initial difficulties were due to the novelty of the procedure and the special character of the International Labour Conventions.

Prior to 1919 all international Conventions, whatever their object, were invested with the traditional diplomatic forms. The text was drafted by means of diplomatic negotiations between plenipotentiaries of the contracting parties and bore their signatures. It was such texts, signed by delegates endowed with full powers, which came before the competent authorities for ratification. It is a noteworthy fact that the traditional procedure was widely modified by the Peace Treaty. In the Conventions provided for under Part XIII the formality of signature is replaced by a two-thirds majority vote, in which not only Government delegates—who, it should be observed, are not plenipotentiaries—but also representatives of the employers' and workers' industrial associations take part. Thus it is that the texts adopted by the International Labour Conference are not Conventions in the accepted sense of the word. The Treaty calls them "Draft Conventions," a term which has been subjected to legal criticism but which, nevertheless, clearly defines the novel character of the texts approved by the International Labour Conference.

It is therefore not astonishing that the novel form of the Conventions caused some surprise in national administrations and Parliaments and gave rise to initial difficulties in several countries, notably in France.

Under the usual constitutional procedure the French Government was accustomed to submit to Parliament, for authorisation to ratify, only conventions or treaties which had previously been signed by French plenipotentiaries and plenipotentiaries of other States. It thus came about that the French Government, after introducing in the Chamber of Deputies, on April 29th, 1920, a number of Bills for the ratification of five of the Washington Conventions, thought well to change its mind. It felt a certain hesitation in submitting to Parliament Draft Conventions adopted merely by two-thirds of the delegates present at the Washington Conference. It felt that it could only accept responsibility for Conventions signed in the usual manner and took steps to transform the Draft Conventions adopted at Washington into Conventions conforming to French constitutional procedure, by proceeding to exchange signatures with other States.

The French attitude was subsequently adopted by the Belgian Government, and six Conventions embodying the text of the provisions of the Conventions adopted at Washington were signed in Paris on January 24th, 1921, by the two States, a protocol being attached for the signatures of other States that might wish to adhere. A copy of the Conventions and the protocol was transmitted to the Secretary-General of the League of Nations, who was asked to bring this exchange of signatures and the existence of the protocol to the notice of the other Members of the International Labour Organisation.

Consulted by the Secretary-General of the League of Nations, the International Labour Office declared that it considered the procedure proposed by the French Government to be contrary to the spirit of Part XIII of the Peace Treaty. In its opinion the States signatory to the Treaty had undertaken to follow a new procedure which was complete in itself, and entirely replaced the previous one. The absence of signatures was a characteristic feature of the new procedure and a logical consequence of the tripartite composition of the Conference. The procedure advocated by the French Government would result in placing the Government delegates on a different footing from the employers' and workers' representatives—which was contrary to the spirit and letter of the Treaty—and might have the paradoxical effect of compelling a Government whose delegates had opposed the adoption of a Convention to endorse the same Convention without forwarding it to the competent authorities for ratification. The Secretary-General of the League of Nations concurred with the argument put forward by the Office and replied to the French Government in that sense.

The French Government did not press its view, but it was only on March 17th, 1924, that it informed the Office of its intention, in the case of future Conventions, to refrain from concluding diplomatic agreements with other Members of the International Labour Organisation. In this manner the first difficulty was overcome.

The novel form of the International Labour Conventions was, however, not the only innovation introduced by the procedure set up by Part XIII, nor was it the boldest. The

Treaty also imposed on States Members an obligation connected with Conventions which is not to be found in pre-War international law concerning conventions and treaties, namely, that of bringing them within a period of one year (or in exceptional cases eighteen months) from the closing of the Session of the Conference concerned "before the authority or authorities within whose competence the matter lies, for the enactment of legislation or other action."

The object of this provision is to compel Governments to bring the draft regulations adopted by the Conference to the notice of the public. It obviates any risk of the Conventions being passed over without consideration, and ensures that they will come up for discussion before a representative national assembly. Respect for this obligation, which is essential if the work of the International Labour Organisation is to be effective, is secured by the right to appeal to the Permanent Court of International Justice against States which fail to comply with it.

Here again the new procedure led to difficulties. Some countries were in doubt as to whether the authorities to whom the Conventions should be submitted were the authorities competent *to ratify* or those entitled *to legislate*. This is a vital question, as in most States the first is the Government and the second Parliament. When consulted the International Labour Office has consistently replied that in its opinion only the authority competent to bring the national legislation into harmony with the Conventions—that is to say, Parliament—could possibly be intended.

This argument appears to have been adopted gradually by all countries. Nowadays all the industrial States carefully comply with the obligation to submit the Conventions to a legislative authority. Only some of the less industrially developed States, such as Bolivia, the Dominican Republic, Ethiopia, Guatemala, Honduras, Liberia, Peru and Persia, have so far failed to supply the International Labour Office with information as to the measures they have taken to meet this obligation, or the reasons which have prevented them from doing so. But this obligation cannot be shirked by a country because of the state of its industrial development. It is therefore hoped that the desire to respect engagements solemnly undertaken will soon be stronger everywhere than the indifference of the administrative authorities.

It is thus clear that the Governments are required regularly to bring to the notice of the legislative authorities the texts adopted by the International Labour Conference. What, however, is the procedure to be observed? This was the third question raised by several countries when faced with the early Conventions.

It is a recognised fact that the Conventions as such have no binding force on the States Members, and Governments and Parliaments are free to ratify them or not as they deem fit. The Governments are entitled to submit them to Parliament with or without a memorandum recommending ratification or the reverse. Now, in several countries, of which France is a notable instance, parliamentary rules and traditions do not permit the Government to introduce a Convention in Parliament otherwise than in the form of a Bill. A Bill, however, cannot logically have any other meaning than to recommend Parliament to ratify the Convention concerned. The French Government was therefore unable to fulfil its obligations towards those Conventions which it did not feel able to recommend for parliamentary approval.

For some considerable time this new difficulty prevented the French Government from introducing into the Chambers the agricultural Conventions adopted by the 1921 Conference.

Here again the difficulty was finally overcome. The French Government ultimately adopted a method of procedure suggested by the International Labour Office which involved the presentation of Draft Conventions to the Chambers in the form of a brochure. The memorandum to a Bill for the introduction of one of these Conventions which the Government proposed to ratify was then used to show which Conventions it was proposed not to ratify and the reasons for such attitude. This procedure has subsequently been adopted in other countries.

But while the Conventions must be formally placed before the national legislature, the latter must also have an opportunity of expressing an opinion on them. It is not enough to present a Bill or a report to Parliament; it must also be included in the agenda of a Session and come up for discussion. The early post-War period was, however, an extremely busy one for Parliaments in most countries, for they had more than enough to do to deal with important questions of national and international policy and the financial situation. So it came about that the discussion of the Conventions had to be postponed. The result was that Bills for their ratification could not be discussed before the end of the parliamentary Session and were shelved. In most cases these Bills were tabled anew at the beginning of the following Session. In some instances, however, this was not done, either because Governments considered that they had fulfilled their obligations by tabling them once, or because political changes in the composition of Governments or Parliaments prevented any possibility of ratification. In such cases it has always been maintained by the Office that the obligation imposed on the Governments could not be held to be complied with so long as the legislative authority had not had a real opportunity of expressing its opinion, and in the main this argument has been generally recognised. Nowadays, however, Parliaments usually consider the examination of the Conventions as a part of their routine work.

Such are the chief difficulties of the new procedure which the International Labour Organisation has had to overcome and which undoubtedly hampered the progress of ratifications during the early years of the Organisation's existence. They may now, however, be considered as solved and definitely removed.

Difficulties of Principle

The ratification of Conventions also encountered difficulties inherent in the actual principle of the international regulation of conditions of labour. These difficulties varied from country to country, and even with the Conventions themselves. They could not, therefore, as in the case of difficulties of procedure, be overcome by any single solution. Even now, some of them exist and will in all likelihood continue to exist for many years to come. In spite of their diversity, however, they may be classified under a few main heads.

The Conventions adopted up to the present are not restricted to the formulation of general ideas to which the States are simply required to adhere in principle. They lay down positive rules, in many cases highly detailed, such as those for the prohibition of harmful products or dangerous or unhealthy work for certain classes of workers, or those for the adoption of definite methods of organisation of work in industrial or other undertakings. The ratification of such Conventions, implying, as it does, the obligation to bring national law into harmony with their provisions, nearly always necessitates the amending of existing legislation. Now, it may happen, for example, that these amendments affect the provisions of a labour or a social insurance code, or even several laws of a country. It may even be necessary to prepare entirely fresh legislation. The requisite legislative measures are likely in some cases to involve a great amount of work for the Government departments concerned. Work of this kind takes a long time in many countries, so that ratification procedure is often delayed.

Again, the ratification of a Convention usually entails—indeed, this is its real object—changes in the working conditions and life of the workers. The result may be to alter an existing labour system, or even to replace it by a new one. These changes may in turn lead to fresh difficulties. In some cases the workers themselves have imagined—and even when their imagination has been at fault the risk has nevertheless been present to some extent—that the adoption of legislation or practices in harmony with a given Convention might endanger a labour system with which they were content.

Finally, a ratification may, directly or indirectly, entail consequences of an economic character for the industries to which the Convention applies, or even for the country as a whole, by leading to increased national expenditure. Hence the opposition of the circles affected.

To quote a few examples : the Washington Hours Convention, the principles of which are now universally accepted, deals with a number of points on lines which have not yet been adopted in all countries, e.g. the regulations concerning overtime and its payment at not less than one-and-a-quarter times the normal wage; the Convention concerning the use of white lead in painting, which prohibits the use of that product in interior painting work, has been considered by white lead manufacturers as a direct menace to their business, and has roused them into opposition; the Convention on the employment of women before and after childbirth, which stipulates that the maintenance allowances payable to women at confinement and their children shall be paid out of public funds or guaranteed by an insurance system, is likely to lead to fresh demands on the State budget; other Conventions, such as those concerning health insurance and seamen's articles of agreements, undoubtedly have more or less important effects on the organisation of certain departments or on certain methods of administration.

In the great majority of cases the ratification of the International Labour Conventions is for Governments not merely a question of making a demonstration in favour of certain humanitarian principles—it really implies the undertaking of a definite scheme of social reform. This is no mere gesture, but an act, and, to give the fullest meaning to that act, the countries ratifying during the past ten years have had to surmount real difficulties, and in many cases to overcome obstinate resistance.

In addition to these difficulties of a national character there are also international complications.

The object of the International Labour Conventions is, in addition to improving working conditions, to standardise them as far as possible in the different countries. "Whereas," states the Preamble of Part XIII of the Peace Treaty, "the failure of any nation to adopt humane conditions of labour is an obstacle in the way of other nations which desire to improve the conditions in their own countries. . . ." Here, as already stated, we have an attempt to prevent "social dumping." The principle is nowadays adopted practically everywhere, but its enforcement has been found in some cases to be somewhat difficult. When a Convention directly affects conditions in countries competing with each other, Governments sometimes express their readiness to ratify only on the understanding that the Convention will come into force in rival States at the same time as in their own. Each State hesitates to take the first step, feeling that delayed ratification by its rivals may temporarily place it at a disadvantage in trade competition.

Various measures have been tried to obviate this difficulty, but all are attended by such serious disadvantages that it has not appeared advisable to recommend their general adoption.

In the first place, certain adjoining countries, mutually bound by close political and economic relationships, have agreed to make a joint examination once a year of the Conventions adopted by the Conference with a view to taking up, where possible, an identical attitude towards them. This procedure was initiated by the northern countries. Representatives of Denmark, Finland, Norway and Sweden have met, after every Session of the Conference, to study the texts adopted in the light of the legislation of their respective countries. Perhaps these States have derived some advantage from these meetings, but what has been the result as regards the success of the Conventions? In some cases it appears that the mere evidence of a difference, sometimes even slight, between the laws of one of these countries and a Convention has been sufficient to delay, and even to prevent, ratification by the whole group.

Another measure adopted is that of "conditional" ratification. In order not to risk finding themselves the only party to a Convention some States, when registering their ratification with the Secretariat of the League of Nations, have stipulated that it is to come into force only when the ratification of certain other States has been received. Such ratifications do at least testify to the good-will of the States making them, but it seems obvious that this procedure should only have been adopted when the dangers of competition were particularly great. From the very outset, however, there has been a growing tendency to use it more generally by applying it even to Conventions which could not in any way affect commercial competition, and to multiply the number of States whose ratification was a stipulated condition. For instance, the French Chamber of Deputies made France's ratification of the three Washington Conventions concerning night work of women, night work of children and unemployment conditional on prior ratification by Czechoslovakia, Germany, Great Britain, Italy, Poland, and even of the United States, which is not a Member of the International Labour Organisation. Again, in 1926 the Latvian Government's ratification of the Convention concerning unemployment indemnity in the case of loss or foundering of the ship was subordinated to prior ratification by "the Powers of chief importance in maritime trade." In this case the vagueness of the phraseology constituted a particularly dangerous precedent. It is true that it was inspired by the provision of Part XIII, under which the eight States "of chief industrial importance" are entitled to seats on the Governing Body of the International Labour Office. But whereas Part XIII defines the procedure to be followed, when necessary, to decide which are these eight States, there are no such means of establishing a list of the Powers of chief importance in maritime trade. It was therefore doubtful when, if ever, the Latvian ratification would become operative.

It was certainly the duty of the International Labour Office to warn States against the dangers which might possibly result from an excessive extension of the system of conditional ratifications. Whenever the occasion arose, this was done by the Office, which used the following arguments:

In the case of a reform which has already been generally accepted by legislation and practice, the inclusion of a suspensory clause in the instrument of ratification can have no value for

Governments and only hinders the general progress of ratifications. Even in the case of Conventions which may have far-reaching economic consequences, and which States may well hesitate to ratify without the assurance that their rivals will undertake similar engagements, it is going too far to subordinate ratification to similar action by an excessive number of States. Such methods can only result in paralysing the whole work of ratification and rendering useless the machinery set up by Part XIII.

Fortunately the arguments of the Office did not fall on deaf ears, with the result that the number of conditional ratifications has fallen and continues to fall. France has ratified unconditionally the three Washington Conventions which the French Parliament had previously demanded should be ratified conditionally. The Latvian Government recently gave its unconditional assent to the Convention concerning unemployment indemnity for shipwrecked seamen and thereby annulled its former conditional ratification. The Italian Government has declared its intention of suppressing the condition originally attached to its ratification of the Washington Hours Convention. At the present time, out of a total of 408 ratifications, only 8 are conditional, of which 5 (Austria, France, Italy, Latvia and Spain) refer to the Convention which, from the standpoint of national competition, is undoubtedly the most important of all, i.e. the Washington Hours Convention. This proportion is clearly very small, and it certainly cannot be said that conditional ratifications have been abused.

There is still a third procedure used to overcome ratification difficulties due to the fear of competition; this consists in interpreting the provisions of the Conventions. Experience has shown that certain articles or paragraphs of some of the Conventions may have more than one interpretation, this being the result of imperfect drafting or, in some cases, of differences in the French and English texts, both of which, it may be recalled, are authentic.

When a State perceives that a provision of the Convention may be interpreted in two different ways, and that one meaning perhaps entails stricter obligations than the other, it naturally desires to ascertain how that provision will be interpreted by the other States, especially those whose competition it fears. It also has the legitimate desire to see a common interpretation adopted by all the States likely to ratify the Convention. How, then, may it satisfy these desires, and what are the means at its disposal?

Part XIII explicitly stipulates that all questions or difficulties connected with the interpretation of Conventions are to be submitted to the Permanent Court of International Justice. There can be no doubt that this procedure should be useful to Governments faced with difficulties of interpretation, but so far no use has been made of it. In every case the Governments have preferred to ask the International Labour Office for its advice. Now, the Treaties have conferred no special competence in this matter on the Office, which has, therefore, never been able to give an official interpretation. It has always pointed out in its replies to the Governments that the information or advice supplied by it is subject to that reservation. In most cases, however, it has been able, by basing its opinion on the preparatory work or discussions which have taken place at the Conference, either in committees or in plenary sittings, to supply the Governments with information calculated to throw light on the point in question. Such action by the Office has generally had good results and facilitated ratification.

As has already been pointed out, the difficulties arising from the necessity for adapting legislation and practice to the provisions of the Conventions or to the requirements of competition cannot be met by any one general solution. The International Labour Office has had to examine them one by one as they arose, and to endeavour in each case, in collaboration with the Government concerned, to find the appropriate solution. Through the goodwill of the Governments a number of these difficulties have been overcome. But, like the difficulties of procedure, they have certainly retarded the progress of ratifications. Moreover, a number of these difficulties still exist, and this must be borne in mind in studying the survey of results which follows.

II. Progress of Ratifications

Total Number of Ratifications

The diagram below shows the number of ratifications registered with the Secretariat of the League of Nations on October 1st of each year since October 1st, 1921—that is to say, two years after the First Session of the International Labour Conference at Washington.

The most noteworthy feature of this table is the regularity with which the ratifications have increased. Taking the good and bad years together, the average yearly increase has been roughly forty. This in itself is no mean achievement, especially when we recall the initial obstacles encountered, several of which will probably not recur in future decades.

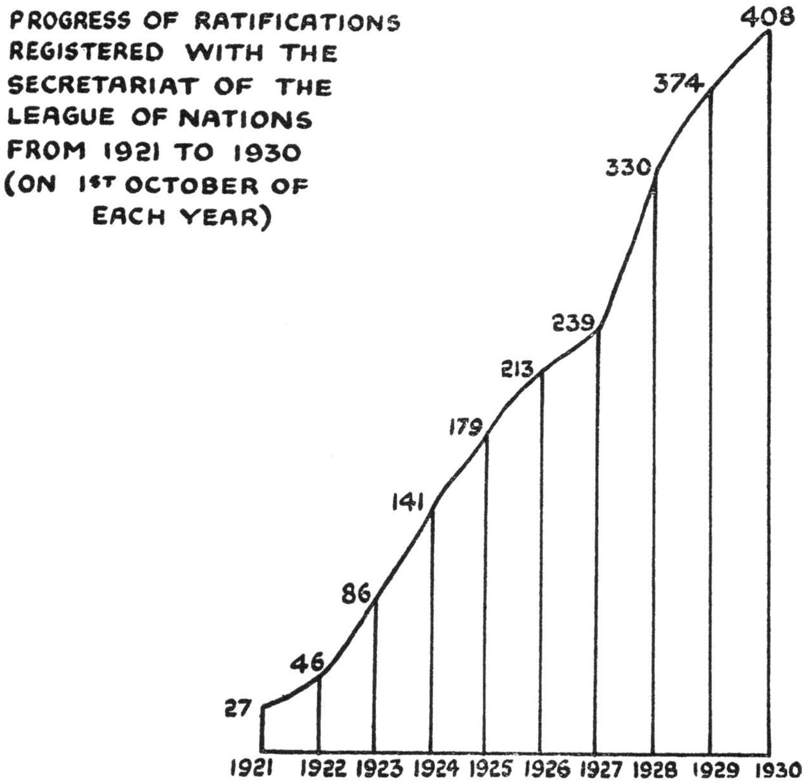

The total number of ratifications registered on October 1st, 1930, was 408, including eight conditional ratifications. This total has often been commented on, sometimes unfavourably. Comparisons have been made with the total number of possible ratifications—that is to say, with the figure that would have been attained had all the States Members of the Organisation ratified all the Conventions. If the number of Conventions adopted so far by the Conference (30) be multiplied by the number of States Members (55), a total of 1,650 possible ratifications is obtained. The 408 ratifications registered thus represent only 25 per cent., which is but a small proportion of the total number possible. But a moment's reflection will show that such a calculation is neither exact nor fair, because it disregards certain essential facts.

In the first place no account is taken of the age of the Conventions. Ratification procedure generally occupies several years, and the two Conventions voted by the Conference in June 1930 cannot fairly be included in any calculation of the results obtained, for the simple reason that the Governments have not had enough time since their adoption to examine them or make up their minds on the subject. For similar reasons the two Conventions adopted in 1929 must also be excluded.

Secondly, there is also the number of States Members to be considered, as several of these have not belonged to the Organisation since its foundation. Joining several years later they suddenly found themselves confronted with a large number of Conventions to which it was naturally more difficult for them to give effect than it was for those States which had had time to deal with them from the date of their adoption. It is true that this factor defies arithmetical expression, but there can be no doubt as to its influence.

Then there is a third factor, the relevance of which can perhaps be more accurately calculated. Certain Conventions undoubtedly have no chance of immediate ratification in a number of States. Take, for example, the seven maritime Conventions. It is unreasonable to expect their ratification by all the non-maritime States, or even by those States which have a seaboard, but little mercantile shipping.

Many Conventions fix a minimum standard of labour conditions intended for countries which have already reached or are on the way to reaching a high level of industrial development. It would be against all reason to expect their immediate ratification by States where industry is in its infancy—for instance, it is highly unlikely that in the near future a country like Ethiopia will ratify the Hours Convention or the Unemployment Convention.

Finally, some account must be taken of the constitutional

position of Federal States. When in one of these States the subject-matter of a Convention comes within the competence not of the Federal Government but of its constituent States, the Federal authority may find it impossible to give its ratification. In several Federal States, as for instance Australia and Canada, efforts have been made to deal with this difficulty, which so far has been a great obstacle to ratification.

The number 408 comprises only ratifications actually registered with the League of Nations. The procedure leading up to ratification includes, however, a number of stages each of which entails positive decisions by Governments or Parliaments, and as such may be considered as partial results. When a Government is empowered by Parliament to ratify a Convention the ratification can be considered as almost registered even although no international obligation has as yet been undertaken. On October 1st, 1930, the number of authorised ratifications was nineteen,[1] a figure that might well be added to the number of registered ratifications. Consideration might even be given to ratifications which Governments have recommended to Parliaments, and which, on the same date, amounted to 144. Although it is always difficult to say how Parliaments will vote, past experience has shown that the vast majority of the ratifications recommended become effective in a relatively short time.

When the above factors are taken into account it has to be recognised that it would be unfair to disparage the 408 registered ratifications by comparing them with the 1,650 possible ratifications. The Chairman of the Governing Body of the International Labour Office, Mr. Arthur Fontaine, considers, after a most minute evaluation of the various factors described above, that the results acquired amount not to 25 but to 62 per cent. of the total possible results.[2]

[1] The number of authorised ratifications is shown as twenty-eight in the table of ratifications published with *Industrial and Labour Information* of October 6th, 1930. This figure, however, includes nine ratifications considered as having been authorised by the Parliament of the Netherlands, but which we have thought it inadvisable to include. Under current procedure in the Netherlands the initial parliamentary decision which "reserves for the Crown the right to adhere to a Convention" is really only a method of postponing the examination of the Convention. It merely implies that Parliament has no objection to future ratification, and for this reason we have added these nine to the 135 ratifications recommended.

[2] Cf. Mr. Arthur Fontaine's article in *The International Labour Organisation*, 1919–1929, published by the International Labour Office, Geneva, 1930.

Ratifications obtained for each Convention

It is not without interest to note the distribution of the ratifications over the various branches of labour legislation.

In the following table the Conventions are arranged in accordance with the number of ratifications obtained during the period under review, the date of the adoption of the Convention being shown in each case.

Conventions	*Ratifications*
Equality of treatment as regards workmen's compensation for accidents (1925)	27
Unemployment (1919)	24
Minimum age for admission of young persons to employment as trimmers or stokers (1921)	23
Compulsory medical examination of children and young persons employed at sea (1921)	23
Minimum age for admission of children to employment at sea (1920)	22
Night work of children (1919)	21
Rights of association and combination of agricultural workers (1921)	21
Night work of women (1919)	19
White lead (1921)	19
Workmen's compensation for occupational diseases (1925)	19
Minimum age for admission of children to industrial employment (1919)	18
Weekly rest in industrial undertakings (1921)	18
Facilities for finding employment for seamen (1920)	17
Unemployment indemnity in case of loss or foundering of the ship (1920)	16
Hours of work in industrial undertakings (1919)	14
Workmen's compensation in agriculture (1921)	14
Minimum age for admission of children to employment in agriculture (1921)	12
Simplification of the inspection of emigrants on board ship (1926)	12
Maternity (1919)	11
Workmen's compensation for accidents (1925)	11
Seamen's articles of agreement (1926)	11
Repatriation of seamen (1926)	10
Sickness insurance for workers in industry and commerce (1927)	8

Conventions	*Ratifications*
Minimum wages (1928)	7
Night work in bakeries (1925)	5
Sickness insurance for agricultural workers (1927) . . .	4
Marking of the weight on heavy packages transported by vessels (1929)	1
Protection of workers engaged in loading and unloading vessels (1929)	1
Forced or compulsory labour (1930)	0
Hours of work of salaried employees (1930)	0

Thus, 22 Conventions have been ratified by at least 10 States, 14 have been ratified by at least 15 States and 7 by at least 20 States. The average is roughly 15 ratifications per Convention.

At first sight this figure may not appear very large. But if the result is compared with that obtained by other Conventions of the same character it will be found that the comparison is distinctly in favour of the International Labour Conventions.

Let us first compare it with the results obtained before the War by the so called Berne Labour Conventions. By 1912 the Berne Convention of 1906 prohibiting the use of white phosphorus in the match industry had been made effective in only six countries. By 1913 it had obtained thirteen ratifications, but for four of these the five years laid down for its introduction had not yet expired. Yet this was an extremely simple Convention which dealt with a clearly defined question of industrial hygiene in an industry of definitely secondary importance. On the other hand, Conventions voted by the International Labour Conference, of an infinitely more complex character and entailing much greater sacrifices, such as the Conventions concerning equality of treatment as regards workmen's compensation for accidents, the minimum age for admission of children to employment at sea, and night work of children, have obtained over twenty ratifications each.

Consider, again, the Conventions and agreements concluded under the aegis of the League of Nations. Some of these, drafted by technical conferences, have been ratified by States which, not being Members either of the League of Nations or the International Labour Organisation, are not entitled to ratify the International Labour Conventions; no account should therefore be taken of these ratifications in making a comparison. When this factor is taken into consideration it is found that the average number of ratifications of the League of Nations Conventions is for all practical purposes the same as for the International Labour Conventions. It is true that several of the Conventions of the League of Nations have been ratified by over thirty States, whereas the most widely ratified Labour Convention—that concerning equality of treatment as regards workmen's compensation for accidents—has received only twenty-seven signatures. This fact is, however, easily explained. In most cases the ratification of a Labour Convention necessitates the introduction of amendments in national legislation, and States frequently hesitate when faced with this obligation. In the case of many of the League of Nations Conventions, ratification does not entail anything more than administrative action. It may therefore be said that the rate of ratification is practically the same for all post-War Conventions—a fact that may be considered complimentary to the Labour Conventions when the material obligations which have to be undertaken by the ratifying States are remembered.

A final basis of comparison is offered by a great State which does not belong to the International Labour Organisation—the United States. There is in that country an institution called the National Federation of Commissioners on Uniform State Laws which, although not very well known, has a certain analogy with the International Labour Conference. It meets, for instance, once a year, is composed of representatives of the different Federal States, and is empowered to take steps to standardise their legislation by preparing model laws for their approval. Like the Conference, therefore, it has the right to propose the introduction of legislation in Parliament. Texts drafted by it are treated by the legislative authorities of the Federal States in the same way as private Bills which Members of Parliament are entitled to submit to the legislature in certain countries. The position in 1926 as regards a number of model laws put forward by this body may be gathered from the following facts: a Child Labour Bill, drafted in 1911, had been adopted by four States; a Workmen's Compensation Bill of 1914 by two States; while a Bill of 1920 on compensation for occupational diseases had not been adopted by a single State.[1] Thus in the United States during a period of fifteen years a model law on child labour

[1] *Handbook of the National Conference of Commissioners on Uniform State Laws and Proceedings of the 36th Annual Meeting, Denver, Colorado, July 6th–12th, 1926*, pp. 26–27.

was approved by only four States, whereas the Conventions of the International Labour Conference concerning night work of children and the minimum age for admission of children to industry obtained twenty-one and eighteen ratifications respectively in a period of ten years; a model law on workmen's compensation for accidents was adopted by two States in twelve years, whereas the International Labour Convention on the same matter was ratified by eleven countries in a period of five years; a model law on workmen's compensation for occupational diseases did not receive a single signature in six years, as against the nineteen ratifications obtained in five years for a similar Convention adopted by the International Labour Conference. And yet the standardisation of the legislation of the States belonging to one federation, however large the federation may be, should certainly meet with fewer obstacles than an attempt to standardise the legislation of countries politically independent of each other and separated by tariff barriers, as is the case with the States Members of the International Labour Organisation.

A classification of the Conventions according to the field covered shows that the largest average number of ratifications falls to the Conventions concerning child labour, for which the average is 20 ratifications; next in order come the maritime Conventions (including three Conventions concerning the employment of children and young persons at sea), with an average of 17 ratifications; then come the Conventions concerning female labour, with an average of 15 ratifications; the social insurance Conventions, with 14 ratifications, and the agricultural Conventions with an average of 13 ratifications. All the other Conventions, with the exception of those adopted in 1929 and 1930, for which there has not yet been sufficient time for ratification, have obtained an average of 14 ratifications.

It may thus be seen that it is the Conventions in which the humanitarian character is most obvious, namely, those for the protection of women and children, which head the list. At the same time it must be remembered that they are among the oldest of the Conventions and have had time on their side. If the Conventions are arranged according to age, then it will be found that the average number of ratifications obtained was as follows:

		Ratifications
Conventions adopted	1919–1921	18
,, ,,	1925	15
,, ,,	May 1926	12
,, ,,	October 1926	10
,, ,,	1927	6
,, ,,	1928	7

Ratifications registered by each State

The following table shows the number of Conventions ratified by each State on October 1st, 1930:

	Ratifications		Ratifications
Luxemburg	25	Spain	12
Bulgaria	23	Finland	12
Belgium	20	Rumania	12
Irish Free State	20	India	11
Yugoslavia	19	Netherlands	11
Estonia	18	Czechoslovakia	11
Latvia	17	Japan	9
Germany	16	Chile	8
Cuba	16	Denmark	8
France	16	Norway	8
Italy	16	Switzerland	6
Great Britain	15	Portugal	5
Poland	14	Canada	4
Greece	13	South Africa	3
Hungary	13	Australia	1
Sweden	13	China	1
Austria	12		

At the same date no Convention had been ratified by the following countries: Albania, the Argentine Republic, Bolivia, Brazil, Colombia, the Dominican Republic, Ethiopia, Guatemala, Haiti, Honduras, Liberia, Lithuania, Nicaragua, New Zealand, Panama, Portugal, Peru, Persia, Salvador, Siam, Uruguay and Venezuela.

The above table shows that three-fifths of the States Members have now ratified one or more Convention, and that sixteen States have ratified at least one-half of the Conventions adopted between 1919 and 1928.

The States which have ratified the largest number of Conventions are States of average rather than of chief industrial importance. This can perhaps be explained by the fact that, their social legislation being of recent date, they have been able to base it from the very outset on the Conventions, without having, as in the more advanced countries, to modify existing laws.

Of the 33 ratifying States 25 are in Europe, and 355 ratifications emanate from these States, as against 53 from non-European States. Only 2 European States—Albanian and Lithuania—have no ratification to their credit. Among the non-European States, on the other hand, 20 of the 28 States Members have not ratified a single Convention. This may possibly be explained by the fact that the majority of these States have not yet attained a sufficiently high standard of industrial development or that working conditions are entirely different from those obtaining in Europe. It should, however, be noted that some of the non-European Governments which have so far failed to ratify a single Convention have recommended several ratifications to the competent authorities, the number of recommended ratifications being 16 in the Argentine Republic, 6 in Brazil, 26 in Colombia, 6 in Paraguay and 28 in Uruguay.

When considering the conclusions which can be drawn from the foregoing study of the ratifications obtained during the first decade of the International Labour Organisation we may ask whether a true impression of the actual results can be conveyed by quoting columns of figures. Must not some account also be taken of the efforts made to overcome difficulties and opposition? Ratification is not merely a demonstration made under the influence of an international environment. The decision to ratify is sometimes taken, long after the adoption of the Convention, by persons who in most cases have not themselves taken part in the work of the Conference. It is in no way due to that "Geneva atmosphere" which it is sometimes alleged favours concessions alien to national interests. It is adopted in national surroundings, generally after long consideration and negotiations with the different interests concerned. Often ratification of a Convention shows that the Government and Parliament of a country have given the Convention in question precedence over numerous national questions. Each ratification is a symbol of difficulties overcome and opposition vanquished.

A figure, which merely expresses a material result, cannot

well convey an idea of such intangible elements. The figure 408 does indeed show the actual number of ratifications deposited in the archives of the League of Nations, but does it really and completely represent all the results obtained? In addition to material results, there are a certain number of moral results, mayhap of even greater importance, which no mere figures can express. There is surely some value in the revolution in international habits and customs which follows from the mere existence of a close network of agreements between States for the regulation of labour questions. Account must be taken of the desire for better things and the progress towards them which each individual ratification denotes.

The will to carry out social reforms by an international adjustment of labour problems which is expressed by each ratification is perhaps the most important result of all, for it is a guarantee of fresh progress in the future.

Finally, results are also reflected in the actual progress made in different countries as a direct or indirect consequence of the Conventions, and no appreciation of the work of the International Labour Organisation is or can be complete which does not take this progress into account.

CHAPTER II

THE EFFECTIVE RESULTS OF THE CONVENTIONS

IN the preceding chapter an account has been given of the actual ratification figures. A moment's reflection will show that those figures cannot be accepted as an adequate expression of the material or effective results secured by and through the Conventions. Several of the Conventions have been widely ratified simply because their ratification involves little or no change in the national law and practice; others have secured comparatively few ratifications because they set a standard which is in advance of that obtaining in most or all of the States Members at the time of their adoption by the Conference, but yet, simply by setting such a standard, are instrumental in bringing about an almost universal advance. Not all the widely ratified Conventions set a low standard, nor do all the poorly ratified Conventions set a high one, but experience will probably, in the long run, show that the real effectiveness of the respective Conventions is on the whole inversely rather than directly proportionate to the rapidity with which they are ratified by the States Members.

After showing the ratification figures it is essential to demonstrate the effective results of the Conventions, but the reader must not expect a complete and concrete record. It would indeed be virtually impossible to express in statistics—number of workers affected, value of benefits secured, number of hours added to the workers' leisure and so forth—the concrete results of international labour legislation. Figures for the various countries are for the most part lacking; and even if they could be obtained no adequate basis for co-ordinating them internationally would be available.

The most that can be done is to attempt to estimate the effects of the Conventions on national legislation. But even here too much must not be expected. It is easy enough to take each Convention separately and to enumerate the various modifications undergone by the laws of the various countries in the direction of the Convention's provisions subsequently to its adoption by the Conference. But the argument of *post hoc, ergo propter hoc* is logically worthless. On the other hand, in order to decide whether, and if so to what extent, the Convention could reasonably be said to have influenced the decisions of the national legislatures in each case, it would be necessary to conduct minute researches into the Press and the parliamentary documents of anything up to fifty or sixty different States, a long and complicated piece of work which the International Labour Office has been unable to undertake. It should therefore be realised that the study of the effective results of the Conventions contained in the following pages has a strictly limited aim—to give a very general outline of the results achieved in terms of national legislation, illustrated by a few relatively striking instances, and to draw a few conclusions from the picture thus presented.

The Conventions may be roughly grouped according to the extent of their effective results down to the time of writing in the following manner (the number of ratifications up to October 1st, 1930, being shown in brackets in each case):

1. *Conventions widely ratified and involving serious legislative progress.* (*a*) the 1920 and 1921 Maritime Conventions: trimmers and stokers (23); compulsory medical examination (23); minimum age (22); employment for seamen (17); unemployment indemnity (16); (*b*) the 1919 Conventions for the protection of women, young persons and children: night work, young persons (21); night work, women (19); minimum age, industry (18); (*c*) the industrial hygiene Conventions: white lead (19); workmen's compensation for industrial diseases (19).

2. *Conventions sparsely ratified, but having inspired considerable legislative progress:* hours (9 unconditional, 5 conditional); maternity (11); night work in bakeries (5).

3. *Conventions widely ratified, but involving relatively slight legislative progress:* Draft Convention concerning equality of treatment for national and foreign workers as regards workmen's compensation for industrial accidents (27); unemployment (24); right of association of agricultural workers (21); weekly rest (18).

4. *Conventions poorly ratified and having inspired relatively slight legislative progress:* minimum age, agriculture (12); workmen's compensation, agriculture (12); workmen's compensation, accidents (11).

In the above summary no account has been taken of the

Conventions adopted by the Conference since 1925, on the ground that it is still too early to attempt to classify them even provisionally.

Such a classification is open to many objections. The lines of demarcation between the various groups are undoubtedly somewhat arbitrary, and the whole classification is valid only for a particular stage or date, seeing that, for instance, the situation as regards the Hours Convention may entirely change in the near future. Nevertheless, such as it is, it enables us to group the Conventions in a certain logical order, and provides a framework for our enquiry.

I. Conventions Widely Ratified and Involving Serious Legislative Progress

The 1920 and 1921 Maritime Conventions

The results achieved by the 1920 and 1921 Maritime Conventions are a legitimate ground for satisfaction. Each of them embodies a definite and necessary reform; and each of them has been both ratified and applied by a large number of maritime countries.

Judged by their intent these five Conventions may be said to fall into two distinct groups: three Conventions each embodying a relatively modern reform for the protection of young persons employed at sea, and ratified respectively by 23, 23 and 22 States; and two Conventions embodying more considerable reforms (from the point of view at least of the legislative or administrative effort involved) and ratified respectively by 17 and 16 countries.

The 23 countries which have ratified the *Convention fixing the minimum age for the admission of young persons to employment as trimmers or stokers* are Belgium, Bulgaria, Canada, Cuba, Denmark, Estonia, Finland, France, Germany, Great Britain, Greece, Hungary, India, the Irish Free State, Italy, Latvia, Luxemburg, Norway, Poland, Rumania, Spain, Sweden, and Yugoslavia. With the exception of France and Yugoslavia, fresh legislation had to be introduced in every maritime country in this list for the purpose of enforcing the prohibition prescribed by the Convention. Further, the Convention has been approved by the Netherlands Parliament, and legislation for the purpose of giving full effect to its provisions is in preparation. Japanese legislation has already been brought into harmony with the Convention, and ratification is foreshadowed.

The *Convention concerning the compulsory medical examination of children and young persons employed at sea* has been ratified by the same twenty-three countries, except that Japan and the Netherlands take the place of Denmark and Norway. In this case also ratification has involved fresh legislation in every maritime country except France and Yugoslavia.

In Denmark the Seamen's Act of May 1st, 1923, empowers the Minister of Commerce to issue regulations ordering the medical examination of ships' crews, so that no fresh legislation is now required in order to permit ratification.

Each of these two Conventions may thus be considered as having effected the quasi-universal adoption and enforcement among the maritime States Members of the Organisation of a new and humane standard on the subject with which it deals.

In submitting its preliminary (blue) report to the Genoa Conference in 1920 on the employment of children at sea, the International Labour Office pointed out that "the most important maritime Powers have already adopted, under one form or another, provisions which seem to indicate that a Convention fixing at fourteen the age of admission of children to the sea-service will not encounter very numerous difficulties. It would be sufficient, generally speaking, to make comparatively slight modifications in existing legislation in order to establish the international rule." In fact, the provisions inserted in the *Convention fixing the minimum age for admission of children to employment at sea* were probably to a large extent already observed in a considerable number of countries. Such observance was, however, more generally based on custom or on the operation of school attendance laws than on legislation specifically adopted for the purpose, and was, therefore, of a somewhat precarious nature. The twenty-two countries which have ratified the Convention are : Belgium, Bulgaria, Canada, Cuba, Denmark, Estonia, Finland, Germany, Great Britain, Greece, Hungary, the Irish Free State, Japan, Latvia, Luxemburg, the Netherlands, Norway, Poland, Rumania, Spain, Sweden and Yugoslavia. In order to make ratification completely effective, fresh legislation was passed in Belgium, Canada, Denmark, Estonia, Finland, Germany, Great Britain (then including the Irish Free State), Greece, Japan, Latvia, the Netherlands, Norway, Rumania, Spain, Sweden and

Yugoslavia—seventeen countries, including most of the more important maritime States. It may further be noted that in Italy the Legislative Decree of May 19th, 1924, has raised the minimum age for the admission of children to employment at sea from ten to fourteen years. Ratification of the Convention by Italy may therefore be confidently expected at an early date.

The *Convention concerning unemployment indemnity in the case of loss or foundering of the ship*, under the terms of which a seaman is entitled, in case of unemployment due to the loss or foundering of his ship, to an indemnity at the rate of his agreed wages for the duration of his unemployment (up to a maximum period of two months), represents a considerable advance on the legislation of any State Member at the time that the Convention was adopted at Genoa in 1920, when in most, if not all, countries a seaman lost all further claim to wages in case of shipwreck. The fact that the Convention has now been ratified by sixteen countries (Belgium, Bulgaria, Canada, Cuba, Estonia, France, Germany, Great Britain, Greece, the Irish Free State, Italy, Latvia, Luxemburg, Poland, Spain and Yugoslavia) and that fresh legislation on the lines of the Convention has been adopted in all the maritime countries which have ratified it, shows what progress has been made through the Convention.

The results of the Convention in the four northern countries, which have not yet ratified it, deserve special note. Conditions of work at sea are determined by more or less identical Acts adopted in Denmark in 1923, in Finland in 1924, in Norway in 1923, and in Sweden in 1923, after mutual consultation. Each of these Acts contains a clause covering a national seaman's rights in case of shipwreck. The provisions in question may be summarised as follows:

> *Denmark:* in case of shipwreck abroad, free passage with maintenance to the seaman's domicile in Denmark, with wages during the voyage home up to a maximum limit of two months' wages for a mate or engineer, or one month's wages for a member of the ordinary crew.
>
> *Finland:* in case of shipwreck in Finnish territorial waters, wages for the period of the agreement up to a maximum of a fortnight; in case of shipwreck abroad, free passage with maintenance to the seaman's domicile in Finland, with wages during the voyage home.

Norway: as for Denmark, but with a uniform maximum limit of two months' wages for all seamen.

Sweden: as for Denmark and Norway, but with no maximum limit as to wages during the voyage home.

The extension of these provisions to cover foreign seamen, subject to reciprocity, is also prescribed in each Act.

There would appear to be no doubt as to the part played by the Convention in securing the adoption of the above provisions. It is interesting to note that in Norway the Judicial Committee reporting on the new Seamen's Bill in 1922 recommended that the provisions of section 91 of the existing Maritime Code (under which a seaman's claims in respect of wages and maintenance ceased immediately in case of shipwreck) should be maintained until it had been seen whether other maritime States would ratify the Draft Convention. Notwithstanding this recommendation, the clause summarised above was inserted in the Act as finally passed. The introductory memorandum to the Finnish Bill states that the competent Committee had not found it expedient to incorporate in the Bill the full provisions of the Convention, but that "they recognised the inadequacy of the existing law, under which seamen receive wages for a period corresponding to the ordinary period of notice for the cancellation of contracts, provided that it may not exceed fourteen days in the case of shipwreck on the high seas." The Committee therefore proposed that provisions similar to those of the Swedish Act should be inserted in the Bill.

Further, in the Netherlands the Government has recommended the ratification of the Convention, and the necessary legislation for the amendment of the Code is in preparation.

It would, in short, be difficult to find a clearer case of the effects of an International Convention in improving working conditions already regulated by national legislation.

The object of the *Convention for establishing facilities for finding employment for seamen* is to abolish the carrying on of the business of placing seamen in employment for pecuniary gain, and to substitute public employment agencies under joint supervision. The importance of this reform needs no emphasis.

The seventeen countries which have ratified the Convention are the following: Australia, Belgium, Bulgaria, Cuba, Estonia, Finland, France, Germany, Greece, Italy, Japan, Latvia, Luxemburg, Norway, Poland, Sweden and Yugoslavia. The direct effects of the Convention are easily traceable in most of these countries. Thus, in Belgium, while the practice was already largely in conformity with the Convention, ratification has involved the insertion of several sections in the Act of June 5th, 1928, concerning seamen's articles of agreement, with a view to giving full legal sanction to the Convention's provisions, and also the institution, under a Royal Order of January 20th, 1926, of a system of joint supervision of employment-finding for seamen. In Bulgaria special clauses were inserted in the Act of April 12th, 1925, relating to employment and unemployment insurance, with a view to giving effect to the Convention. The Act abolishes the business of finding employment for profit, and contains special provisions concerning the finding of employment for seamen. In Estonia provisions in accordance with the Convention have been inserted in the Seamen's Institute Act of January 31st, 1928, and the Seamen's Act of March 22nd, 1928. In Finland, ratification has been followed by measures for the extension of the system of public employment offices for seamen and by the institution of a system of joint supervision. In France, the charging of fees for finding employment for seamen has been prohibited by the Act of December 13th, 1926, while employment exchanges for seamen under joint supervision are organised by a Decree of January 29th, 1928. In Germany, the charging of fees for the finding of employment has been prohibited as from the beginning of 1931 by the Act of July 16th, 1927, while the Act of July 22nd, 1922, lays down that "the institution of seamen's employment exchanges shall be regulated in accordance with the Convention concluded at Genoa." In Greece, the provisions of the Convention have been incorporated as they stand in national law. In Italy, the charging of fees has been prohibited by the Decree of May 26th, 1925, which regulates the finding of employment for seamen on a public basis, with joint advisory committees. In Japan, a special Act has been passed and Orders have been issued with the object of giving effect to the Convention. In Latvia, the finding of employment for pecuniary gain has been prohibited, and a system of public employment exchanges has been set up by the Order of February 3rd, 1927, concerning the placing of seamen in employment. In Norway, private employment agencies have been abolished by an Act of June 14th, 1929. In Sweden, the Government states that "as a result of various circumstances, including the adoption of the present Convention, the Swedish Government endeavoured in 1922 with considerable success to transfer the business of finding employment from private agencies to the public employment exchanges."

In the Netherlands, ratification has been approved by Parliament, and legislation for giving effect to the Convention's provisions is in preparation.

It is of interest to note that in 1924 steps were taken by the Japanese Seamen's Union to set in motion in connection with this Convention the procedure laid down in Article 409 of the Treaty of Versailles for the lodging of a complaint with the Governing Body of the International Labour Office concerning the application of a Convention by a particular Government. The Union complained that, notwithstanding Japan's ratification of the Convention, the activities of the private fee-charging agencies (or crimps) were continuing on a considerable scale. As the Government explicitly allows the temporary maintenance of such agencies, and lays down no precise time limit within which they must be abolished, the Governing Body was obliged to conclude that no case had been made out for carrying the matter further. Nevertheless, it is noteworthy that since 1924 rapid progress has been made in Japan. In 1926 a Joint Maritime Committee (constituted by representatives of the shipowners and seamen) was set up, and this body has since been maintaining free agencies in the principal Japanese ports. At the end of 1928 there were only twenty-eight persons still holding permits to carry on fee-charging agencies for seamen.

The 1919 Conventions for the Protection of Women, Young Persons and Children

This group of Conventions (with the exception of the Maternity Convention discussed below) is closely comparable with the Maritime Conventions. Each embodies a relatively modest but definite measure of social protection, and each has led to modifications in the national law of a considerable number of countries.

The *Convention fixing the age limit for night work at eighteen* has now been ratified by the following twenty-one countries : Austria, Belgium, Bulgaria, Chile, Cuba, Denmark, Estonia, France, Great Britain, Greece, Hungary, India, the Irish Free State, Italy, Latvia, Luxemburg, the Netherlands, Poland, Rumania, Switzerland and

Yugoslavia. Even before the adoption of the Convention, an eighteen-year limit was already in force in Austria, Bulgaria, Denmark, France, Great Britain, Norway, Sweden and Switzerland. Among these countries those which subsequently ratified the Convention have, however, had to extend the scope of their legislation in one direction or another, particularly as regards the industries covered. In the other countries the legislative progress has, *a fortiori*, been in most cases still more considerable. The Irish Free State has ratified on the basis of the same legislation as Great Britain. For India the Convention makes special provision, the term "industrial undertaking" being defined as including only "factories" as defined in the Indian Factory Act, and the age limit for male workers being reduced to fourteen years.

In a number of other States which have not yet ratified the Convention, substantial progress has also been made during the last ten years. In the Argentine Republic, the Act of September 3rd, 1924, prohibits night work for young persons under eighteen. In Western Australia, the Factories and Shops Act, 1920, raises the age limit for night work from fourteen to sixteen years. In Bolivia a Decree issued on October 2nd, 1929, prohibits night work for young persons under sixteen. In Brazil, the Minors' Code of 1926–1927 fixes eighteen years as the minimum age for night work. In several Canadian Provinces, the law on the subject has been made stricter. In China, regulations issued by the Pekin Government on October 21st, 1927, prohibit night work for children, and other Chinese Governments have taken similar measures. In Colombia, an Act of November 29th, 1924, prohibits the employment in collieries at night of children under fourteen years old. In Ecuador, an Act of October 6th, 1928, prohibits night work for children under sixteen. In Finland, an Act passed in July 1929 prohibits night work for young persons under eighteen. In Guatemala, the Labour Act of April 30th, 1926, contains a similar prohibition. In Japan, the night work of young persons under sixteen is now prohibited by the 1923 Factory Act, as amended on March 27th, 1929. In Portugal, the Decree of October 29th, 1927, prohibits night work for young persons under eighteen, as does the Venezuelan Labour Act of July 23th, 1928.

Finally, it may be noted that legislation is in preparation in Czechoslovakia and Germany on the lines of the Convention, while in Panama a Draft Labour Code submitted to the National

Assembly in 1926 prohibits night work for young persons under eighteen.

Thus it may justly be claimed that in the course of ten years the Convention has come very near to establishing an effective and quasi-universal rule against the night work of young persons.

The *Convention concerning the minimum age for admission of children to employment in industry* fixes fourteen years as an age limit. This standard had already been attained in nine[1] States Members when the Convention was adopted by the Conference, while in two other countries Bills were already before the legislatures for raising the age to fourteen. The Convention may therefore justly be regarded as a particularly moderate reform, and the number of States by which it has so far been ratified—eighteen, including eight of the nine States referred to above, where legislation was already in harmony with the Convention—may be thought unduly low. It should, however, be borne in mind that the full application of the Convention would in many cases imply the raising of the school-leaving age—a reform which requires careful preparation. This fact has so far hindered a certain number of States from ratifying. Further, it is a significant fact that the number of States Members whose laws prescribe a minimum age of less than fourteen years for the employment of children in factories and mines is now extremely small—perhaps half-a-dozen—and that in nearly all countries the raising of the minimum age to the Convention standard is the subject of proposed legislation. It can hardly be doubted that the Convention is largely responsible for this gratifying progress.

The countries which already had a fourteen-year standard before the Washington Conference, and which have subsequently ratified the Washington Convention, are Belgium, Bulgaria, Czechoslovakia, Denmark, Great Britain, Greece, Switzerland and Yugoslavia. In each of these countries some extension of the previously existing national law was necessary—particularly in regard to its scope—in order to permit ratification. The Irish Free State, which has become an individual State Member since 1923, has, as in the case of the Night Work Convention, ratified on the basis of the same legislation as Great Britain. In the remaining countries which have ratified (Chile, Cuba, Estonia, Japan, Latvia, Luxemburg, the Netherlands, Poland and Rumania) a raising of standards has, *a fortiori*, taken place since 1919.

[1] Ten, if the Irish Free State be included.

In certain other countries which have not yet ratified the Convention, progress along the lines of the Convention's provisions is known to have been made. Thus, in Argentina, the age for admission to industrial work was twelve years until 1924, and a lower limit was allowed in the case of children whose work was necessary for the support of their families. In 1924 an Act was passed raising the age to fourteen, and permitting no exceptions in the case of industrial employment. In Brazil, at the time of the Washington Convention, there was no regulation except in the province of São Paulo, where a general limit of twelve years was in force. The Minors' Code of 1927, which applies throughout the Republic, forbids the employment of children under fourteen in industry unless they have been granted a certificate of primary education, in which case the age limit is reduced to twelve. In India, again, the age limit for factories was nine, while there was no absolute limit for mines. In 1922 the age limit for factories was raised to twelve, and in 1923 the employment of any child under thirteen in a mine—above or below ground—was prohibited.

The *Convention concerning employment of women during the night* is substantially identical with the Berne Convention of 1906, except that the exemption of undertakings employing ten or less workers is omitted. The Berne Convention has been ratified by Austria, Belgium, the British Empire (including New Zealand and a number of colonial territories), France (including Algeria and Tunis), Germany, Italy, the Netherlands, Portugal, Spain, Sweden and Switzerland. The Convention adopted by the International Labour Organisation has now been ratified by the following nineteen States: Austria, Belgium, Bulgaria, Cuba, Czechoslovakia, Estonia, France, Great Britain, Greece, Hungary, India, the Irish Free State, Italy, Luxemburg, the Netherlands, Rumania, South Africa, Switzerland and Yugoslavia. This list, it will be noted, includes eleven countries which had not previously adhered to the Berne Convention. Fresh legislation has been necessary in order to permit ratification in the following countries: Belgium, Estonia, France, Great Britain (including the Irish Free State), Greece, Hungary, Italy, the Netherlands, Rumania, Switzerland and Yugoslavia.

It is further to be noted that since 1919 legislation prohibiting the night work of women, either generally or in certain undertakings, has been passed in the following States: Argentina,

Australia (South Australia, New South Wales, Western Australia and Queensland), Bolivia, Canada (British Columbia, Manitoba, Saskatchewan), China, Ecuador, Japan, Poland, Portugal, Salvador, Spain and Venezuela.

The case of Japan is of particular interest. This country has not ratified either the Berne or the Washington Conventions; but in 1911 a Factory Act was enacted, one clause of which prescribed that "no women . . . shall be employed between the hours of 10 p.m. and 4 a.m. in a factory." The preamble to the Bill contained the following reference to the Berne Convention: "At the International Conferences for the protection of labour (Berne, 1901, 1905, 1906) it was agreed to regulate the night work of women and children by means of an agreement which has been signed by nearly every European Power. Quite apart from the question as to whether Japan is to sign this agreement hereafter or not, it cannot be denied that sooner or later the restriction or prohibition of night work will be necessary." The application of the night work clause in the Act was delayed for eighteen years, and the clause finally came into force only on July 1st, 1929. The occasion was regarded throughout Japan as one of great significance, and was celebrated in various ways. The Acting-Chief of the Labour Division of the Bureau of Social Affairs broadcast a message emphasising the importance of the prohibition of night work; the Chairman of the Board of Directors of the Japanese Cotton Spinners' Association published a declaration welcoming the reform; and handbills were distributed and a public meeting organised in Tokyo by the Commission on Women's Labour Problems of the Japanese Association for the International Labour Organisation. The Industrial Association of the Okayama Prefecture decided to celebrate July 1st in future years as "Health Day," and this example has been followed in a number of other Prefectures. There is abundant reason for believing that the adoption of the Washington Convention in 1919 hastened the effective application of the prohibition of night work in Japan.

The Industrial Hygiene Conventions

The effective results of the *Convention concerning the use of white lead in painting* fall very far short, as regards completeness, of those obtained by the other Conventions so far considered. In a considerable number of countries which have ratified it the legislative progress involved has been relatively slight, or the use of lead paints is in any case so small as not to constitute a problem of first-class importance. The Convention has, however, been ratified by the following nineteen countries: Australia, Belgium, Bulgaria, Chile, Cuba, Czechoslovakia, Estonia, Finland, France, Greece, Hungary (conditionally upon ratification by certain other countries), Latvia, Luxemburg, Norway, Poland, Rumania, Spain, Sweden and Yugoslavia. Fresh legislation or regulations have been, or will be, necessary in all of these countries except Greece and Yugoslavia. Prior to the adoption of measures for the purpose of ratifying the Convention the use of lead paints was, so far as is known, entirely unregulated in Bulgaria, Chile, Estonia, Finland, Latvia, Luxemburg, Norway, Rumania, Spain and Sweden.

In Belgium, ratification of the Convention has involved introducing for the first time the prohibition of the use of lead paints in interior painting and of the employment of women and young persons in painting-work involving the use of such paints. In France, ratification has involved the extension of the measures previously in force to cover paints with a basis of sulphate of lead and has entailed the publication of a Decree prohibiting the employment of women and young persons in industrial-painting work in which lead paints are used.

In certain other countries, which have not yet ratified it, the Convention has also led directly to important progress. Thus, in Great Britain, after prolonged controversy centring round the Convention, the Lead Paint (Protection against Poisoning) Act, 1926, was passed. This Act, and the Orders issued under it, give substantial effect to the provisions of the Convention, except that the use of lead paints for interior painting is regulated, not prohibited. In Switzerland, again, the question of white lead is (mainly, it would appear, in connection with the Convention) still under discussion, and a general report is to be submitted to the Federal Parliament before the end of 1931. Meanwhile, it has been decided to make all painting establishments compulsorily insurable against accidents so as to bring them directly under the supervision of the Swiss National Insurance Fund.

It is not difficult to account for the relative ease and rapidity with which the Conventions in the above three groups have borne fruit in national legislation. The shipping industry is by its very nature international, and from the beginnings of history conditions in the industry have been regulated by codes of an international character. As regards the other two groups, the questions involved are of the same nature (white phosphorus, night work of women and young persons) as those discussed in pre-War days by the Berne Conferences.

The conscience of most civilised communities had been struck by the dangers arising from international competition which, in the interests of cheap production, exploited the defenceless and undermined the health of the workers. In this direction the path to further social conquest had been opened up before the War. The International Labour Organisation enthusiastically seized the opportunity with the means at its disposal, and positive results have not been long delayed.

II. Conventions Sparsely Ratified, but Having Inspired Considerable Legislative Progress

Washington Hours Convention

The assertion that the Washington Hours Convention has exercised a positive influence will hardly be contested by anyone who has followed the evolution of the question of hours of work in the various countries since 1919. At the same time it is not easy to assess the exact extent of that influence. After the end of the War a world-wide movement in the direction of the eight-hour day began. One of the first steps of the provisional or revolutionary Governments in most of the newly established countries was to introduce, by law or decree, the eight-hour day and forty-eight-hour week. At Versailles, the High Contracting Parties incorporated in the Treaty of Peace a clause to the effect that among the most urgent and important methods and principles for regulating labour conditions which all industrial communities should endeavour to apply was "the adoption of an eight-hour day or a forty-eight-hour week as the standard to be aimed at where it had not already been attained." They also decided to place on the agenda of the Washington Conference the "application of the principles of the eight-hour day or of the forty-eight-hour week." The Hours Convention thus consolidated, in the form of a solemn international agreement containing a number of detailed provisions applicable to industrial undertakings, a principle which had already won general approval and which was already inspiring a powerful world-wide movement.

Since 1919 this movement has so spread that in the great majority of States Members of the International Labour Organisation the bulk of the industrial workers enjoy, in virtue either of legislation or of collective agreements, a maximum working week not exceeding forty-eight hours. Moreover, the advance has, in all but a few cases, been maintained; there have been few instances of serious regression in respect of hours.

We have only to look back through the past decade with its periodical Press campaigns around the question of the eight-hour day, or to peruse the records of parliamentary debates where the same problem was discussed as much in countries which have not ratified the Washington Convention as in those which have, in order to comprehend the important part played by the provisions of the Convention in all these controversies, and the extreme care taken, even by Governments which repudiated all possibility of immediate ratification, to avoid any unnecessary departure from the Convention and, in some cases, to give a transitional character to exemptions deemed necessary at the moment. Would, it may be asked, the position of those who through the vicissitudes of the last ten years have striven for the maintenance or the extension of the eight-hour day have been so strong had they been unable to rally round a common and definite plan or to make use of the means put at their disposal by the moral undertaking embodied in the Washington Conference decisions?

The Convention has been ratified unconditionally by nine countries: Belgium, Bulgaria, Chile, Czechoslovakia, Greece, India, Luxemburg, Portugal and Rumania. In Bulgaria, Czechoslovakia, Luxemburg and Portugal, ratification took place on the basis of legislation enacted before the Washington Conference, though in Czechoslovakia the Convention strengthens the previously existing legislation by requiring payment for overtime at the rate of not less than time-and-a-quarter (the national law simply specifies that overtime shall be "specially remunerated").

In most of the remaining countries which have ratified the Convention unconditionally, not only was the legislation, in virtue of which the Convention's provisions are applied, introduced for the specific purpose of permitting ratification, but it was also the first legislation to be enacted limiting the hours of work of adult workers. This is true of Belgium, Chile, Greece and Rumania. In India, the maximum working hours previously allowed under the Indian Factories Act, 1911, were eleven hours per day for all women workers, and twelve hours for male workers in textile factories. Ratification of the Convention has involved legislation introducing a maximum sixty-hour week in factories, mines and certain classes of railway work.

The direct influence of the Convention (or—what amounts to the same thing—of the approval in Part XIII of the Peace Treaty of the eight-hour day or forty-eight-hour week) can be traced in a number of other countries.

In France, hours of work are regulated by the Act of April 23rd, 1919. When this Act was first submitted to the French Parliament it was accompanied by an explanatory statement pointing out that the object of the projected legislation was to incorporate the principles laid down by the Commission on International Labour Legislation of the Peace Conference. The Act is on substantially the same lines as the Convention. In a report submitted to the Senate on March 27th, 1926, on behalf of the Finance Committee, Mr. L. Pasquet, Senator, gave the following information on the application of the Act: "During the seven years that it has been in force, the Act has been applied to about five million workers in industry and commerce who could be covered by the Act, not including the mining industry and employment at sea, which are dealt with by special Acts. Forty-five public administrative regulations have been issued,[1] bringing most industries and very many branches of commerce under the operation of the Act." The Convention was ratified by France on June 2nd 1927, ratification to take effect as soon as the Convention is ratified by Germany and Great Britain. Such legislative changes as are necessary to bring the Act entirely into harmony with the Convention (particularly in regard to the statutory payment for overtime) are to be introduced as soon as the conditions for making ratification effective are realised.

In Italy, the Royal Decree of March 15th, 1923, introduced the legal eight-hour day and forty-eight-hour week. In the following year the Convention was ratified conditionally upon

[1] The number is now very much larger.

ratification by Belgium, France, Germany, Great Britain and Switzerland. On March 7th, 1930, the Minister of Corporations, Mr. Bottai, laid before the Senate a Bill concerning hours of work in industrial undertakings, the object of which is to secure full application of the provisions of the Convention and permit the Government to abandon the conditions previously attached to its ratification.

In the case of Japan, Article 9 of the Convention provides specially for a fifty-seven-hour weekly limit (sixty hours in the raw silk industry) for adults working above ground, and a maximum forty-eight-hour week for underground workers. The Government has declared its inability to recommend ratification of the Convention owing to the post-War business depression followed by the earthquake. Nevertheless, the Factories Act of March 29th, 1923, reduced the maximum hours of work for women and young persons under sixteen years of age from twelve to eleven per day, including a break of at least one hour (subject to certain exceptions). Figures published by the Statistical Bureau of the Cabinet show that, in the factories covered by the Factories Act, hours of work are generally within the limits laid down by the Convention. Further, regulations for mines issued in September 1928, which came into force at the beginning of 1930, limit the hours of work of adult male underground workers to ten per day, no limit having been previously imposed in the case of such workers.

In the Argentine Republic, an eight-hour-day Bill (in general harmony with the Convention, and going further than the Convention in some respects) was adopted by the Chamber of Deputies on September 19th, 1928, and by the Senate on August 29th, 1929. On the latter occasion Mr. Serrey, Chairman of the Committee responsible for presenting the Bill, observed that "the Washington Conference, at which the Argentine Republic was represented, was called on to determine the methods of regulating hours of work in industry. As the Committee of the Chamber of Deputies has approved the Convention adopted at that Conference, it is hoped that ratification will follow." The Act came into force on March 12th, 1930.

On the North American continent also the Convention has produced satisfactory effects. In the Canadian province of British Columbia the Hours of Work Act, 1923 (which came into force on January 1st, 1925), embodies the provisions of the Convention and to a large extent reproduces them textually. In the neighbouring province of Alberta the Factories Act, 1926, prescribes maximum working hours (nine per day and fifty-four per week) and also provides for the appointment of a commission "to consider the questions involved in the establishment of a forty-eight-hour working week."

In addition to the above cases, where the direct influence of the Convention is particularly plain, an eight-hour day and/or a forty-eight-hour week has been introduced by law since the Washington Conference in the following countries: Bolivia (for salaried employees in industry and commerce), Guatemala, Honduras (under the Political Constitution of September 10th, 1924), Latvia (which on August 15th, 1925, ratified the Convention conditionally upon ratification by three of the States of chief industrial importance within the meaning of Article 393 of the Treaty of Versailles), Lithuania, the Netherlands, Poland, Sweden and Yugoslavia.

Further, any estimate of the influence of the Convention would be incomplete without a mention of the part that it has played in certain countries where no legislation has as yet been passed for the purpose of bringing its provisions into force. In Germany, where the eight-hour day was introduced by the Order of November 23rd, 1918, the critical economic situation in 1923 induced the Government to issue a fresh Order allowing substantial exceptions. Since that time the supporters of the eight-hour day have made the Washington Convention the corner-stone of their policy. In 1927 they succeeded in securing the passing of an Emergency Act for the purpose of reducing the extent of the exceptions allowed under the 1923 Order. They have also succeeded in having inserted in the Labour Protection Bill now before the Reichstag clauses which, in the opinion of successive Governments, will permit the ratification of the Convention.

In Great Britain, also, the Convention has stood in the foreground of political life ever since its adoption. The last Government (Conservative) was prepared to recommend ratification if the Convention could be revised in such a way as explicitly to permit certain British practices and to dissipate certain ambiguities. The present Government (Labour) is prepared to recommend ratification without such revision, and has introduced a Bill for the purpose of permitting ratification to take place.

In the meanwhile it would probably be no exaggeration to say that, despite the difficult economic circumstances of the last few years, almost every attempt to prolong working hours beyond the limits permitted by the Convention has been held in check by the general desire to leave the way open for ratification.

Finally, in Switzerland, where the Factory Act was amended in 1919 so as to reduce the maximum working week in factories to forty-eight hours, Parliament decided in 1922 once more to amend the Act so as to increase the maximum to fifty-four. The amending Act was, however, opposed by the trade unions, and on being submitted to a referendum was rejected. The Convention was undoubtedly instrumental in bringing about this result.

Thus, both by stimulating progress and by stiffening resistance to regression the Hours Convention has already exercised a most powerful influence in a great number of countries, despite the fact that the hesitation of the chief industrial Powers of Europe to ratify it effectively has prevented it from yielding its full results. Whether the situation in this respect will be modified in the immediate future depends on the fate of the Bills at present before the German Reichstag and the British Parliament.

The Maternity Convention

This Convention has been ratified by a relatively small number of countries (eleven). When it is borne in mind that the provisions of the Convention go considerably beyond the protection afforded to women workers before and after childbirth in any of the States Members before 1919, the paucity of the ratifications cannot be considered surprising. On the other hand, few Conventions have resulted in a greater or more general raising of national standards, as expressed in legislation.

The Convention, it may be recalled, provides that any woman employed in an industrial or commercial undertaking (*a*) shall not be permitted to work during the six weeks following her confinement, (*b*) shall have the right to leave her work if she produces a medical certificate stating that her confinement will probably take place within six weeks, (*c*) shall be entitled to maintenance and medical benefit, provided out of public funds or by means of a system of insurance, during the twelve weeks of her absence from work, (*d*) shall, if nursing her child, be allowed half-an-hour twice a day during working hours for this purpose, and (*e*) shall be protected against dismissal during the twelve weeks of her absence from work, or for a longer period, to be fixed by the national authorities, in case of illness arising out of her pregnancy or confinement.

What actually was the position before the adoption of the Convention? For information on this matter let us turn to the report prepared by the Organising Committee for the Washington Conference. According to that document a compulsory rest period at childbirth was prescribed in twenty-nine States or Provinces. In only one of those countries—South Africa—was the period as long as twelve weeks (four before and eight after). After confinement a rest period of thirty days or less was allowed in fourteen countries and one of five weeks or more in fifteen countries. In the two countries where a rest period of six weeks was allowed that period might be reduced to four weeks on production of a medical certificate; and the shorter rest periods allowed in other countries might in many cases be reduced on the same condition. A rest period of four weeks or less (compulsory in only one case) before confinement was prescribed in some half-dozen States. Twelve States had a system of benefits or grants to cover the legal period of exclusion from work. In six States the law expressly required that a woman's place should be kept open for her during her absence; and in a similar number of States a nursing mother was legally entitled to time off during working hours in order to feed her infant.

The present position, as shown by the information at the Office's disposal, is that legislation (not necessarily identical in scope with the Convention) for the protection of women workers at confinement has been enacted in forty-three States Members of the Organisation.[1] The period of rest after confinement is at least six weeks in the following twenty-three States: Argentina, Austria, Bulgaria, Canada (British Columbia), Czechoslovakia, Finland (commercial employees), France, Hungary, Japan (four weeks in certain cases), Latvia, Lithuania, Luxemburg, the Netherlands, Norway, Peru, Poland, Rumania, South Africa, Spain, Sweden, Switzerland, Western Australia and Yugoslavia. The rest period after confinement is five weeks in Guatemala and four weeks or slightly less in Australia (New South Wales), Belgium, Brazil, China, Denmark, Greece, India (Bombay), the Irish Free State, Italy, New Zealand, Norway, Portugal and

[1] Such legislation is also known to have been enacted in Ecuador, Turkey, the Soviet Union and six States of the American Union.

Salvador (commercial employees). A voluntary, or in some cases compulsory, rest period of not less than six weeks before confinement is prescribed in seventeen States: Argentina, Australia (Western Australia), Austria (commercial employees), Bulgaria, Canada (British Columbia), Chile, Czechoslovakia, France, Germany, Hungary, the Netherlands, Poland, Portugal, Rumania, Salvador (commercial employees), Spain and Yugoslavia. A four weeks' rest period is allowed in Brazil, China, Greece, Guatemala, Italy, Japan, Latvia, Norway and South Africa; three weeks are allowed in Bombay and Peru, two weeks in Sweden and from two to six weeks in Lithuania. In twenty States a woman's employment must be kept open for her during her legal rest period; and in twenty-six States nursing mothers must be allowed time off during working hours to feed their infants.

As regards the essential question of benefits or allowances during the legal rest period, the progress has been perhaps even more striking. In nineteen States maternity benefits are granted under a system of social insurance. In Denmark, New Zealand, Sweden and Switzerland, benefits are provided under a voluntary insurance system. In Italy and Spain, systems of maternity insurance have been set up. In Australia, Brazil and South Africa, grants are made out of public funds. The rate at which such benefits or allowances are usually paid has also considerably increased—in certain countries the full basic wage is paid.

The Convention has actually been ratified by the following eleven countries: Bulgaria, Chile, Cuba, Germany, Greece, Hungary, Latvia, Luxemburg, Rumania, Spain and Yugoslavia. In each of these countries, ratification has involved, or is involving, important improvements in the national law.

Night Work in Bakeries

The results of this Convention have, it must be admitted, been disappointing in certain respects. At the same time they are by no means insignificant.

A large number of countries possess legislation on the subject, but only five have so far found it possible to ratify. Of these five only Finland already possessed a law (dating from 1908) prohibiting night work in bakeries; in order to be able to ratify, however, the Finnish Parliament had to pass a new Act so as to extend the existing prohibition to cover baking by machinery. The four remaining countries—Bulgaria, Cuba, Estonia and Luxemburg—have had to adopt entirely fresh legislation in order to ratify.

Certain results can also be attributed to the influence of the Convention in other countries. Thus, in 1925 (i.e. after the first reading of the Convention) an Act was passed in Latvia which, according to a statement made by the Latvian Government delegate at the following Session of the Conference, regulated the problem of night work in bakeries "in the fullest accordance with the aspirations expressed by the Sixth Session of the International Labour Conference." In Portugal, a Decree intended by the Government as a move towards ratification, and dated May 17th, 1929, prohibits night work in Lisbon bakeries. In Switzerland, the Federal Parliament decided against ratification, but at the same time requested the Federal Council to prepare a Bill regulating night work in bakeries so as to ensure a nightly rest from 8 p.m. to 4 a.m. Finally, it may be noted that in the Argentine Republic an Act which came into force on September 9th, 1926, prohibits night work in bakeries, a certain latitude being allowed to undertakings where bread is made by machinery.

It should be pointed out that when the question was placed on the agenda of the Conference, seventeen countries possessed legislation prohibiting night work in bakeries; nowadays twenty-eight countries possess such legislation.

III. Conventions Widely Ratified, but Involving Relatively Slight Legislative Progress

The Conventions grouped under this heading are all Conventions which aim rather at the general establishment of a particular principle than at the introduction of important legislative reforms. The widespread acceptance of the principles respectively involved, represented by the numerous ratifications of these Conventions, is not by any means to be regarded as a negligible result; but it is naturally a result less easy to define in terms of legislative progress. In certain cases, however, it is possible to indicate positive and concrete results.

Unemployment

In the case of the *Convention concerning unemployment*, for instance, it is noteworthy that since the adoption of the Convention by the Washington Conference in 1919 measures for the organisation or extension of the system of free public employment agencies have been taken in Austria, Bulgaria, Denmark, Finland, France, Germany, Greece, Italy, Japan, Rumania, South Africa, Spain,

Switzerland and Yugoslavia (all of which countries have ratified the Convention).

An interesting example of the effectiveness of this Convention is afforded by Switzerland. When that country ratified the Convention a Decree of the Federal Council (issued by virtue of the special powers conferred upon it during the War period), dated October 29th, 1919, formed the principal legal basis for ratification. It provided for a system of unemployment relief and the establishment of Cantonal employment offices. It was, however, only provisional in character and its abrogation in 1924 left Switzerland's ratification of the Convention unsupported by adequate legislation. Accordingly, on November 11th, 1924, the Federal Council issued a circular pointing out that the Convention, having been ratified, had force of law in Switzerland, that failing Federal legislation the Cantons were bound to comply with the Convention's provisions and that the Federal Council, in virtue of its constitutional responsibility for securing the fulfilment of international obligations, had power to call upon the Cantons to take the necessary measures. By an Order issued on the same date the Federal Council therefore restored the obligation upon the Cantons to set up joint free employment offices. The preamble to the Order recalls Switzerland's obligations under the Convention.

Equality of Treatment

A number of agreements for reciprocal treatment in respect of unemployment insurance benefits have been concluded between States Members in the last ten years. It is not always possible to establish a direct causal relationship between these agreements and the Convention, but it is interesting to note that the Declaration exchanged by the Swiss and Italian Governments on February 9th, 1927, establishing equality of treatment in respect of unemployment, is expressly based on the desire of both parties to fulfil their obligations under Article 3 of the Convention (which provides for the making of arrangements entitling workers belonging to one of the States Members and employed in the territory of the other to receive the same insurance benefit as national workers). The same Article is also specifically mentioned in the exchange of notes between Switzerland and Denmark (September 28th to December 13th, 1927).

Finally, it may be pointed out that Switzerland's ratification of the *Convention concerning equality of treatment for national and foreign workers as regards workmen's compensation for accidents* automatically conferred the right to equal treatment with Swiss workers on the nationals of the twenty-six other States which are parties to the Convention—a right which had previously been withheld.

Weekly Rest

Again, in the case of the Convention concerning the application of the weekly rest in industrial undertakings, special Sunday rest legislation was enacted in Estonia, Rumania and Spain in order to permit ratification. It is also noteworthy that in India, between the 1921 Conference and the date of ratification, the Indian Mines Act, 1923, which provides *inter alia* for a weekly rest day for mine workers, was enacted. Further, a Bill to amend the Indian Railways Act so as to empower the Government to make rules for regulating the hours of work and rest periods for railway servants has recently been introduced and is expected to become law. (The Convention leaves the Indian Government free to specify the branches of railway work to which the weekly rest is to apply.)

In Switzerland (which has not yet ratified the Convention) a Bill was drafted in 1929 by the Federal Labour Office for the purpose of bringing the regulation of weekly rest periods entirely under Federal control, so as to enable ratification to take place. This Bill was submitted to the workers' and employers' organisations for their observations and the Federal Council has since (on May 27th, 1930) submitted a Bill to the Federal Parliament. In the memorandum accompanying the Bill the Federal Council specifically affirms that Switzerland is under an international obligation to pass such legislation in order to be able to ratify the Convention.

IV. The Practical Results of Conventions and their Formal Ratification

The Objects of International Labour Legislation

The above outline of the concrete effects of the Conventions will convey a clearer picture if we briefly analyse on theoretical grounds the nature of the objects pursued in international labour legislation.

The first object of the Conventions as a whole is to set up a certain social standard, acceptable to the conscience of civilised communities, and to further the general attainment of that standard by providing a means of concerted action, thus spreading a feeling of mutual confidence and averting the danger of unfair competition. These are the reasons set forth in the Peace Treaty to justify the International Labour Conventions.

Secondly, the exchange of workers and even of commodities between one country and another raises labour problems which can only be settled by agreement between the respective Governments. Several of the International Labour Conventions are multilateral labour treaties in the strict sense.

Thirdly, social legislation in general is a new subject for scientific study and research. During the last ten years the practice of holding international gatherings for the common study of scientific problems relating to labour has become increasingly general. The object of such gatherings is to pool knowledge and experience and to agree upon the most suitable lines for further action. In every sphere of economic life, and especially in that of labour, the mechanisation of life has involved the elimination of particularities and the increasing uniformisation of conditions. An International Labour Conference is thus, to a large extent, a conference of technical experts bent on finding solutions for common technical problems. Such solutions, when found, are often embodied in international conventions, and one of the objects of the International Labour Conventions is consequently to set up a standard suitable for general adoption, but more particularly for adoption by "new" countries instituting measures of social reform for the first time. (It is hardly necessary to add that no Convention pursues this object alone; where the Conference desires merely to suggest a model, it adopts a Recommendation and not a Draft Convention.)

It is therefore possible to group the effects of the Conventions under the following three heads:

(1) The generalisation of a higher standard of life and working conditions;
(2) The facilitating of international movement and exchanges;
(3) The adoption of modern and effective methods of dealing with labour problems.

If we now glance back at the results described for the various Conventions we shall find that they fall naturally and logically under one of these three heads. For instance, effect number (1) has been abundantly secured by the Maritime Conventions, the Conventions for the protection of women and young persons, and the Hours Convention. Effect number (2) has been attained by the Convention concerning equality of treatment in respect of accident compensation, the Unemployment Convention, and certain of the Maritime Conventions. Effect number (3) has been secured by various Conventions—e.g. Luxemburg has embodied most of the Conventions as they stand in her national law, British Columbia has taken over most of the provisions of the Hours Convention unchanged, Greece has incorporated the text of several Conventions in her legislation, a number of countries have scheduled the text of various Maritime Conventions, South Africa has drafted social insurance legislation on the Geneva model—and the list of instances could be prolonged almost indefinitely.

Outstanding Importance of the Ratifications

In conclusion, emphasis must be laid on the importance of the ratification of Conventions, especially in connection with the practical attainment of their different objects. For the attainment of the third object, ratification has clearly no relevance at all, as that could equally well be secured by a Recommendation. The second can hardly be attained without ratification, and it is probably no mere coincidence that the highest ratification figures have been attained by Conventions solely or mainly pursuing it—the ratification of an agreement holding out the prospect of reciprocity would naturally be particularly tempting to most Governments. The first object cannot be fully secured without general ratification, which alone can create the requisite fullness of mutual confidence and security. Nevertheless, the results of several of the Conventions prove that, quite apart from ratification, the setting up of a high standard by the International Labour Conference may, in the case of a reform appealing directly to the public conscience (reduction of working hours, protection of maternity, safeguarding of health) contribute effectively to the launching of a general forward movement and to maintaining intact such progress as is realised.

But there should be no misunderstanding as to the vital importance, in the case of all the Conventions, of the fact that they *are* Conventions which, once ratified, constitute a network of binding mutual obligations. If in a number of cases a Convention assists the supporters of the standard embodied in it to defend that standard successfully, even in countries which have not ratified, it is the Convention, rather than the standard, which plays an effective part. The upholders of the eight-hour day in Germany and Great Britain, for instance, have been assisted in their campaigns principally because they have been able to argue (*a*) that a certain number of countries have already entered into a binding compact to maintain the provisions adopted at Washington, and (*b*) that it is in the interests of their own countries at any rate to retain the possibility of becoming parties to that compact. The standard embodied in the Convention, like those embodied in the various Recommendations, no doubt exercises a certain psychological attraction, but no Recommendation would appear ever to have provided the rallying cry for a campaign in any country. It is the embodiment of the standards in a binding international instrument, and the guarantees provided in the Peace Treaty for the execution of the Conventions, that supply arguments of really convincing force.

Application of Article 408

Further, the provisions contained in the Treaties for securing the effective application of the Conventions by the countries that ratify them are certainly among the most powerful factors in the influence of the Conventions as a whole. One of the most interesting results of the Conventions is beyond doubt the development of the system of mutual supervision for which Article 408 of the Treaty of Versailles provides.

A summary of this Article was given in the first part of this book, but it is worth while referring to it again. It is laid down in Article 408 that "each of the Members agrees to make an annual report to the International Labour Office on the measures which it has taken to give effect to the provisions of the Conventions to which it is a party. These reports shall be made in such form and shall contain such particulars as the Governing Body may request. The Director shall lay a summary of these reports before the next meeting of the Conference."

In 1926 it was decided, very tentatively and after much hesitation, to appoint a Committee of Experts to examine the annual reports sent in under Article 408, and in the same year the practice of setting up a Committee of the Conference at each Session to examine the summaries of the reports was initiated. These two bodies—the Committee of Experts and the Conference Committee—have since carried out their duties year by year with increasing care and competence. Every State which ratifies a Convention now knows that the measures by which it applies the Convention's provisions will be closely scrutinised by authorised bodies at Geneva, and that any serious discrepancy will in all probability be discussed in public debate. The discussions at the Conference have been more and more frank and more and more thorough, and time after time the undertaking of a Government representative that a point in his Government's report that has given rise to criticism will be carefully considered has been followed by the adoption of fresh legislative or administrative measures with a view to securing a more exact application of the Convention in question. The development of such a system is bound as time goes on greatly to strengthen the effective influence of the Conventions by increasing public confidence in their practical efficacy.

CHAPTER III

THE RECOMMENDATIONS

THE Conventions constitute a network of binding international obligations, and the ratifying States are required to report yearly on the measures which they have adopted in order to fulfil those obligations. The reports supply an excellent basis for a study of the effective results to which the Conventions have led in the various countries. On the other hand, States are in no way bound to report periodically on the measures, if any, adopted in order to give effect to the Recommendations. The International Labour Office recently embarked upon a systematic study of the results of the Recommendations, but in the absence of periodical reports from the States Members such a study must necessarily be long and difficult, and no complete information can be embodied in this volume.

The Different Forms of Recommendations

A certain change is already noticeable in the attitude of the International Labour Conference towards Recommendations.

In 1919 and 1920 the Conference adopted a considerable number of Recommendations, some in the form of a pendant to a Convention, others standing alone and intended to prepare the way for the adoption of a Convention in the future. Leaving on the one side the Recommendation to adhere to the Berne White Phosphorus Convention, these Recommendations appear to possess one common feature—each was in some sense a confession of impotence. For one reason or another the Conference felt unable to draft a suitable Convention on the various subjects concerned; it therefore tried to shelve the difficulty by adopting a formal decision, embodying certain definite proposals, but with no binding character.

In 1921 a new kind of Recommendation appeared. The Conference adopted a Recommendation concerning the prevention of unemployment in agriculture, which contained no definite proposals, but simply advised the States Members to "examine the advisability" of adopting various methods of dealing with agricultural unemployment. This precedent was followed in 1924, when the Conference adopted a similar kind of Recommendation concerning the "development of facilities for the utilisation of workers' spare time." Further, at each of the Sessions held respectively in 1922, 1923 and 1924, the Conference contented itself with adopting a single Recommendation on a single question figuring on its agenda for the first time. Its practice in these years would appear to indicate that the Conference had come to regard the Recommendation as a form of decision parallel but subordinate to the Convention, suitable for the formulation of general principles or model methods for dealing with problems on which a Convention appeared inadvisable or impossible.

It may well be that in the future the Conference will again adopt Recommendations of this sort; but the fact remains that during the years 1925–1930 it has never adopted a Recommendation except in conjunction with a Convention. It is true that in 1929 the two Conventions adopted dealt with subsidiary aspects of the main question (prevention of industrial accidents) which was made the subject of a Recommendation; but the Conference does seem to have set its face against dealing with any question by way of a Recommendation alone. A further indication of this tendency is provided by the fact that on every occasion when a Draft Convention has failed to secure the requisite two-thirds majority, the Conference has refused to adopt the proposals contained in the Draft Convention in the form of a Recommendation.

The present tendency therefore seems to be to consider the Convention and the Recommendation as mutually complementary. The relationship between the two may take various forms; for instance, the Recommendation may suggest the application of the provisions of the Convention to additional classes of workers, or propose supplementary measures of protection, or lay down general principles for the guidance of Governments in applying the Convention, or it may simply serve to emphasise the intention of the Conference as soon as the time is ripe to adopt a further Convention on some special aspect of the question concerned. Such an intention is indeed frequently present even where the Recommendation has other practical objects.

This tendency to use Recommendations as a means of preparing the way for Conventions found expression in the Report of the Committee set up by the Fourteenth Session of the Conference

(1930) to examine the annual reports supplied by Governments on the application of the Conventions ratified by them. In this Report the following passage occurs:

> It was pointed out to the Committee that it would be of interest were practical reports (for example, once in two years) on the application of the Recommendations also to be furnished by the Governments and submitted to the Conference. Provision for such reports might be made in the Recommendations themselves. Several members of the Committee expressed the opinion that this method would permit a consideration of the possibility of transforming after some years certain Recommendations into Conventions. Other members suggested that if such a system of checking the results, and thereby increasing the practical value of the Recommendations, were adopted, the Conference might have more frequent recourse to them for the solution of certain questions brought before it for the first time.

For practical reasons the Governing Body has not felt able to approve the proposal to call for periodical reports on the application of the Recommendations, but it has instructed the Office to devote particular attention to the effective results of the Recommendations in the various countries.

Another decision taken by the Governing Body at the same Session lends additional point to the observation of the Conference Committee quoted above. In 1919 the Conference supplemented the Convention concerning unemployment by a Recommendation containing, among other suggestions, one to the effect that measures should be taken to prohibit the establishment of employment agencies which charge fees or which carry on business for profit. The Governing Body has now decided to place this question on the agenda of the Session of the Conference to be held in 1932, with a view to the adoption of a Draft Convention. Since the Recommendation was adopted at Washington in 1919, steps have been taken in a number of countries towards carrying out the provision concerning the prohibition of private fee-charging agencies. In Germany, the complete abolition of such offices not later than December 31st, 1930, is prescribed by the Act of July 16th, 1927. Such abolition has been enacted in Bulgaria and Rumania by laws passed in 1925 and 1921 respectively. In Yugoslavia and Italy, measures have been taken for the partial abolition of fee-charging offices, while in France, Japan, Mexico, Poland and South Africa, stricter measures of supervision have been introduced. This is an excellent example of the manner in which a Recommendation may serve to prepare the way for a Convention in dealing with a problem of particular difficulty.

Results of the Recommendations

Under the Peace Treaty the States are bound to inform the Secretary-General of the League of Nations of the action taken on the Recommendations. The information thus supplied has been reproduced or summarised from time to time in the publications of the International Labour Office, particularly in the Director's Annual Report to the Conference. To obtain a general idea of the effective results of the Recommendations it will be necessary in the first place to study and collate this information. The Office is at present engaged on such a study, and we are convinced that it will show that the Recommendations have, by their results, contributed most usefully to the development of national legislation on labour questions, and that, particularly in conjunction with the Conventions, they have been an important factor in international social progress.

That this is so is exemplified by the fact that all the principles which found expression in the Recommendations adopted in 1923 on factory inspection have been incorporated in factory inspection laws or regulations subsequently enacted in Bulgaria (1924) and during 1927 in China, Finland, Poland and Rumania.

Similarly, the adoption in 1924 of the Recommendation concerning workers' spare time has been followed everywhere by the rapid development of institutions, whether public or private, local or regional, denominational or secular, set up to improve the workers' minds and promote interest in libraries, theatrical performances and sports. In Belgium, for example, the introduction in Parliament of a Bill to establish a State service to direct and promote such institutions was sufficient to bring together advocates and opponents of the Bill, both equally anxious to find in the text of the Recommendation the necessary justification for their conceptions, which, moreover, differed not on the principles involved but only in respect of their application. Again, in China, the Factory Act of December 30th, 1929, contains a chapter on welfare in which it is definitely specified that the factories must "whenever possible provide means of education for workers deprived of such facilities" and "provide suitable means of recreation for their workers."

Finally, a Recommendation which has not only had satisfactory results but has also paved the way for a Convention, is that adopted by the Washington Conference in 1919 concerning the protection of women and children against lead poisoning. Thus, in Austria, three Orders dealing with lead and lead compounds, issued on March 8th, 1923, embodied many provisions contained in the Recommendation. In Estonia, the employment of children under fifteen years of age in the processes mentioned in the Recommendation has been prohibited by an Act passed in 1928. In France, the regulations were amended in 1926 so as to exclude women and young persons from employment in the processes defined in the Recommendation. In Great Britain, an Act was passed in 1920 and three Orders were issued in 1921 to give effect to the Recommendation. In India, the terms of the Recommendation were inserted verbatim in the Indian Factories Act of 1921. In the Netherlands, full effect has been given to the Recommendation by two Orders issued in 1920 and by an amendment introduced in the Workers' Accident Insurance Act in 1921. In Poland, an Order issued in September 1930 prohibits the employment of women and young persons under eighteen years of age on work involving the use of lead products, with certain exceptions. In Switzerland, approval of the Recommendation has involved an extension of the list of processes previously prohibited for women and young persons, and the raising of the age limit of the young persons protected from sixteen to eighteen years of age. Further, in Germany, the provisions necessary to give effect to the Recommendation have been inserted in the general Workers' Protection Bill which is at present before the Reichstag.

The part played by this Recommendation in preparing the way for the insertion in the 1921 Convention concerning the use of white lead in painting of a provision prohibiting the employment of women and young persons under eighteen years of age in painting-work involving the use of lead pigments must also be noted. The Office expressly proposed the insertion of the clause in question by the 1921 Session of the Conference on the ground that "it is a logical extension of the provisions as regards white lead of the Washington Recommendation against lead poisoning."

It may therefore be said, even in the absence of the report now being prepared by the Office, that the Recommendations, with their varied form and elasticity of procedure, have fulfilled the hopes placed in them by the authors of the Peace Treaty.

PART IV

RELATIONS

In the two preceding parts an attempt has been made to give an idea of the work of the International Labour Organisation and the results obtained since it was set up. Neither work nor results would have been the same if it had not tried from the first to create that collective spirit which alone can infuse life into an inanimate institution. In accordance with its threefold nature, there were three ways in which it could work towards this end.

As an association of States, the Organisation had to accustom the Governments of the States Members to international collaboration, their traditional tendency being that of work in isolation, on the national plane. They had to be made to understand how they might benefit in their ordinary work by such collaboration.

As a democratic institution based on the participation of workers and employers, it had to organise unbroken relations, not only with the more important industrial bodies statutorily represented in the Organisation, but with all associations, whatever their aims, that had a valid claim to speak on behalf of the groups in question.

As an institution for social progress with a definite mission, it had to seek the support of all other institutions, official or private, whose action tended in the same direction, and to fuse all the activities that might assist it in achieving each of the points in its programme, by helping to create an enlightened public opinion.

In a word, the International Labour Organisation had to become the sounding-board, so to speak, for the whole social movement. On the basis of a close network of relations covering the whole world, it had to make itself felt, not only through the regular working of its constitutional organs—the Conference, the Governing Body and the Office—but through the action of all who in every country sought with it to establish social justice in the world.

CHAPTER I

RELATIONS WITH STATES

IF the International Labour Organisation were not merely to comply with the strict letter of its constitution, but to act in full accordance with the spirit that had created it, it was necessary to establish relations with all countries, and not only with the States Members of the Organisation. For the work of the latter to be fully effective, it must be universal. Though its administrative relations had to be confined to the States Members of the Organisation, what may be called its general relations could not be allowed to be exclusive. Such exclusion would have been all the more inadmissible, since, in addition to a few other countries, two great industrial communities, the United States of America and the Union of Socialist Soviet Republics, were outside the Organisation. Furthermore, by its threefold composition it is in practice fully international, for the workers and employers of the non-Member States have the same power as those of the Member States to make their influence felt through the international associations with which the Organisation is bound to be in touch.

1. RELATIONS WITH STATES MEMBERS

> The Government Departments of any of the Members which deal with questions of industry and employment may communicate directly with the Director through the Representative of their Government on the Governing Body of the International Labour Office, or failing any such Representative, through such other qualified official as the Government may nominate for the purpose.

This is the only indication, brief though it is, that Article 397 of the Treaty of Peace gives concerning the organisation of the relations of the Office with the Governments of the States Members; brief but precise. It means that the Treaty of Peace itself recognises the right of the Office to communicate directly with the Government departments dealing with labour questions in the different countries, without passing through the ordinary diplomatic channels.

Now, after ten years, the official relations of the Office with the large majority of the States Members may be regarded as firmly established. But the creation of these many and varied contacts has called for much patient work during this period. To-day, many Ministers of State know the way to Geneva; most of the important national officials follow closely the varied activities of the Organisation, by attending the Conference or the meetings of the Governing Body or the committees it has set up; on the other hand, many of the officials of the Office have had an opportunity by tours of investigation and otherwise to establish useful relations and make valuable friendships.

The relations of the Office with the States Members are now organised at both ends: in the different countries and in Geneva itself.

Labour Ministries

All the Governments have responded to an appeal made to them by the Office in February 1920, some by setting up ministerial departments, some by appointing officials with whom the Office can correspond. The growing activity of the Office year by year has made the need for special liaison services felt in most countries. In the great industrial countries, where ministries of labour had long been in existence, the creation of offices, departments or institutions to centralise communications with the Office raised no difficulty.

On the other hand, since 1920 many countries have set up ministries or ministerial departments of labour or social welfare. This movement has been specially marked in Latin America. The Argentine Republic, for instance, has created, in addition to the National Labour Department, a special service for questions connected with the International Labour Organisation in its Ministry of Foreign Affairs. Brazil has set up a National Labour Council; Chile, a Ministry of Hygiene, Social Assistance, Welfare and Labour, which is now the Ministry of Social Welfare; Colombia, a General Labour Office; Cuba, an International Labour Organisation Service in the Secretariat of Agriculture, Commerce and Labour; Guatemala, a General Labour Department subordinate to the Ministry of Public Works; Haiti, a Labour Department; Panama, a Labour Office; Ecuador, a Ministry of Labour.

The Union of South Africa has established a State Department of Labour. As to Europe, a Ministry of Social Affairs has been created in Denmark, and in Portugal the Ministry of Foreign Affairs has set up a General Secretariat of Portuguese League of Nations Services with a special section for the International Labour Office.

Co-ordinating Bodies

These institutions were soon found insufficient. The fact is that labour questions are not within the competence of one administrative department only. Agricultural labour questions, for instance, may be dealt with by a ministry of agriculture, seamen's questions by a merchant shipping department. Various Governments have therefore thought it expedient to co-ordinate the work of these different departments by establishing interministerial committees or even new departments.

Italy, early in 1920, created an International Labour Organisation Section, now the Permanent Committee for Co-ordinating International Labour Questions, which is presided over by the Minister of Foreign Affairs. This Committee includes representatives of the various State departments interested in labour questions.

Soon after, France set up a Consultative Committee on International Conventions, attached to the Ministry of Labour. It ensures the co-ordination of the various departments concerned in studying, ratifying, and enforcing International Labour Conventions. Similarly, Great Britain set up an interdepartmental Committee composed of representatives of the ministries concerned in the work of the International Labour Organisation, its secretarial work being performed by the International Labour Division of the Ministry of Labour, which is specially responsible for relations between the British Government and the Office.

The Scandinavian countries followed the example; Denmark with its Department for International Co-operation in Social Questions, attached to the Ministry of Social Affairs; Sweden with its Delegation for International Co-operation in Questions of Social Policy, which, temporarily suspended, resumed activity in 1928, and includes, in addition to officials of the departments concerned, representatives of employers and workers. Finally, the Rumanian Government recently set up a Committee for Relations with the International Labour Organisation and Office. It includes employers' and workers' representatives and has been given very definite duties to ensure effective Rumanian collaboration in the work of the International Labour Office, ranging from replies to enquiries and questionnaires to the enforcing of ratified Conventions.

Delegations in Geneva

For the furtherance of their relations with the International Labour Office, many countries have nominated permanent delegates to Geneva. They were in fact adapting to the International Labour Organisation an established tradition: that of social attachés. In 1920, Sweden had a Social Attaché in Berlin, Germany a Social Attaché in Rome. It was thought that instead of increasing the number of social attachés at the different embassies and legations, it would be more expedient to accredit them to the International Labour Office in Geneva. Here the example was set by Japan, which appointed a Japanese Government delegation to Geneva, presided over by the representative of that Government on the Governing Body. Next, Poland accredited to the Office its representative on the Governing Body, and Sweden appointed a Social Adviser accredited to the Office; finally, Peru appointed a delegate specially accredited to the Office.

The brevity of this list might give a wrong idea of the permanent delegations in Geneva. For, in point of fact, many countries have set up legations in that city under the direction of ministers plenipotentiary, their duty being to maintain liaison with all the official international institutions at Geneva, the General Secretariat of the League of Nations and the International Labour Office. Thus, the delegation of the Polish Government to the Governing Body has now become a Polish Delegation under a Minister and with a complete legation staff, its duty being to ensure the representation of the Polish Government on the Council of the League of Nations and the Governing Body of the Office. Other countries have followed suit, attaching complete legations to the League of Nations. Yet others have specially accredited to the Secretariat and the Office their Ministers at Berne, or set up in Geneva special offices for questions relating to the international institutions.

At the time of writing, Canada, China, Colombia, Cuba, Denmark, Finland, Hungary, the Irish Free State, Latvia, Persia, Poland, Portugal, Rumania, the Union of South Africa and Yugoslavia have permanent delegations or representatives in Geneva.

The Governments of the Argentine Republic, Bulgaria, Czechoslovakia, Greece, Italy, Norway and Venezuela have instructed their diplomatic or consular representatives in Berne or Geneva to represent them also in their dealings with the League of Nations and the International Labour Office, or the Office alone. The National Labour Office of Uruguay keeps in touch with the Office through the Uruguayan Consul-General in Geneva.

Correspondence Offices and National Correspondents

The International Labour Office itself has established several "correspondence offices" and appointed "national correspondents."

The first was the Paris Office opened in January 1920, which had at once to help with the general organisation of the International Labour Office, being responsible for the recruiting of French officials and the collection of the official material and information required. Next came the Washington Office (May 1920), which, as a matter of fact, had been active ever since the First Session of the International Labour Conference in October and November 1919. This was immediately followed by the creation of the London and Rome Offices (July 1920). Next year an office was opened in Berlin (March 1921). Three years later the first Correspondence Office for a Far Eastern country was opened in Tokyo (January 1924); the second was opened in Delhi (October 1928), and the third in Nankin (April 1930).

In other countries, where it was impossible or not wholly essential to set up a complete office, permanent correspondents, with the same functions as the offices, but on a reduced scale, were appointed in Prague, Madrid, Brussels, Vienna, Budapest, Warsaw, Rio de Janeiro and Bucharest.

The creation of these offices and the appointment of national correspondents were due to the need of maintaining regular relations between the Office and the Governments and public administrative departments of the countries concerned, and of supplementing these relations by establishing contact with Parliaments, following social policy and social movements by means of relations with workers' and employers' organisations, making the International Labour Organisation known, popularising the conceptions on which it is based, describing its activities and achievements and correcting any misconceptions with regard to its work.

An enumeration of the reasons for appointing national correspondents is equivalent to an enumeration of their duties, the performance of which has proved most useful to the Organisation. This usefulness was recently recognised by a committee set up by the Governing Body to study the system. This committee, which held meetings in December 1929 and March 1930, was unanimous in its opinion of the value of the correspondence offices and the national correspondents as links with the countries concerned, and as centres of information enabling the Office to collect without delay the information needed for its work. It also recognised the expediency of contemplating an extension of the system. After studying the possibility of opening an office in Moscow and recognising that this proposal would have to wait until conditions were such as to ensure the permanent existence and independent activity of such an office, it expressed itself in favour of opening offices at Belgrade and Buenos Aires, a proposal accepted by the Governing Body for 1931.

Missions

Besides facilitating the regular performance of the administrative duties on which the working of the Organisation depends, and enabling the States Members and Office to keep in touch with each other's activities, the various institutions for maintaining relations which have been set up by the States on the one hand and the Office on the other have made those relations more fruitful owing to the daily contact so established. But more was needed to create and maintain the atmosphere of mutual interest and understanding. For this purpose members of the Directorate of the International Labour Office have visited different countries, had interviews with persons in leading positions, attended important conferences, examined and discussed on the spot the questions and tendencies of the day. During the past ten years this has been done whenever possible. The Director and Deputy-Director, to mention no others, have frequently paid visits to the principal European capitals; they have also visited oversea countries, including non-Member States. In 1922, after visiting Canada, the Director went to the United States. In 1925 he visited several Latin-American countries: Brazil, Uruguay, the Argentine Republic and Chile. In 1928–1929 he visited Russia, China and Japan. The Deputy-Director was in the United States in 1926 and in South Africa in 1927–1928.

It is impossible here to describe the relations of each country with the International Labour Office; it will be sufficient to note certain facts proving the solidity of these relations.

Two States, Spain and Brazil, were able to leave the League of Nations—the former only for a brief period—without any effect on their participation in the International Labour Organisation. The misunderstandings with Italy that arose out of the question of the credentials of the Workers' Delegate to the Conference were removed by frank and complete explanations. More recently, the difficulties resulting from the fact that the Norwegian Storting refused to pass the necessary votes for the sending of a delegation to the Sessions of the Conference during the financial year 1929–1930, which had somewhat disturbed relations with Norway, now appear to be on the way to settlement. A similar reason for concern existed for a longer time in the case of the Argentine Republic, for that country decided, after active participation in the work of the Organisation up to last year, to withdraw its contribution to the League of Nations until the question of its constitutional position in the League had been settled. The representative of the Argentine Government was present, however, at the session of the Governing Body held in October 1930.

Taken as a whole, the life of the Organisation is developing on normal lines. There is increasing reason to hope that its activities will soon extend to certain countries which still do not belong to it—the United States, the U.S.S.R., Mexico, Turkey and Egypt.

II. Relations with Non-Member States

The United States

The United States played a part in the history of the Organisation even before the latter had entered on its activities. The Commission on International Labour Legislation, which was set up at the end of January 1919 by the Peace Conference to draft the Constitution of the Organisation, elected as its president Mr. Samuel Gompers, President of the American Federation of Labor, who took a very active part in the work of the Commission. Soon after, on October 29th, 1919, the First Session of the Conference opened at Washington, convened by President Wilson; a member of his Cabinet, Mr. William B. Wilson, Secretary of Labor, was elected as president. Mr. Gompers,

Professor J. H. Shotwell and Mr. J. B. Andrews were members of the Organising Committee.

Though the United States have not ratified the Treaty of Versailles and have taken no official part in the work of the Organisation since 1919, they have been in frequent touch with it. At the Second Session of the Conference, at Genoa in 1920, Mr. A. Furuseth was present, and in 1921 Dr. M. Dorset, of the Department of Agriculture, was chosen by the United States Government to represent it on the Advisory Committee on Anthrax set up by the Governing Body. In the same year several Americans were appointed to the Committee on Industrial Hygiene. Since that date the various advisory bodies set up by the Office have always included Americans.

It was stated above that the Director of the International Labour Office paid a visit to the United States in 1922, and the Deputy Director in 1926. Both found much evidence of interest in the work of the Organisation.

The Office has in turn had frequent opportunity to render useful service to the United States Government. Thus, in 1922, information on conditions in European coal mines was officially supplied to the American Coal Commission. In the following year a quantity of material was submitted to a Senate Commission appointed to draft a federal measure on child labour. In 1926, the Office undertook an important research into migration statistics at the request of the National Bureau of Economic Research, which helped to finance the enquiry. On several other occasions Washington has had recourse to the scientific research work of Geneva. When in 1921 the Governing Body appointed a Permanent Emigration Commission, its meetings were attended by Americans on several occasions. In 1926, conversations with Mr. E. A. Filene and Mr. H. S. Dennison, of the Twentieth Century Fund, led to the creation in Geneva of an International (Scientific) Management Institute. In 1930, at the request of the Ford Company, the Office undertook an enquiry, financed by Mr. Filene, into the wages which would have to be paid to workers in different European cities to ensure them the same standard of life as an average worker in Detroit, an enquiry previously mentioned in another part of this book.

With the passing of time the attitude of the United States towards the Organisation has become more and more one of "friendly co-operation without participation," as it was described by Mr. Magnus Alexander, President of the National Industrial Conference Board. Since 1927 the Industrial Counselors Inc. have accredited an official to the International Labour Office, who, while maintaining a contact which is of great value with the United States, makes enquiries into industrial relations in different countries and has published studies of much interest. Finally, the United States took an active part in the Silicosis Conference held in Johannesburg in August, 1930.

The U.S.S.R.

It was explained in the first part of this work that from the outset the International Labour Office has attentively followed developments in the Union of Socialist Soviet Republics. An attempt was even made in 1920 to send a special committee of enquiry to Russia, but it had to be given up for reasons for which the Office was not responsible.

Nevertheless, the Office has been able to get into direct touch with a large number of Government and trade union institutions and to obtain in exchange for its publications most of the important periodical and other Soviet publications. With this full, and in its way unique, supply of material it has been able to carry out a systematic study of social and economic conditions in the U.S.S.R.

The attitude of the Soviet Union towards the International Labour Office is determined by the general policy of the Government, with which it naturally fluctuates. About two years ago the Office was entitled to think that collaboration had been established in the field of scientific research. It had, for instance, published in the *International Labour Review*, with the assistance and full approval of the U.S.S.R. Commissariat of Labour, information on wages in Moscow compared with those in the principal world centres. Since then a change has taken place in the home and foreign policy of the U.S.S.R. At present the Soviet Government considers that the fundamental differences between the political and social conceptions of the U.S.S.R. on the one hand and the League of Nations and the International Labour Office on the other are too great to allow of any collaboration. The activities of the International Labour Office are regarded in the U.S.S.R. as *a priori* sterile and useless. Hence the usually unfriendly comments of the Soviet Press on these activities. The position is different, however, for the scientific work of the International Labour Office. The official Soviet Press has often agreed that it constitutes a valuable source of information.

Mexico

The Federative Republic of Mexico is one of the countries of Latin America where social legislation has made most progress. With a view to co-ordinating the social legislation of the different States and giving effect to Articles 73 and 123 of the National Constitution adopted in 1917, the Government submitted to the Chamber a draft Federal Labour Code, subsequently amended, which began to be discussed in 1929. The draft gives expression in the main to the principles adopted by the International Labour Conference at its various Sessions and laid down in Part XIII of the Treaty of Peace. In June 1930, at the Fourteenth Session of the Conference, Mexico sent an observer who, in replying to the welcome addressed to him by the President of the Conference, declared that outside the International Labour Organisation Mexico had carried on a work that in more than one respect coincided with the work of the Organisation, and that it could not but feel gratified at following a path parallel to that of the Organisation.

Turkey

The Turkish Republic, which is making a noteworthy and systematic attempt to introduce social legislation, was also semi-officially represented at recent Sessions of the Conference.

Egypt

With Egypt, whose membership of the League of Nations, and therefore of the International Labour Organisation, depends on the negotiations in progress between the British and the Egyptian Governments, the International Labour Office has been on cordial terms, the culminating point being the visit paid to it by King Fuad in July 1929. Previously, on his return from the Far East, the Director of the Office met at Cairo the Under-Secretary of State in the Ministry of Justice, Rida Pasha, from whom he obtained information on the preparation of a Labour Code that will give Egypt a labour legislation in conformity with the principles of the International Labour Organisation.

These principles are now known in every country. By its relations, the International Labour Organisation is helping to create an atmosphere favourable to the adoption of measures in the spirit of Part XIII of the Treaty of Peace, and may thus hope to become world-wide in its moral influence while still waiting to achieve constitutional universality.

CHAPTER II

RELATIONS WITH WORKERS' ORGANISATIONS

The Need of these Relations and their Origin

The fact that the Charter constituting the International Labour Organisation was part of the Treaty of Peace could not by itself endow the Organisation with full power of effective action. Not even the building up, by several years of effort, of a highly organised system of study and action was enough. It also needed the support of public opinion, especially of those directly interested—in other words, the confident and active assistance of the world of labour.

Representatives of the trade union movement had taken part in drafting Part XIII of the Treaty of Peace. It was, indeed, in that movement that the campaign originated which led the negotiators of the Treaty to set up the International Commission on Social Legislation that drafted Part XIII. Without that movement the Organisation which it had helped to bring into being could hardly prosper.

As early as September 1914 the American Federation of Labour had passed a resolution urging that when the Peace Conference that would put a stop to the War was held, the representatives of the organised workers of all countries should hold a Conference at the same place as the Congress for the purpose of taking the necessary steps to protect the rights of labour, thus making their contribution to the establishment of a lasting peace.

At the end of the same year the French General Confederation of Labour approved this resolution in a public manifesto. In July 1916 the Socialist organisations of Great Britain, Belgium, France and Italy, at a Conference held in Leeds, discussed the economic clauses to be inserted in the Peace Treaty, and drew up a programme of labour demands. In June 1917 the trade unions of the Central European and Scandinavian countries approved the Leeds programme at a Conference in Stockholm, and they confirmed this decision at a second Conference, held in Berne in October of the same year.

Finally, soon after the Armistice, in February 1919, a Conference, attended by representatives of the trade unions of both belligerent and neutral States, was held in Berne and adopted an International Labour Charter, which it demanded should be made by the League of Nations an integral part of international law when peace was concluded.

The Berne Conference was held at the very time when the drafting of Part XIII of the Treaty of Peace was beginning. The Commission of fifteen members appointed for this purpose included workers' delegates and advisers from the Allied countries, under the chairmanship of Mr. Samuel Gompers, President of the American Federation of Labor.

Part XIII was drafted, but it deviated in important respects from the terms of the Leeds and Berne programme. It nevertheless constituted such an advance in the field of social policy that there could be no doubt of the support of the world of labour. At the International Trade Union Congress held in Amsterdam in July 1919, the Berne Charter was confirmed, but it was decided to invite the national trade union organisations to attend the First Session of the International Labour Conference, which was to be held in Washington, on condition, however, that Germany and Austria were also allowed to attend. This decision was duly carried into effect.

Since that date the workers' unions have constantly and regularly collaborated with the three organs of the Institution: the Conference, the Governing Body and the International Labour Office.

When the Information and Relations Division was first organised, the Director of the Office set up in it a service for relations with workers' organisations, which has always been in close touch with the international trade union organisations and the central national unions.

I. Relations with the International Federation of Trade Unions

First Stage (1920–1924)

The year 1920 was for the International Labour Office a period of organisation. For the trade unions it was a year of disturbance and conflict. The International Federation of Trade Unions, which in 1919 and 1920 had 25 million members, suffered a serious reduction in membership. This reduction was accompanied by a certain hesitation in the views of trade union leaders. At the London Congress in 1921, the Federation's collaboration with the International Labour Office was much criticised, but a very large majority rejected a proposal to break off relations. Thereby the International Labour Office may be said to have won its cause in the trade union movement. The international federations had already begun to send in numerous requests for information on such subjects as night work in bakeries, agricultural questions and the conditions of work in chemical factories. The period of "relations" had begun.

At the Rome Congress in 1922, the International Federation of Trade Unions invited the Director of the International Labour Office to attend, and he used this opportunity to explain to the workers' representatives his view on the nature of the relations between the Geneva institutions and the trade union movement. At the Vienna Congress in 1923 he was again present, and since then he has attended practically all the Congresses of the Federation. At the same time there was a steady increase in the requests for information from the organisations. Twenty-eight were received in 1921, 48 in 1922, 116 in 1923, and the number and importance of the requests have steadily grown since then.

Normal Relations Established (1924–1930)

Normal relations may be said to date from 1924, since when they have become firmly consolidated. At first, however, there was some uncertainty. The Russians, who had affirmed their hostility to the International Labour Organisation, had been invited to attend the British Trades Union Congress in Hull. The Director of the International Labour Office had also been invited, and was present. During the discussion, the Secretary of the Congress (Mr. Bramley) noted that much of the workers' programme for international legislation was identical with the programme of the International Labour Organisation defined in Part XIII.

Soon after, the Director of the International Labour Office, during a visit to the Balkans, was able to get into touch with the workers' organisations there, and heard their complaints in the matter of freedom of association. These complaints, as formulated by the Trade Union Conference of the Balkan Countries held at Sofia in April 1925, gave rise to the inclusion of freedom of association in the agenda of the International

Labour Conference, with the result which has been described in another part of this book.

Since then there have been several occasions on which a workers' organisation has deliberated on a question, and, by means of its relations with the International Labour Organisation, has succeeded in having the question placed before the Conference, or at least referred to the International Labour Office for study.

There can be no doubt, for instance, that the conversations inaugurated in 1924 between the International Labour Office and the International Transport Workers' Federation gave rise to the renewed activity of the Organisation in favour first of seamen, then of railwaymen (the question of automatic coupling), and then of workers employed in inland navigation.

The similar, and perhaps even more regular, negotiations between the Office and the International Federation of Miners in 1925 gave rise to the steps taken by the International Labour Organisation, and later by the League of Nations itself, to try to reach a social and economic solution of the coal problem.

Similarly, when the World Migration Congress met in London in 1926, the International Federation of Trade Unions had recourse to the assistance of the International Labour Office and used its material in support of a demand that the International Labour Organisation should follow a bolder and more active policy in the matter of workers' migration. The renewal of activity described above was the result of this resolution.

Finally, in 1929 the International Federation of Textile Workers, at its Congress in Ghent, requested the Office to carry out its proposed enquiry into conditions of work in the principal textile industries.

These facts have been chosen from among many others as examples to show that between 1924 and 1930 the relations between the Organisation and the trade union movement increased steadily in volume and strength. At first they were confined to simple requests for information, but soon they turned into definite attempts at collaboration for the protection of the workers. Following the transport workers, the miners and textile workers, the federations of workers in the wood, glass, food and metal industries, and in agriculture, have in turn made use of their opportunity to profit by the resources of the International Labour Organisation for the collection of information and active collaboration.

II. Relations with the Christian Trade Unions

The International Federation of Christian Trade Unions

In June 1920 a congress of Christian trade unions held at The Hague founded an International Federation. Even before the War these unions had had an international secretariat at Cologne. By 1920 they had acquired a substantial membership in Austria, Belgium, Czechoslovakia, France, Germany, Hungary, Italy, Luxemburg, the Netherlands, Poland, Spain and Switzerland. At the first two Sessions of the International Labour Conference, in Washington and Genoa, several delegations included representatives of the Christian trade unions as advisers. The movement was already gaining power.

The International Labour Office sent a representative to The Hague Congress in 1920, as well as to the congress of the most important branch of the new Federation—the Federation of German Christian Trade Unions—held in Essen. After a delegation of the International Federation had visited the Office in May 1921, the Director appointed a special official to maintain regular relations with the Christian trade union movement. The International Labour Office was thus in a position to draw the attention of the Christian unions to the International Labour Organisation and its work.

Difficulties

Hardly had these relations been opened when a first difficulty arose. For the Third Session of the Conference, in 1921, the Netherlands Government had designated as workers' delegate a representative of the Netherlands Catholic unions who was at the same time General Secretary of the International Federation of Christian Trade Unions. The International Federation of Trade Unions of Amsterdam protested at the Conference against the credentials of this delegate. The matter was not finally settled until 1922 by the advisory opinion given by the Permanent Court of International Justice, which recognised the regularity of the procedure followed by the Netherlands Government. Even before the Session opened and the official protest was made by the Amsterdam International, the Director of the

International Labour Office had tried to bring about an agreement between the two Federations.

In the meantime, the second International Congress of Christian Trade Unions held at Innsbruck in June 1922 demanded "fair" representation on the different organs of the International Labour Organisation. Now, the constitution of the Organisation does not provide expressly for the representation of trade union minorities. It merely allows the Office on occasion to apply a sort of moral corrective to the strict rule of majority representation: for instance, when setting up committees which are more or less independent of the official machinery of the Organisation. For the official bodies, it will be recalled that the delegates to the Conference are designated by the Governments, the members of the Workers' Group of the Governing Body by the Workers' Group of the Conference, and the worker members of the official committees by the Workers' Group of the Governing Body.

So far, therefore, the Christian unions have not obtained the official position they desire in the Organisation. But the publication of the advisory opinion of the Permanent Court has led other Governments to follow the example of the Netherlands Government and to designate representatives of the Christian unions as workers' delegates or advisers to the Conference. In this way, as well as through the unofficial committees and the direct relations of the International Labour Office with the organisations themselves, collaboration has been made possible and has been found fruitful.

The First Results of Collaboration

Few congresses of Christian unions have been held without touching on the International Labour Organisation. They have passed resolutions in favour of the ratification of Conventions, or demanded the inclusion of certain special questions in the agenda of the Conference, or expressed demands more or less closely connected with the work and aims of the Organisation.

As early as 1922 the Innsbruck Congress adopted a wide economic programme, in which it gave the International Labour Organisation a place of its own. The International Federation of Christian Agricultural Workers' Unions, the International Federation of Christian Miners' Unions, the International Federation of Christian Factory, Transport and Food Workers' Unions, the International Federation of Christian Railwaymen's Unions have in turn displayed an interest in the activities of the

International Labour Organisation. Following the example of the Amsterdam Federation, the Federation of Christian Textile Workers' Unions is assisting the Office in its enquiry into conditions of work in the textile industry.

Here again relations with the International Labour Organisation are established under the twofold head of documentation and collaboration.

III. Relations with Other Trade Unions

The Fascist Unions

The Italian Federation of National Corporations, which at first represented the trade unions in the new Fascist movement, took part in the work of the International Labour Conference in 1922 through the medium of a workers' adviser. The Fascist Party having come to power, the President of the Federation has presided over the Italian workers' delegation since the Fifth Session of the Conference in 1923. This was the rule for several years, even after the Act of April 3rd, 1926, which determines the legal status of the unions, up to the date on which the joint Federation of Fascist Workers was replaced by seven autonomous national federations, each with its own president. Since then the Italian workers have been represented at the Conference by one of these presidents.

Relations between the International Labour Office and the Fascist unions have been quite normal: an exchange of documents and information on both sides; on the part of the Office, a thorough study of Fascist trade union institutions, the publication of descriptions of their work, visits, etc.; on the part of the Fascist unions, the creation of a special section for relations with the Office, and a critical study of its work.

At every Session of the Conference since 1923 the Workers' Group has protested against the credentials of the Italian workers' delegate, but the majority of the Conference has always accepted those credentials.

The Unions of the British Dominions

The Australian trade union movement had occasionally been in touch with the Office before 1924, but it was not until after that year that more continuous relations were established. In 1925 an Australian workers' delegate attended the Seventh Session of the International Labour Conference. In 1927 the Australasian Council of Trade Unions took steps to ensure a more co-ordinated system of appointing workers' delegates to the International Labour Conference. The Australian trade unions have at times been attracted to Moscow and the Pan-Pacific Secretariat, but they now seem to be entering on a path that will bring them closer to the International Labour Organisation.

From the Union of South Africa, workers' delegates have attended nearly all the Sessions of the International Labour Conference. The South African Industrial and Commercial Workers' Union, an organisation of native workers, is affiliated to the International Federation of Trade Unions. The proposal to amalgamate the two main organisations of white workers, the Cape Federation of Labour and the South Africa Trades Union Congress, has lately been carried out.

In Canada, the Trades and Labour Congress has collaborated with the Organisation from its inception. It has always had delegates at the Conference and on the Governing Body. The satisfactory relations with the Canadian workers call for no comment.

A similar interest has been displayed by the New Zealand unions. The Alliance of Labour, which since its congress held at Wellington in the spring of 1927 has gained in prestige and authority, makes much use of the publications and documentation of the International Labour Office in the course of its activities.

The Unions of the Far East

In Japan, organised seamen, workers in arsenals, State employees, officers in the mercantile marine, and the Japanese Federation of Labour together form a solid block of 300,000 workers, among whom the influence of the programme of the International Labour Organisation is gradually making itself felt.

From China, complete delegations have recently taken part in the work of the International Labour Conference, thus enabling representatives of Chinese labour to estimate the importance and efficacy of the work of the Organisation. Any increase in the co-ordination of the trade union movement of that vast country will lead to closer contact with the Organisation.

The American Unions

In Latin America, relations were opened by way of personal correspondence with certain trade union leaders. The opportunities for establishing contact have since been increased by the publications of the Office issued in Spanish. This applies to Argentina, Chile, Brazil, Uruguay, Cuba and the Central American States. In the Argentine Republic, a central trade union federation is affiliated to the International Trade Union Federation and accepts the programme of the International Labour Organisation.

From Mexico, workers' representatives have attended certain Sessions of the International Labour Conference as observers.

In the United States, the American Federation of Labor has always kept in touch with the International Labour Office. Its late President, Mr. Samuel Gompers, was a friend of the Organisation, and relations have continued since his death. The present President of the Federation declared at the Toronto Congress in 1929 that Samuel Gompers had been an enthusiastic supporter of the International Labour Organisation and had firmly expected that some day the American Federation of Labor would be officially represented in it.

This survey of the labour world may be terminated by noting that the International Labour Office is in touch with the trade union federations of Palestine, Egypt and the Dutch East Indies.

IV. Relations with Trade Unions of Special Groups of Workers

Seamen

It will be recalled that when Part XIII of the Treaty of Versailles was being drafted the International Seafarers' Federation—in which most of the European seamen's unions were then grouped about the organisations in Great Britain and the United States of America—asked that there should be a special institution for the regulation of conditions of work at sea. In this form their demand could not be approved as a practical proposition, but within the general framework of the Organisation seamen have in actual fact obtained a special position which is by no means negligible. The creation of a Joint Maritime Commission and a special technical service, the work of four Sessions of the Conference, three of which took the form of special Maritime Conferences, and seven Draft Conventions, which have obtained 112 ratifications, are eloquent proof of the attempts made and the results achieved on behalf of seamen.

It seems therefore that collaboration with the seamen's leaders ought to have been easy. Yet there have been difficulties, for although all have recognised that the Office could assist them, there has not been the same unanimity on the action to be expected of it. Some organisations have doubted whether the best way of achieving their demands was to develop legislative action in every country. Some of them, in Anglo-Saxon or Scandinavian countries, being firmly convinced that the Governments should meddle as little as possible in maritime questions, would in certain cases have preferred that the Office should intervene only in order to lead to further agreement with shipowners. Others, believing above all in the virtue of direct action, were inclined to make use of the international negotiations as an opportunity to accentuate the clash between interests or classes. There has been a more or less conscious conflict between these various tendencies, which has been intensified by the splits in various national and international federations and even by personal disagreements.

The unity, and therefore the strength, of the International Seafarers' Federation has in fact often suffered. The International Federation of Transport Workers, which now groups most of the national unions, won them over only by degrees. The important British organisation of seamen is still outside, just as it has for long been outside the Trades Union Congress. Similarly, in the case of officers, the International Association of Mercantile Marine Officers, which was not formed until 1925, has not had time, in spite of the rapidity of its progress, to attract all the existing organisations and put a stop to the divisions that still hamper joint action. Notwithstanding the importance of these two great international organisations and their devotion to the work of the Office, it was necessary to obtain the support of independent or purely national associations such as the British unions of seamen and ships' officers, the Italian Fascist Federation and the Christian unions of seamen and fishermen in various countries. The Office, by wholehearted devotion to the accomplishment of its task, has finally succeeded in gaining the confidence and good-will of nearly all.

Agricultura Workers

During 1920 and 1921 two international federations of agricultural workers were formed, one affiliated to the International Federation of Trade Unions, the other to the International Federation of Christian Unions.

The first of these, the International Land Workers' Federation, which is the larger and more active, held its fourth Congress at Geneva in September 1926, precisely for the purpose of entering into closer touch with the International Labour Organisation. The three resolutions it voted on that occasion made an appeal to the Organisation or related to the work done or in progress. Since then, relations with the two Federations have been normal, and have naturally helped the International Labour Office to keep in touch with the national federations.

On several occasions agricultural workers, not content with applying to the Office for information and support in the matter of International Labour Conventions, have asked for its assistance in obtaining admission to the other institutions of the League of Nations which deal with agricultural matters; for instance, the Sub-Committee of Agricultural Experts, which forms an advisory institution of the Economic Committee. Thanks to the Office, this request was ultimately granted.

Professional Workers

The relations of the International Labour Organisation with the organisations of professional workers cannot be said to have taken shape until the International Federation of Professional Workers was founded in April 1923. This new institution soon felt the need of being in close touch with the International Labour Office. At its second Congress, held in Paris in December 1923, it instructed its Secretary-General to get into touch with the International Labour Office with a view to establishing permanent relations. The various national and international organisations of professional workers that have since sprung up or developed have tried to establish similar relations.

The International Federation of Journalists, the International Federation of Authors and Composers and the Federation of Unions of Professional Workers were formed in 1926, followed by the International Professional Association of Medical Men, the International Union of Dramatic Artistes, the World Theatre Society, etc. By 1927 there were forty-five of these bodies in existence, and they have all established relations with the International Labour Office. During this initial period nearly all of them expressed a wish that the International Labour Organisation should admit them and protect their interests, for they were not always quite clear as to the legal conditions underlying the work of the Geneva institutions. This in itself was proof of the need for creating a lasting link between these organisations and the International Labour Office, so that the latter could understand them and they in turn could learn to know and understand the Office.

Following on its third Congress in Paris in 1925, the International Federation of Professional Workers addressed a letter to the Governing Body of the International Labour Office, in which it suggested, in accordance with a Resolution of the International Labour Conference, that professional workers should be included as experts in the delegations of the most representative associations of workers or the Government delegations at the Sessions of the Conference. This was a first attempt to give a legal basis to the relations between the International Labour Organisation and the organisations of professional workers. The very delicate question of the representation of these workers in the Organisation was not finally settled until 1927. At the end of 1926, the Italian Government Delegate on the Governing Body proposed that it should set up a Committee on Professional Workers. The principle of this suggestion was approved, and in 1927 the Committee was actually created.

Relations with the professional workers' organisations thus entered on a new stage. Up to then, what had been sought was mainly a method of collaboration; thenceforward, collaboration has existed and proved fruitful. The various professional workers' organisations, in constant touch with the International Labour Office, draw the attention of the Advisory Committee to the questions of the day; they make reasoned proposals and carry out preparatory enquiries that greatly facilitate the work of the Office. Reference may be made for instance to the work done on these lines by the International Federation of Journalists for that profession, and in general by the International Federation of Professional Workers in such difficult questions as those raised by employees' inventions or the placing in employment of theatrical performers.

Relations with the various organisations of professional

workers are now well established. This does not mean, however, that all difficulties have been removed. As will be clear from the debates that took place at the Congress of the International Federation of Professional Workers at The Hague in 1929, some concern was expressed at the creation by the International Labour Office of a Committee on Salaried Employees, which they feared would tend to undermine the organisations of professional workers. Experience has shown these fears to be exaggerated. The work done by the Advisory Committee on Professional Workers at its second Session in December 1929 was sufficient to convince the professional workers' organisations that it was indispensable for them to enter into even closer touch with the International Labour Organisation.

Salaried Employees and Civil Servants

During the last few years the activities of salaried employees, though connected with those of the workers, have developed in a field of their own. In many countries employees have organised more slowly, and they have not always been able to obtain the benefits of social legislation. Before the War, especially in countries where collective agreements were not the custom, no measures had been taken to protect the hours of work of salaried employees, the hygienic conditions in shops and offices, or the work of women and children. As soon as employees understood the need of co-operating more closely for the protection of their professional interests, they acted accordingly, at first independently of other workers.

Another factor is that since the War the proportion of salaried employees to workers has increased in nearly all undertakings as a consequence of rationalisation. The employees have had more and more to do with the management of the undertaking and have been given greater responsibility and power of initiative. Here is yet another reason in their eyes for no longer submitting to conditions of work and life that in many cases are worse than those of manual workers. The result is that the organisations of salaried employees have recently made great progress; their aggregate membership is now about two millions. These organisations soon understood the need for international action. It is true that there had to be much adjustment before relations with the International Labour Office became regular and profitable. Employees were grouped in organisations representing three different shades of opinion: "free" unions, Christian unions and neutral unions, which were not necessarily in agreement with each other. The situation called for an attempt at establishing an understanding on questions of common interest. The first step was taken at Montreux, at a meeting organised in connection with the first Congress of the International Association for Social Progress, held in September 1926. A programme was drawn up, the details of which have been described elsewhere. It has also been shown above that in 1930 the Conference adopted a Draft Convention and three Recommendations concerning hours of work. The organisations of salaried employees, however, have constantly demanded permanent representation in the International Labour Office. The fact is that they are not represented on the Governing Body nor on the Advisory Committee on Professional Workers. In February 1929, the German Government delegate on the Governing Body submitted to it a proposal for the appointment of an advisory committee on salaried employees. This proposal gave rise to prolonged discussion and was finally adopted in June 1929. The functions of the Committee have been defined as follows: "The Committee on Salaried Employees shall serve as a basis for the consultation of employees in questions concerning them and for permanent contact with their organisations." This Committee, which consists of twelve employee members, three representatives of the Governing Body, and two representatives of employers, was to hold its first meeting early in 1931.

Public Servants

Civil servants and salaried employees in public services have displayed increasing interest in the work of the International Labour Office. As in the case of private employees, the Director of the Office, when making a selection of the questions concerning civil servants, on two occasions consulted persons connected with the international organisations of civil servants, employees in the postal, telegraph and telephone services, teachers, and employees in municipal public services. This collaboration is purely technical. Several studies have already been made relating to the regulation of the hours of work of civil servants, maternity leave for women officials, the working of bodies set up to ensure collaboration between public departments and their staffs, and the welfare institutions set up by organisations of public servants.

Handicraftsmen

In certain countries, handicraftsmen have for a long time had their own organisations. In others, the movement towards organisation is beginning, and special legislation is being prepared to regulate and sometimes to protect handicrafts of all kinds and degrees.

In all those countries where they have a long tradition of craftsmanship, or where handicrafts are now being revived, craftsmen are anxious to ascertain the conditions under which their fellows live and work in other lands. As they do not yet possess a well-established international organisation, they naturally turn to the International Labour Office for information on social questions. In addition, their organisations, in safeguarding the interests of their members, are confronted with various problems, some of which relate to handicrafts as such, others to production and labour in general. Hence they take a growing interest in the activities of the International Labour Conference, sometimes not unmixed with a certain anxiety. A desire has been expressed for collaboration and for some means of influencing the decisions of the Conference.

On two occasions already, in 1928 and 1929, the National Congress of French Craftsmen voiced this desire, which was reiterated in 1929 at a small conference attended by Belgian, French and Italian representatives. This desire is manifested chiefly by countries where handicrafts are being revived, while other countries, especially Germany, encourage the Office to continue its investigations into craftsmen's problems. As a matter of fact, the Office had begun, even before such requests were addressed to it, to collect material for giving information on the living and working conditions of craftsmen. The problems concerning this class of workmen are bound up with those affecting production and labour in general. All of them are closely interrelated, each throwing light on the others, and developments in one direction having effects on conditions in all or nearly all others. Any kind of social regulation may have direct or indirect effects on undertakings in a scattered industry. It is in this spirit that a Sub-Committee of the Governing Body, with the assistance of experts on craftsmen's problems, is carrying out this work of investigation.

CHAPTER III

RELATIONS WITH EMPLOYERS' ORGANISATIONS

The Attitude of Employers

One of the reasons that may help to explain the extreme caution that has often been observed in the attitude of the representatives of employers' organisations when faced with the question of labour legislation and with problems of social policy in general is no doubt to be found in their self-declared obligation to protect the interests of production. This obligation has been very clearly defined, as it appears to have been understood by employers in all countries, by Mr. Carlier, Belgian employers' delegate (and for many years Employers' Vice-President of the Governing Body of the International Labour Office), when he said at the Fourth Session of the Conference in 1922: "The spirit which animated the employers at Washington, and which is the spirit of Part XIII of the Treaty of Peace, still lives in them. Employers have never departed from their determination to do everything in their power to improve the lot of their fellow-workers nationally as regards their own individual countries and also internationally through the medium of the Permanent International Labour Organisation. But it must not be forgotten that it is above all with employers that rests the responsibility of providing the means of national existence. It is not upon deficient production nor upon production at excessive cost that a nation can live, and it is not from these that a Government can provide the means of maintaining State services."

I. Collaboration in the International Labour Organisation

This state of mind did not necessarily entail a purely negative and prejudiced attitude on all questions. Cases may be noted in which the Employers' Group as a whole or some of its members have made interesting suggestions. It was, for instance, on the initiative of the Employers' Group of the Governing Body, and in particular of the Italian delegate, that it was decided in 1920 to make an enquiry into production. At the Eleventh Session of the Conference, in 1928, the French employers' delegate sketched in outline a positive programme of action for the International Labour Office.

The reports of the Director of the International Labour Office to the Conference are evidence of the evolution in industrial relations that has been described above, which is tending towards systematic and reasoned collaboration between the two principal factors of production, both within undertakings and in the national field. In Great Britain there has been the so-called Mond–Turner Conference: similar steps have been taken in some of the British Dominions. In Sweden there has been the Social Peace Conference. In the Old World, as in the New, there have been other manifestations, which, without attracting so much attention, have still made their contribution to the establishment of that peace which it is hoped may be built up on the ruins of the past.

The International Organisation of Employers

Direct and normal relations with employers were much facilitated and improved by the creation in March 1920 of the International Organisation of Industrial Employers. The aim of this Organisation is "the study in common of all social problems affecting industry and labour throughout the world, and in particular the study and preliminary investigation of all questions dealt with or capable of being dealt with by the International Labour Conference and the International Labour Office." With its active and enlightened secretariat, this Organisation speedily became a most effective interpreter between the International Labour Office and the world of employers.

All, or nearly all, the employers on the Governing Body and their substitutes are members of the Executive Committee of the International Organisation, and at the same time have leading positions in the affiliated national organisations. The result is that the representation in the International Labour Organisation of the interests of employers in the States Members of the League of Nations is as complete and authoritative as could be desired.

Working in close touch with the International Organisation of Employers there is a Central Office of the Employers' Federations of the Northern Countries, which was set up in Brussels in 1921.

During 1929 the Federation of Japanese Chambers of Commerce appointed a representative in Europe with the special duty of keeping in touch with the Organisation of Employers and the International Labour Organisation.

To-day the Organisation of Industrial Employers also has the duty of representing and defending the interests of agricultural employers. For maritime questions, the centralisation of employers' interests is in the hands of the International Shipping Federation.

The Service for Relations with Employers' Organisations

As regards the International Labour Office, the Director opened in 1922 a special service to maintain relations with the international organisations of employers and some of the national federations affiliated to them. From time to time these national centres have sent temporary workers to the service, and they have thus obtained a closer acquaintance with the work of the International Labour Office.

Furthermore, during the last two years the International Labour Office has established relations with international organisations of employers with which it had previously not been in touch: the international federations for the building, woollen, cotton and silk industries, associations of employers in the transport industry, motor-car manufacturers, publishers, hotel and restaurant keepers, managers of cinemas, etc. It has followed the publications of the technical Press, most of which are connected with the employers' movement. Finally, it gives information in its publications on the employers' associations and their opinions.

These particulars concerning employers' organisations appear periodically in *Industrial and Labour Information* and the *International Labour Review*, which has published articles on employers' organisations in the northern countries, Germany, France and Italy. Finally, in 1926, the International Labour Office published a *Directory of Employers' Organisations*, concerning which the General Confederation of French Production and the Union of Metal and Mining Industries have stated that "it was the most interesting attempt hitherto made to give in concise and orderly form a general survey of employers' organisations in France and elsewhere."

II. Relations with Certain Special Groups of Employers

Shipowners

Under the heading of relations with workers, the importance and difficulty of the maritime relations of the Office on the labour side have been described. On the employers' side, the difficulties have been greater, though different in origin.

Here the International Labour Organisation was faced from the first by powerful and decided economic organisations. In point of fact, it had to deal mainly with one federation only, specially responsible for labour questions, namely, the International Shipping Federation, which groups around the British Shipping Federation most of the national shipowners' associations, besides being in touch with non-affiliated groups.

It was no doubt a great moral satisfaction to the Office when, immediately after the failure of Genoa, shipowners consented to continue discussing with seamen the questions of hours of work at sea under the chairmanship of the Director. But the discussion was broken off, and a movement against the Office became evident, which even threatened to turn into the adoption of a hostile attitude as a matter of principle irrespective of the aims pursued by the International Labour Organisation. Since then, the task of bringing the shipowners into the work of the Organisation has often proved ungrateful; but it could never be, and has never been, abandoned.

How far have the untiring efforts of the Office succeeded? The quality of its technical work has often received public recognition. In the Joint Maritime Commission, members of the shipowners' group have in certain cases displayed a spirit of conciliation and agreed to enquire into the most suitable methods of preparing the material for the Sessions of the Conference. Similarly, most national organisations have effectively assisted in centralising information. But any extension of protective legislation for seamen has met with obstinate resistance. This is a case in which special stress has been laid on the argument that national agreements between the parties directly concerned should suffice. When the Conference turned to the discussion of hours of work at sea, the problem of collaboration arose in an acute form. Even more than seamen, shipowners had always maintained that questions affecting their industry should be dealt with at special Sessions of the Conference with an exclusively maritime agenda and so composed as to represent only countries and organisations really concerned in maritime questions. At the Thirteenth Session, the composition of the British delegation was used by the shipowners as a pretext for the introduction of a resolution, declaring that for maritime conferences the designation of the non-Government delegates should be made in agreement with the most representative organisations of shipowners and seamen. On the rejection of this resolution, the Employers' Group declared its intention of not taking any further part in the work of the Conference, and prolonged negotiations were needed before it agreed to return and the work of the Session could be completed in a calmer atmosphere.

What are the prospects for the near future? Judging only from certain shipping periodicals, which too often condemn not only the eight-hour day but nearly all the work of the Organisation, some anxiety would appear to be justified. Ten years' experience have shown, however, that very often a spirit of conciliation, maintained in the face of all difficulties, can ultimately overcome the most stubborn opposition.

Agricultural Employers

It was during the Third Session of the International Labour Conference in 1921 that the idea arose of forming an international organisation to represent employers in agriculture—an idea that had previously been discussed by the International Organisation of Industrial Employers. In 1922, the International Farmers' Union was founded for the purpose of studying questions of agricultural labour. Its secretarial work was entrusted to the National Farmers' Union of Great Britain. The only occasion on which this organisation really came into touch with the Office was the meeting held by its Executive in 1928 at Geneva in connection with the Eleventh Session of the International Labour Conference, when the question arose of the possible inclusion of agriculture in the Recommendation on the prevention of industrial accidents.

In 1927, the Union came into conflict with the International Commission of Agriculture, then being reorganised, as will be described below, on a question of competence. The matter was at last settled in December 1929 by an agreement that when a question of agricultural labour came up for discussion at Geneva, the two institutions should consult each other before taking any action.

The number of institutions affiliated to the International Farmers' Union was never very great, and some of them were dissolved after they had joined; for instance, the Danish Farmers' Union. In May 1930 the International Union itself decided to dissolve at a meeting held in Paris. Since then the International Organisation of Industrial Employers again considers itself to be the representative of the interests of agricultural employers with respect to the Geneva institutions.

In the meantime, the International Commission of Agriculture, which was set up some forty years ago, had been reconstituted. In 1921, when the question of the competence of the International Labour Office in the matter of agricultural labour was taken to the International Court at The Hague, the Commission was among those who denied that competence. But it loyally accepted the decision in favour of the Office. Although the prejudice of agricultural employers against the Office gradually disappeared, the relations between the Commission and the International Labour Office remained for some time purely formal. It was not until the question arose of reorganising the Commission so as to make it truly representative of agricultural organisations in many countries that collaboration became effective. At the meeting of the Commission held in Vienna in 1928 an address was given by the Director of the Office on "Agriculture and the International Labour Organisation," after which a resolution was adopted declaring that "the International Commission of Agriculture is ready to take an active part in the work of realising systematic collaboration between all the bodies which deal with agricultural interests, more especially in collaboration with the International Labour Office as regards all questions of agricultural labour and social questions." At the meeting held at Bucharest in 1929, the Executive of the Commission was instructed to set up a special committee for studying questions of labour in agriculture. The Executive considered this decision in 1930 and proposed to set up the committee in the near future.

CHAPTER IV

THE INTERNATIONAL LABOUR ORGANISATION AND VARIOUS SOCIAL INSTITUTIONS

THE organisations or institutions with social interests or aims which have come into touch with the International Labour Organisation during the last ten years are legion, and they cannot all be mentioned here. From the first the Organisation has naturally maintained relations with the International Federation of League of Nations Societies, which a few years ago set up an Economic and Social Committee whose resolutions help the Organisation year by year by indicating the support and trends of an enlightened public opinion. Similarly, the Red Cross has never ceased to be in sympathetic touch with the International Labour Office. This is also true of numbers of international associations of students of varying shades of opinion and denominations interested in the League of Nations.

The present chapter will consider in rather more detail the relations of the International Labour Organisation with those private institutions whose aims and methods of work are more or less directly related to its own.

I. ORGANISATIONS FOR SOCIAL PROGRESS

The International Association for Social Progress

Since the International Association for Social Progress was set up in 1925 as an outcome of the Congress on Social Policy held at Prague in 1924, the Office has established with it constant and useful working relationships.

As provided by the rules of the Association, the Office, like several Governments, has been regularly represented at each of its meetings, where questions closely concerning the International Labour Organisation have been thoroughly and competently discussed: accident prevention, social insurance, protection of salaried employees, credit control as a remedy for unemployment, unemployment insurance, the status of foreign workers, the social effects of rationalisation, protection of the family, raising of the school age, methods of remuneration, international migration. On all these questions the Association has done pioneer work, preparing the way for the official action of the International Labour Organisation, in respect of which it plays a similar part to that played by the Federation of League of Nations Societies in respect of the League.

This close collaboration is not surprising when it is remembered that the Association for Social Progress was the result of the amalgamation of the three great international social organisations in existence before the War, which specialised respectively in the questions of labour legislation, unemployment and social insurance, and acted as forerunners in the field of activity defined by Part XIII of the Treaty of Versailles.

Other Institutions or Social Progress

The Office has also received useful support from the International Conference of Private Associations for the Protection of Migrants, which was formed in 1924 and numbers some fifty associations of the most varied kinds in Europe, America, and the Far East.

II. The Co-operative Movement

Co-operation and the International Labour Organisation

The relations of the International Labour Organisation with co-operative organisations date back to its earliest days, as was natural in view of the similarity which exists, and which the co-operative organisations immediately perceived, between their aims and objects and the work assigned to the Organisation. Being in close touch with the interests of the workers by reason of the composition of the classes of persons forming their membership, co-operative societies of all sorts, urban and rural, have shown by their attitude towards labour problems and by their achievements, which have so often anticipated legislation, that their members and the workers they employ are associated in a common desire for emancipation and progress.

By a unanimous decision of the Governing Body, taken at its Third Session (March 1920), a special service was set up in the International Labour Office to collect information on the co-operative movement and to keep in touch with co-operative organisations. This decision anticipated the intentions of the International Labour Conference, which in two consecutive Sessions defined the programme of work of the Co-operation Service: to keep in touch with co-operative organisations so as to ensure the presentation of their point of view on the questions of interest to them submitted to the Conference, and to collect information on the varied forms and progress of the co-operative movement in different countries.

Collaboration with Co-operative Organisations

The investigations of the Office have been effectively seconded by the collaboration of the co-operative organisations themselves. By 1922, it was already receiving some fifty periodicals of co-operative federations; now the number is nearly 200. It also receives every year from 250 to 300 publications and annual reports on co-operation. It has thus obtained information on 728 central co-operative organisations in forty-eight different countries, comprising over 280,000 societies and 65 million members.

It should be added that the Office has not confined its investigations to distributive and housing societies, which are of interest mainly to urban workers' households. It has extended them to all the fields covered by the movement and all forms of societies. Co-operative organisations being often the only or principal means of association of certain special groups or for certain important, if little-known, methods of production, the Office has been able to get into touch not only with peasant farmers, but with small rural industries, the many forms of home work, small traders, fishermen, etc.

These multiple contacts have not only given the International Labour Office a better idea of the structure of the co-operative movement in the different countries, but have helped it to understand more clearly the complex needs and aims of the movement, which are influenced alike by the aspirations of the masses, theoretical considerations and the practical work of management. It has learned the point of view of co-operative organisations on the questions concerning them and dealt with in enquiries or Draft Conventions. As early as the Third Session of the Conference, in 1921, some delegations, such as those of Bulgaria, Czechoslovakia, Finland, Germany, Italy and the Netherlands, included representatives of co-operative organisations. At nearly every subsequent Session this practice has been repeated. In 1924, the most representative co-operative organisations set up a Correspondence Committee of experts for their relations with the International Labour Office. This enabled co-operators to estimate from their own point of view the probable effects of the measures contemplated by the Organisation.

The first occasion for consulting the members of this Committee arose when the question of night work in bakeries was placed on the agenda of the Sixth Session in 1924. The International Labour Office obtained definite expressions of opinion from co-operative organisations in many countries. Furthermore, representatives of the International Co-operative Alliance were able to convey the views of the movement on certain questions: night work in bakeries, utilisation of workers' spare time, etc.

Similarly, the International Labour Office has been able to offer its services to co-operative organisations in their relations with the economic institutions of the League of Nations. In 1926, when the Council of the League appointed a committee to prepare for the World Economic Conference, it convened two co-operators, members of the Central Committee of the International Co-operative Alliance. In 1927, the International Economic Conference itself included a fair number of co-operators, among them the General Secretary of the Alliance.

By its relations with all forms of co-operative organisations, the International Labour Office is in a position to help to harmonise the various tendencies of the movement. Without encroaching on the functions of the International Alliance, it has been able to promote the desire of co-operative societies to establish economic and general collaboration among themselves. During the next few years it will be one of the tasks of the International Labour Office, in conjunction with the Secretariat of the League of Nations, to support the agricultural and distributive co-operative societies in their efforts to link up, in a continuous chain, all the operations in which they are concerned and to eliminate certain sources of waste in the process of distribution.

Collaboration with Study Centres

Finally, the International Labour Office is in touch with the co-operative study centres that have been set up during the last few years for research into special questions: the *Seminar für Genossenschaftswesen* of Halle University; the Horace Plunkett Foundation of London; the American Institute of Co-operation; the research departments of the great federations of Great

Britain, Germany, Sweden, Finland, Switzerland, etc., whose growing need of information has made of them centres of international study; the auxiliary bodies of the International Co-operative Alliance; the International Co-operative Wholesale Society, the International Co-operative Banking Committee, the International Women's Guild, the International Committee of Co-operative and Labour Insurance Societies, the International Co-operative Summer School.

This variety of international centres of co-operative study is a satisfactory sign of growth, and each of the centres corresponds to a definite aim or meets a definite need. Still, the question arises whether better results would not be obtained by establishing closer and more continuous relations between them all. It would no doubt be useful to enquire into the possibility of ensuring, without prejudice to the independence of the different study centres, the collaboration of all in each particular field of research. The International Labour Office, true to the principles that inspire its action here as elsewhere, will do all in its power to promote more systematic relations and concentration of effort.

III. Women's Organisations

Women's Work in the Trade Union Movement

All that has been said on the subject of trade unions applies also to women workers, since the principal international labour organisations, the International Federation of Trade Unions of Amsterdam, the International Federation of Christian Trade Unions and the International Trade Secretariats include women in the same unions as men.

The International Labour Organisation has attentively studied all the independent activities of women workers. The Office has followed all their congresses, taken part in their work, assisted them in obtaining the documentation they needed, and whenever they have asked for information it has tried to give them satisfaction.

An attempt was made in 1919 by the United States National Union of Women's Trade Unions to organise women workers internationally and independently, but this attempt has not succeeded. The Women's Federation so formed held two congresses, at Geneva in 1921 and at Vienna in 1923. But the majority of women workers in European countries were not in favour of trade union organisation for women distinct from the general organisations, and the Federation was dissolved after the Vienna Congress. Nevertheless, in order to represent women's interests in the workers' organisations, an International Women Workers' Committee was set up in its place and attached to the International Federation of Trade Unions of Amsterdam. In the national unions, too, the tendency is gaining ground to entrust the special interests of women to women's committees. In the Federation of Christian Trade Unions a committee entitled "Christian Women's Social Work" deals with questions relating to the organisation of Christian women workers.

Except in some of the northern countries, where women workers do not yet suffer so severely from the effects of industrial development as in the great industrial countries, women trade unionists have, whenever an occasion arose, always expressed their desire that the protection given to women by the International Conventions should be maintained, and have even demanded its extension.

Relations with Other Women's Organisations

The feminist movement, which before the War concentrated principally on obtaining the right to vote, developed after the War—the right to vote having been won by women in most of the great countries of Europe and America—a programme of action covering all important social problems. Among these, protective legislation for women holds a predominant place.

In consequence, the International Labour Office, which from the first was in close touch with the organisations of women workers, also established direct relations with the great international women's organisations, such as the International Council of Women, the International Alliance of Women for Suffrage and Equal Citizenship, the Young Women's Christian Association, the International Girls' Friendly Society, the International Council of Nurses, the International Federation of University Women, the International Committee of Social Service Schools, the Permanent Committee of International Women's Organisations, etc.

These women's organisations usually take a lively interest in the Conventions adopted by the International Labour Conference. In certain feminist circles, however, the problems of protective legislation for women workers are regarded from a point of view different from that held by the women workers themselves. The primary objective is considered to be the attainment of absolute equality in conditions as between men and women, whatever the conditions may be. This tendency resulted in 1929 in the formation of a new international organisation, the Open Door International, which aims at the economic emancipation of women workers by the absolute equalisation of the conditions of employment of the two sexes.

In seeking contact with all the social forces that may be employed and co-ordinated for the success of its work, the Office can observe but one principle, untrammelled by the conflict of theories, and that is to defend the Conventions adopted by the International Labour Conference and work for their ascendancy. Inspired by this principle, it carries out its task with all the more ardour and faith for being convinced that the protection of women workers, together with the protection of children and insurance against invalidity and old age, constitutes the most humane and generous part of the programme entrusted to it.

IV. Religious Organisations

The International Labour Office has followed in a spirit of wide sympathy the activities of religious bodies, on whose attention social problems have a strong claim.

The International Catholic Organisations

The great movement which was originated in the Roman Catholic Church by the Encyclical *Rerum Novarum* of 1891 has proved extremely fruitful. This Catholic labour charter has inspired a number of associations, which aim at establishing social equity. Not only does it express the "current doctrine" confirmed in turn by the Popes succeeding Leo XIII; but the Catholic hierarchy, faced with the changed and unforeseen conditions of the last few years and the economic conflicts of the War and post-War periods, has applied itself to completing and expanding the traditional teaching on such questions as an adequate wage, social insurance, the intervention of the law, trade unionism and mutual understanding between capital and labour. Even when so limited by traditional principles, the field of enquiry remains a very large one, in which Catholics, both thinkers and men of action, may develop their work on their own responsibility in the face of changing industrial conditions; and thus a variety of tendencies have been produced, though always within the framework of the Encyclical, and schools of thought have been formed with a special interest in the maintenance of international human solidarity.

Catholics as such have been able to participate in the work of labour protection defined by Part XIII and in the aspirations of which it is the outcome. In May 1929, in the course of the ceremony in which the Catholics of Rome celebrated the anniversary of the Encyclical *Rerum Novarum*, Father Balduzzi, Director and Secretary of the Catholic Institute, referred to the results obtained by Leo XIII's denunciation of the rising tide of individualism and added that the principles of justice then laid down had been adopted in the social legislation of the various nations in turn and formed one of the most striking instances of the intervention of the State in connection with labour. The same ideas after the War had brought about the setting up of a permanent international organisation attached to the League of Nations, for the extension and universal adoption of labour legislation.

The International Labour Organisation has received frequent proofs of the sympathy of Catholic organisations in the work they have carried out, the researches they have made and their social propaganda.

Very soon it got into touch with the "Social Weeks" of France, that educational movement which for twenty-seven years has sought to deepen the doctrine of the Catholic Church on social questions, and which has been imitated by Catholics in the Irish Free State, Italy, Poland, Belgium, Switzerland, Uruguay, and for many years Mexico. As early as 1922, the International Labour Office was officially represented at the Strasburg Week, and it is now the accepted tradition for it to send a representative every year. In 1929, the Director of the Office, in a message to the Besançon Week, greeted the "strong moral forces" of the Catholic Social Movement and their readiness to assist the International Labour Office in carrying out its task. The Social Weeks, in particular that held at Le Havre, which dealt specially with international questions, and the Catholic Union of International Studies, which is closely related to them, have openly recognised the need for a League of Nations and an International Labour Organisation.

In this spirit of understanding, the International Labour Office has had no difficulty in getting into touch with the various international Catholic movements of a social nature. Since 1928 it has been invited to send a delegate to the congress of the International Catholic Organisation (IKA), which in Central Europe, with methods of its own and more general aims, is inaugurating propaganda on the lines of the Social Weeks.

In its immediate action the International Labour Office has been supported not only by the intellectual sympathy of Catholics but by their practical work. An account has been given of what has been done by the Christian Unions. In 1925 the Catholic Workers' International was founded, which—while leaving labour demands to the Christian trade unions though working in close collaboration with them—aims at organising the workers in the widest sense of the word on a class, or more exactly, an "estate" (*Stände*) basis, and thus to guide them and prepare them for a new economic and social order.

In a narrower field, the Office has developed its action in touch with the Association of Catholic Students (*Pax Romana*) and with the International Bureau of Catholic Journalists. In the International Conference of Private Organisations for the Protection of Migrants it has collaborated, for instance, with the International Catholic Association for the Protection of Girls. In the question of workers' welfare and leisure, it has been in touch with a permanent centre for documentation and joint action set up by the Catholic institutions of various countries interested in charitable work, hygiene and social service, the *Caritas Catholica*. The Basle Congress (1928) of this institution supported the work of the International Labour Conference in favour of children and young persons, particularly in new countries. In the same year it approved the proposals of the International Labour Office in connection with the International Congress of Social Work held during the Social Fortnight of Paris. As early as 1925, the International Labour Office had entered into relations with the new-born movement of the International Catholic Social Service Union, which now comprises twenty-five schools and over 1,600 social workers. This Union closely follows the decisions of Geneva relating to women's work.

The recent initiative taken by the Organisation in the matter of forced labour has met with warm encouragement on the part of missionaries and their friends. On the occasion of the Twelfth Session of the International Labour Conference, the Catholic

Union of International Studies published a memorandum on the Draft Convention that was approved by the great international Catholic organisations—the International Union of Catholic Women's Associations, the International Catholic Social Service Union, the *Caritas Catholica*, etc. The Union declared that in the proposed regulations (since adopted) lay "the effective means . . . of extending to all workers of the world the rules of law that establish labour protection and that . . . in most cases merely apply to labour legislation the principles of Christian social morality."

The Churches Supporting the Stockholm Movement

The relations of the International Labour Office with the Anglican, Orthodox, Lutheran, Reformed and Old Catholic Churches date from 1925, the year in which the World Conference for Practical Christianity was held at Stockholm. This Conference was an attempt to induce the Churches to adopt a united attitude on social questions. The message to the Christian world with which it terminated revealed identical intentions and possibilities of collaboration. The Conference declared that human personality should be respected, that the soul, which is the highest of all values, should not be subordinated to blind machinery or to property, that no social order can endure or satisfy human aspirations unless it is just, and that in all economic problems the human factor is of more importance than material gain. It made an appeal for that collaboration which alone can lead to a social state where employers and employed alike may find in their daily work a means of fulfilling their true vocation on earth. Finally, it affirmed the responsibility of all in the face of social problems, which had become too complicated for solution by individual effort, and urged that these conditions called for the checking of unbridled individualism for the sake of the common weal. The Conference also adopted certain special conclusions arising out of these general principles, for instance, the abolition of child labour, the principle of the eight-hour day, the weekly rest, regular holidays and a more equitable regulation of wages.

This is the foundation on which the relations of the International Labour Office with the Churches and religious institutions represented at Stockholm have developed. It is in touch with the Continuation Committee, now the Œcumenical Council of Practical Christianity, with the International Institute of Social

Christianity, the committees on "The Churches and Labour," "Young Persons," "The Press," etc. These relations have helped these new bodies in defining their methods of work, and have influenced the increasingly positive tendencies of the social activities of the Churches. They have also placed the problem of social reform in closer connection with spiritual demands by bringing out the deep-rooted need for collaboration and proving that any measure for greater welfare and protection has not only immediate material effects for the individual, but much wider repercussions of a higher nature.

It was not long before these relations were made to serve purposes of information and study. It is characteristic of the Churches adhering to the Stockholm movement that they should display such an interest in obtaining an exact knowledge of facts, in estimating social realities, appraising the value of systems and discerning more clearly what reforms are possible. This need for objective study explains the creation in most Churches of committees for social action, which, in addition to churchmen, include economists, secretaries of social institutions, employers and workers. It has led to the foundation, by the Stockholm Committee, of the International Institute of Social Christianity, which was set up at Geneva in 1928. All these bodies find the documentation of the International Labour Office, its work, the Sessions of the Conference, the discussions and the questions of principle involved a source of valuable information, serving as a guide for the research work of the Churches. Information on the work of the International Labour Organisation is given with more and more fullness and regularity in their publications; for instance, the periodicals of the Institute, in France the special numbers of the *Revue du Christianisme social*, in the United States the *Information Service* published by the Federal Council of the Churches of Christ and so forth.

These various religious committees and institutions have undertaken thorough investigations into the problems of unemployment, the effects of rationalisation, the right of association, the welfare of the workers. The interest to the Stockholm movement of the Labour Conventions and their ratification is not confined to national studies of immediate difficulties and advantages, but rises to a consideration of the moral aspect of the obligations assumed.

CONCLUSION

The history of the first ten years of the International Labour Organisation is the story of a period rich in events, fruitful of results and still full of promise.

Part XIII of the Treaties of Peace had given the Organisation its legal structure. The work of the Organisation during this period has infused life into that structure. In other words, the Organisation has become a living organism; it grows and evolves in the field defined for it by international law; it absorbs one by one the departments assigned to it, creating as occasion arises the organs it needs for the purpose. This first stage may be said to have been accomplished. The institution is alive, possessing all the essential organs, created for and tested by action. It is probable that the International Labour Organisation will evolve like other living beings and acquire yet other subsidiary organs, adopting new methods of procedure to meet new needs. But the main body of the institution has now been created, and the essential features of its activity have been outlined. Henceforward, it is fitted to perform all the tasks entrusted to it by the Treaties of Peace.

Though the Organisation entered from the outset upon these various duties, it is clear that everything could not be completed during the ten years of its early youth. It is possible to conceive of the ultimate and complete realisation of the ideal for which the Organisation is patiently working, a world in which conditions of labour are governed by international conventions that do justice to all needs of protection and are ratified and applied by every State. In such a world, the "social justice," which by the Treaties of Peace is the aim of the Organisation, will have been finally and fully established. This end has not been attained, if indeed it is at all attainable in a changing world always concerned for the maintenance of its unstable economic equilibrium. But those who conceive of an ideal worthy of the name will work steadily for its realisation even without the stimulus of the hope that it will one day be achieved. The first result of the constant efforts of the Organisation is that to-day its competence is no longer contested. The objections raised some years ago to its intervention in questions of non-industrial labour are past history. To-day there is no one to dispute its right to work for the protection of all labour, in the fields as in the factory, in transport as in commerce and shipping, in offices as in workshops, in professional as in manual occupations; in a word, of all workers, irrespective of race and the climatic conditions under which they work. This first point has now been gained.

The foregoing pages have described which sections of this vast field the Organisation has merely explored, which it has cleared for action, in which it has sown, and in which it has already reaped in the form of thirty International Conventions and thirty-nine Recommendations covering nearly all conditions of labour: hours of work, wages, the weekly rest and holidays, night work, the minimum age for employment, health and safety, housing and the utilisation of spare time, the protection of women and children. Side by side with these international instruments there is all the documentation for preparing similar instruments in the future: collections of social legislation and collective agreements, a complete library, so to speak, of comparative studies on national legislation and practice in all labour matters, defining the possibility of, and the conditions for, future international agreements.

The results obtained have been shown: 408 ratifications on October 1st, 1930 (414 at the time of writing), by thirty-three States, including the principal industrial States of the world, with the exception of the United States and the Soviet Union, which, not being members of the Organisation, are not called upon to ratify its Conventions. And this leaves out of account the many national laws which have been amended in the light of these Conventions or have been called into being by their example and cast in the same mould. Even if not perfect, these results are of a nature to reassure the anxious friends of the Organisation, and to prove that it is performing no barren task in a waste of indifference, but is finding support and co-operation in many quarters.

Without this essential factor of support and collaboration, the work of the Organisation would indeed be nothing. And the existence of this factor is due to the efforts of the Organisation analysed in the last section of this historical survey. From its inception, the Organisation has tried to create contacts, to become known, understood and appreciated, to find support, encouragement, a stimulus and a guide in its relations with all the elements of international life. It is fair to say that it has succeeded. Not the least interesting and vivid chapter of this ten years' record is that describing the work done and the results obtained by the Organisation in creating a network of friends and collaborators. The first to help, and that from the very outset, were representatives of all concerned in production, and of the institutions for labour legislation. They were followed by members of the different religious denominations. Soon—and we may close with this final aspiration—the Organisation will be able to count on every State and every nation without exception.

APPENDIX

PART XIII (LABOUR) OF THE TREATY OF VERSAILLES OF JUNE 28, 1919[1]

SECTION I

ORGANISATION OF LABOUR

WHEREAS the League of Nations has for its object the establishment of universal peace, and such a peace can be established only if it is based upon social justice;

And whereas conditions of labour exist involving such injustice, hardship and privation to large numbers of people as to produce unrest so great that the peace and harmony of the world are imperilled; and an improvement of those conditions is urgently required: as, for example, by the regulation of the hours of work, including the establishment of a maximum working day and week, the regulation of the labour supply, the prevention of unemployment, the provision of an adequate living wage, the protection of the worker against sickness, disease and injury arising out of his employment, the protection of children, young persons and women, provision for old age and injury, protection of the interests of workers when employed in countries other than their own, recognition of the principle of freedom of association, the organisation of vocational and technical education and other measures;

Whereas also the failure of any nation to adopt humane conditions of labour is an obstacle in the way of other nations which desire to improve the conditions in their own countries;

The HIGH CONTRACTING PARTIES, moved by sentiments of justice and humanity as well as by the desire to secure the permanent peace of the world, agree to the following:

[1] The provisions of Part XIII of the Treaty of Versailles are reproduced in full in Part XIII of the Treaty of Saint-Germain of September 10th, 1919 (Articles 332–372), Part XIII of the Treaty of Trianon of June 4th, 1920 (Articles 315–355), and Part XII of the Treaty of Neuilly of November 27th, 1919 (Articles 249–289).

CHAPTER I

ORGANISATION

Article 387

1. A permanent organisation is hereby established for the promotion of the objects set forth in the Preamble.

2. The original Members of the League of Nations shall be the original Members of this organisation, and hereafter membership of the League of Nations shall carry with it membership of the said organisation.

Article 388

The permanent organisation shall consist of:

1. A General Conference of Representatives of the Members and

2. An International Labour Office controlled by the Governing Body described in Article 393.

Article 389

1. The meetings of the General Conference of Representatives of the Members shall be held from time to time as occasion may require, and at least once in every year. It shall be composed of four Representatives of each of the Members, of whom two shall be Government Delegates and the two others shall be Delegates representing respectively the employers and the workpeople of each of the Members.

2. Each Delegate may be accompanied by advisers, who shall not exceed two in number for each item on the agenda of the meeting. When questions specially affecting women are to be considered by the Conference, one at least of the advisers should be a woman.

3. The Members undertake to nominate non-Government Delegates and advisers chosen in agreement with the industrial organisations, if such organisations exist, which are most representative of employers or workpeople, as the case may be, in their respective countries.

4. Advisers shall not speak except on a request made by the Delegate whom they accompany and by the special authorisation of the President of the Conference, and may not vote.

5. A Delegate may by notice in writing addressed to the President appoint one of his advisers to act as his deputy, and the adviser, while so acting, shall be allowed to speak and vote.

6. The names of the Delegates and their advisers will be communicated to the International Labour Office by the Government of each of the Members.

7. The credentials of Delegates and their advisers shall be subject to scrutiny by the Conference, which may, by two-thirds of the votes cast by the Delegates present, refuse to admit any Delegate or adviser whom it deems not to have been nominated in accordance with this Article.

ARTICLE 390

1. Every Delegate shall be entitled to vote individually on all matters which are taken into consideration by the Conference.

2. If one of the Members fails to nominate one of the non-Government Delegates whom it is entitled to nominate, the other non-Government Delegate shall be allowed to sit and speak at the Conference, but not to vote.

3. If in accordance with Article 389 the Conference refuses admission to a Delegate of one of the Members, the provisions of the present Article shall apply as if that Delegate had not been nominated.

ARTICLE 391

The meetings of the Conference shall be held at the seat of the League of Nations, or at such other place as may be decided by the Conference at a previous meeting by two-thirds of the votes cast by the Delegates present.

ARTICLE 392

The International Labour Office shall be established at the seat of the League of Nations as part of the organisation of the League.

ARTICLE 393[1]

1. The International Labour Office shall be under the control of a Governing Body consisting of 24 persons, appointed in accordance with the following provisions:

[1] At its Nineteenth Sitting, held on November 2nd, 1922, the Fourth Session of the International Labour Conference adopted by 82 votes to 2, with 6 abstentions, the following draft amendment to Article 393, which is at present before the States Members of the International Labour Organisation, in accordance with the provisions of Article 422 of the Treaty of Versailles. [*Continued at foot of p.* 370.

2. The Governing Body of the International Labour Office shall be constituted as follows—

> Twelve persons representing the Governments;
> Six persons elected by the Delegates to the Conference representing the employers;
> Six persons elected by the Delegates to the Conference representing the workers.

3. Of the twelve persons representing the Governments eight shall be nominated by the Members which are of the chief industrial importance, and four shall be nominated by the Members selected for the purpose by the Government Delegates to the Conference, excluding the Delegates of the eight Members mentioned above.

4. Any question as to which are the Members of the chief industrial importance shall be decided by the Council of the League of Nations.

5. The period of office of the members of the Governing Body will be three years. The method of filling vacancies and other similar questions may be determined by the Governing Body subject to the approval of the Conference.

6. The Governing Body shall, from time to time, elect one of its members to act as its Chairman, shall regulate its own procedure and

"The International Labour Office shall be under the control of a Governing Body consisting of thirty-two persons:

> *"Sixteen representing Governments,*
> *"Eight representing the Employers, and*
> *"Eight representing the Workers.*

"Of the sixteen persons representing Governments, eight shall be appointed by the Members of chief industrial importance, and eight shall be appointed by the Members selected for that purpose by the Government Delegates to the Conference, excluding the Delegates of the eight Members mentioned above. Of the sixteen Members represented six shall be non-European States.

"Any question as to which are the Members of chief industrial importance shall be decided by the Council of the League of Nations.

"The persons representing the Employers and the persons representing the Workers shall be elected respectively by the Employers' Delegates and the Workers' Delegates to the Conference. Two Employers' representatives and two Workers' representatives shall belong to non-European States.

"The period of office of the Governing Body shall be three years.

"The method of filling vacancies and of appointing substitutes and other similar questions may be decided by the Governing Body subject to the approval of the Conference.

"The Governing Body shall, from time to time, elect one of its number to act as its Chairman, shall regulate its own procedure, and shall fix its own times of meeting. A special meeting shall be held if a written request to that effect is made by at least twelve of the representatives on the Governing Body."

shall fix its own times of meeting. A special meeting shall be held if a written request to that effect is made by at least ten members of the Governing Body.

ARTICLE 394

1. There shall be a Director of the International Labour Office, who shall be appointed by the Governing Body, and, subject to the instructions of the Governing Body, shall be responsible for the efficient conduct of the International Labour Office and for such other duties as may be assigned to him.

2. The Director or his deputy shall attend all meetings of the Governing Body.

ARTICLE 395

The staff of the International Labour Office shall be appointed by the Director, who shall, so far as is possible with due regard to the efficiency of the work of the Office, select persons of different nationalities. A certain number of these persons shall be women.

ARTICLE 396

1. The functions of the International Labour Office shall include the collection and distribution of information on all subjects relating to the international adjustment of conditions of industrial life and labour, and particularly the examination of subjects which it is proposed to bring before the Conference with a view to the conclusion of international conventions, and the conduct of such special investigations as may be ordered by the Conference.

2. It will prepare the agenda for the meetings of the Conference.

3. It will carry out the duties required of it by the provisions of this Part of the present Treaty in connection with international disputes.

4. It will edit and publish in French and English, and in such other languages as the Governing Body may think desirable, a periodical paper dealing with problems of industry and employment of international interest.

5. Generally, in addition to the functions set out in this Article, it shall have such other powers and duties as may be assigned to it by the Conference.

ARTICLE 397

The Government Departments of any of the Members which deal with questions of industry and employment may communicate directly with the Director through the Representative of their Government on the Governing Body of the International Labour Office, or failing any such Representative, through such other qualified official as the Government may nominate for the purpose.

ARTICLE 398

The International Labour Office shall be entitled to the assistance of the Secretary-General of the League of Nations in any matter in which it can be given.

ARTICLE 399

1. Each of the Members will pay the travelling and subsistence expenses of its Delegates and their advisers and of its Representatives attending the meetings of the Conference or Governing Body, as the case may be.

2. All the other expenses of the International Labour Office and of the meetings of the Conference or Governing Body shall be paid to the Director by the Secretary-General of the League of Nations out of the general funds of the League.

3. The Director shall be responsible to the Secretary-General of the League for the proper expenditure of all moneys paid to him in pursuance of this Article.

CHAPTER II

PROCEDURE

ARTICLE 400

The agenda for all meetings of the Conference will be settled by the Governing Body, who shall consider any suggestion as to the agenda that may be made by the Government of any of the Members or by any representative organisation recognised for the purpose of Article 389.

ARTICLE 401

The Director shall act as the Secretary of the Conference, and shall transmit the agenda so as to reach the Members four months before the meeting of the Conference, and, through them, the non-Government Delegates when appointed.

ARTICLE 402

1. Any of the Governments of the Members may formally object to the inclusion of any item or items in the agenda. The grounds for such objection shall be set forth in a reasoned statement addressed to the Director, who shall circulate it to all the Members of the Permanent Organisation.

2. Items to which such objection has been made shall not, however, be excluded from the agenda, if at the Conference a majority of two-thirds of the votes cast by the Delegates present is in favour of considering them.

3. If the Conference decides (otherwise than under the preceding paragraph) by two-thirds of the votes cast by the Delegates present that any subject shall be considered by the Conference, that subject shall be included in the agenda for the following meeting.

ARTICLE 403

1. The Conference shall regulate its own procedure, shall elect its own President, and may appoint committees to consider and report on any matter.

2. Except as otherwise expressly provided in this Part of the present Treaty, all matters shall be decided by a simple majority of the votes cast by the Delegates present.

3. The voting is void unless the total number of votes cast is equal to half the number of the Delegates attending the Conference.

ARTICLE 404

The Conference may add to any committees which it appoints technical experts, who shall be assessors without power to vote.

ARTICLE 405

1. When the Conference has decided on the adoption of proposals with regard to an item in the agenda, it will rest with the Conference to determine whether these proposals should take the form: (*a*) of a recommendation to be submitted to the Members for consideration with a view to effect being given to it by national legislation or otherwise, or (*b*) of a draft international convention for ratification by the Members.

2. In either case a majority of two-thirds of the votes cast by the

Delegates present shall be necessary on the final vote for the adoption of the recommendation or draft convention, as the case may be, by the Conference.

3. In framing any recommendation or draft convention of general application the Conference shall have due regard to those countries in which climatic conditions, the imperfect development of industrial organisation, or other special circumstances make the industrial conditions substantially different and shall suggest the modifications, if any, which it considers may be required to meet the case of such countries.

4. A copy of the recommendation or draft convention shall be authenticated by the signature of the President of the Conference and of the Director and shall be deposited with the Secretary-General of the League of Nations. The Secretary-General will communicate a certified copy of the recommendation or draft convention to each of the Members.

5. Each of the Members undertakes that it will, within the period of one year at most from the closing of the session of the Conference, or if it is impossible owing to exceptional circumstances to do so within the period of one year, then at the earliest practicable moment and in no case later than eighteen months from the closing of the session of the Conference, bring the recommendation or draft convention before the authority or authorities within whose competence the matter lies, for the enactment of legislation or other action.

6. In the case of a recommendation, the Members will inform the Secretary-General of the action taken.

7. In the case of a draft convention, the Member will, if it obtains the consent of the authority or authorities within whose competence the matter lies, communicate the formal ratification of the convention to the Secretary-General and will take such action as may be necessary to make effective the provisions of such convention.

8. If on a recommendation no legislative or other action is taken to make a recommendation effective, or if the draft convention fails to obtain the consent of the authority or authorities within whose competence the matter lies, no further obligation shall rest upon the Member.

9. In the case of a federal State, the power of which to enter into conventions on labour matters is subject to limitations, it shall be in the discretion of that Government to treat a draft convention to which such limitations apply as a recommendation only, and the provisions of this Article with respect to recommendations shall apply in such case.

10. The above Article shall be interpreted in accordance with the following principle:

11. In no case shall any Member be asked or required, as a result of the adoption of any recommendation or draft convention by the Conference, to lessen the protection afforded by its existing legislation to the workers concerned.

ARTICLE 406

Any convention so ratified shall be registered by the Secretary-General of the League of Nations, but shall only be binding upon the Members which ratify it.

ARTICLE 407

1. If any convention coming before the Conference for final consideration fails to secure the support of two-thirds of the votes cast by the Delegates present, it shall nevertheless be within the right of any of the Members of the Permanent Organisation to agree to such convention among themselves.

2. Any convention so agreed to shall be communicated by the Governments concerned to the Secretary-General of the League of Nations, who shall register it.

ARTICLE 408

Each of the Members agrees to make an annual report to the International Labour Office on the measures which it has taken to give effect to the provisions of conventions to which it is a party. These reports shall be made in such form and shall contain such particulars as the Governing Body may request. The Director shall lay a summary of these reports before the next meeting of the Conference.

ARTICLE 409

In the event of any representation being made to the International Labour Office by an industrial association of employers or of workers that any of the Members has failed to secure in any respect the effective observance within its jurisdiction of any convention to which it is a party, the Governing Body may communicate this representation to the Government against which it is made, and may invite that Government to make such statement on the subject as it may think fit.

Article 410

If no statement is received within a reasonable time from the Government in question, or if the statement when received is not deemed to be satisfactory by the Governing Body, the latter shall have the right to publish the representation and the statement, if any, made in reply to it.

Article 411

1. Any of the Members shall have the right to file a complaint with the International Labour Office if it is not satisfied that any other Member is securing the effective observance of any convention which both have ratified in accordance with the foregoing Articles.

2. The Governing Body may, if it thinks fit, before referring such a complaint to a Commission of Enquiry, as hereinafter provided for, communicate with the Government in question in the manner described in Article 409.

3. If the Governing Body does not think it necessary to communicate the complaint to the Government in question, or if, when they have made such communication, no statement in reply has been received within a reasonable time which the Governing Body considers to be satisfactory, the Governing Body may apply for the appointment of a Commission of Enquiry to consider the complaint and to report thereon.

4. The Governing Body may adopt the same procedure either of its own motion or on receipt of a complaint from a Delegate to the Conference.

5. When any matter arising out of Article 410 or 411 is being considered by the Governing Body, the Government in question shall, if not already represented thereon, be entitled to send a representative to take part in the proceedings of the Governing Body while the matter is under consideration. Adequate notice of the date on which the matter will be considered shall be given to the Government in question.

Article 412

1. The Commission of Enquiry shall be constituted in accordance with the following provisions:

2. Each of the Members agrees to nominate within six months of the date on which the present Treaty comes into force three persons of industrial experience, of whom one shall be a representative of employers, one a representative of workers, and one a person of

independent standing, who shall together form a panel from which the members of the Commission of Enquiry shall be drawn.

3. The qualifications of the persons so nominated shall be subject to scrutiny by the Governing Body, which may by two-thirds of the votes cast by the representatives present refuse to accept the nomination of any person whose qualifications do not in its opinion comply with the requirements of the present Article.

4. Upon the application of the Governing Body, the Secretary-General of the League of Nations shall nominate three persons, one from each section of this panel, to constitute the Commission of Enquiry, and shall designate one of them as the President of the Commission. None of these three persons shall be a person nominated to the panel by any Member directly concerned in the complaint.

Article 413

The Members agree that, in the event of the reference of a complaint to a Commission of Enquiry under Article 411, they will each, whether directly concerned in the complaint or not, place at the disposal of the Commission all the information in their possession which bears upon the subject-matter of the complaint.

Article 414

1. When the Commission of Enquiry has fully considered the complaint, it shall prepare a report embodying its findings on all questions of fact relevant to determining the issue between the parties and containing such recommendations as it may think proper as to the steps which should be taken to meet the complaint and the time within which they should be taken.

2. It shall also indicate in this report the measures, if any, of an economic character against a defaulting Government which it considers to be appropriate, and which it considers other Governments would be justified in adopting.

Article 415

1. The Secretary-General of the League of Nations shall communicate the report of the Commission of Enquiry to each of the Governments concerned in the complaint, and shall cause it to be published.

2. Each of these Governments shall within one month inform the Secretary-General of the League of Nations whether or not it accepts

the recommendations contained in the report of the Commission; and if not, whether it proposes to refer the complaint to the Permanent Court of International Justice of the League of Nations.

ARTICLE 416

In the event of any Member failing to take the action required by Article 405, with regard to a recommendation or draft convention, any other Member shall be entitled to refer the matter to the Permanent Court of International Justice.

ARTICLE 417

The decision of the Permanent Court of International Justice in regard to a complaint or matter which has been referred to it in pursuance of Article 415 or Article 416 shall be final.

ARTICLE 418

The Permanent Court of International Justice may affirm, vary or reverse any of the findings or recommendations of the Commission of Enquiry, if any, and shall in its decision indicate the measures, if any, of an economic character which it considers to be appropriate, and which other Governments would be justified in adopting against a defaulting Government.

ARTICLE 419

In the event of any Member failing to carry out within the time specified the recommendations, if any, contained in the report of the Commission of Enquiry, or in the decision of the Permanent Court of International Justice, as the case may be, any other Member may take against that Member the measures of an economic character indicated in the report of the Commission or in the decision of the Court as appropriate to the case.

ARTICLE 420

The defaulting Government may at any time inform the Governing Body that it has taken the steps necessary to comply with the recommendations of the Commission of Enquiry or with those in the decision of the Permanent Court of International Justice, as the case may be, and may request it to apply to the Secretary-General of the League to constitute a Commission of Enquiry to verify its contention. In this case the provisions of Articles 412, 413, 414, 415, 417 and 418 shall apply and if the report of the Commission of Enquiry or the decision of the Permanent Court of International Justice is in favour of the defaulting Government, the other Governments shall forthwith discontinue the measures of an economic character that they have taken against the defaulting Government.

CHAPTER III

GENERAL

Article 421

1. The Members engage to apply conventions which they have ratified in accordance with the provisions of this Part of the present Treaty to their colonies, protectorates and possessions which are not fully self-governing:

(1) Except where owing to the local conditions the convention is inapplicable, or
(2) Subject to such modifications as may be necessary to adapt the convention to local conditions.

2. And each of the Members shall notify to the International Labour Office the action taken in respect of each of its colonies, protectorates and possessions which are not fully self-governing.

Article 422

Amendments to this Part of the present Treaty which are adopted by the Conference by a majority of two-thirds of the votes cast by the Delegates present shall take effect when ratified by the States whose representatives compose the Council of the League of Nations and by three-fourths of the Members.

Article 423

Any question or dispute relating to the interpretation of this Part of the present Treaty or of any subsequent convention concluded by the Members in pursuance of the provisions of this Part of the present Treaty shall be referred for decision to the Permanent Court of International Justice.

CHAPTER IV

TRANSITORY PROVISIONS

Article 424

1. The first meeting of the Conference shall take place in October 1919. The place and agenda for this meeting shall be as specified in the Annex hereto.

2. Arrangements for the convening and the organisation of the first meeting of the Conference will be made by the Government designated for the purpose in the said Annex. That Government shall be assisted in the preparation of the documents for submission to the Conference by an International Committee constituted as provided in the said Annex.

3. The expenses of the first meeting and of all subsequent meetings held before the League of Nations has been able to establish a general fund, other than the expenses of Delegates and their advisers, will be borne by the Members in accordance with the apportionment of the expenses of the International Bureau of the Universal Postal Union.

Article 425

Until the League of Nations has been constituted all communications which under the provisions of the foregoing Articles should be addressed to the Secretary-General of the League will be preserved by the Director of the International Labour Office, who will transmit them to the Secretary-General of the League.

Article 426

Pending the creation of a Permanent Court of International Justice, disputes which in accordance with this Part of the present Treaty would be submitted to it for decision will be referred to a tribunal of three persons appointed by the Council of the League of Nations.

ANNEX

First Meeting of Annual Labour Conference, 1919

1. The place of meeting will be Washington.

2. The Government of the United States of America is requested to convene the Conference.

3. The International Organising Committee will consist of seven Members, appointed by the United States of America, Great Britain, France, Italy, Japan, Belgium and Switzerland. The Committee may, if it thinks necessary, invite other Members to appoint representatives.

4. Agenda:

(1) Application of principle of the 8-hours day or of the 48-hours week.
(2) Question of preventing or providing against unemployment.
(3) Women's employment:
  (*a*) Before and after child-birth, including the question of maternity benefit;
  (*b*) During the night;
  (*c*) In unhealthy processes.
(4) Employment of children:
  (*a*) Minimum age of employment;
  (*b*) During the night;
  (*c*) In unhealthy processes.
(5) Extension and application of the International Conventions adopted at Berne in 1906 on the prohibition of night work for women employed in industry and the prohibition of the use of white phosphorus in the manufacture of matches.

SECTION II

GENERAL PRINCIPLES

Article 427

The High Contracting Parties, recognising that the well-being, physical, moral and intellectual, of industrial wage-earners is of supreme international importance, have framed, in order to further this great end, the permanent machinery provided for in Section I, and associated with that of the League of Nations.

They recognise that differences of climate, habits and customs, of economic opportunity and industrial tradition, make strict uniformity in the conditions of labour difficult of immediate attainment. But, holding as they do that labour should not be regarded merely as an article of commerce, they think that there are methods and principles for regulating labour conditions which all industrial communities should endeavour to apply, so far as their special circumstances will permit.

Among these methods and principles, the following seem to the High Contracting Parties to be of special and urgent importance:

First.—The guiding principle above enunciated that labour should not be regarded merely as a commodity or article of commerce.

Second.—The right of association for all lawful purposes by the employed as well as by the employers.

Third.—The payment to the employed of a wage adequate to maintain a reasonable standard of life as this is understood in their time and country.

Fourth.—The adoption of an eight-hour day or a forty-eight-hour week as the standard to be aimed at where it has not already been attained.

Fifth.—The adoption of a weekly rest of at least twenty-four hours, which should include Sunday wherever practicable.

Sixth.—The abolition of child labour and the imposition of such limitations on the labour of young persons as shall permit the continuation of their education and assure their proper physical development.

Seventh.—The principle that men and women should receive equal remuneration for work of equal value.

Eighth.—The standard set by law in each country with respect to the conditions of labour should have due regard to the equitable economic treatment of all workers lawfully resident therein.

Ninth.—Each State should make provision for a system of inspection in which women should take part, in order to ensure the enforcement of the laws and regulations for the protection of the employed.

Without claiming that these methods and principles are either complete or final, the High Contracting Parties are of opinion that they are well fitted to guide the policy of the League of Nations; and that, if adopted by the industrial communities who are Members of the League, and safeguarded in practice by an adequate system of such inspection, they will confer lasting benefits upon the wage-earners of the world.

For Product Safety Concerns and Information please contact our EU
representative GPSR@taylorandfrancis.com
Taylor & Francis Verlag GmbH, Kaufingerstraße 24, 80331 München, Germany

www.ingramcontent.com/pod-product-compliance
Ingram Content Group UK Ltd.
Pitfield, Milton Keynes, MK11 3LW, UK
UKHW022214190926
475702UK00003B/349